Honour Killings and Criminal Justice

AF734715

Despite recent reforms to the Turkish Penal Code, the country retains a high level of honour-based violence. This book analyses the motives behind honour-based violence in Turkey and examines the criminal justice system's approach to this type of crime. The work takes a socio-legal approach to explore the concepts of honour, patriarchy, and hierarchy, along with the roles of culture and tradition. It also examines how the legal system deals with this phenomenon, focusing on the decisions of the criminal courts in honour killing cases and drawing on prisoner interviews. These analyses show the extent to which the State follows a patriarchal approach when dealing with honour killings and inform recommendations for improving the legal and criminal justice system so as to deter crimes of this nature.

Ferya Taş-Çifçi is Principal Lecturer in Law and Criminal Justice and Criminology Programme Leader, University of Hertfordshire, UK.

Honour Killings and Criminal Justice

Social and Legal Challenges in Turkey

Ferya Taş-Çifçi

Routledge
Taylor & Francis Group
LONDON AND NEW YORK

First published 2020 by Routledge

2 Park Square, Milton Park, Abingdon, Oxon OX14 4RN
605 Third Avenue, New York, NY 10017

Routledge is an imprint of the Taylor & Francis Group, an informa business

First issued in paperback 2021

Copyright © 2020 Ferya Taş-Çifçi

The right of Ferya Taş-Çifçi to be identified as author of this work has been asserted by her in accordance with sections 77 and 78 of the Copyright, Designs and Patents Act 1988.

All rights reserved. No part of this book may be reprinted or reproduced or utilised in any form or by any electronic, mechanical, or other means, now known or hereafter invented, including photocopying and recording, or in any information storage or retrieval system, without permission in writing from the publishers.

Notice:
Product or corporate names may be trademarks or registered trademarks, and are used only for identification and explanation without intent to infringe.

Publisher's Note

The publisher has gone to great lengths to ensure the quality of this reprint but points out that some imperfections in the original copies may be apparent.

British Library Cataloguing-in-Publication Data
A catalogue record for this book is available from the British Library

Library of Congress Cataloging-in-Publication Data
A catalog record for this book has been requested

ISBN: 978-1-138-34847-9 (hbk)
ISBN: 978-1-03-217309-2 (pbk)
DOI: 10.4324/9780429436642

Typeset in Galliard
by Apex CoVantage, LLC

To my mother Hacer Taş and my father İsmet Taş

Contents

Acknowledgements

First, I would like to express my sincere gratitude to Professor Maleiha Malik for her support and pastoral care, her motivation, and her knowledge. Her constant support has guided me and her care has made me believe that life is harmonious. I also would like to extend my thanks to Professor Elaine Player for her direction and assistance during my challenging fieldwork.

I owe huge thanks to my friends and colleagues for being by my side throughout this manuscript. I thank Ece Pekdinç Yıldız, Rabia Ünaldı, and Cemil Çelik for working so hard to help me during my fieldwork.

Most importantly, I would like to express my deepest gratitude to my family: My mother Hacer Taş and my father İsmet Taş for always believing in me, supporting me, and encouraging me to study, learn, and discover; my sisters Derya Taş Subaşı and Hülya Pekdinç for holding my hand whenever I needed; and my husband Dr Deniz Çifçi for his love, kindness, and patience. Without his love and understanding, I would not have been able to finish this book. Lastly, I would like to thank my daughter Arîn Aryen Çifçi for bringing happiness and joy into my life.

1 Introduction

1. Honour-based violence and honour killings

Honour-based violence (HBV) is a reality in most parts of the Middle East, Asia, the Muslim world, and Western countries. The severity of HBV has been widely realised over the past few decades and the conceptualisation of HBV has been developing. A wide range of definitions have been offered in order to frame and conceptualise the crime, but there is still no definitional consensus on either HBV or honour killings[1] (or so-called honour killings).[2]

Some of these definitions address HBV as type of violence that is committed either to protect or to restore 'honour,'[3] and any behaviour that challenges

1 For criticism about the term of 'honour killing,' see Lynn Welchman and Sara Hossain, 'Introduction: "Honour", Rights and Wrongs' *'Honour': Crimes, Paradigms, and Violence Against Women* (London, Zed Books 2005) 8; see also Sercan Tokdemir, 'Honor Crimes in Turkey: Rethinking Honour Killings and Reconstructing the Community Using Restorative Justice System' (2013) 4 Law & Justice Review 257, 258.

2 Rochelle L Terman, 'To Specify or Single Out: Should We Use the Term "Honor Killing"?' (2010) 7 Muslim World Journal of Human Rights 1, 7; Aisha K Gill, 'Honor Killings and the Quest for Justice in Black and Minority Ethnic Communities in the United Kingdom' (2009) 20 Criminal Justice Policy Review 474; Welchman and Hossain (n 1) 4; Joanne Payton, '"Honour," Collectivity, and Agnation: Emerging Risk Factors in "Honor"-Based Violence' (2014) 29 Journal of Interpersonal Violence 2863, 2864–67; Lindsey N Devers and Sarah Bacon, 'Interpreting Honor Crimes: The Institutional Disregard Towards Female Victims of Family Violence in the Middle East' (2010) 3 International Journal of Criminology and Sociological Theory 359, 360–62; Moira Dustin and Anne Phillips, 'Whose Agenda Is It?: Abuses of Women and Abuses of "Culture" in Britain' (2008) 8 Ethnicities 405, 412; Karl Anton Roberts, Gerry Campbell, and Glen Lloyd, *Honor-Based Violence: Policing and Prevention* (London, CRC Press 2014) 1–2; Mohammad Mazher Idriss, 'Key Agent and Survivor Recommendations for Intervention in Honour-Based Violence in the UK' (2018) 42 International Journal of Comparative and Applied Criminal Justice 321; Gökçe Yurdakul and Anna C Korteweg, 'State Responsibility and Differential Inclusion: Addressing Honor-Based Violence in the Netherlands and Germany' (2019) Social Politics: International Studies in Gender, State & Society <https://doi.org/10.1093/sp/jxz004> accessed 06 February 2020; İhsan Çetin, 'Gelenek ve Modernite Arasında Türkiye'de Son Dönem Kadın Cinayetleri' (2014) 30 Sosyoloji Dergisi 41, 45.

3 Christina Julios, *Forced Marriage and 'Honour' Killings in Britain: Private Lives, Community Crimes and Public Policy Perspectives* (Surrey, Ashgate 2015) 7; Nazand Begikhani, Aisha K Gill, and Gill Hague, *Honour-Based Violence: Experiences and Counter-Strategies in Iraqi*

patriarchal authority or that may be accepted as sexual misconduct by the society are considered as an honour violation.[4] As discussed in Chapters 3 and 4, this society involvement provides evidence of cultural and traditional norms that create honour codes allowing and sometimes even legitimising different forms of violence. The literature also highlights that HBV as a wider concept encompasses different types of violence, including but not limited to domestic violence, forced marriage, female genital mutilation, and honour killings;[5] this last is the most severe form of HBV and is committed in order to restore honour.

In looking at the literature, it is evident that individual and/or collective honour and honour/shame relationships form the common ground of concepts of female sexuality, patriarchy, culture, and traditions.[6] HBV is considered to be a form of gender-based violence in general – violence against women (VAW) in particular – and considers women to be the primary victims of this violence.[7] Apart from these conceptual definitions, the literature also provides important information about the regions in which HBV is committed,[8] emphasising that HBV cannot be attributed to one region: It is committed worldwide.[9]

Kurdistan and the UK Kurdish Diaspora (Surrey, Ashgate 2015) 6–8; Welchman and Hossain (n 1) 4–10; Rupa Reddy, 'Domestic Violence or Cultural Tradition? Approaches to "Honour Killing" as Species and Subspecies in English Legal Practice' in Aisha K Gill, Carolyn Strange, and Karl Roberts (eds), *'Honour' Killing & Violence: Theory, Policy & Practice* (Hampshire, Palgrave Macmillan 2014) 30.

4 Welchman and Hossain (n 1) 5; David Tokiharu Mayeda, Sunmin Rachel Cho, and Raagini Vijaykumar, 'Honour-Based Violence and Coercive Control Among Asian and Youth in Auckland, New Zealand' (2019) 25 Asian Journal of Women's Studies 159, 160.

5 Julios (n 3) 7; Begikhani, Gill, and Hague (n 3) 4–5.

6 Anna Korteweg and Gokce Yurdakul, 'Religion, Culture and Politicization of Honour-Related Violence: A Critical Analysis of Media and Policy Debates in Western Europe and North America' (United Nations Research Institute for Social Development 2010) Gender Development Programme Paper 12 2; Unni Wikan, *In Honour of Fadime: Murder and Shame* (Chicago, The University of Chicago Press 2008) 70, 73; Aisha K Gill and Avtar Brah, 'Interrogating Cultural Narratives About "Honour"-Based Violence' (2014) 21 European Journal of Women's Studies 72, 73; Anna Korteweg, '"Honour Killing" in the Immigration Context: Multiculturalism and the Racialization of Violence Against Women' (2014) Politikon: South African Journal of Political Studies 183, 2; Lila Abu-Lughod, 'Seductions of the "Honor Crime"' (2011) 22 Differences: A Journal of Feminist Cultural Studies 17, 17; Amnesty International, 'Culture of Discrimination: A Fact Sheet on Honor Killings' (2005) <https://www.amnestyusa.org/files/pdfs/honor_killings_fact_sheet_final_2012.doc> accessed 06 February 2020.

7 Begikhani, Gill, and Hague (n 3) 6–8; Aisha K Gill, '"Crimes of Honour" and Violence Against Women in the UK' (2011) 32 International Journal of Comparative and Applied Criminal Justice 243; Welchman and Hossain (n 1) 4; Korteweg and Yurdakul (n 6) 3; Mohammad Mazher Idriss, 'Not Domestic Violence or Cultural Tradition: Is Honour-Based Violence Distinct From Domestic Violence?' (2017) 39 Journal of Social Welfare and Family Law 3.

8 Radhika Coomaraswamy, 'Integration of the Human Rights of Women and the Gender Perspective: Violence Against Women' (United Nations Economic and Social Council Commission on Human Rights 2002) E/CN.4/2002/83 <https://undocs.org/E/CN.4/2002/83> accessed 06 February 2020.

9 'So-Called "Honour Crimes"' (Council of Europe Parliamentary Assembly Committee on Equal Opportunities for Women and Men 2003) 9720.

Some definitions of HBV, especially honour killings, specifically include family members as perpetrators. For instance, one of the earlier definitions of honour killings provided by Abu-Odeh states: "Killing of a women by her father or brother for engaging in, or being suspected of engaging in, sexual practices before or outside marriage."[10] Warrick, Sev'er and Yurdakul, Korteweg, and Khan also highlight in their conceptualisations the involvement of family members in perpetrating these killings.[11] As this book analyses in Chapters 4, 5, and 6, court records consider honour killings to be a form of violence committed by family members. Research conducted in the Turkish context by Bağlı and Özensel, Dogan, Onal, and Fındıkçı also underline the fact of family members' involvement in committing these crimes.[12] As Appendix 2.1 shows, the majority of honour killings are committed by relatives; however, it is also evident that non-relative perpetrators (especially intimate partners and ex-husbands) also commit these killings for the sake of honour. Therefore, conceptualising HBV and honour killings by only considering family member involvement places limits on HBV.

The literature also shows some evidence of conceptualising honour killings as premeditated murders, that is, committed with planning in advance.[13] As discussed in detail in Chapter 6, the Turkish courts aimed to follow this approach in their decisions to criminalise honour killings with using a specific term: customary killings. The Turkish literature also makes this differentiation and considers pre-planning (especially family council decisions) as a condition of customary killings.[14] However, the prison interviews for this research reveal that the majority of perpetrators declared that murdering their victim was a sudden decision, which shows that not all honour killings are pre-planned. This problem is further analysed in depth in Chapter 6.

Another problematic issue related to the conceptualisation of HBV and honour killings is the differentiation between passion and honour killings. Patriarchal violence against women is a global problem and cannot be attributed only to

10 Lama Abu-Odeh, 'Crimes of Honour and Construction of Gender in Arab Societies' in Mai Yamani (ed), *Feminism and Islam: Legal and Literary Perspectives* (Reading, Garnet Publishing Limited 1996) 141.

11 Catherine Warrick, 'The Vanishing Victim: Criminal Law and Gender in Jordan' (2005) 39 Law & Society Review 315, 232; Aysan Sev'er and Gokcecicek Yurdakul, 'Culture of Honor, Culture of Change: A Feminist Analysis of Honor Killings Rural Turkey' (2001) 7 Violence Against Women 964; Korteweg (n 6) 184; Tahira S Khan, *Beyond Honour: A Historical Materialist Explanation of Honour Related Violence* (Oxford, Oxford University Press 2006) 42–68.

12 Mazhar Bağlı and Ertan Özensel, *Türkiye'de Töre ve Namus Cinayetleri: Töre ve Namus Cinayetleri İşleyen Kişiler Üzerine Sosyolojik Bir Araştırma* (Istanbul, Deistek Yayınevi 2011); Aydın Fındıkçı, *Töre Cinayetleri Kürt Kültürünün Bir Parçası Mı: Arama Sonuçları* (Ankara, İmaj Yayınları 2010); Ayse Onal, *Honour Killing: Stories of Men Who Killed* (London, Saqi Books 2008); Recep Dogan, 'The Profiles of Victims, Perpetrators, and Unfounded Beliefs in Honor Killings in Turkey' (2014) 18 Homicide Studies 389.

13 Sev'er and Yurdakul (n 11) 964; Korteweg (n 6) 184.

14 Detailed analysis and discussion on the difference between honour killings and customary killings will be provided in Chapter 6.

Middle Eastern and Turkish societies.[15] As discussed in Chapter 2, the concept of male authority over females exists in every society; any behaviour that challenges this authority and puts men in a position of being less masculine and patriarchal may result in violent reactions. As discussed by Abu-Odeh, the patriarchal roots of these types of violence usually have been formulated in a way that creates Oriental and Occidental distinctions[16] as well as a stigmatised approach to non-Western communities.[17] In this sense, 'passion' is used in the West and 'honour crimes' in the East to define very similar motivated incidents against women.[18] Certain characteristics are created in the literature to provide differences between honour killings and passion killings, for instance that honour killings represent the orient, barbaric traditions, and backwardness, whereas passion killings represent both the occident and orient and are not necessarily barbaric.[19] Also, while honour killing includes the concept of collective honour and the involvement of different family members, passion killing is more individualised and is committed by the victims' sexual partners. Lastly, honour killings are premeditated, whereas passion killings are committed with a sudden loss of control.[20] As Welchman and Hossain argue, this differentiation creates different legal and social responses to similar incidents committed with motives of patriarchal ideology.[21]

In the Turkish context, it is evident that this differentiation is still considered by some scholars, leading to considerable limitation of the concept of honour killings.[22] Instead of considering the concept of patriarchy and the concept of male ownership over women's sexuality, this approach mainly focuses on the difference between the concepts of customary law and sudden loss of control and makes a distinction between collective and individual honour.[23] As discussed in detail in Chapter 6, the State's approach to criminalising honour killings also follows this differentiation and limitation in separating customary killings, honour killings, and passion killings. Chapter 6 also highlights how this differentiation creates injustice for the victims of honour killings when the State conceptualises the crime.

15 Ruth Sanberg and Janine HLJ Janssen, 'The Spectacle of the Feminine Other: Reading Migrant Women's Autobiographies About Honour-Based Violence' (2018) 68 Women's Studies International Forum 55.

16 Abu-Odeh (n 10) 141.

17 Terman (n 2) 5–6.

18 Welchman and Hossain (n 1) 10–13.

19 Abu-Lughod (n 6) 18; Purna Sen, 'Crimes of "Honour", Value and Meaning' in Lynn Welchman and Sara Hossain (eds), *'Honour': Crimes, Paradigms, and Violence Against Women* (London, Zed Books 2005) 45; Recep Dogan, 'The Dynamics of Honour Killings: Perpetrators' Experiences' (2016) 20 Homicide Studies 53, 365.

20 Welchman and Hossain (n 1) 11.

21 Ibid. 12.

22 Bağlı and Özensel (n 12) 55–59; Mahmut Tezcan, *Turkiye'de Tore (Namus) Cinayetleri: Sosyo Kulturel Antropolojik Yaklasim* (Ankara, Naturel 2003) 15–20; Fındıkçı (n 12) 102–20.

23 Bağlı and Özensel (n 12) 55; Leyla Pervizat, 'Tackling Honour in the Aftermath with Good Practice' (United Nations Division for the Advancement of Women United Nations Economic Commission for Africa 2009) Expert Paper EGM/GPLHP/2009/EP .02 7–9.

This book aims to follow a broad definition of HBV and honour killings that avoids ethnic, cultural, traditional, and religious stigmatisation and accepts HBV and honour killings as a form of gender-based violence that is applied in order to protect and/or restore individual and family honour.[24] This allows me to consider honour killings as a wider concept that also includes, but is not limited to, customary killings and passion killings.

Based on this, HBV can be defined as a form of patriarchal violence that is used either to protect or to restore honour; honour killings are the most severe form of HBV, used in response to alleged sexual misconduct against male authority and patriarchal social norms.[25]

2. Main focus of the book

This book makes a distinct contribution to academic and policy analysis by focusing on the gap between the criminalisation of so-called honour killings and the judiciary process in Turkey. Although considerable research has been done and advances made in terms of how HBV is tackled within the context of criminal law regionally (i.e. in the Middle East and South Asia), the area still needs further research, especially in Turkey, considering the Penal Code reforms.

This research aims to answer the following question(s):

> *How and under which conditions are honour killings committed in Turkey, and how does the Turkish Penal Code deal with them?*

Within the context of this question, the research aims to explore the following tentative hypothesis:

> *Since women's honour is considered to be the honour of the family and society, is violence against women in the name of honour legitimised by society?*
>
> *Although there have been considerable developments in the Turkish legal system in terms of recognition of gender equality, the existing Penal Code is still insufficient in deterring and denouncing honour killings.*

3. Theoretical framework and methodology

Since the study aims to answer how and under which conditions honour killings are committed in Turkey, and how the Turkish Penal Code deals with

24 Gill, 'Honor Killings and the Quest for Justice in Black and Minority Ethnic Communities in the United Kingdom' (n 2) 2; Reddy (n 3) 305, 306; Welchman and Hossain (n 1) 4–10; Fadia Faqir, 'Intrafamily Femicide in Defence of Honour: The Case of Jordan' (2001) 22 Third World Quarterly 65, 69.

25 A similar approach has been taken by Natasha Mulvihill and others in 'The Experience of Interactional Justice for Victims of "Honour"-Based Violence and Abuse Reporting to the Police in England and Wales' (2019) 29 Policing and Society: An International Journal of Research and Policy 640.

them, it requires a theoretical approach that supports analysis of variable, complex concepts related to HBV and honour killings. Therefore, this book is based on two main theories: hermeneutics[26] and feminist theory (the former is discussed in the following section; the latter is explained in detail in Chapter 3). The book also follows the methodological approaches of case study, doctrinal, and socio-legal analysis, including analysis of court cases and interviews.

3.1 Hermeneutics of HBV as a research method

The art of interpretation, or hermeneutics, is perhaps a good start for creating a contextual circle around HBV; this leads us to create a hermeneutical circle of HBV. Schleiermacher defines hermeneutics as the "art of understanding, particularly the written discourse of another person correctly."[27] Similarly, Ricoeur defines it as "the theory of operations of understanding in their relation to the interpretation of texts."[28]

Although hermeneutics theory was much concerned with theology and philosophy in the 19th century, it gradually became a part of all human sciences.[29] Schleiermacher and his follower, Dilthey, were two Romantic German philosophers who analysed the theory of interpretation by focusing on the importance of understanding the relationship between the parts and the whole, the reader and the author, during the process of interpretation.[30] Dilthey stressed that knowledge of a person – which has a historical relation – is very much dependent on the success of transforming oneself to occupy the other person's mental life.[31] However, this epistemological approach was highly criticised by Heidegger and Gadamar, who discussed hermeneutics within the context of ontology.[32] According to Heidegger, we all start to understand and interpret by using our fore-conception; in other words, with our pre-understanding or pre-conception.[33] With this pre-conception, we create the relationship between the subject and the object; it is this relationship that

26 A similar approach in a Pakistan context was followed by Amir H Jafri, *Honour Killing: Dilemma, Ritual, Understanding* (Oxford, Oxford University Press 2008) 36–45.

27 Paul Ricoeur, *From Text to Action: Essays in Hermeneutics, II* (Kathleen Blamey and John Thompson trs, London, The Athlone Press 1991) 63–64.

28 Paul Ricoeur, *Hermeneutics and the Human Sciences* (John Thompson tr, Cambridge, Cambridge University Press 1981) 43.

29 Hans-Georg Gadamer, *Truth and Method* (London, Bloomsbury 2013) 182.

30 Ronald Bontekoe, *Dimensions of the Hermeneutic Circle* (New York, Humanity Books 2000) 24–25.

31 Wilhelm Dilthey, *Hermeneutics and the Study of History*, vol 4 (Rudolf Makkreel and Frithjof Rodi eds, Princeton, Princeton University Press 1996) 230.

32 Ricoeur (n 27) 63–64.

33 Martin Heidegger, *Being and Time* (John Macquarrie and Edward Robinson trs, Oxford, Blackwell 1962) 191; Gadamer (n 29) 280.

determines how we self-understand the subject and how we understand the world/object, and this understanding stands as a circle, which is described as 'vicious.'[34]

Although this theory was dismissed as an "epistemological failure" by Ricoeur,[35] it is the ideal situation that I would like to emphasise during this research. While analysing the hermeneutical circle of HBV, I would like the reader to approach the text without breaking the circle. My aim is, as Heidegger explains, "not to get out of the circle but to come into it in the right way."[36] Of course, as Heidegger argues, while coming into the circle people will also bring their prior knowledge or presumptions about the topic/whole.[37] Gadamer also focuses on the importance of prior knowledge/understanding during the process of interpretation,[38] arguing that in order to avoid misunderstanding and prejudice while interpreting the text, we need to be "sensitive to the text's alterity."[39] This leads us to consider the whole text and its parts, and then we need to go back to the whole as if we have a circle,[40] which reminds us of Dilthey's analysis of the hermeneutical circle.

Taylor also analyses hermeneutics and the hermeneutical circle, adopting a combined approach to dealing with the problem of achieving the correct interpretation. Taylor argues that the parts constitute the whole; he creates the circle based on understanding the parts in order to understand the whole, and vice versa.[41] However, at the same time he talks about how individuals interpret using their pre-knowledge or assumptions. He acknowledges that interpretation exists within a circle, where we constantly refer to the parts and the whole.[42] In addition, Taylor also stresses the importance of subjective and intersubjective meaning during the process of hermeneutics,[43] which I will come back to later on.

Taylor not only refers to the relationship between the parts and the whole but also highlights the fact that every subject's meaning is related to other subjects' meanings.[44] According to Taylor:

> Things only have meaning in a field, that is, in relation to the meanings of other things. This means that there is no such thing as a single, unrelated

34 Heidegger (n 33) 193–94.
35 Ricoeur (n 28) 57.
36 Heidegger (n 33) 195.
37 Ibid. 191.
38 Gadamer (n 29) 305.
39 Ibid. 281–82.
40 Ibid. 302.
41 Charles Taylor, 'Interpretation and the Science of Man' (1971) 25 The Review of Metaphysics 3, 6.
42 Ibid.
43 Ibid. 27–31.
44 Ibid. 11.

meaningful element; and it means that changes in the other meanings in the field can involve changes in the given element.[45]

Taylor's analysis is very much related to my aim in interpreting HBV, not only because it allows us to remain within the right context, Turkey, but also because it shows us the importance of interpreting the parts of HBV. As we will see in the analysis of the hermeneutical circle of HBV, this type of violence contains different elements: the concepts of honour, patriarchy, and hierarchy; culture and tradition; and the law. Guiding the reader to an understanding of these elements requires[46] fabricating the right hermeneutic circle. Otherwise, the reader may easily interpret these elements as she understands them, which may affect the whole meaning of HBV. Therefore, as I underlined earlier, I am not much concerned that my interpretation of HBV might become a vicious circle, as Bontekoe describes.[47] Quite the reverse: It is, in fact, ideal for my analysis of HBV, because by using a hermeneutical circle I can be sure that the reader will not have a direct link beyond it, to other HBV circles; also, should any part of my circle's meaning change, the reader can easily modify the whole accordingly. In this way, I can focus the reader within the specific context, which is HBV in Turkey. As Taylor argues, "we have to be within the circle."[48] By remaining in a certain circle, I am also trying to create a common meaning for my readers when they follow my interpretation. Taylor says that "interpretation lays a claim to make a confused meaning clearer; hence there must be some sense in which the same meaning is expressed, but differently."[49] And so, by creating a circle that includes its common meaning, I will avoid misinterpretation and misunderstanding.

However, during this interpretation process, the reader may also realise that this common meaning sometimes coincides with their pre-knowledge/understanding of HBV, and if this is the case, they could use this pre-knowledge to make comparisons. Creating this common meaning also enables me to analyse not only the subjective meaning but also the intersubjective meaning of HBV. Taylor argues that intersubjective meaning is usually described beneath the umbrella of consensus.[50] However, it is actually more than consensus; it is, in fact, about being able to share a common understanding.[51] It requires more than one subject and aims to reach a common meaning between these different subjects.[52] Therefore,

45 Ibid.
46 Ibid. 6.
47 Bontekoe (n 30) 5–6.
48 Taylor (n 41) 13.
49 Ibid. 14.
50 Ibid. 27.
51 Varun Gauri, Michael Woolcock, and Deval Desai, 'Intersubjective Meaning and Collective Action in Developing Societies: Theory, Evidence and Policy Implications' (2013) 49 The Journal of Development Studies 160.
52 Matthew Peter Unger, 'Intersubjectivity, Hermeneutics, and the Production of Knowledge in Qualitative Mennonite Scholarship' (2005) 4 International Journal of Qualitative Methods 1, 3.

as Gauri et al. argue, it is impossible to talk about individuals when dealing with intersubjective meaning.[53] When applying this to HBV in Turkey, I try to highlight commonalities when considering different subjective elements/different participants. As the following chapters argue, the aim of this study is not to reach a subjective interpretation of HBV. Although my aim is to keep the readers in the circle of intersubjective meaning by analysing the common meanings of HBV, the research also provides some evidence of how HBV has been interpreted by different participants in Turkey, especially by the State.

3.1.1 Hermeneutical circle of HBV

In terms of the hermeneutical circle, it is crucial to make references to the whole while trying to read the parts, just as it is crucial to make reference to the parts while trying to understand the whole.[54] At this point, it is important to ask what constitutes the parts and what the whole is when dealing with the hermeneutical circle of HBV. If we consider HBV as a whole, it contains four different parts: honour; patriarchy/hierarchy/masculinity; culture/tradition; and law. Each part also has its own hermeneutical circle that needs interpretation. The first part of the circle is related to honour, which includes its own parts: *şeref*, *namus*, and chastity.[55] The second part is related to the linked concepts of patriarchy/hierarchy/masculinity. In order to analyse these within the context of HBV in Turkey, we also need to analyse its constituent parts: person, family, society, and the State. After considering honour and patriarchy, hierarchy, and masculinity, the circle reaches its third part: culture and tradition. The terms 'culture' and 'tradition' are too broad in themselves, and so, in keeping with the other parts of the hermeneutical circle of HBV, we will focus on the secondary concepts of gender relations and family life. The circle is completed with law, including State and customary law. Analysing the relationship of the parts within the circle enables us to realise how they actually affect each other when dealing with HBV. When we combine the parts, the hermeneutical circle of HBV appears as shown in Diagram 1.1.

Keeping this diagram in mind, one of the aims of this research is to interpret HBV within the depicted circle in order to reach what I call a 'principled interpretation' of HBV. What I mean by principled interpretation is not an 'ideal' or 'supportive of women' interpretation. The principled interpretation has no specific purpose of 'othering' certain societies, minorities, cultures, or traditions. What I mean by a principled interpretation is an interpretation that allows readers, especially Western ones, to fully understand the concept.[56] With this aim in

53 Gauri, Woolcock, and Desai (n 51) 161.

54 Dilthey (n 31) 231.

55 Detailed analysis of these Turkish terms will be made in the next chapter.

56 A similar approach was also supported by Alinia's consideration of masculinity and manhood (Minoo Alinia, *Honor and Violence Against Women in Iraqi Kurdistan* (New York, Palgrave Macmillan 2013) 53.

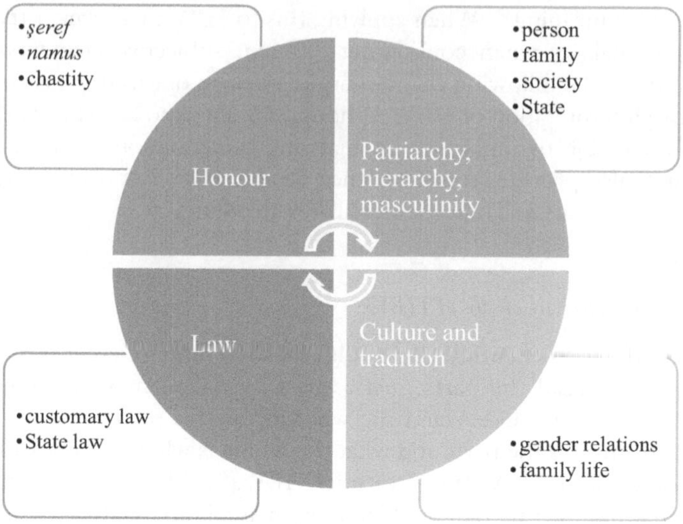

Diagram 1.1 Hermeneutical circle of HBV

mind, it is essential to create both the parts and the whole of a concept of honour and to understand that there is a complex relationship between each conceptual level. As the discussion in the following sections suggests, while ‘honour’ stands as the ‘whole’ in the circle, it also has constitutive parts, which can be defined as *şeref*, *namus*, and chastity. In order to understand and interpret ‘honour,’ we must therefore look at *şeref*, *namus*, and chastity, and vice versa. However, being in the circle of honour will be insufficient for us to reach the right interpretation and conceptualisation of HBV. We also need to realise that honour itself is only one of the parts of the whole. Therefore, it is crucial that we understand the relationship between honour and HBV.

Diagram 1.1 illustrates the hermeneutical circle of HBV and honour’s position in this circle. Abu-Odeh also introduced a similar interpretation,[57] describing the concept of honour crimes with a triangle that includes “social violence (the crime of honor itself), State violence (the attempt to regulate this crime), and the response by contemporary men and women.”[58] My use of the hermeneutical circle not only provides visual clarification of HBV but also creates the base for my main research question: *How and under which conditions are honour killings committed in Turkey, and how does the Turkish Penal Code deal with them?* This hermeneutical circle of HBV also provides a guide

57 Abu-Odeh (n 10) 287.
58 Ibid.

to the sequence in which this research question needs to be broken down into further analytical enquiries focusing on honour, patriarchy, culture and tradition, and law.

It should be also remembered during the process of interpreting the circle that even the hermeneutical circle of HBV can be located within different circles and become part of them. For instance, feminism can include the hermeneutical circle of HBV. In the following chapters, I will use feminism as just such a wider hermeneutical circle, and I will base my interpretation of HBV on certain feminist theories. I emphasise the word 'certain' here for a specific reason. Chapter 3, which analyses the theoretical background of VAW within the context of Turkey, aims to reflect the importance of applying feminist approaches.

During the interpretation of the hermeneutical circle, the reader should be aware of the fact that each part of this circle may share common meanings,[59] both when considering HBV in different contexts and when addressing it as a multinational problem. For instance, although the concept of honour would be completely different when taken out of the circle of HBV, its meaning is common to all the societies that occupy that circle. Therefore, my aim in interpreting honour is to target certain protagonists who are actually located outside this circle. In order to make this interpretation as successful as possible, I intend to tighten the hermeneutical circle of HBV by mainly considering and analysing a particular territory: Turkey and the people who live there. Although Taylor alleges that outsiders can only guess at or imagine actual meaning,[60] my aim is to provide the reader with a tool to look at the inside of the circle and see what she cannot see from the outside without this tool. Therefore, in the following sections, where I interpret the meaning of honour by considering its parts, the interpretation and conceptualisation of honour will help the reader to understand the subjective meaning of honour depending on which circles it belongs to, and its intersubjective meaning, when considering HBV.[61]

Following honour, the hermeneutical circle of HBV involves the interpretation of patriarchy. This includes individual patriarchy and collective patriarchy, family, society, and the State. Chapter 3 specifically deals with the interpretation of patriarchy, excluding State patriarchy, as this is mainly dealt with under the section on legal analysis of HBV. Interpretation of culture and tradition does not have its own section; however, these concepts are also interpreted throughout the research under different sections. It is important to note here that while I use the terms 'traditional' or 'tradition,' I am not trying to suggest that traditional societies are backwards and barbaric. I agree with the argument raised by Abu-Lughod, Grewal, and Fournier that there is an assumption that

59 Taylor (n 41) 13.
60 Ibid.
61 Ibid. 27.

Western societies are modern and Eastern/Muslim societies are backwards.[62] However, I try to emphasise here, by using 'traditions,' that the latter are strongly tied up with their 'cultural norms' and strictly deny women's autonomy and rights.[63] Although this approach was criticised by Volpp for having a Western (in her context 'hegemonic') cultural approach,[64] I do not consider westernisation as an ideal, or that non-westernised cultures, because they are traditional, 'lag'[65] behind and are uncivilised. My intention in using 'tradition' and 'traditional' is to underline the strong connection with the cultural 'norms' that deny that men and women are equals. Yet, I do not follow the path of Gozdecka et al. who argue that 'culture' is very much reflected in its attitude to minority women, whose cultural behaviours are consequently bad and need to be changed.[66] Along with Volpp, I am not suggesting that Western women are developed, secular, and liberated and that Eastern women, 'the other,' should achieve this state by following the same path.[67] I agree that 'cultures' and 'traditions' that allow and legitimate violence against women in the name of honour need to be changed; however, I do not wish to 'other' these societies. As Phillips argues, this would result in a stereotypical interpretation of non-Western cultures.[68] In other words, my interpretation of culture and tradition during the entire work should not be considered as supporting cultural racism or Orientalism. In the following chapters, I aim to show how the common understanding of terms related to HBV are considered by different actors by looking at their intersubjective meanings. As mentioned earlier, I also aim to provide some evidence as to how the State sometimes takes a culturally racist and Orientalist position when interpreting HBV. My aim in this

62 Lila Abu-Lughod, *Do Muslim Women Need Saving?* (Cambridge, MA, Harvard University Press 2013) 114; Inderpal Grewal, 'Outsourcing Patriarchy' (2013) 15 International Feminist Journal of Politics 1, 3–8; Pascale Fournier, 'The Ghettoisation of Difference in Canada: "Rape by Culture" and the Danger of a "Cultural Defence" in Criminal Law Trials' (2002) 29 Manitoba Law Journal 1, 7.

63 Susan Moller Okin, 'Is Multiculturalism Bad for Women?' in *Is Multiculturalism Bad for Women* (Princeton, Princeton University Press 2001) 21–22; see also Withaeckx and Coene for discussions about conceptualising HBV as a cultural problem (Sophie Withaeckx and Gily Coene, '"Glad to Have Honour": Continuity and Change in Minority Women's Lived Experience of Honour' (2013) 23 Journal of Gender Studies 376, 377–78).

64 Leti Volpp, 'Blaming Culture for Bad Behavior' (2000) 12 Yale Journal of Law & the Humanities 89, 96.

65 Ibid.

66 Dorota A Gozdecka, Selan A Ercan, and Magdalena Kmak, 'From Multiculturalism to Post-Multiculturalism: Trends and Paradoxes' (2014) 50 Journal of Sociology 51, 54; Janet Batsleer and others, 'Domestic Violence and Minoritisation: Supporting Women to Independence' (Women's Studies Research Centre, the Manchester Metropolitan University 2002) 94–95 <e-space.mmu.ac.uk/e-space/bitstream/2173/ . . . /978-0-954155-01-8.pdf> accessed 8 July 2019.

67 Leti Volpp, 'Feminism versus Multiculturalism' (2001) 101 Columbia Law Review 1181, 1198.

68 Anne Phillips, 'When Culture Means Gender: Issues of Cultural Defence in the English Courts' (2003) 66 Modern Law Review 510, 515.

work is to scrutinise tradition using principles of gender equality for a formative understanding, not alleging that tradition reflects backwardness because it shows non-Westernism.

In its last part, the hermeneutical circle of HBV deals with the interpretation of law in the context of HBV. Chapters 5 and 6 of this research analyse the law, considering it as a challenge to women's liberation. I divide the legal challenges into 'customary' and State law in order to show the different degrees of oppression and patriarchy.

3.2 Methods and design

3.2.1 Qualitative method

When considering the book's question once again – *How and under which conditions are honour killings committed in Turkey, and how does the Turkish Penal Code deal with them?* – the research aims are, first, to understand and analyse the social and legal conditions that pave the way to the committing of honour killings. This requires not only looking at the existing laws on honour killing but also analysing the concept of honour itself, the social environment that exists before HBV is committed, and the cultural norms that trigger this violence; as a result, this research focuses on Yin's first feature of qualitative research: "studying the meaning of people's lives, under real world conditions."[69] Considering the case study and the deductive approach this study adopts, the best way of conducting this research is to use the qualitative research method, which allows the researcher to deal with a social inquiry in specific conditions while focusing on the real world.[70] In order to answer the research question using the qualitative method, the research adopts certain approaches to gather the necessary data and to analyse it, which will be explained in the following sections.

3.2.2 Deductive method

The book uses to an extent the deductive method, but it does not fully follow the steps explained by Bryman: "theory, hypothesis, data collection, findings, hypothesis confirmed or rejected, and revision of theory."[71] The deductive method aims to answer a research question by using theory or theories to explain a specific hypothesis or hypotheses and research finding(s). The data obtained from the deductive method is collected to test the hypothesis/hypotheses and to revise the existing theory or theories. Unlike the inductive method, which aims

69 Robert K Yin, *Qualitative Research From Start to Finish* (New York and London, The Guildford Press 2011) 7.

70 Robert E Stake, *Qualitative Research: Studying How Things Work* (New York and London, The Guildford Press 2010) 14–17.

71 Alan Bryman, *Social Research Methods* (4th edn, Oxford, Oxford University Press 2012) 24.

Table 1.1 The deductive process of this research

Theories	Question Hypothesis/hypotheses Data collection Findings Revising research question and hypothesis/hypotheses

to create a theory by using finding(s), the deductive method relies on the existing theories on the subject. As Table 1.1 shows, the book uses theories, explained in Chapter 3, in order to answer the question, analyse the hypothesis, gather data, analyse the findings, and, finally, revise the research question and the main hypothesis. In other words, unlike Bryman's deductive process, in this research the aim is not to test the theories but to use them to complete each process of the research.

3.3 Case selection

The book is limited to considering honour killings committed in Turkey. Although some attention was given in the research to Middle Eastern countries because of cultural and religious similarities with Turkey, the situation in those countries was not analysed in detail.

Apart from the case of Turkey, the book's main limitation is a focus on female victims. While this book accepts that HBV is gender-based violence and can be committed against anyone who behaves or allegedly behaves against patriarchal honour codes and/or traditional gender norms, the main victim group is of female victims. This is in the line with the existing literature and case law from Turkey, which consider females as the main victims of honour killings and males as the main perpetrators.[72] This led me to consider HBV as a form of VAW as well. This classification has two justifications. First, the existing literature on HBV also considers males as the perpetrators and females as the victims when dealing with HBV. This does not mean that men are never victims and women are never become perpetrators. The literature proves that, although it is a small number, men also become the victims of this crime.[73] Also, women, especially

72 Aisha K Gill, 'Introduction: "Honour" and "Honour"-Based Violence: Challenging Common Assumptions' in Aisha K Gill, C Strange, and K Roberts (eds), *'Honour' Killing & Violence: Theory, Policy & Practice* (London, Palgrave Macmillan 2014) 3; Resul Çakır, M Fatih Yavuz and Y Tunç Demircan, 'Türkiye'de Namus Saikiyle İşlenen Adam Öldürme Suçlarının Değerlendirilmesi' (2004) 18 Adli Tıp Dergisi 27.

73 Suruchi Thapar-Bjorkert, 'Conversations Across Borders: Men and Honour-Related Violence in the UK and Sweden' in Mohammad Mazher Idriss and Tahir Abbas (eds), *Honour, Violence, Women and Islam* (Oxon, Routledge 2011) 188–90. Sen (n 19) 48.

older women, either directly or indirectly take part on committing HBV.[74] Nevertheless, statistics provided by Emniyet Genel Müdürlüğü Asayiş Dairesi and Başkanlığı in Turkey show that men are the primary perpetrators of detected honour killings in Turkey.[75] Therefore, this case study research is designed around considering men as primary perpetrators and women as primary victims of HBV in Turkey.

Although the book is limited to Turkey, it does not only cover ethnically Turkish people, nor does it focus on any particular ethnicity. In order to avoid a stereotypical interpretation of HBV that targets specific groups in Turkey, especially the Kurds, no attention was given to ethnic groups living in Turkey. This caused a huge challenge in terms of writing and identifying research groups; however, to clarify the meaning of the terminology used for this book, the reader should be aware that the term 'Turkish' includes not only Turkish ethnic groups but also other ethnic groups and citizens of Turkey.

3.4 Data collection

Two sets of primary data were collected during this research: court cases related to honour killings and interviews. The first set, the court cases, constitute the official data of this book; as mentioned earlier, this data aims to strengthen reliability, authenticity, and credibility.[76]

The second set comprises the interviews. Since the book aims to answer the question by focusing on a social phenomenon in a real-world context, it was thought that the best way to gather information was to reach out to people and talk to them. Qualitative interviews, as Yin highlights, provide an environment in which the researcher and the participants can have a conversation, and in which their relationships are not strictly framed.[77] Also, preparing semi-structured interviews and asking open-ended questions allows the researcher to be more flexible and to gather more information that can be used for deep analysis. The interviews were carried out with two groups: prisoners and elites in Turkey. The interview structures were designed as semi-structured interviews. Only the prisoner interviews were designed as surveys, in case the prisoners were not willing to be interviewed but preferred filling the survey, which happened with one prisoner. Although the prisoners' sample questions were designed as a survey, during the interviews I was able to ask further questions to clarify their answers or to go into the subject in more depth.

74 Gill, 'Introduction: "Honour" and "Honour"-Based Violence: Challenging Common Assumptions' (n 72) 3; Khan (n 11) 56.

75 'Emniyet Genel Müdürlüğü Asayiş Dairesi Başkanlığı Töre ve Namus Cinayetleri Raporu' (Emniyet Genel Müdürlüğü Asayiş Dairesi Başkanlığı 2006) 5.

76 Bryman (n 71) 549–50.

77 Yin (n 69) 134.

3.4.1 Court case collections

The book's question – ***how and under which conditions are honour killings committed in Turkey, and how does the Turkish Penal Code deal with them?*** – required deep socio-legal analysis. It was essential to gain accurate information about the background of honour killings committed in Turkey, including the motives, perpetrators, and victims. Also, it was necessary to analyse how current criminal law relating to honour killings is applied and how the courts deal with these crimes. One way of getting this necessary data for deep analysis was to look at court cases in Turkey. This is because the court cases provide not only information about the law's implementation but also necessary detailed information about motives, perpetrators, and victims. Therefore, 259 court cases (102 First Degree Courts, 125 Appeal Courts, 30 Assembly of the Criminal Chambers, 1 European Court of Human Rights (ECtHR), 1 UK Criminal Court Case) were collected for this research between 2012 and 2019. These cases were collected by visiting the courts (Adana, Ankara, Batman, Bakırköy, Bursa, Diyarbakir, Gaziantep, Istanbul, Kartal, Mardin, Sanliurfa, Trabzon, Van), using two main Turkish databases for the case research (UYAP[78] and KAZANCI[79]), and accessing the ECtHR's official website.[80] Comparative analysis of the court cases within the context of HBV and Turkish criminal law made a fresh contribution to the existing literature.

3.4.1.1 FIRST DEGREE COURT CASES

The First Degree Court cases were collected and used considering strict confidentiality rules. Therefore, no personal information that would enable the identification of the perpetrators or their victims was disclosed in the research. As Appendix 2.1 shows, such personal information was removed from the data, and only the gender of these people remained in order to allow for some analysis of the conditions under which honour killings are committed. Appendix 2.1 provides detailed information about the perpetrators and victims, the relationship between the perpetrators and victims, the motives of the crime, and the sentence that the perpetrators received. According to this data, 90 cases had male perpetrators; seven of them involved male and female perpetrators and five had female perpetrators[81] When looking at the victims, it shows that 51 cases had only female victims, 14 cases had both female and male victims, 33 had only male victims, and 4 cases had new-born baby victims.[82] The data collected from the First Degree Court cases show variation in the relationship

78 <www.uyap.gov.tr/> accessed 24 January 2020.
79 <www.kazanci.com/> accessed 24 January 2020.
80 <www.echr.coe.int/Pages/home.aspx?p=home> accessed 24 January 2020.
81 Please see Appendix 2.1.
82 Ibid.

between the victims and perpetrators. In only 22 cases were the perpetrators unacquainted with the victims or had no family relationship. The rest of them had a relationship as either first-degree or extended relatives.[83] The motives show a strong connection between female sexuality, the concept of patriarchy, and problems related to women's sexual autonomy in Turkey. Appendix 2.2 shows the variation between the motives that were considered by the First Degree Courts in Turkey.

The First Degree Court cases also provide detailed information about how the courts deal with these crimes. First of all, the data shows how the courts conceptualise these cases. The evidence of this conceptualisation comes from the Turkish Penal Code sections that the judges applied to the cases. According to the data, in 43% of the cases, the crimes were defined as murder; 25% as premeditated murder; 26% as customary killings; and 5% as attempted murder.[84] This is important data, as it provides a foundation for the analysis of problems related to the courts' conceptualisation of honour killings in Turkey, which is covered in detail in Chapter 6. This further analysis involves using the Appeal Court's and the Assembly of the Criminal Chambers' decisions, as well as the Turkish Penal Code and the literature related to it.

Second, the data provided information about the defences and mitigating circumstances in the cases. The main defences were unjust provocation (s.29 of the Turkish Penal Code); matters of discretionary mitigation (s.62 of the Turkish Penal Code); attempt (s.35 of the Turkish Penal Code); and minority (s.31 of the Turkish Penal Code).[85] Of 102 First Degree Court decisions, the unjust provocation defence was applied in 42 cases; matters of discretionary mitigation in 91 cases; minority in 13 cases; and attempt in 9 cases. No defence or reduction was made in seven cases. Detailed analysis of these reductions, especially the unjust provocation defence and matters of discretionary mitigation, is developed in Chapter 6 while examining the consequences of decisions taken by the First Degree Courts in honour killing cases.

Finally, the court records provide information about the sentences that the perpetrators received. According to s.82 of the Turkish Penal Code, honour killing perpetrators (customary killing, as defined by the Code) should receive a sentence of aggravated life imprisonment on conviction, which is a mandatory sentence in s.82. However, the data shows a huge variation in the sentences imposed, which reflects the variable significance the courts attach to the previously mentioned defence and mitigating circumstances.

This is again very important data, especially for analysing the deterrent effect of the prison sentence on honour killing cases in Turkey. More detail and analysis of this is given in Chapter 6.

83 Please see Appendix 2.1. For a similar finding, please see Dogan (n 12) 396.
84 Please see Appendix 2.5.
85 Full texts of all the sections used for this research can be found in Appendix 3.

Table 1.2 Sentences that the defendants received

Sentence	*Number of offenders in 102 First Degree Courts cases*
Acquitted	72
Less than 10 years	26
10–20 years	57
20 years–life imprisonment	91
Case closed; no sentence decided[86]	10
Total	256

3.4.1.2 APPEAL COURT AND ASSEMBLY OF THE CRIMINAL CHAMBERS

The Appeal Court and the Assembly of the Criminal Chambers not only act as Supreme Courts but also produce precedents for the First Degree Courts, as well as conceptualise honour killing in a way that is influential in shaping the perceptions and understandings of the First Degree Courts. In order to provide a better analysis of how the Appeal Court and the Assembly of the Criminal Chambers approach honour killing, cases were collected not only from the time period of the new Penal Code (which came into force in 2005) but also from the time period of the abolished Penal Code. This provides a comparative perspective which facilitates consideration of whether the courts' approach to honour killings has changed over time (Table 1.2).[87]

3.4.2 Interviews

Two sets of interviews were conducted for this research in Turkey. The first group was with prisoners who committed honour killings and the second group was with elites.

3.4.2.1 PRISONER INTERVIEWS

The prisoners were selected through the case records collected from the courts and information received from NGO representatives. Twelve prisoners convicted of HBV (1 woman, 11 men) were interviewed in 2012. Permission was obtained from the Ministry of Justice–General Directorate of Prisons and Detention Houses to interview the prisoners. For security reasons, the Directorate provided access to only six high security prisons.[88] Again, due

86 Cases were closed due to the death of the defendants during the trials or insufficient reason to proceed.

87 Due to the limited space for this research, attention was primarily given to the New Penal Code and the cases from 2005.

88 Badırma Type M, Bakırköy Women's Prison, Bursa Type H, Kocaeli Type F and T, Metris Type T, Silivri Type L No: 3, 5.

to internal security reasons, the research was only conducted in Bakırköy, Kocaeli, Bursa, and Silivri. A request to participate in the research and the full list of questions to be asked were sent to each prisoner and delivered by the prison staff. They also received an information sheet, which set out the purpose of the research and the role they were being asked to play, assuring them of confidentiality and anonymity in the final report. However, due to the strict security in the prisons, the interviews were conducted in the presence of one prison guard. It is likely that this lack of confidentiality may have affected their responses to certain questions, especially those related to how they were treated in prison.

Before starting the interviews, the participants were asked to read the information sheet again and sign the consent form. They were also reminded that participation was voluntary. Because the information sheet did not include any information about the guards' presence, the participants were reminded before starting the interviews that they could withdraw their consent and decide not to be interviewed.

The participants were asked about the crime they had committed, their trial and sentence, and the concept of honour. The perpetrators were between 21 and 65 years old, and all of them were literate; two of them had university degrees. Appendix 1.1 provides detailed information about the perpetrators, their crimes, their victims, their motives, and the sentences they were serving. Appendix 1.2 details how the crime was committed, whether spontaneously or pre-planned. This is an important analysis: As will be seen later on in Chapter 5, there is an approach that associates customary killing with premeditation and collective family decision-making.

3.4.2.2 ELITE INTERVIEWS

The elite interview participants comprised seven NGO representatives and one Appeal Court Judge. The NGOs chosen for this study were women's rights organisations, and the interviews conducted with their representatives were mainly considered preliminary research, useful for gathering some information on current affairs in Turkey on gender relations and HBV. Since the research follows a feminist approach to analysing HBV in Turkey, it was crucial to understand how NGOs, as the main representatives of feminist movements in Turkey, conceptualised HBV and evaluated the State's approach to this violence. Therefore, apart from the interviews with Aylin from VAKAD and Tülay and Nilüfer from KAMER, they were not used as primary data for this research. However, the information gathered from these NGOs was highly beneficial in creating the hermeneutical circle of HBV and conceptualising HBV by highlighting real examples from current incidents and crimes.

The interview with the Appeal Court Judge was used to gain some insight into, and provide some discussion about, the Appeal Court's approach to honour killings. As seen in Chapter 6, this revealed the Appeal Court's changing attitudes towards these crimes (Table 1.3).

Table 1.3 Elite interviews

Name	*Organisation*	*Place*	*Time*
Aylin Çelik	VAKAD	Van	26.06.2012
Nilüfer Yilmaz	KAMER	Diyarbakir	28.06.2012
Tülay Elcioglu	KAMER	Mardin	30.06.2012
Aynur Yildiran	KAMER	Gaziantep	05.07.2012
Cigdem Akca	AKDAM	Adana	09.07.2012
Emine Ciftci	Yeni Yasam Dernegi	Sanliurfa	19.07.2012
Ilke	Mor Cati	Istanbul	24.07.2012
Judge Muzaffer Ozdemir	Department No:1 of the Criminal Appeal Court	Ankara	08.07.2013

3.4.3 Observations

The research also used direct[89] and participant observation as a method to gather information about the research participants in a real-life environment.[90] The observations made in prisons were direct observations and included observing the participants and the prison officers in order to better understand the participants' lives in the prison. During the observation process in prison, I was a passive observer who simply followed the conversations[91] and watched the behaviours of the prisoners and the staff.

3.5 Data analysis

During the data analysis process, two methods were used: qualitative data analysis (mainly grounded theory) and computer-based qualitative data analysis (NVivo 10).

As mentioned earlier, the book does not fully follow the deductive approach, and it is different from the ordinary deduction process through its application of the theories. Keeping that in mind, this book focuses on a grounded theory approach to analysing the data collected through the fieldwork, which has enabled me to code the data and analyse it using my field notes during the empirical study.[92] The data gathered from the courts is categorised by type of court, decision year, perpetrators, victims, type of crime committed, and sentence. This categorisation system allows me to make comparisons between different variables and to analyse the phenomenon in depth. The prison interviews were categorised in different forms and analysed with pie charts, which can be seen in Appendix 1. This categorisation was extremely useful for providing a general overview of the participants' answers.

89 Robert K Yin, *Case Study Research: Design and Methods* (5th edn, London, Sage 2014) 113–15.

90 Eugene J Webb and others, *Unobtrusive Measures: Nonreactive Research in the Social Sciences* (Chicago, Rand McNally & Company 1966) 112.

91 For the importance of listening during the observation, see Yin (n 89) 74.

92 Yin (n 89) 74; Anselm L Strauss, *Qualitative Analysis: For Social Scientists* (Cambridge, Cambridge University Press 1993) 22–23.

4. Outline

This book consists of seven chapters. The second chapter analyses the concept of honour and the honour-related terms chastity, virginity, *namus*, and *eref*. This forms the first part of the hermeneutical circle of HBV. The third chapter introduces the feminist theories related to HBV and compares Western and Eastern feminist movements and how they explain HBV. This chapter also analyses gender relations in Turkey and how patriarchal and hierarchal social structures trigger the committing of violence against women. Chapter 4 examines why honour, as one of the prominent social values, becomes problematic in societies. In order to identify this problem effectively, the chapter follows two different approaches. First, it deals with the possessing mechanism and the possessors of honour; following this, protecting honour and its protectors are examined. The chapter also focuses on the specific behaviours that are commonly accepted as threats to honour and to families' reputations. Chapters 5 and 6 analyse Turkish law and its relation to society when dealing with honour killings. Chapter 6 uses a feminist interpretation of the existing criminal law; it looks at how the law is practiced by the authorities and highlights how feminist interpretation contradicts the State's and society's patriarchy by using primary data: court cases collected from Turkey. Chapter 7 includes concluding remarks and further recommendations.

Bibliography

Abu-Lughod L, 'Seductions of the "Honor Crime"' (2011) 22 Differences: A Journal of Feminist Cultural Studies 17

———, *Do Muslim Women Need Saving?* (Cambridge, MA, Harvard University Press 2013)

Abu-Odeh L, 'Crimes of Honour and Construction of Gender in Arab Societies' in Mai Yamani (ed), *Feminism and Islam: Legal and Literary Perspectives* (Reading, Garnet Publishing Limited 1996)

———, 'Comparatively Speaking: The "Honor" of the "East" and the "Passion" of the "West"' (1997) Utrecht Law Review 287

Alinia M, *Honor and Violence Against Women in Iraqi Kurdistan* (New York, Palgrave Macmillan 2013)

Amnesty International, 'Culture of Discrimination: A Fact Sheet on Honor Killings' (2005) <https://www.amnestyusa.org/files/pdfs/honor_killings_fact_sheet_final_2012.doc> accessed 06 February 2020.

Bağlı M and Özensel E, *Türkiye'de Töre ve Namus Cinayetleri: Töre ve Namus Cinayetleri İşleyen Kişiler Üzerine Sosyolojik Bir Araştırma* (Istanbul, Destek Yayınevi 2011)

Batsleer J and others, 'Domestic Violence and Minoritisation: Supporting Women to Independence' (Women's Studies Research Centre, the Manchester Metropolitan University 2002) <e-space.mmu.ac.uk/e-space/bitstream/2173/ . . . /978-0-954155-01-8.pdf> accessed 8 July 2019

Begikhani N, Gill AK and Hague G, *Honour-Based Violence: Experiences and Counter-Strategies in Iraqi Kurdistan and the UK Kurdish Diaspora* (Surrey, Ashgate 2015)

Bontekoe R, *Dimensions of the Hermeneutic Circle* (New York, Humanity Books 2000)

Bryman A, *Social Research Methods* (4th edn, Oxford, Oxford University Press 2012)

Çakır R, Yavuz MF and Demircan YT, 'Türkiye'de Namus Saikiyle İşlenen Adam Öldürme Suçlarının Değerlendirilmesi' (2004) 18 Adli Tıp Dergisi 27

Çetin İ, 'Gelenek ve Modernite Arasında Türkiye'de Son Dönem Kadın Cinayetleri' (2014) 30 Sosyoloji Dergisi 41

Coomaraswamy R, 'Integration of The Human Rights of Women and the Gender Perspective: Violence Against Women' (United Nations Economic and Social Council Commission on Human Rights 2002) E/CN.4/2002/83 <http://lastradainternational.org/lsidocs/95%20UN%20Report%20on%20trafficking%20migration%20and%20violence%20against%20women.pdf> accessed 06 February 2020

Devers LN and Bacon S, 'Interpreting Honor Crimes: The Institutional Disregard Towards Female Victims of Family Violence in The Middle East' (2010) 3 International Journal of Criminology and Sociological Theory 359

Dilthey W, *Hermeneutics and the Study of History*, vol 4 (Rudolf Makkreel and Frithjof Rodi eds, Princeton, Princeton University Press 1996)

Dogan R, 'The Profiles of Victims, Perpetrators, and Unfounded Beliefs in Honor Killings in Turkey' (2014) 18 Homicide Studies 389

———, 'The Dynamics of Honour Killings: Perpetrators' Experiences' (2016) 20 Homicide Studies 53

Dustin M and Phillips A, 'Whose Agenda Is It?: Abuses of Women and Abuses of "Culture" in Britain' (2008) 8 Ethnicities 405

'Emniyet Genel Müdürlüğü Asayiş Dairesi Başkanlığı Töre ve Namus Cinayetleri Raporu' (Emniyet Genel Müdürlüğü Asayiş Dairesi Başkanlığı 2006)

Faqir F, 'Intrafamily Femicide in Defence of Honour: The Case of Jordan' (2001) 22 Third World Quarterly 65

Fındıkçı A, *Töre Cinayetleri Kürt Kültürünün Bir Parçası Mı:* (Ankara, İmaj Yayınları 2010)

Fournier P, 'The Ghettoisation of Difference in Canada: "Rape by Culture" and the Danger of a "Cultural Defence" in Criminal Law Trials' (2002) 29 Manitoba Law Journal 1

Gadamer H-G, *Truth and Method* (London, Bloomsbury 2013)

Gauri V, Woolcock M and Desai D, 'Intersubjective Meaning and Collective Action in Developing Societies: Theory, Evidence and Policy Implications' (2013) 49 The Journal of Development Studies 160

Gill AK, 'Honor Killings and the Quest for Justice in Black and Minority Ethnic Communities in the United Kingdom' (2009) 20 Criminal Justice Policy Review 474

———, '"Crimes of Honour" and Violence Against Women in the UK' (2011) 32 International Journal of Comparative and Applied Criminal Justice 243

———, 'Introduction: "Honour" and 'Honour'-Based Violence: Challenging Common Assumptions' in Aisha K Gill, C Strange and K Roberts (eds), *'Honour' Killing & Violence: Theory, Policy & Practice* (London, Palgrave Macmillan 2014)

Gill AK and Brah A, 'Interrogating Cultural Narratives About "Honour"-Based Violence' (2014) 21 European Journal of Women's Studies 72

Gozdecka DA, Ercan SA and Kmak M, 'From Multiculturalism to Post-Multiculturalism: Trends and Paradoxes' (2014) 50 Journal of Sociology 51

Grewal I, 'Outsourcing Patriarchy' (2013) 15 International Feminist Journal of Politics 1

Heidegger M, *Being and Time* (John Macquarrie and Edward Robinson trs, Oxford, Blackwell 1962)

Idriss MM, 'Not Domestic Violence or Cultural Tradition: Is Honour-Based Violence Distinct From Domestic Violence?' (2017) 39 Journal of Social Welfare and Family Law 3

———, 'Key Agent and Survivor Recommendations for Intervention in Honour-Based Violence in the UK' (2018) 42 International Journal of Comparative and Applied Criminal Justice 321

Jafri AH, *Honour Killing: Dilemma, Ritual, Understanding* (Oxford, Oxford University Press 2008)

Julios C, *Forced Marriage and 'Honour' Killings in Britain: Private Lives, Community Crimes and Public Policy Perspectives* (Surrey, Ashgate 2015)

Khan TS, *Beyond Honour: A Historical Materialist Explanation of Honour Related Violence* (Oxford, Oxford University Press 2006)

Korteweg A, '"Honour Killing" in the Immigration Context: Multiculturalism and the Racialization of Violence Against Women' (2014) Politikon: South African Journal of Political Studies 183

Korteweg A and Yurdakul G, 'Religion, Culture and Politicization of Honour-Related Violence: A Critical Analysis of Media and Policy Debates in Western Europe and North America' (United Nations Research Institute for Social Development 2010) Gender Development Programme Paper 12

Mayeda DT, Cho SR and Vijaykumar R, 'Honour-Based Violence and Coercive Control Among Asian and Youth in Auckland, New Zealand' (2019) 25 Asian Journal of Women's Studies 159

Mulvihill N and others, 'The Experience of Interactional Justice for Victims of "Honour"-Based Violence and Abuse Reporting to the Police in England and Wales' (2019) 29 Policing and Society: An International Journal of Research and Policy 640

Okin SM, 'Is Multiculturalism Bad for Women?' in *Is Multiculturalism Bad for Women* (Princeton, Princeton University Press 2001)

Onal A, *Honour Killing: Stories of Men Who Killed* (London, Saqi Books 2008)

Payton J, '"Honour," Collectivity, and Agnation: Emerging Risk Factors in "Honor"-Based Violence' (2014) 29 Journal of Interpersonal Violence 2863

Pervizat L, 'Tackling Honour in the Aftermath with Good Practice' (United Nations Division for the Advancement of Women United Nations Economic Commission for Africa 2009) Expert Paper EGM/GPLHP/2009/EP .02

Phillips A, 'When Culture Means Gender: Issues of Cultural Defence in the English Courts' (2003) 66 Modern Law Review 510

Reddy R, 'Gender, Culture, and the Law: Approaches to Honour Crimes in the UK' (2008) 16 Feminist Legal Studies 305

———, 'Domestic Violence or Cultural Tradition? Approaches to "Honour Killing" as Species and Subspecies in English Legal Practice' in Aisha K Gill, Carolyn Strange and Karl Roberts (eds), *'Honour' Killing & Violence: Theory, Policy & Practice* (Hampshire, Palgrave Macmillan 2014)

Ricoeur P, *Hermeneutics and the Human Sciences* (John Thompson tr, Cambridge, Cambridge University Press 1981)

———, *From Text to Action: Essays in Hermeneutics, II* (Kathleen Blamey and John Thompson trs, London, The Athlone Press 1991)

Roberts KA, Campbell G and Lloyd G, *Honor-Based Violence: Policing and Prevention* (London, CRC Press 2014)

Sanberg R and Janssen JHLJ, 'The Spectacle of the Feminine Other: Reading Migrant Women's Autobiographies About Honour-Based Violence' (2018) 68 Women's Studies International Forum 55

Schleiermacher F, *Hermeneutics and Criticism and Other Writings* (Andrew Bowie tr, Cambridge, Cambridge University Press 1998)
Sen P, '"Crimes of Honour", Value and Meaning' in Lynn Welchman and Sara Hossain (eds), *'Honour': Crimes, Paradigms, and Violence Against Women* (London, Zed Books 2005)
Sev'er A and Yurdakul G, 'Culture of Honor, Culture of Change: A Feminist Analysis of Honor Killings Rural Turkey' (2001) 7 Violence Against Women 964
'So-Called "Honour Crimes"' (Council of Europe Parliamentary Assembly Committee on Equal Opportunities for Women and Men 2003) 9720
Stake RE, *Qualitative Research: Studying How Things Work* (New York and London, The Guildford Press 2010)
Strauss AL, *Qualitative Analysis: For Social Scientists* (Cambridge, Cambridge University Press 1993)
Taylor C, 'Interpretation and the Science of Man' (1971) 25 The Review of Metaphysics 3
Terman RL, 'To Specify or Single Out: Should We Use the Term "Honor Killing"?' (2010) 7 Muslim World Journal of Human Rights 1
Tezcan M, *Turkiye'de Tore (Namus) Cinayetleri: Sosyo Kulturel Antropolojik Yaklasim* (Ankara, Naturel 2003)
Thapar-Bjorkert S, 'Conversations Across Borders: Men and Honour-Related Violence in the UK and Sweden' in Mohammad Mazher Idriss and Tahir Abbas (eds), *Honour, Violence, Women and Islam* (Oxon, Routledge 2011)
Tokdemir S, 'Honor Crimes in Turkey: Rethinking Honour Killings and Reconstructing the Community Using Restorative Justice System' (2013) 4 Law & Justice Review 257
Unger MP, 'Intersubjectivity, Hermeneutics, and the Production of Knowledge in Qualitative Mennonite Scholarship' (2005) 4 International Journal of Qualitative Methods 1
Volpp L, 'Blaming Culture for Bad Behavior' (2000) 12 Yale Journal of Law & the Humanities 89
———, 'Feminism versus Multiculturalism' (2001) 101 Columbia Law Review 1181
Warrick C, 'The Vanishing Victim: Criminal Law and Gender in Jordan' (2005) 39 Law & Society Review 315
Webb EJ and others, *Unobtrusive Measures: Nonreactive Research in the Social Sciences* (Chicago, Rand McNally & Company 1966)
Welchman L and Hossain S, 'Introduction: "Honour", Rights and Wrongs' in Lynn Welchman and Sara Hossain (eds), *'Honour': Crimes, Paradigms, and Violence Against Women* (London, Zed Books 2005)
Wikan U, *In Honour of Fadime: Murder and Shame* (Chicago, The University of Chicago Press 2008)
Withaeckx S and Coene G, '"Glad to Have Honour": Continuity and Change in Minority Women's Lived Experience of Honour' (2013) 23 Journal of Gender Studies 376
Yin RK, *Qualitative Research From Start to Finish* (New York and London, The Guildford Press 2011)
———, *Case Study Research: Design and Methods* (5th edn, London, Sage 2014)
Yurdakul G and Korteweg AC, 'State Responsibility and Differential Inclusion: Addressing Honor-Based Violence in the Netherlands and Germany' (2019) Social Politics: International Studies in Gender, State & Society <https://doi.org/10.1093/sp/jxz004> accessed 26 July 2019

Part I

Honour killings and social challenges

2 Conceptual analysis of honour

1. Introduction

Since honour is a variable term that can be defined in different ways, both from culture to culture and in different time periods,[1] how it is conceptualised in this book is highly important if we are to understand HBV. Merely considering its lexical meaning – respect, pride, esteem – is not enough; we can interpret honour in different structures: universal, historical, Western, Eastern, and so on. We might think of honour in terms of military success,[2] economic power,[3] and physical strength,[4] which I will sometimes refer to in a wider context.[5] And so, in order to analyse the concept of honour within the context of HBV, this chapter focuses on the crucial and related terms *şeref*, *namus*, and chastity. Analysing these terms will provide the necessary foundation for our further socio-legal analysis on HBV.

2. The hermeneutical circle of honour: *şeref*, *namus*, chastity

As discussed in the introduction, the book is constructed around hermeneutics, specifically a hermeneutical circle of HBV, in order to be able to sustain a clearly

1 Tahira S Khan, *Beyond Honour: A Historical Materialist Explanation of Honour Related Violence* (Oxford, Oxford University Press 2006) 46; Aisha K Gill and Avtar Brah, 'Interrogating Cultural Narratives About "Honour"-Based Violence' (2014) 21 European Journal of Women's Studies 72, 74.

2 Mika LaVaque-Manty, 'Dueling for Equality: Masculine Honor and the Modern Politics of Dignity' (2006) 34 Political Theory 715, 716; Paul Robinson, *Military Honour and the Conduct of War: From Ancient Greece to Iraq* (Oxon, Routledge 2006) 1–6; Simon Lloyd, *English Society and the Crusade: 1216–1307* (Oxford, Clarendon Press 1988) 101–03, 198–200; Carl Erdmann, *The Origin of the Idea of Crusade* (Surrey, Princeton University Press 1977) 270; Ronald C Finucane, *Soldiers of the Faith: Crusaders and Moslems at War* (London and Melbourne, JM Dent & Sons Ltd 1983) 30–49.

3 Andrew Kimbrell, *The Masculine Mystique: The Politics of Masculinity* (New York, Ballantine Books 1995) 320–22.

4 Julio Caro Baroja, 'Honour and Shame: A Historical Account of Several Conflicts' in JG Peristiany (ed), *Honour and Shame: The Values of Mediterranean Societies* (London, Weidenfeld and Nicolson 1965) 110.

5 This concept of honour is identified as gender-neutral by Dogan (Recep Dogan, 'Different Cultural Understandings of Honor That Inspire Killings: An Inquiry Into the Defendant's Perspective' (2014) Homicide Studies 1, 5.

defined interpretation of behaviours. The hermeneutical circle of HBV shows that the concept of honour has its own circle; this circle includes three different but interconnected elements: *şeref*, *namus*, and chastity.

2.1 Şeref

In Turkish, *şeref* is used in many different contexts; it can be translated and used to mean dignity, purity, chastity, pride, prestige, honesty, respect, status, and esteem.[6] While there are various different interpretations of *şeref*, the Western interpretation of it usually centres on one: dignity. For instance, Kant argues that honour (he reflects on 'love of honour') is very much related to dignity,[7] and he claims that love of honour is the ground for human dignity.[8] Kant further argues that while honour is related to dignity, dignity itself is very much related to autonomy.[9] According to Kant, human beings are autonomous, and even if they live under certain laws, they have the right to contribute to law-making, so that each person is actually bound by her or his own will.[10] The key component of Kant's concept of dignity is that, in order to treat someone with dignity, one should accept the existence of that person's autonomy. This leads Kant to a fundamental question: If we need to accept another person's autonomy in order to reach the ideal interpretation of dignity, can everybody in society have autonomy? At this stage of our argument, I will simply say that, when considering *şeref* within the circle of HBV, it is clear that not everybody has the same level of autonomy. As argued by Friedman, traditionally, levels of autonomy are based on gender and hierarchy.[11]

If we accept the premise that dignity is related to autonomy, then in traditional Turkish societies, as a result of being fully autonomous individuals, men hold *şeref* but not women.[12,13] On first examining *şeref*, we see that it is based on a man's

6 Clementine Van Eck, *Purified By Blood: Honour Killings Among Turks in the Netherlands* (Amsterdam, Amsterdam University Press 2003) 19–20.

7 Taylor contradicts this idea by considering dignity as against earlier version of honour (Charles Taylor, 'The Politics of Recognition' in Amy Gutmann (ed), *Multiculturalism: Examining the Politics of Recognition* (Princeton, Princeton University Press 1994) 27).

8 Rachel Bayefksy, 'Dignity, Honour, and Human Rights: Kant's Perspective' (2013) 41 Political Theory 809, 825–26.

9 Immanuel Kant, *Groundwork for the Metaphysics of Morals* (Allen W Wood ed, Yale University Press 2002) 4:332–36; Paul Formosa, 'Dignity and Respect: How to Apply Kant's Formula of Humanity' (2014) 45 The Philosophical Forum, Inc. 49, 51; Michael Rosen, *Dignity: Its History and Meaning* (Cambridge, MA, Harvard University Press 2012) 25; Oliver Sensen, *Kant on Human Dignity* (Göttingen, Hubert & Co GmbH & Co KG 2011) 180–88.

10 Kant (n 9) 4:431–32, 4:441.

11 Marilyn Friedman, *Autonomy, Gender, Politics* (Oxford, Oxford University Press 2003) 101.

12 In the Turkish language, a man or his family can be either *şerefli* (honourable) or *şerefsiz* (dishonourable), whereas the same words are not used for women. Even if a woman's family loses its honour/*şeref*, this situation does not result in her being named *şerefsiz*. As will be seen below, in a situation where a woman loses honour, the word *namussuz* is used instead of *şerefsiz*.

13 It is worth noting here that although the Turkish interpretation of *şeref*/dignity leads us to consider gender difference and discrimination, scholars like Adler stress that "the dignity

behaviour and is usually linked to the wider meaning of honour.[14] He can possess this *şeref* by being masculine, reliable, honest, faithful, and diligent, providing for or fulfilling his family's needs, and protecting them from any risks and dangers.[15] In societies where men have dominant positions, providing food and housing and protecting the family are some of the duties of men.[16] Thus, failing in these duties simply results in the man no longer possessing *şeref*.

The second aspect of *şeref* is not confined solely to male behaviour. While not directly attached to women, it is strongly linked to certain behaviours of women within their families and communities. In Turkish societies, men are responsible for their female relatives and children. Having modest, reverential, and *namuslu*[17] wives and kinswomen who bring their children up properly contributes to men acquiring or maintaining their *şeref*. Women's chastity, purity, modesty, shyness, and obedience, and their relationships with kinsmen and outsiders, are strongly related to *şeref*;[18] they bring their kinsmen and family *şeref*/dignity when they are practiced and damage it when they are not, which shows that honour is a gendered concept within Turkish society.

2.2 Namus

Within the hermeneutical circle of HBV, *namus* mostly represents sexual behaviours such as virginity, purity, chastity, sexual modesty, and virtue;[19] therefore, it is identified as a gendered term.[20] In this regard, unlike *şeref*, women can acquire

---

of man is the dignity of the human being as a person," which demonstrates an egalitarian approach (Mortimer J Adler, *The Difference of Man and the Difference It Makes* (New York, Holt, Rinehart and Winston 1968) 17).

14 Pınar Ecevitoğlu, *Namus Töre ve İktidar: Kadının Çıplak Hayat Olarak Kuruluşu* (Ankara, Dipnot 2012) 316.

15 Van Eck (n 6) 19–20.

16 For instance, it was stated under the abolished Turkish Civil Code Numbered 743 Dated: 1926 Article 151 that the husband is the head of the family with the duty of providing for the family's needs, whereas women are responsible for the domestic work. The status of men as heads of their families is also argued by Ghada Karmi, 'Women, Islam, and Patriarchalism' in Mai Yamani (ed), *Feminism and Islam: Legal and Literary Perspectives* (Reading, Garnet Publishing Limited 1996) 79.

17 The meaning of *namus* and its relation to honour will be analysed in detail under the subheading of "*Namus*."

18 Pascale Fournier, Pascal McDougall, and Anna R Dekker, 'Dishonour, Provocation and Culture: Through the Beholder's Eye?' (2012) 16 Canadian Criminal Law Review 161, 182; Ruşen Işık and Nuray Sakallı-Uğurlu, 'Development of "Attitudes Toward Honor" and "Violence Against Women in the Name of Honor" Scales' (2009) 12 Türk Psikoloji Yazıları 1, 2.

19 Yvette van Osch and others, 'A Different Kind of Culture: Family Honor and Aggression in Turks' (2013) 16 Group Process & Intergroup Relations 334, 335; Ecevitoğlu (n 14) 305; Meltem Müftüler-Bac, 'Turkish Women's Predicament' (1999) 22 Women's Studies International Forum 303, 309; Derya Tekin, 'Victims of Law: The Efficiency of Turkish Penal System on Honour Killings' (2012) Strategic Outlook.

20 Michael Boiger and others, 'Defending Honour, Keeping Face: Interpersonal Affordances of Anger and Shame in Turkey and Japan' (2014) Cognition & Emotion 1, 3–4; Bethany A Corbin, 'Between Saviors and Savages: The Effect of Turkey's Revised Penal Code on the Transformation of Honor Killings Into Honor Suicides and Why Community Discourse

or lose their own *namus*; like *şeref*, both men's and the family's *namus* are dependent on women's *namus*.[21] If a woman's *namus* is tainted (*namusu lekelenmek*) or damaged, it is not possible for her family to have *namus* and dignity.[22] This is because families are responsible for her *namus* in society. Moreover, if a woman's *namus* is tainted, it is not only kinsmen and the family that are affected; kinswomen can lose their *namus*, especially the mothers and sisters of the tainted woman. This is because, in societies where *namus* has an important value, it is the most important domestic duty for a mother to raise her daughters in an appropriate way. If her daughter's *namus* is questioned by society, it shows that she has failed in her duty.

To avoid this danger, how can a woman be honourable (*namuslu*)? The difficulty of answering this question is inherent in the variable meanings of *namus*. For a woman, *namus* is a combination of different behaviours. It is not only one behaviour that can result in her being *namuslu*: she must be surrounded by a network of values and behaviours that intersect in order to be *namuslu*.[23]

The first value that all women must have in order to be *namuslu* is virginity.[24] Virginity is explained perfectly by Lama Abu-Odeh as determined by three categories: vaginal, bodily, and social virginity.[25] In real terms, in most situations virginity only refers to vaginal virginity, because the combination of these three categories (vaginal, bodily, and social) is usually accepted to be the outcome of chastity.[26] According to Abu-Odeh's vaginal virginity approach, a woman must be a virgin until she gets married, and the evidence of bodily virginity is the hymen.[27] It is believed that the most important value that a woman and her family should carefully preserve until the nuptial night is virginity; this is the source

Is Necessary for Honor Crime Eradication' (2014) 29 Emory International Law Review 277, 282; Bekir Kocadaş, 'Sosyolojik Açıdan Gençlerin Namus ve Şiddet Değerlendirmeleri' (2016) 1 Sosyolojik Düşün 27, 30.

21 Serap Ozgur and Diane Sunar, 'Social Psychological Patterns of Homicide in Turkey, A Comparison of Male and Female Convicted Murders' in Cigdem Kagitcibasi (ed), *Sex Roles, Family, and Community in Turkey* (Indiana, Indiana University Turkish Studies 1982) 350.

22 Kıymet Yeşilçiçek Çalik, 'Attitudes of Turkish Academics Regarding Violence Against Women in the Name of Honor' (2018) 33 Journal of Interpersonal Violence 3232, 3233.

23 Suzan Ceylan, Canay Doğulu, and Gülçin Akbaş, 'Namus Adına Kadına Yönelik Şiddete Dair Sosyal Temsiller: Karma Yöntemli Bir Çalışma' (2016) 2016 Türk Psikoloji Yazıları 56, 51; Elif Gürsoy and Hediye Arslan-Özkan, 'Türkiye'de Üniversite Öğrencilerinin Kadına İlişkin "Namus" Algısı (Turkish Youth's Perception of Sexuality/"Honor" on Relation to Women' (2014) 5 Psikiyatri Hemşireliği Dergisi 149, 149–50.

24 Müftüler-Bac (n 19) 309.

25 Lama Abu-Odeh, 'Crimes of Honour and Construction of Gender in Arab Societies' in Mai Yamani (ed), *Feminism and Islam: Legal and Literary Perspectives* (Reading, Garnet Publishing Limited 1996) 149–51.

26 The well-known Turkish phrase "*namus iki bacak arasındadır*" (*namus* is between two legs) refers to vaginal virginity. See also Sultan Komut, 'Women, Sexuality and Virginity in Turkey' (2011) 3 Sosyal ve Beşeri Bilimler Dergisi 87, 90.

27 Abu-Odeh (n 25) 149–51; Zeliha Kaygisiz Ertug, 'Individual Differences on the Importance of Virginity in Turkish Society: An Application on Turkish University Students' (2013) 10 International Journal of Human Sciences 610, 611.

of the family's honour.[28] At this stage, two questions arise. First, how can virginity be proved, and second, to whom should this virginity be proved?

The answer to the first question is always the bloodstain on the white sheets after the nuptial night,[29] and it is usually accepted that these sheets need to be seen by the families as proof of virginity.[30] Failure to bleed on the nuptial night is accepted as a failure to prove *namus* and chastity,[31] a sign that the woman has had premarital sexual intercourse; she is then considered *namussuz*. At this stage, it is worth asking what happens if a woman has lost her virginity before marriage. If defloration is discovered by her family and society, it is certain that she and, of course, her family will be named *namussuz* by society, and violence may take place against her for the sake of the family's *namus* and honour.[32] However, if this situation has not been discovered, she may still be able to 'prove' her virginity during her nuptial night through hymen reconstruction surgery. This plastic surgery is performed on a woman to reconstruct her broken hymen a few days before her wedding day, and the operation results in successful bleeding on the nuptial night, just as if the woman had been a virgin.

Although from a medical perspective this is only relatively minor cosmetic surgery, from a social perspective it creates a major dilemma. From one aspect, this surgery is necessary in a society driven by *namus* because failure to prove virginity on the wedding night may threaten the bride's life and disgrace the family.[33] In other words, in societies where violence is applied in order to protect or regain honour, hymen reconstruction surgery is often vital in protecting women from potential violent practices (including serious injuries, permanent disability, and even murder) that could be committed against them.[34] But from the other aspect, this surgery can be easily considered deceitful behaviour against the groom and his family.[35] However, although this dilemma among doctors exists, hymen reconstruction surgery is very common in Turkey.[36] Cindoglu, in her analysis of this topic, touches on one important point regarding the approach of medical

28 Pinar Ilkkaracan, 'How Adultery Almost Derailed Turkey's Aspiration to Join the European Union' in Pinar Ilkkaracan (ed), *Deconstructing Sexuality in the Middle East* (Aldershot, Ashgate 2008) 49; Khan (n 1) 90; Tekin (n 19).

29 Altan Eşsizoğlu and others, 'Double Standard for Traditional Value of Virginity and Premarital Sexuality in Turkey: A University Student Case' (2011) 51 Women & Health 136, 136, 142.

30 Eşsizoğlu and others (n 29) 136.

31 Nancy Lindisfarne, 'Variant Masculinities, Variant Virginities: Rethinking "Honour and Shame"' in Andrea Cornwall (ed), *Dislocating Masculinity: Comparative Ethnographies* (London, Routledge 2003) 94.

32 More detailed analysis regarding this violence is set out at the end of this chapter and in the following chapter.

33 Pelin Aytemiz, 'Lost and Found Virginity: A Critical Look to the "Reappearing Hymen" in Consumer Culture' (2015) 23 İLETİ-Ş-İM 97, 102, 105.

34 HA Saraiya, 'Surgical Revirgination: Four Vaginal Mucosal Flaps for Reconstruction of a Hymen' (2015) 48 Indian Journal of Plastic Surgery 192.

35 Erdem Akkay, 'Ülkemizde Kızlık Zarı ve Adlı Tıp Sorunları' (2011) 48 İstanbul Üniversitesi Hukuk Fakültesi Mecmuası 325, 329.

36 Dilek Cindoglu, 'Virginity Tests and Artificial Virginity' in Pinar Ilkkaracan (ed), *Women and Sexuality in Muslim Societies* (Istanbul, Women for Women's Human Rights (WWHR) 2000).

professionals to hymen reconstruction surgery. Cindoglu argues that there is a high tendency within the medical professions to call the surgery 'repair.'[37] This approach clearly proves that even surgeons share the idea that women who have had premarital sexual relationships are damaged and need to be fixed. It also shows how women's autonomy is ignored, and that their bodily integrity is tied to their hymen. If their hymen is broken, they are considered 'blemished.'

At the beginning of this section, virginity was divided into three categories: vaginal, bodily, and social.[38] As mentioned earlier, bodily and social virginity actually determine the meaning of chastity: A woman must also meet other conditions that are set by the community. Behaving in a certain way so as to avoid any suspicion, or any allegations that question her vaginal virginity, is one of the strict conditions that a maiden has to meet. How to meet these conditions, however, does vary. First of all, a virgin should suppress her sexuality and ignore her sexual desires until her marriage. And not only before the marriage: Even during the first days of her marriage she should preserve her shyness, her inhibitions, and even her sexual desires towards her husband.[39] Otherwise, even if she proves her virginity on her nuptial night, if she is sexually too indecent in her behaviour towards her husband in the first few days of her marriage, suspicions regarding her pre-marriage sexuality can easily arise. In this matter, it can be said that a maiden has to prove that her vaginal virginity is also based on having refrained from any sexual activity before marriage. This illustrates that the potential question of a woman's virginity is not restricted to the nuptial night but also continues after the marriage and expands from the hymen to encompass the whole body.[40]

Not only the unmarried but also married women have a duty to protect their *namus*. It is obvious that questioning the virginity of a married woman is not applicable because one of the crucial conditions of marriage is for a woman to surrender her virginity to her husband.[41] A married woman's *namus* is instead based on sexual obedience to her husband[42] and is thus linked to her chastity, which will be explained in the following section.

2.3 Chastity

Chastity may be strongly related to *namus* and honour, but the meaning of it is actually broader than *namus*. While *namus* is merely related to virginity

37 Ibid. 222.

38 Ibid.

39 Liz Ercevik Amado, 'Promoting Sexual Rights Through Human Rights Education: Experiences at Grassroots in Turkey' (2006) 17 Institute of Development Studies Bulletin 117, 119. Unni Wikan explains that it is also shameful for a woman to kiss her husband on her own initiative (Unni Wikan, 'Shame and Honour: A Contestable Pair' (1984) 19 Man, New Series 635, 641).

40 Abu-Odeh (n 25) 151.

41 John P Mason, 'Sex and Symbol in the Treatment of Women: The Wedding Rite in a Libyan Oasis Community' (1975) 2 American Ethnologist 649, 89.

42 Işık and Sakallı-Uğurlu (n 18) 2.

and sexuality, chastity is a value that encompasses *namus* but extends beyond it: *Namus* can be explained as a subordinate category of chastity.[43] Chastity is a combination of all behaviours that women should have and protect in their families and societies; these behaviours are linked not necessarily only to sexuality but also to purity, modesty, and decency.

As with *namus*, gender discrimination and powerful patriarchy concerning honour govern chastity as well. In societies where honour has an important role, chastity is linked to women, not men. Men's sexual behaviours and heterosexual sexual experiences before marriage are not normally questioned by others; they are usually tolerated and even sometimes encouraged[44] (with the exception of adultery, rape, and same-sex relationships). The main reason for this lack of scrutiny of men's sexual relationships with women is because men's chastity is attached to and dependent on their kinwomen's chastity.[45] Men and women both share the responsibility of protecting this chastity: Women should protect their chastity, and men should control, protect, and secure it.[46]

Analysing societies' beliefs on how to be chaste and decent does not lead to any sole definition; in honour-based societies, it is the combination of traditions, customs, and beliefs that creates the whole concept of chastity. From childhood until death, different societies create their own specific behaviours that women must follow in order to prove, protect, and maintain their chastity. Some of these behaviours are common to both virgins and married women; however, some of them are applicable only to one or the other.

Submitting to patriarchal authority is one of the behaviours that can be displayed by both maidens and married women. However, the nature of this authority changes before and after the marriage. Before the marriage, it is expected that a virgin obeys her kinsmen's authority, whereas after the marriage she should follow only her husband's path. The set of rules and behaviours (which can also be defined as customary rules) are established in one way to prove that the patriarchal system works efficiently, and in another way to restrict and control the female agnates as well as to protect the family's reputation and honour in the community.[47] For instance, it is always thought

43 As previously explained, *namus* is more related to sexuality. The Turkish phrase we encountered above, "*namus iki bacak arasındadır*" refers to how *namus* is specifically related to virginity and sexuality.

44 Cindoglu (n 36) 216; Pinar Ilkkaracan, 'Exploring the Context of Women's Sexuality in Eastern Turkey' in Pinar Ilkkaracan (ed), *Women and Sexuality in Muslim Societies* (Istanbul, Women for Women's Human Rights (WWHR) 2000) 238; Ipek Ilkkaracan and Gulsah Seral, 'Sexual Pleasure as a Woman's Human Right: Experiences From Grassroots Training Program in Turkey' in Pinar Ilkkaracan (ed), *Women and Sexuality in Muslim Societies* (Istanbul, Women for Women's Human Rights (WWHR) 2000) 187.

45 Aylin Akpinar, 'Honour/Shame Complex Revisited: Violence Against Women in the Migration Context' (2003) 26 Women's Studies International Forum 425, 431.

46 Ibid.; Aliye Çınar Köysüren, *Kültürel ve Dini Algıda Toplumsal Cinsiyet* (Bursa, Sentez 2013) 107, 125.

47 Nikki Keddie and Lois Beck, *Women in the Muslim World* (Cambridge, Cambridge University Press 1978) 24.

proper that a maiden should sit, eat, and dress in certain ways by her parents.[48] A maiden should also behave in such a way in society that she does not draw any attention to herself; in other words, she should preserve her anonymity.[49] It is mostly the style of dress and their behaviour outside the family home that have a major role in demonstrating this conservatism, chastity, and *namus*. If a woman dresses revealingly or if she walks or talks to strangers on the street, if she speaks loudly or laughs, then all of these provide sufficient evidence to question her *namus* and chastity.[50]

A married woman, on the other hand, always represents her husband in society. As a result of this, her engagement with outsiders should be at a formal level at all times, even if she works or is continuing in education. Otherwise, her social peers will readily suspect and question these relations, seeing them as adulterous and betrayals of her husband. Even if these allegations are not supported by sufficient evidence, unfortunately in many cases they may be taken seriously by husbands and their families, and as a result of these allegations, women's husbands may commit violent actions or even homicide against their wives to cleanse this dishonour.

As with maidens, a married woman is expected to prove and protect her chastity with her behaviours in society; she should also dress and talk in a modest way. Although in those societies it is usually believed that women are supposed to meet their husband's sexual desires according to their husband's wishes, they need to preserve their attractiveness in front of others and be obedient towards their husbands' boundaries,[51] and they should not appear in society with their sexualities and desires.[52]

3. Conclusion

The aim of this chapter has been to analyse the term of 'honour' conceptually. Although *şeref*, *namus*, and chastity have their counterparts in patriarchal Western societies, as mentioned in the previous chapter, these terms have been considered here within the hermeneutical circle of HBV. Since conceptualising honour

48 Ilkkaracan and Seral (n 44) 187.

49 Miki Suzuki Him and Ayse Gunduz Hosgor, 'Reproductive Practises: Kurdish Women Responding to Patriarchy' (2011) 34 Women's Studies International Forum 335, 338; Mehtap Hamzaoğlu and Emrah Konuralp, 'Geleneksel Toplumlarda Namus Olgusu ve Namus Cinayeti: Türkiye Örneği' (2019) 1 İstanbul Üniversitesi Kadın Araştırmaları Dergisi 51, 53.

50 Sabina Faiz Rashid and Stephanie Michaud, 'Female Adolescents and Their Sexuality: Notions of Honour, Shame, Purity and Pollution During the Floods' (2000) 24 Overseas Development Institute Disasters 54, 57.

51 Fatma Umar Naseef, *Women in Islam: A Discourse in Rights and Obligations* (New Delhi, Sterling Publishers Private Limited 1999) 202–03.

52 Him and Gunduz Hosgor (n 49) 338; Ayesha M Imam, 'The Muslim Religious Right ("Fundamentalists") and Sexuality' in Haideh Moghissi (ed), *Women and Islam: Critical Concepts in Sociology* (Oxon, Routledge 2005) 58–59.

and HBV has been done using an inductive approach, I have conceptualised the term starting from its constituent parts. Therefore, I created the concept of honour's own hermeneutical circle, where honour itself stands as a whole. Within this circle, honour's constituent parts are *şeref*, *namus*, and chastity.

The analysis in this chapter has examined the importance of honour, as well as the importance of its related terms, such as chastity, virginity, purity, *namus*, and *şeref*. It has also identified specific traditions, customs, and beliefs that have an impact on shaping the value of honour in Turkey. For instance, proving virginity on the nuptial night is one of the most important, traditional, and customary practices that persists related to honour. This practice is also important to prove that honour is not personal but communal and social. It is the honour of not only persons but also families and societies.

In addition to this, honour-related terms illustrate the significant segregation between genders. As we will see later on, this segregation can be distinguished from possessing, maintaining, and protecting honour. For instance, while women do not possess honour individually, every woman is under the burden of protecting and maintaining it. This protection can be provided only with certain behaviours and actions that are accepted by societies. Men, by comparison, have different roles and responsibilities regarding honour; they are responsible for their female agnates' visibility outside of their family home and their behaviours and relationships towards strangers.

This is an introductory chapter that sets out a way to conceptualise honour. This conceptualisation will be the starting point for examining gender relations, VAW, domestic violence, and HBV in Turkey. It is important to highlight and clarify what honour means at the beginning of this research. In light of this conceptualisation, the following chapters will deal with the background of HBV, i.e. the social environment within which the crimes are committed. This will also help us to understand and analyse how laws in Turkey are shaped and interpreted when it comes to HBV. Without conceptualising and interpreting honour within the hermeneutical circle of HBV, our further analysis of legal challenges would be misleading and, perhaps, confused.

Bibliography

Abu-Odeh L, 'Crimes of Honour and Construction of Gender in Arab Societies' in Mai Yamani (ed), *Feminism and Islam: Legal and Literary Perspectives* (Reading, Garnet Publishing Limited 1996)

Adler MJ, *The Difference of Man and the Difference It Makes* (New York, Holt, Rinehart and Winston 1968)

Akkay E, 'Ülkemizde Kızlık Zarı ve Adlı Tıp Sorunları' (2011) 48 İstanbul Üniversitesi Hukuk Fakültesi Mecmuası 325

Akpinar A, 'Honour/Shame Complex Revisited: Violence Against Women in the Migration Context' (2003) 26 Women's Studies International Forum 425

Aytemiz P, 'Lost and Found Virginity: A Critical Look to the "Reappearing Hymen" in Consumer Culture' (2015) 23 İLETİ-Ş-İM 97

Baroja JC, 'Honour and Shame: A Historical Account of Several Conflicts' in JG Peristiany (ed), *Honour and Shame: The Values of Mediterranean Societies* (London, Weidenfeld and Nicolson 1965)

Bayefksy R, 'Dignity, Honour, and Human Rights: Kant's Perspective' (2013) 41 Political Theory 809

Boiger M and others, 'Defending Honour, Keeping Face: Interpersonal Affordances of Anger and Shame in Turkey and Japan' (2014) Cognition & Emotion 1

Ceylan S, Doğulu C and Akbaş G, 'Namus Adına Kadına Yönelik Şiddete Dair Sosyal Temsiller: Karma Yöntemli Bir Çalışma' (2016) 2016 Türk Psikoloji Yazıları 56

Çınar Köysüren A, *Kültürel ve Dini Algıda Toplumsal Cinsiyet* (Bursa, Sentez 2013)

Cindoglu D, 'Virginity Tests and Artificial Virginity' in Pinar Ilkkaracan (ed), *Women and Sexuality in Muslim Societies* (Istanbul, Women for Women's Human Rights (WWHR) 2000)

Corbin BA, 'Between Saviors and Savages: The Effect of Turkey's Revised Penal Code on the Transformation of Honor Killings Into Honor Suicides and Why Community Discourse Is Necessary for Honor Crime Eradication' (2014) 29 Emory International Law Review 277

Dogan R, 'Different Cultural Understandings of Honor That Inspire Killings: An Inquiry Into the Defendant's Perspective' (2014) Homicide Studies 1

Ecevitoğlu P, *Namus Töre ve İktidar: Kadının Çıplak Hayat Olarak Kuruluşu* (Ankara, Dipnot 2012)

El Saadawi N, *The Hidden Face of Eve* (London, Zed Books Ltd 1980)

Ercevik Amado L, 'Promoting Sexual Rights Through Human Rights Education: Experiences at Grassroots in Turkey' (2006) 17 Institute of Development Studies Bulletin 117

Erdmann C, *The Origin of the Idea of Crusade* (Surrey, Princeton University Press 1977)

Eşsizoğlu A and others, 'Double Standard for Traditional Value of Virginity and Premarital Sexuality in Turkey: A University Student Case' (2011) 51 Women & Health 136

Finucane RC, *Soldiers of the Faith: Crusaders and Moslems at War* (London and Melbourne, JM Dent & Sons Ltd 1983)

Formosa P, 'Dignity and Respect: How to Apply Kant's Formula of Humanity' (2014) 45 The Philosophical Forum, Inc. 49

Fournier P, McDougall P and Dekker AR, 'Dishonour, Provocation and Culture: Through the Beholder's Eye?' (2012) 16 Canadian Criminal Law Review 161

Friedman M, *Autonomy, Gender, Politics* (Oxford, Oxford University Press 2003)

Gill AK and Brah A, 'Interrogating Cultural Narratives About "Honour"-Based Violence' (2014) 21 European Journal of Women's Studies 72

Gürsoy E and Arslan-Özkan H, 'Türkiye'de Üniversite Öğrencilerinin Kadına İlişkin "Namus" Algısı (Turkish Youth's Perception of Sexuality/"Honor" on Relation to Women' (2014) 5 Psikiyatri Hemşireliği Dergisi 149

Hamzaoğlu M and Konuralp E, 'Geleneksel Toplumlarda Namus Olgusu ve Namus Cinayeti: Türkiye Örneği' (2019) 1 İstanbul Üniversitesi Kadın Araştırmaları Dergisi 51

Him MS and Gunduz Hosgor A, 'Reproductive Practises: Kurdish Women Responding to Patriarchy' (2011) 34 Women's Studies International Forum 335

Ilkkaracan I and Seral G, 'Sexual Pleasure as a Woman's Human Right: Experiences From Grassroots Training Program in Turkey' in Pinar Ilkkaracan (ed), *Women and Sexuality in Muslim Societies* (Istanbul, Women for Women's Human Rights (WWHR) 2000)

Ilkkaracan P, 'Exploring the Context of Women's Sexuality in Eastern Turkey' in Pinar Ilkkaracan (ed), *Women and Sexuality in Muslim Societies* (Istanbul, Women for Women's Human Rights (WWHR) 2000)

———, 'How Adultery Almost Derailed Turkey's Aspiration to Join the European Union' in Pinar Ilkkaracan (ed), *Deconstructing Sexuality in the Middle East* (Aldershot, Ashgate 2008)

Imam AM, 'The Muslim Religious Right ("Fundamentalists") and Sexuality' in Haideh Moghissi (ed), *Women and Islam: Critical Concepts in Sociology* (Oxon, Routledge 2005)

Işık R and Sakallı-Uğurlu N, 'Development of "Attitudes Toward Honor" and "Violence Against Women in the Name of Honor" Scales' (2009) 12 Türk Psikoloji Yazıları 1

Kant I, *Groundwork for the Metaphysics of Morals* (Allen W Wood ed, New Haven & London, Yale University Press 2002)

Karmi G, 'Women, Islam, and Patriarchalism' in Mai Yamani (ed), *Feminism and Islam: Legal and Literary Perspectives* (Reading, Garnet Publishing Limited 1996)

Kaygisiz Ertug Z, 'Individual Differences on the Importance of Virginity in Turkish Society: An Application on Turkish University Students' (2013) 10 International Journal of Human Sciences 610

Keddie N and Beck L, *Women in the Muslim World* (Cambridge, Cambridge University Press 1978)

Khan TS, *Beyond Honour: A Historical Materialist Explanation of Honour Related Violence* (Oxford, Oxford University Press 2006)

Kimbrell A, *The Masculine Mystique: The Politics of Masculinity* (New York, Ballantine Books 1995)

Kocadaş B, 'Sosyolojik Açıdan Gençlerin Namus ve Şiddet Değerlendirmeleri' (2016) 1 Sosyolojik Düşün 27

Komut S, 'Women, Sexuality and Virginity in Turkey' (2011) 3 Sosyal ve Beşeri Bilimler Dergisi 87

LaVaque-Manty M, 'Dueling for Equality: Masculine Honor and the Modern Politics of Dignity' (2006) 34 Political Theory 715

Lindisfarne N, 'Variant Masculinities, Variant Virginities: Rethinking "Honour and Shame"' in Andrea Cornwall (ed), *Dislocating Masculinity: Comparative Ethnographies* (London, Routledge 2003)

Lloyd S, *English Society and The Crusade: 1216–1307* (Oxford, Clarendon Press 1988)

Mason JP, 'Sex and Symbol in the Treatment of Women: The Wedding Rite in a Libyan Oasis Community' (1975) 2 American Ethnologist 649

Müftüler-Bac M, 'Turkish Women's Predicament' (1999) 22 Women's Studies International Forum 303

Naseef FU, *Women in Islam: A Discourse in Rights and Obligations* (New Delhi, Sterling Publishers Private Limited 1999)

Osch Y van and others, 'A Different Kind of Culture: Family Honor and Aggression in Turks' (2013) 16 Group Process & Intergroup Relations 334

Ozgur S and Sunar D, 'Social Psychological Patterns of Homicide in Turkey, A Comparison of Male and Female Convicted Murders' in Cigdem Kagitcibasi (ed), *Sex Roles, Family, and Community in Turkey* (Indiana, Indiana University Turkish Studies 1982)

Rashid SF and Michaud S, 'Female Adolescents and Their Sexuality: Notions of Honour, Shame, Purity and Pollution During the Floods' (2000) 24 Overseas Development Institute Disasters 54
Robinson P, *Military Honour and the Conduct of War: From Ancient Greece to Iraq* (Oxon, Routledge 2006)
Rosen M, *Dignity: Its History and Meaning* (Cambridge, MA, Harvard University Press 2012)
Saraiya H, 'Surgical Revirgination: Four Vaginal Mucosal Flaps for Reconstruction of a Hymen' (2015) 48 Indian Journal of Plastic Surgery 192
Sensen O, *Kant on Human Dignity* (Göttingen, Hubert & Co GmbH & Co KG 2011)
Taylor C, 'The Politics of Recognition' in Amy Gutmann (ed), *Multiculturalism: Examining the Politics of Recognition* (Princeton, Princeton University Press 1994)
Tekin D, 'Victims of Law: The Efficiency of Turkish Penal System on Honour Killings' (2012) Strategic Outlook
Van Eck C, *Purified By Blood: Honour Killings Among Turks in the Netherlands* (Amsterdam, Amsterdam University Press 2003)
Wikan U, 'Shame and Honour: A Contestable Pair' (1984) 19 Man, New Series 635
Yeşilçiçek Çalik K, 'Attitudes of Turkish Academics Regarding Violence Against Women in the Name of Honor' (2018) 33 Journal of Interpersonal Violence 3232

3 Theoretical background of gender relations and violence against women in Turkey

1. Introduction

This chapter focuses on the concerns common to feminist approaches to gender relations, identifying which aspects will better serve to explain and provide a critical analysis. Here, again, we will realise the importance of understanding the hermeneutical circle of HBV. This theoretical analysis will ultimately create the necessary groundwork for the following chapters to build on relating to the motives behind HBV and to show how the State and society tackle this type of violence.

While this chapter mainly deals with gender relation theories and how patriarchy, hierarchy, and masculinity shape gender difference, it also aims to draw a picture of the traditional Turkish nuclear family, in order to show how patriarchy and hierarchy shape this family structure. Making this structural relationship explicit at this stage is highly important, as it is instrumental in identifying the perpetrators of HBV and showing how their assumptions about gender role divisions affect their behaviour – and in particular their use of violence. This analysis is also an important conceptual technique for supporting the legal analysis later on in this study, particularly in understanding specific cases and how judges interpret the social code of honour.

2. Feminist movements in the Middle East and Turkey

This section focuses on feminist movements in the Middle East and Turkey. Although Middle Eastern feminist movements in general and Turkish feminism in particular have followed Western feminism, there are still huge differences between Western and Eastern feminism. This section focuses on these differences by analysing secular and non-secular feminist movements.

2.1 Non-secular feminist movements in the Middle East and Turkey

Huma Ahmed-Ghosh clearly defines Islamic and secular feminism and adds a third form of feminism: 'hybrid feminism.'[1] According to Ahmed-Ghosh,

1 Huma Ahmed-Ghosh, 'Dilemmas of Islamic and Secular Feminists and Feminisms' (2008) 9 Journal of Women's Studies 99, 101–02.

"Islamic feminists seek Muslim women's emancipation within rubrics of Islamic patriarchy."[2] Haideh Moghissi, on the other hand, emphasises that Islamic feminism is used to denote any activities and/or beliefs on the part of Muslim women who are trying to improve conditions for their sex within a faith-based system.[3] Both scholars are in agreement on the influence of faith on gender inequality.[4] However, Ahmed-Ghosh's argument is mainly directed towards the patriarchy that has been created within the context of Islam. Some Islamic feminists in the Middle East take this argument seriously. For instance, Amina Wadud and Asma Barlas specifically tackle dilemmas arising from the institution of patriarchal Islam and patriarchal interpretations of Islam.[5] They strongly argue that Islam is not patriarchal, and so cannot be cited as the main source of inequality between men and women; what causes inequality is not the Qur'an but the patriarchal interpretation of it, which has been affected by culture and traditions.[6] Asma Barlas's critical analysis is based on the importance of reading the Qur'an without patriarchal influence and from a woman's perspective.[7] Like Barlas, Amina Wadud also pays attention to reading the Qur'an from a woman's perspective, but she highlights the gender equality that she believes the Qur'an actually creates.[8] However, Ziba Mir-Hosseini argues, more in line with Barlas, that legal and social inequality are human constructs rather than the product of religion.[9]

Feminist movements from the Islamic perspective have a unique character in Turkey: they aim not only to provide an interpretation of Islam in favour of women but also to separate women from the secular identity that Ataturk and the Turkish Republic created in the 1920s. Gülnaz and Şişman emphasise the need

2 Ibid. 103.

3 Haideh Moghissi, *Feminism and Islamic Fundamentalism: The Limits of Postmodern Analysis* (London, Zed Books Ltd 1999) 134.

4 The relationship between faith and gender equality has also been analysed by Miriam Cooke, who considers the relationship between faith and women's rights as a difficult double commitment (Miriam Cooke, *Women Claim Islam: Creating Islamic Feminism Through Literature* (London, Routledge 2001) 59).

5 In fact, Asma Barlas does not call herself a 'feminist' but rather a 'believing woman' (Asma Barlas, 'Engaging Islamic Feminism: Provincializing Feminism as a Master Narrative' in *Islamic Feminism: Current Perspectives* (Tampare, Juvenes Print 2008) 16.

6 For further information see Asma Barlas, *Believing Women in Islam: Unreading Patriarchal Interpretations of the Qur'an* (Austin, University of Texas Press 2003); Amina Wadud, *Qur'an and Woman: Rereading the Sacred Text From a Woman's Perspective* (Oxford, Oxford University Press 1999). See also Ahmed-Ghosh (n 1); Ziba Mir-Hosseini, 'Muslim Women's Quest for Equality: Between Islamic Law and Feminism' (2006) 32 Critical Inquiry 629, 633.

7 Barlas (n 6). See also Margot Badran, *Feminism in Islam: Secular and Religious Convergences* (Oxford, One World Publications 2009) 244.

8 Wadud (n 6) 15.

9 Mir-Hosseini (n 6) 642. In contrast, Shaheen Sardar Ali argues that although the Qur'an promotes equality between men and women in terms of fulfilling religious obligations, there is a hierarchy between the sexes that makes men higher than women (Shaheen Sardar Ali, *Gender and Human Rights in Islam and International Law: Equal Before Allah, Unequal Before Man?* (The Hague, Kluwer Law International 2000) 42–91).

for an Islamic interpretation of gender relations in Turkish society.[10] One of the main arguments of Islamic feminists in Turkey is that a modernising and westernising society causes more problems for gender relations and has turned women into sex objects, making them more vulnerable.[11]

The appearance of the Islamic feminist movement in Turkey has mainly remained in the shadow of political movements. In fact, instead of being independent, the Islamic feminist movement has acted as a branch of certain right-wing political parties and some Islamic movements.[12] Although conservative women have been working on women's rights, their activities do not really fit the wider context of feminism. As Serpil Sancar mentions, the main difference between feminism in general and women's movements depends on their aims.[13] While feminism criticises the system as a whole and aims to make substantial changes to it, women's movements aim to improve women's rights and conditions within a specific society without necessarily aiming to change the system as a whole.[14] Whether we call non-secular feminism in Turkey 'Islamic feminism' or the 'Islamic women's movement,' it has unfortunately fallen behind secular feminist movements in Turkey, and their activism has mostly focused on freedom of religion and religious rights.[15] Because the main concern of the Islamic feminist movement is how to enjoy the Islamic way of life, rather than address the lack of sexual autonomy for women or the problem of HBV, it has not fundamentally challenged patriarchal society.[16]

2.2 Secular feminist movements in the Middle East and Turkey

Secular feminist movements explore their arguments within the human rights and women's rights arenas and aim to separate religion from the analysis.[17] For instance, Valentine Moghadam states that "women's rights and human rights are best promoted and protected in an environment of secular thought and secular institutions."[18] Like Moghadam, Kandiyoti also extensively deals with secular feminism and secular feminist movements in the Middle East. Kandiyoti divides

10 Ozlem Ingun, 'Feminizm ve Islam Iliskisi: "Islami Feminizm"' (Uludag Universitesi 2005) 112.

11 Ibid. 113.

12 Rusen Cakir, 'Dindar Kadinin Seruveni' (2000) 137 Birikim <www.rusencakir.com/Dindar-kadinin-seruveni/292> accessed 24 January 2020.

13 Yasemin Akis and Ulku Ozakin, 'Türkiye'de Feminizm ve Kadın Hareketi' *BiaMag* (16 May 2009) <http://bianet.org/biamag/diger/114551-turkiye-de-feminizm-ve-kadin-hareketi> accessed 24 January 2020.

14 Ibid.

15 Cagla Diner and Sule Toktas, 'Waves of Feminism in Turkey: Kemalist, Islamist and Kurdish Women's Movements in Era of Globalization' (2010) 12 Journal of Balkan and Near Eastern Studies 41, 42.

16 Ibid. 50.

17 Ahmed-Ghosh (n 1) 106.

18 Valentine M Moghadam, 'Islamic Feminism and Its Discontents: Toward a Resolution of the Debate' (2002) 27 Journal of Women, Culture, and Society 1135, 1160.

feminist movements in the Middle East into three categories: the first wave: feminism and nationalism; the second wave: the rise of social paradigms and developmentalism; and the third wave: dialogues within feminism.[19] Kandiyoti's first wave feminism coincides with the era of social reforms, modernisation, and the formation of the postcolonial state.[20] Her second wave of feminism, on the other hand, refers to awareness of the family and women's roles in social discourse, mainly in modernisation theory and Marxism.[21] This conceptualisation provides an insight into how early interpretations of Marxist feminist theories explored existing gender issues in the Middle East and the Muslim world. Kandiyoti's third wave refers to the dialogues within feminism and reflects the work that has been carried out by Western scholars or Western-trained scholars in the Middle East.[22] Kandiyoti's early work on feminist movements in the Middle East and the Muslim world is still relevant and applicable in many aspects and still highlights the current debates on gender relations. However, they are far from reflecting another issue that has affected many Middle Eastern and Muslim women and their lives in the Western world: multiculturalism. Middle Eastern women's problems and the issue of gender inequality go beyond concepts of regionality in the contemporary world. Many Middle Eastern and Muslim women who live in Western countries suffer the effects of multiculturalism, and I will come back to this point in the following section.

Middle Eastern and North African feminists have framed their arguments using different paradigms, *inter alia* gender inequality, patriarchy, and lack of women's autonomy. Turkish feminists and scholars have followed a similar approach. Secular feminism in Turkey can be seen in different forms: Kemalist, socialist, and Kurdish feminism. The following paragraphs provide a historical background of Turkish secular feminist movements and how they tackle gender issues.

Since the 1920s, a series of political and legal improvements have been established in Turkey, and the women's movements have been shaped by this. Feminist movements, especially between the 1920s and 1980s, shared a parallel ideology with the Kemalist movement.[23] During this time, Turkish feminism was not very effective and remained under the shadow of the strong Kemalist ideology, which aimed to create a nation without any links to the Ottoman Empire.[24] Although Kemalism has had an undeniable role in improving women's status,

19 Deniz Kandiyoti, 'Contemporary Feminist Scholarship and Middle East Studies' in Deniz Kandiyoti (ed), *Gendering the Middle East: Emerging Perspectives* (London, Tauris &Co Ltd 1996) 8–15.

20 Ibid. 8.

21 Ibid. 10.

22 Ibid. 12–13.

23 Sevin Unlu, 'Turk Toplumunda Feminizm: Universiteli Gencler Uzerinde Bir Arastirma' (Gazi Universitesi 2000) 68.

24 Pinar Ilkkaracan, 'Reforming the Penal Code in Turkey: The Campaign for the Reform of the Turkish Penal Code from a Gender Perspective' (2007) Institute of Development Studies Bulletin 1, 7.

it is debatable whether women have achieved that status.[25] According to some scholars, Kemalist reforms did not provide an environment for women to gain their rights themselves: it conferred rights on women, and this can be described as man-made equality.[26] By providing legislative improvement in women's rights, Sancar suggests that this was part of an era when women were not expected to fight for their rights.[27] Arat critically argues that Kemalism did not actually wish to be feminist. According to Arat, Kemalist reforms did not aim to make women free and improve women's consciousness and self-identity, but rather to serve to the 'Republican patriarchy' that supported traditional gender roles, whereby women make good mothers and wives[28] and remain pure and chaste.[29] It gave women rights and aimed to improve their status because women were considered to be the main source of Kemalist re-evaluation:[30] in other words, the sign of Turkey's modernisation and civilisation.[31] And, because the Kemalist movement was more nationalist than feminist, tackling HBV was not the main purpose of it.

Since the beginning of the 1980s, Turkish feminist movements have become highly effective.[32] Women's rights activists started to raise many questions about equality between men and women and the necessity of recognising women's rights as human rights. This includes rights related to women's sexual autonomy.[33] This period can be referred to as the second wave of feminism in Turkey. Since the 1980s, women have raised their voices against state patriarchy and patriarchal laws;[34] this was the perfect moment for women to become activists because of the coup d'état in Turkey.[35] During this time, many political parties

25 Meltem Müftüler-Bac, 'Turkish Women's Predicament' (1999) 22 Women's Studies International Forum 303, 304.

26 Seda Cosar, *The Reflections of the Ottoman-Turkish Feminism on the Literary Works of Nezihe Muhittin* (Ankara, Graduate School of Social Sciences of Middle East Technical University 2006) 18.

27 Serpil Sancar, *Türk Modernleşmesinin Cinsiyeti: Erkekler Devlet, Kadınlar Aile Kurar* (Istanbul, İletisim 2012) 162.

28 Zehra Arat, 'Kemalizm ve Turk Kadini'' in *75 Yilda Kadinlar ve Erkekler* (Istanbul, Tarih Vakfi Yayinlari 1998) 52; Simten Cosar, 'Women in Turkish Political Thought: Between Tradition and Modernity' (2007) 86 Feminist Review 113, 117–20; Müftüler-Bac (n 25) 307.

29 Nevin Yıldız Tahincioğlu, 'Namus Olgusunun Bir Biyo-Politik Olarak Düşünülebilirliği: Şanlıurfa Örneği' (2010) 13 Akdeniz iletişim Fakültesi Dergisi 1, 7.

30 Elvan Ozdemir, 'Kemalist Tradition and Kemalist Women's Movement in Turkey After 1980' (2010) 1 Turkish Journal of Politics 99, 101; Necla Arat, 'Women's Studies in Turkey' (1996) 24 Women's Studies Quarterly 400, 401.

31 Cosar (n 26) 117–20; Ayşe Durakbaşa, 'Kemalism as Identity Politics in Turkey' in Zehra Arat (ed), *Deconstructing Images of 'The Turkish Woman'* (London, Macmillan 1998) 141.

32 'Türkiye'de Toplumsal Cinsiyet Eşitsizliği: Sorunlar ve Çözüm Önerileri' (Istanbul, TUSIAD and KAGIDER 2008) 245.

33 Yesim Arat, 'Toward a Democratic Society: The Women's Movement in Turkey in the 1980s' (1994) 17 Women's Studies International Forum 241, 244.

34 Ibid. 244–45.

35 Saime Ozcurumez and Feyda Sayan Cengiz, 'On Resilience and Response Beyond Value Change: Transformation of Women's Movement in Post-1980 Turkey' (2011) 34 Women's

were shut down and there was a political gap in the country that was ideal for women to create their own new groups.[36] This period was highly fruitful for the raising of gender consciousness in general and for fighting against VAW, including HBV, in particular.

After the 1980s, it was not only socialist and Kemalist feminist movements that emerged: the people also witnessed the establishment of Kurdish feminism in Turkey.[37] This represents the third wave of feminism, with a Kurdish nationalist ideology or 'Kurdishness.'[38] The main argument within the Kurdish feminist movement is to improve Kurdish women's rights and conditions within not only society but also the State. Although the Kurdish feminist movement has been accused of being a part of the Kurdish Worker's Party (PKK), their activism has had considerable effect on raising awareness about HBV, especially within the Kurdish communities in Turkey.

3. Gender relation theories and violence against women

The aim of this section is to analyse gender relation theories that interpret HBV and how these theories create a bridge between honour and HBV. Therefore, patriarchy, hierarchy, masculinity, and femininity will be the main subjects of this section.

The common ground linking all types of violence is the creation of an imbalance of power between the victims and the offenders, or the maintaining of an existing imbalance. Patriarchy, hierarchy, and masculinity are some of the key factors for creating this imbalance and making victims weak and the offenders powerful. Before analysing the motives behind VAW, it is important to highlight why women are the primary victims of such violence. The first possible interpretation, which is the patriarchal interpretation, is because women are weak and cannot protect themselves.[39] Moreover, patriarchal and hierarchal societies try to keep women weak and powerless. Using VAW is one of the ways to maintain this weakness and preserve the superiority of men over women. In strict patriarchal families, one of the factors that ensures men's power is the continuity of women's weakness. If women become powerful, then men's power is questioned or, as Kandiyoti terms it, 'bargained.'[40] Stabilising women's inferiority by applying violence is one way to protect men's power and superiority.

Studies International Forum 20, 24; Ömer Çaha, *Sivil Kadın: Türkiye'de Sivil Toplum ve Kadın* (Ankara, Vadi Yayınları 1996) 142.

36 Unlu (n 23) 671.

37 Shahrzad Mojab, 'The Politics of "Cyberfeminism" in the Middle East: The Case of Kurdish Women' (2001) 8 Race, Gender, Class 42, 47.

38 Diner and Toktas (n 15) 48.

39 Jamie R Abrams, 'The Collateral Consequences of Masculinizing Violence' (2010) 16 William and Mary Journal of Women and the Law 703, 717; Nancy Lindisfarne, 'Variant Masculinities, Variant Virginities: Rethinking "Honour and Shame"' in Andrea Cornwall (ed), *Dislocating Masculinity: Comparative Ethnographies* (London, Routledge 2003) 85.

40 Deniz Kandiyoti, 'Bargaining With Patriarchy' (1988) 2 Gender and Society 274, 274.

3.1 Gender relations in Turkey: cultural and traditional roots

3.1.1 Patriarchy and hierarchy

Patriarchy and hierarchy are two important systems to apply to gender relations. The hermeneutical circle of HBV, as we have seen, includes patriarchy, culture, and tradition. These parts are firmly connected to each other, and in many cases, it is impossible to separate them. They create the link between the concept of honour and the law and complete the hermeneutical circle of HBV by introducing the social background of these crimes. Despite Dogan's contrary argument, without attempting to interpret these terms, it will be difficult to analyse the concept of HBV within the context of Turkey properly.[41]

Living in a patriarchal social structure alone does not cause domestic violence. However, patriarchy plays a leading part in triggering it. Both Western and Middle Eastern researchers agree that patriarchy is not a phenomenon unique to Middle Eastern and Muslim societies. Patriarchy can be seen in any type of society; indeed, as Ahmed-Ghosh explains, all women – whether they are religious or non-religious – live in patriarchal societies.[42] It is a matter of the degree and shape of patriarchy, how it affects individual and society's behaviour, and how it causes violence.[43]

Like the Western concept of patriarchy, the basic principle of patriarchy within Turkish societies is to accept men's superior and dominant position over women in every aspect of life. However, it is not only patriarchy that causes the oppression but also hierarchy. Therefore, women feel a dual oppression: One is patriarchal and the other is hierarchal. In fact, the main difference between patriarchy and hierarchy is that while patriarchal structure is based on gender relations, hierarchy is usually based on age division.[44] With both combined, this can create a type of family structure defined as 'classic patriarchy' by Kandiyoti in 'Bargaining with Patriarchy.'[45] Kandiyoti describes men's oppression of women as a form of patriarchy and women's superiority over other women as a form of hierarchy and combines them under the same rubric: 'classic patriarchy.'[46] As will be seen later, this patriarchal and hierarchal gender division has a crucial role to play in identifying the victims and perpetrators of HBV.

This patriarchal and hierarchal family structure has serious consequences for women in Turkey. First, it creates clear inequality and discrimination between men and women. In patriarchal families, both males and females feel pressure from the heads of the families. What is problematic here is the degree of that

41 Recep Dogan, 'Do Women Really Kill for Honor? Conceptualizing Women's Involvement in Honor Killings' (2018) 39 Deviant Behavior 1247.
42 Ahmed-Ghosh (n 1) 100.
43 Kalwant Bhobal, *Gender, 'Race' and Patriarchy: A Study of South Asian Women* (Aldershot, Ashgate 1997) 50–51.
44 Kandiyoti, 'Bargaining With Patriarchy' (n 40) 278.
45 Ibid.
46 Ibid. 279.

pressure. The degree of pressure applied to males and females is different. Especially within the concept of honour and the family's reputation, women feel a strong patriarchal pressure, but men do not. Second, while both females and males are collectively responsible for the protection and maintenance of family honour, this responsibility is not divided equally between the genders. Men fulfil this duty by putting pressure on women, thereby making sure that women remain inferior and obedient and avoid shame.[47] Women, on the other hand, feel a dual pressure: pressure from their patriarchal families to protect the family honour and pressure from their male kin in order to guarantee that the male kin fulfil their duties properly within the 'classic patriarchy' context described by Kandiyoti.[48]

At this stage, it may be useful to sketch the structure of patriarchal and hierarchal families in traditional Turkish societies. The concept of extended family structure is evident in Turkey but not as common as it is used to be; although two or three generations do not always live under the same roof, they either live very close to each other or remain in very close relationships.[49]

If the family structure is considered as a pyramid, at the top of it stands the father, who is the patriarchal and hierarchal head. Below him, the mother and brothers take their places. While the brothers' position is based on the patriarchy, the mother's position is based on hierarchy within this structure. Mothers who share the responsibility of bringing up the children have authority over their children. The oppression and pressure are always more effective and visible on the daughters than on the sons.[50] Whereas a mother's control over her daughter is unlimited and lasts forever, her influence on her sons is reduced considerably when they reach adulthood. However, even though sons are less oppressed than daughters, this does not mean that mothers lose all their authority over them.[51] This authority is not exercised in the form of discipline but comes from sons respecting motherhood and the age hierarchy. Even so, when they reach adulthood, sons remain under the oppressive discipline of their fathers as a result of patriarchal and hierarchical structure.[52]

What needs to be understood about this structure is that although sons occupy a place in a patriarchal pyramid under their fathers and mothers, their position in relation to their mothers is not stable but rather dynamic. However, this

47 Aisha K Gill and Avtar Brah, 'Interrogating Cultural Narratives About "Honour"-Based Violence' (2014) 21 European Journal of Women's Studies 72, 74; Michelle Lowe and others, 'Attitudes towards Intimate Partner "Honor" Based Violence in India, Iran, Malaysia and Pakistan' (2018) 10 Journal of Aggression, Conflict and Peace Research 283, 284.

48 Kandiyoti, 'Bargaining With Patriarchy' (n 40) 278.

49 Orhan Bingöl, 'Toplumsal Cinsiyet Olgusu ve Türkiye'de Kadınlık' (2014) 16 KMÜ Sosyal ve Ekonomik Araştırmalar Dergisi 108, 112.

50 Lila Abu-Lughod, *Veiled Sentiments: Honor and Poetry in a Bedouin Society* (Berkley, University of California Press 1999) 109.

51 Ibid. 81.

52 Aysel Günindi Ersöz, 'Türk Atasözleri ve Deyimlerde Kadına Yönelik Toplumsal Cinsiyet Rolleri' (2010) 1 Gazi Türkiyat Türkoloji Araştırmaları Dergisi 167, 178.

dynamism does not pertain to brother/sister relationships. This is because brothers have full authority over their sisters irrespective of their sisters' age; even if the sisters are older, they are under the oppressive authority of their younger brothers, which comes from the patriarchal and hierarchical structure.[53] As Abu-Lughod states, even younger brothers are responsible for their older sisters.[54] Because of this, the youngest female member of a family will always feel the heaviest patriarchal pressure, both from her parents and her (male) siblings.

3.1.2 Masculinity and femininity

Masculinity and femininity are two binary concepts in gender relationships, and as expressed by Connell, they are "products of social learning."[55] While men intend to reach the highest level of masculinity by themselves, they aim to guarantee women's femininity, meaning that one is active while the other is passive. If masculinity usually refers oppression, domination, and superiority, then femininity refers to subjection and inferiority.

Why do men act in masculine ways to protect family honour by oppressing their female relatives? This question also leads us to consider the relationship between culture and individual agency. Is it culture that makes men masculine, or do men act in masculine ways 'by themselves,' so that eventually 'being masculine' becomes the part of the culture? If we accept the former, the cultural masculinity approach, then we need to answer Okin's question about essentialism: Is culture bad or not?[56] In doing so, we must also accept that men in that particular cultural group act in a masculine way in order to be part of that group. However, if we accept that problems come from individual agency, then we need to source masculinity back to male conduct rather than cultural attributes, and we need to make distinction between masculine society and masculine culture. And what we mostly see in Turkish societies is that masculine conduct creates a masculine society, and that the people of that society derive that masculinity from their cultures and traditions, and even sometimes from their religion.[57]

In both the Eastern and the Western worlds, men are expected to demonstrate both a public and private masculinity. Public masculinity requires them to display authority and prestige in public; private masculinity requires them to exercise oppression and superiority in their homes. According to Kandiyoti, masculinity – unlike hierarchy – is not an ascribed but an achieved status.[58] The social environment teaches and pushes men to achieve both private and public masculinity

53 Ibid.
54 Abu-Lughod (n 50) 81.
55 RW Connell, *Masculinities* (Cambridge, Polity Press 2011) 22, 43.
56 Susan Moller Okin, 'Is Multiculturalism Bad for Women?' in *Is Multiculturalism Bad for Women* (Princeton, Princeton University Press 2001).
57 John Beynon, *Masculinities and Culture* (Berkshire, Open University Press 2002) 2–3.
58 Deniz Kandiyoti, 'Emancipated But Unliberated? Reflections on the Turkish Case' (1987) 13 Feminist Studies 317, 327.

during their lives. If a man fails to achieve both, he may be driven to become more masculine and even violent in order to prove his masculinity, or to protect what masculinity he has secured at the place where it remains. For instance, according to Anderson, if a man has a lack of power and/or authority in his work environment and in public, he may act more aggressively at home.[59]

What we usually come across in the context of masculinity in Turkey is hegemonic masculinity. Connell defines it as the

> configuration of gender practice which embodies the currently accepted answer to the problem of legitimacy of patriarchy, which guarantees (or is taken to guarantee) the dominant position of men and the subordination of women.[60]

As seen from this definition, hegemonic masculinity is related to gender relations, whereby hegemonic masculinity is the dominant power over all genders.[61] Hegemonic masculinity is usually seen as controlling female kin's private and public behaviour, especially sexual behaviour. Connell and Messerschmidt describe the attitude towards hegemonic masculinity as the belief that it is the most honourable way to be a man.[62] Similarly, Hatty argues that hegemonic masculinity is "the publicly avowed, preferred model of manliness."[63] Hegemonic masculinity has a dual character: It forces men to be strong, protective, superior, and masculine towards women, but at the same time it requires them to control their female family members' behaviours and preserve women's segregation according to society's expectations.[64] As Abram highlights, the characteristics of hegemonic masculinity not only harm women and other men but also lead to violence towards and the subordination of women.[65] He adds that hegemonic masculinity legitimates patriarchy and maintains gender inequality.[66] Connell and Messerschmidt share this viewpoint, saying that "hegemonic masculinity permits collective dominance over women."[67]

As mentioned by Clatterbaugh, masculinity requires specific behaviours that men must follow in order to be powerful.[68] Violence is one way to prove men's

59 Kristin L Anderson, 'Gender, Status, and Domestic Violence: An Integration of Feminist and Family Violence Approaches' (1997) 59 Journal of Marriage and Family 655, 658.
60 Connell (n 55) 77.
61 Richard Howson, *Challenging Hegemonic Masculinity* (Oxon, Routledge 2006) 60.
62 RW Connell and James W Messerschmidt, 'Hegemonic Masculinity: Rethinking the Concept' (2005) 19 Gender and Society 829, 832.
63 Suzanne E Hatty, *Masculinities, Violence, and Culture* (Thousand Oaks, Sage Publications Ltd 2000) 173.
64 R Emerson Dobash and Russel Dobash, *Violence against Wives: A Case Against the Patriarchy* (London, Open Books 1980) 24.
65 Abrams (n 39) 707.
66 Ibid. 712.
67 Connell and Messerschmidt (n 62) 840.
68 Kenneth Clatterbaugh, *Contemporary Perspective on Masculinity: Men, Women, and Politics in Modern Society* (Boulder, Westview Press 1990) 41.

power, but it also works to protect men's reputations. As Julie Peteet highlights in her essay, masculinity is "attained by constant vigilance and willingness to defend honour (sharaf)."[69] Therefore, any danger to masculinity and men's reputations can make men violent in defending their honour.[70] The link between masculinity and honour occurs when this danger appears.

4. Patriarchal and hierarchical violence against women

The terminology of patriarchal and hierarchical domestic violence is deliberately used in this book to identify any types of structural domestic violence (physical, sexual, emotional, mental, and financial) used by (superior) men and women against (inferior) men or women within the same family.[71] This type of violence is also described as 'patriarchal terrorism' by Johnson.[72] Johnson defines 'patriarchal terrorism' as a form of systematic violence within families and a product of the patriarchal tradition of men's right to control 'their' women.[73] This type of violence can be seen in both Western and Eastern countries, especially in societies where patriarchy, class, and gender inequality are significant.

Patriarchal violence takes different forms and can have different victims: It can be violence against partners, children, siblings, in-laws, and elderly relatives. Violence against parents and elderly family members is not common in any Middle Eastern country, including Turkey. The patriarchal family structure demands that great respect is shown to parents and elderly family members. Not only violence but any type of misbehaviour towards them are unacceptable within these societies. There are only some exceptions – which will be discussed further on – where violence against parents and elderly family members do emerge. The above-mentioned pyramidal family structure also shows the direction of the application of domestic violence. People who hold patriarchal or hierarchal authority feel entitled to use violence against those who are placed below them. The following sections focus on the protagonists of this type of violence.

As mentioned previously, the evidence of extended family relationships is seen in traditional Turkish families. When we talk about patriarchal and hierarchal domestic violence, it is not only the members of nuclear families that are counted but also extended family members. Uncles, male cousins, and grandfathers are

69 Julia Peteet, 'Male Gender and Rituals of Resistance in the Palestinian Intifada: A Cultural Politics of Violence' in Mai Ghoussoub and Emma Sinclair-Webb (eds), *Imagined Masculinities: Male Identity and Culture in the Modern Middle East* (London, Al Saqi Books 2000) 107.

70 Douglas Schrock and Irene Padavic, 'Negotiating Hegemonic Masculinity in a Batterer Intervention Program' (2007) 21 Gender and Society 625, 628.

71 Ferdous Jahan, *When Women Protect Women* (New Delhi, South Asian Publishers Pvt Ltd 2008) 27.

72 Michael P Johnson, 'Patriarchal Terrorism and Common Couple Violence: Two Forms of Violence Against Women' (1995) 57 Journal of Marriage and Family 283, 284.

73 Ibid.; Richard J Gelles, *Intimate Violence in Families* (Thousand Oaks, Sage Publications Ltd 1997) 21.

the most prominent extended family members to take part in the perpetration of domestic violence against their female relatives. Irrespective of the situation within a nuclear family, extended family members usually are able to effectively make decisions on whether and how to punish female relatives for their misbehaviour in order to cleanse the family honour. They also take major roles in assisting the nuclear family members to commit HBV.

However, although extended family members do have significant roles to play in domestic VAW, this subsection only focuses on nuclear families. Therefore, first patriarchal domestic violence and then hierarchal domestic violence will be analysed in order to show the different perpetrators and the motives they have for committing this violence. The first part focuses on the male perpetrators, including husbands, fathers, brothers, and sons. The differences between these perpetrators are presented in order to clarify the motives behind their violence. The second part, on the other hand, focuses on mothers as perpetrators. Although in some situations women will even commit violence against their new-born babies, if they have delivered them out of wedlock, in order to protect their family honour and/or save their own lives from becoming victims of honour killing, this situation is not considered in this section; instead, it will be analysed in the next chapter.

4.1 Patriarchal violence against women[74]

4.1.1 Husbands/fathers as perpetrators

When a head of a family uses gender-based violence, his first target is usually his wife. As we saw in the first chapter, a husband has an absolute right to entirely control his wife's behaviour and her appearance in society. This control is a requirement for protecting women's chastity and *namus* as well as for preserving family honour. If a wife behaves in any way that challenges this authority, it may result in violence against her and even honour killings.[75] For instance, 6 out of 12 prisoners who participated in this research committed honour killings against their wives, motivated by extramarital relationships, infidelity, denial of the husband's authority, and jealousy.[76] When looking at the case records collected for this research, in 15 cases husbands committed honour killings because of their wives' extramarital relationships, infidelity, eloping, and dressing against the family's approval.[77]

More than this, a wife can be a victim of domestic violence because of her role in the family. As a mother, she has a duty to bring up the children properly.

74 Although extended family members also commit a high amount of HBV, data from the Turkish First Degree Courts show that first-degree relatives are the primary offenders in honour killings (see Appendix 2.1).

75 Lowe and others (n 47) 284.

76 Please see Appendix 1.1.

77 Please see Appendix 2.1.

Her children's misbehaviour is her responsibility and also makes them share her guilt.[78] As a result of this, she is also criticised and censured by society, with the result that she can become the victim of violence.[79] This situation is most often seen in the case of the misbehaviour of daughters. Especially if daughters behave in such a way to bring shame on the family honour, or if they act against patriarchal authority, not only the daughters but also their mothers may become victims of different types of violence, including HBV. This is because it is accepted that mothers have failed in their duty to bring up their children in an appropriate way.

Another important point to underline here is the extent of the husbands' capacity for oppression and to exert pressure over their wives. In traditional Turkish societies even if the marriage is over and the spouses are divorced, the husband can still feel entitled to control his former wife and restrict her behaviour.[80] This is because a former husband still feels that his honour and reputation depend on her sexual behaviour, her *namus*, her chastity, and her honour. If the marriage produced children, the ex-husband further feels that he has an absolute right to control her, not only because of their former conjugal relationship but also because she is still his children's mother.[81] In this complex relationship, a former wife feels dual responsibilities: to protect the former husband's as well as her natal family's honour and dignity. Any unacceptable behaviour by her can easily tarnish her former husband's reputation and family honour, as well as his children's honour and reputation. In that case, the former husband – as well as his wife's paternal family – feels fully entitled to use violence against her. More than this, the husband may also use violence against his former wife in order to clean the shame from his name if his former wife is engaged, or is even suspected of engaging, in any sexual relationship after him. For instance, the court records collected for this research show four cases where former husbands committed honour killings against their former wives, with the motive of being in a sexual relationship after the divorce.[82]

As well as their wives, men will often also use violence against their daughters. Although in classic patriarchal families a mother, as a producer, is primarily responsible for the children's upbringing, a father also has full authority over his children, and especially his daughters, as they are the main sources of family

78 Phyllis D Coontz and Judith A Martin, 'Understanding Violent Mothers and Fathers: Assessing Explanations Offered By Mothers and Fathers for Their Use of Punishment' in Gerald T Hotaling and others (eds), *Family Abuse and Its Consequences: New Directions in Research* (Newbury Park, Sage 1988) 81; Nevin Yıldız Tahincioğlu, *Namusun Halleri* (Postiga 2011) 246–51.

79 Ibid.; Mohammad Mazher Idriss, 'Not Domestic Violence or Cultural Tradition: Is Honour-Based Violence Distinct From Domestic Violence?' (2017) 39 Journal of Social Welfare and Family Law 3, 5.

80 Nooria Faizi, 'Domestic Violence in the Muslim Community' (2000) 10 Texas Journal of Women and the Law 209, 211.

81 For instance, Salih mentioned during our interview: "Even if we divorced you cannot separate from me." Interview with Salih (3 September 2012).

82 Please see Appendix 2.1.

honour and reputation.[83] Fathers' involvement in committing honour killings is quite common in traditional Turkish societies. The research conducted by Dogan, Onal, and Bağlı and Özensel show cases where the fathers were the perpetrators of honour killings.[84] The prison interviews and the case records of this book also support their findings. In 17 cases, fathers murdered their daughters because of pregnancy out of wedlock, eloping, being raped, infidelity, extramarital relationship, divorcing, rumours, loss of virginity before marriage, and getting married without the family's approval.[85] Two prisoner participants committed honour killings against their daughters because of their extramarital relationships.[86]

4.1.2 Brothers as perpetrators

As a result of the patriarchal and hierarchal social structure, brothers' duties as sons are to follow their fathers, but as brothers they are to control their sisters' behaviour – especially sexual behaviour – and protect them from any danger that may come from the outside world.[87] Fulfilling these duties is also a way to protect and maintain family honour as well as their own masculinities. This duty sometimes results in disciplining and even punishing their sisters by using violence against them, which may cause daughters to be vulnerable to the abuse of the brothers. Brothers use violence against their sisters not only to discipline or punish them but also to prove that they are masculine and strong in their communities. Accepting the argument of Kandiyoti that refers to masculinity, the brothers may also use violence to prove their masculinity. Masculinity is a value that needs to be achieved; this becomes highly crucial for brothers, especially the younger ones in the family.[88] As Abrams contends, if there is no other source available to achieve masculinity, violence can accomplish it.[89] From the gender inequality perspective, using violence against inferior females could easily be a way of achieving this masculinity.

The extreme form of violence that may be applied by the brothers is honour killings. The literature and cases collected for this research often reflect the brothers' involvement in committing honour killings in order to restore family honour

83 Abu-Lughod (n 50) 80; Bertrand Russel, *Marriage and Morals* (London, Unwin Paperbacks 1985) 25.

84 Recep Dogan, 'The Profiles of Victims, Perpetrators, and Unfounded Beliefs in Honor Killings in Turkey' (2014) 18 Homicide Studies 389, 396; Ayse Onal, *Honour Killing: Stories of Men Who Killed* (London, Saqi Books 2008); Mazhar Bağlı and Ertan Özensel, *Türkiye'de Töre ve Namus Cinayetleri: Töre ve Namus Cinayetleri İşleyen Kişiler Üzerine Sosyolojik Bir Araştırma* (Istanbul, Destek Yayınevi 2011) 90–91.

85 Please see Appendix 2.1.

86 Please see Appendix 1.1.

87 Mahmut Tezcan, *Turkiye'de Tore (Namus) Cinayetleri: Sosyo Kulturel Antropolojik Yaklasim* (Ankara, Naturel 2003) 21. Suad Joseph, 'Brother/Sister Relationships: Connectivity, Love, and Power in the Reproduction of Patriarchy in Lebanon' 21 American Ethnologists 50, 58.

88 Kandiyoti, 'Emancipated but Unliberated? Reflections on the Turkish Case' (n 58) 327.

89 Abrams (n 39) 713.

and punish their sisters.[90] The cases collected for this research show that in 29 cases, brothers took part in murdering their sisters in order to clean the family's honour.[91] The prisoners' data, on the other hand, shows that 2 perpetrators out of 12 were brothers of the victims.[92] Gokhan murdered his sister because of her extramarital relationship, whereas Kemal committed the crime because his sister not only had an extramarital relationship but also became pregnant.[93] Linking to this, both participants mentioned that if honour is tarnished, murder is the only solution.[94]

4.1.3 Sons as perpetrators

At first glance, identifying sons as the perpetrators of domestic violence against mothers seems a contradiction to the general theory of the hierarchical and patriarchal family structure of traditional Turkish societies.[95] There are not many situations, however, in which sons use violence against their mothers. In order for them to use violence against mothers, there needs to be a situation where the mothers lose their authority over their sons or the sons feel ashamed of their mothers' behaviours, especially sexual behaviours

Mothers normally have full authority over their sons, which comes from the age hierarchy of the culture. However, as Abu-Lughod emphasises, authority is achieved and can be lost.[96] One circumstance is through the misbehaviour of mothers. Although the husband is primarily responsible for the behaviour of his wife, there are some circumstances where a husband's authority is no longer in force. This can be seen mostly in the case of the husband's death or divorce. In those situations, the older sons may feel responsible for their mothers and even sometimes may act as their guardians. In that case, if the mother misbehaves and tarnishes the family honour, then the son may feel that it is his responsibility to clean the shame. As discussed in the following chapter, there are different motives for the sons feeling that the honour of the family has been tarnished. The case records collected for this research show that in three cases, sons committed honour killings against their mothers with the motives of rumours and delivering a baby out of wedlock.[97] Dogan also provides evidence of how sons involved

90 Tezcan (n 87) 18; Pınar Ecevitoğlu, *Namus Töre ve İktidar: Kadının Çıplak Hayat Olarak Kuruluşu* (Ankara, Dipnot 2012) 362; Bağlı and Özensel (n 84) 90–91; Dogan, 'The Profiles of Victims, Perpetrators, and Unfounded Beliefs in Honor Killings in Turkey' (n 84) 8, 11; Recep Dogan, 'The Dynamics of Honour Killings: Perpetrators' Experiences' (n 90) 53, 13.

91 Please see Appendix 2.1.

92 Please see Appendix 1.1.

93 Please see Appendix 1.1.

94 Please see Appendix 1.17.

95 For more information about the domestic violence committed by sons and grandsons against grandmothers and mothers, please see Nicole Westmarland, *Violence Against Women: Criminological Perspective on Men's Violences* (Oxon, Routledge 2015) 51–60.

96 Abu-Lughod (n 50) 85.

97 Please see Appendix 2.1.

in committing honour killings against their mothers; he provides infidelity and prostitution as the main motives of those killings.[98]

4.2 Hierarchal violence against women: mothers as perpetrators

Although patriarchal families confer absolute authority on fathers over their children, mothers also have full authority over their daughters and even sometimes over their daughters-in-law. In order to raise their children according to the expectations of society or to maintain the family honour, mothers may use different forms of violence against their daughters or daughters-in-law.[99] As Hook mentions, female children as well as daughters-in-law may experience different forms of violence from their mothers and in-laws as a form of control,[100] which is also addressed as a form of HBV.[101] This type of violence can be seen as a form of HBV. The most extreme form of violence that the mothers use against their daughters is honour killings. The data collected from the First Degree Courts for this book shows that in four cases mothers committed honour killings against their daughters, motivated by rumours, extramarital relationship, eloping, and pregnancy out of wedlock.[102]

The main purpose of this section has been to identify the difference between patriarchal and hierarchal VAW in order to create a bridge between the concepts of honour and HBV. The section has shown how the perpetrators of VAW in Turkey have been shaped depending on their gender roles. While males' roles and duties are usually based on controlling females, in order to prevent them from ruining the family name and honour, males are also seen as punishers who restore lost honour. Women, on the other hand, take the role of disciplining other women in order to protect family honour and their reputation. Since the division of roles is seen as both a protection and a punishment, we usually see men as the perpetrators of HBV in general and honour killings in particular.

5. Conclusion

This chapter mainly followed Middle Eastern feminist movements in general and Turkish feminist movements in particular in order to address the Middle Eastern and Muslim concepts of patriarchy, masculinity, hierarchy, and male oppression. Since the non-secular feminist movements in Turkey have not had the desired

98 Dogan, 'The Dynamics of Honour Killings: Perpetrators' Experiences' (n 90) 9–10.

99 Rachel Aplin, 'Exploring the Role of Mothers in "Honour" Based Abuse Perpetration and the Impact on the Policing Response' (2017) 60 Women's Studies International Forum 1, 3–4.

100 bell hooks, 'Violence in Intimate Relationship: A Feminist Perspective' in *Gender Violence: Interdisciplinary Perspective* (New York, New York University Press 2007) 270.

101 Lis Bates, 'Females Perpetrating Honour-Based Abuse: Controllers, Collaborators or Coerced?' (2018) 10 Journal of Aggression, Conflict and Peace Research 293, 299.

102 Please see Appendix 2.1. See also Dogan, 'Do Women Really Kill for Honor? Conceptualizing Women's Involvement in Honor Killings' (n 41).

effect on HBV, the research mainly follows secular feminist approaches and interpretations, and this will provide the necessary analysis, which can be situated within the hermeneutical circle of HBV, when dealing with honour killings and Turkish laws. Since this book mainly focuses on feminist theories in Turkey and in the Middle East, there are some criticisms of these movements. In particular, the lack of consensus and solidarity between the feminist movements in Turkey has become one of the most significant problems in the process of fighting against HBV.

Following the analysis of Turkish feminist movements, the chapter specifically focused on gender relation theories. In this context, patriarchy, hierarchy, and masculinity/femininity were dealt with, specifically how these theories affect gender relations and role division within Middle Eastern societies in general and Turkish societies in particular. Interpretation of the concept of honour was used during this analysis. By creating a view of traditional or, as Kandiyoti identifies it, 'classic'[103] patriarchal family structure, I provided the necessary background information on family relations before violence is committed against women in Turkey. I also highlighted the gender role division, which is created by patriarchy and hierarchy, and how this gender role division actually shows us the common perpetrators of HBV. This clarification was highly important for my further analysis of HBV and legal challenges to it, as without considering this gender role division, it would be impossible to make the right interpretation of the legal challenges, especially when talking about customary law in Turkey.

Bibliography

Abrams JR, 'The Collateral Consequences of Masculinizing Violence' (2010) 16 William and Mary Journal of Women and the Law 703

Abu-Lughod L, *Veiled Sentiments: Honor and Poetry in a Bedouin Society* (Berkley, University of California Press 1999)

Ahmed-Ghosh H, 'Dilemmas of Islamic and Secular Feminists and Feminisms' (2008) 9 Journal of Women's Studies 99

Akis Y and Ozakin U, 'Türkiye'de Feminizm ve Kadın Hareketi' *BiaMag* (16 May 2009) <www.bianet.org/biamag/diger/114551-turkiyede-feminizm-ve-kadin-hareketi> accessed 24 January 2020.

Ali SS, *Gender and Human Rights in Islam and International Law: Equal Before Allah, Unequal Before Man?* (The Hague, Kluwer Law International 2000)

Anderson KL, 'Gender, Status, and Domestic Violence: An Integration of Feminist and Family Violence Approaches' (1997) 59 Journal of Marriage and Family 655

Aplin R, 'Exploring the Role of Mothers in "Honour" Based Abuse Perpetration and the Impact on the Policing Response' (2017) 60 Women's Studies International Forum 1

Arat N, 'Women's Studies in Turkey' (1996) 24 Women's Studies Quarterly 400

Arat Y, 'Toward a Democratic Society: The Women's Movement in Turkey in the 1980s' (1994) 17 Women's Studies International Forum 241

103 Kandiyoti, 'Bargaining With Patriarchy' (n 40).

Arat Z, 'Kemalizm ve Turk Kadini" in *75 Yilda Kadinlar ve Erkekler* (Istanbul, Tarih Vakfi Yayinlari 1998)
Badran M, *Feminism in Islam: Secular and Religious Convergences* (Oxford, One World Publications 2009)
Bağlı M and Özensel E, *Türkiye'de Töre ve Namus Cinayetleri: Töre ve Namus Cinayetleri İşleyen Kişiler Üzerine Sosyolojik Bir Araştırma* (Istanbul, Destek Yayınevi 2011)
Barlas A, *Believing Women in Islam: Unreading Patriarchal Interpretations of the Qur'an* (Austin, University of Texas Press 2003)
———, 'Engaging Islamic Feminism: Provincializing Feminism as a Master Narrative' in *Islamic Feminism: Current Perspectives* (Tampare, Juvenes Print 2008)
Bates L, 'Females Perpetrating Honour-Based Abuse: Controllers, Collaborators or Coerced?' (2018) 10 Journal of Aggression, Conflict and Peace Research 293
Beynon J, *Masculinities and Culture* (Berkshire, Open University Press 2002)
Bhobal K, *Gender, 'Race' and Patriarchy: A Study of South Asian Women* (Aldershot, Ashgate 1997)
Bingöl O, 'Toplumsal Cinsiyet Olgusu ve Türkiye'de Kadınlık' (2014) 16 KMÜ Sosyal ve Ekonomik Araştırmalar Dergisi 108
Çaha Ö, *Sivil Kadın: Türkiye'de Sivil Toplum ve Kadın* (Ankara, Vadi Yayınları 1996)
Cakir R, 'Dindar Kadinin Seruveni' (2000) 137 Birikim <www.rusencakir.com/Dindar-kadinin-seruveni/292> accessed 24 January 2020.
Clatterbaugh K, *Contemporary Perspective on Masculinity: Men, Women, and Politics in Modern Society* (Boulder, Westview Press 1990)
Connell RW, *Masculinities* (Cambridge, Polity Press 2011)
Connell RW and Messerschmidt JW, 'Hegemonic Masculinity: Rethinking the Concept' (2005) 19 Gender and Society 829
Cooke M, *Women Claim Islam: Creating Islamic Feminism Through Literature* (London, Routledge 2001)
Coontz PD and Martin JA, 'Understanding Violent Mothers and Fathers: Assessing Explanations Offered By Mothers and Fathers for Their Use of Punishment' in Gerald T Hotaling and others (eds), *Family Abuse and Its Consequences: New Directions in Research* (Newbury Park, Sage 1988)
Cosar S, *The Reflections of the Ottoman-Turkish Feminism on the Literary Works of Nezihe Muhittin* (Ankara, Graduate School of Social Sciences o Middle East Technical University 2006)
———, 'Women in Turkish Political Thought: Between Tradition and Modernity' (2007) 86 Feminist Review 113
Diner C and Toktas S, 'Waves of Feminism in Turkey: Kemalist, Islamist and Kurdish Women's Movements in Era of Globalization' (2010) 12 Journal of Balkan and Near Eastern Studies 41
Dobash RE and Dobash R, *Violence against Wives: A Case Against the Patriarchy* (London, Open Books 1980)
Dogan R, 'The Profiles of Victims, Perpetrators, and Unfounded Beliefs in Honor Killings in Turkey' (2014) 18 Homicide Studies 389
———, 'The Dynamics of Honour Killings: Perpetrators' Experiences' (2016) 20 Homicide Studies 53
———, 'Do Women Really Kill for Honor? Conceptualizing Women's Involvement in Honor Killings' (2018) 39 Deviant Behavior 1247

DurakbaŞa A, 'Kemalism as Identity Politics in Turkey' in Zehra Arat (ed), *Deconstructing Images of 'The Turkish Woman'* (London, Macmillan 1998)
Ecevitoğlu P, *Namus Töre ve İktidar: Kadının Çıplak Hayat Olarak Kuruluşu* (Ankara, Dipnot 2012)
Ersöz AG, 'Türk Atasözleri ve Deyimlerde Kadına Yönelik Toplumsal Cinsiyet Rolleri' (2010) 1 Gazi Türkiyat Türkoloji Araştırmaları Dergisi 167
Faizi N, 'Domestic Violence in the Muslim Community' (2000) 10 Texas Journal of Women and the Law 209
Gelles RJ, *Intimate Violence in Families* (Thousand Oaks, Sage Publications Ltd 1997)
Gill AK and Brah A, 'Interrogating Cultural Narratives About "Honour"-Based Violence' (2014) 21 European Journal of Women's Studies 72
Hatty SE, *Masculinities, Violence, and Culture* (Thousand Oaks, Sage Publications Ltd 2000)
Hooks B, 'Violence in Intimate Relationship: A Feminist Perspective' in *Gender Violence: Interdisciplinary Perspective* (New York, New York University Press 2007)
Howson R, *Challenging Hegemonic Masculinity* (Oxon, Routledge 2006)
Idriss MM, 'Not Domestic Violence or Cultural Tradition: Is Honour-Based Violence Distinct From Domestic Violence?' (2017) 39 Journal of Social Welfare and Family Law 3
Ilkkaracan P, 'Reforming the Penal Code in Turkey: The Campaign for the Reform of the Turkish Penal Code from a Gender Perspective' (2007) Institute of Development Studies Bulletin 1
Ingun O, 'Feminizm ve Islam Iliskisi: "Islami Feminizm"' (Uludag Universitesi 2005)
Interview with Salih (3 September 2012)
Jahan F, *When Women Protect Women* (New Delhi, South Asian Publishers Pvt Ltd 2008)
Johnson MP, 'Patriarchal Terrorism and Common Couple Violence: Two Forms of Violence Against Women' (1995) 57 Journal of Marriage and Family 283
Joseph S, 'Brother/Sister Relationships: Connectivity, Love, and Power in the Reproduction of Patriarchy in Lebanon' 21 American Ethnologists 50
Kandiyoti D, 'Emancipated But Unliberated? Reflections on the Turkish Case' (1987) 13 Feminist Studies 317
———, 'Bargaining With Patriarchy' (1988) 2 Gender and Society 274
———, 'Contemporary Feminist Scholarship and Middle East Studies' in Deniz Kandiyoti (ed), *Gendering the Middle East: Emerging Perspectives* (London, Tauris &Co Ltd 1996)
Lindisfarne N, 'Variant Masculinities, Variant Virginities: Rethinking "Honour and Shame"' in Andrea Cornwall (ed), *Dislocating Masculinity: Comparative Ethnographies* (London, Routledge 2003)
Lowe M and others, 'Attitudes Towards Intimate Partner "Honor" Based Violence in India, Iran, Malaysia and Pakistan' (2018) 10 Journal of Aggression, Conflict and Peace Research 283
Mir-Hosseini Z, 'Muslim Women's Quest for Equality: Between Islamic Law and Feminism' (2006) 32 Critical inquiry 629
Moghadam VM, 'Islamic Feminism and Its Discontents: Toward a Resolution of the Debate' (2002) 27 Journal of Women, Culture, and Society 1135
Moghissi H, *Feminism and Islamic Fundamentalism: The Limits of Postmodern Analysis* (London, Zed Books Ltd 1999)

Mojab S, 'The Politics of "Cyberfeminism" in the Middle East: The Case of Kurdish Women' (2001) 8 Race, Gender, Class 42

Müftüler-Bac M, 'Turkish Women's Predicament' (1999) 22 Women's Studies International Forum 303

Okin SM, 'Is Multiculturalism Bad for Women?' in *Is Multiculturalism Bad for Women* (Princeton, Princeton University Press 2001)

Onal A, *Honour Killing: Stories of Men Who Killed* (London, Saqi Books 2008)

Ozcurumez S and Cengiz FS, 'On Resilience and Response Beyond Value Change: Transformation of Women's Movement in Post-1980 Turkey' (2011) 34 Women's Studies International Forum 20

Ozdemir E, 'Kemalist Tradition and Kemalist Women's Movement in Turkey After 1980' (2010) 1 Turkish Journal of Politics 99

Peteet J, 'Male Gender and Rituals of Resistance in the Palestinian Intifada: A Cultural Politics of Violence' in Mai Ghoussoub and Emma Sinclair-Webb (eds), *Imagined Masculinities: Male Identity and Culture in the Modern Middle East* (London, Al Saqi Books 2000)

Russel B, *Marriage and Morals* (London, Unwin Paperbacks 1985)

Sancar S, *Türk Modernleşmesinin Cinsiyeti: Erkekler Devlet, Kadınlar Aile Kurar* (Istanbul, İletisim 2012)

Schrock D and Padavic I, 'Negotiating Hegemonic Masculinity in a Batterer Intervention Program' (2007) 21 Gender and Society 625

Tahincioğlu NY, 'Namus Olgusunun Bir Biyo-Politik Olarak Düşünülebilirliği: Şanlıurfa Örneği' (2010) 13 Akdeniz iletişim Fakültesi Dergisi 1

———, *Namusun Halleri* (Postiga 2011)

Tezcan M, Turkiye'de Tore (Namus), *Cinayetleri: Sosyo Kulturel Antropolojik Yaklasim* (Ankara, Naturel 2003)

'Türkiye'de Toplumsal Cinsiyet EŞitsizliği: Sorunlar ve Çözüm Önerileri' (Istanbul, TUSIAD and KAGIDER 2008)

Unlu S, 'Turk Toplumunda Feminizm: Universiteli Gencler Uzerinde Bir Arastirma' (Gazi Universitesi 2000)

Wadud A, *Qur'an and Woman: Rereading the Sacred Text from a Woman's Perspective* (Oxford, Oxford University Press 1999)

Westmarland N, *Violence Against Women: Criminological Perspective on Men's Violences* (Oxon, Routledge 2015)

4 The social environment that exists before HBV is committed

1. Introduction

Following the previous discussion, conceptualising honour, this chapter aims to analyse the social environment that exists before HBV is committed. While keeping the second part of the hermeneutical circle of HBV in mind, this chapter looks at the conditions in which HBV is triggered. Although the hermeneutical circle of HBV does not include any specific section on social environments and the motives behind HBV, these elements are important for our understanding of how and why individuals and families consider committing this crime. In previous chapters, I set out the necessary conceptual clarification of specific concepts without making direct links to HBV. This chapter turns to address the root of how and in what conditions HBV is committed and will cover the first part of the book's question: *How and under which conditions are honour killings committed in Turkey, and how does the Turkish Penal Code deal with them?*

In order to answer the first part of the question, I start by examining why honour, as a prominent social value, becomes problematic in societies. In order to identify this problem effectively, the chapter takes two different but complementary approaches. First, it deals with how honour is gained and who gains it. The aim is to show how patriarchal and hierarchal social structures play the main role in distinguishing the possessors and protectors of honour, and how this leads to discrimination against women and, ultimately, sometimes even triggers the committing of HBV against women.

The chapter also identifies specific behaviours that are commonly accepted as threats to honour and reputation. It is impossible to create an exhaustive list of these behaviours, as any behaviour that has a potential link to women's sexuality, women's bodily autonomy, and patriarchy can be considered dangerous. Thus, this chapter examines the most common threats accepted in every society where honour crimes exist. In order to make this analysis, illicit sexual relationships, seeking divorce, being raped, the spread of rumours, and challenging patriarchal authority will be dealt with as some, though not all, motives behind HBV.

After focusing on how honour causes discrimination and physical and emotional violence, and how some behaviours are treated as if they tarnish honour, the chapter then analyses the concept of loss of honour. This analysis is mainly based on four categories: shame, loss of prestige and reputation, exclusion from the family and society, and applying violence. This analysis shows the unique characteristic of the hermeneutical circle of HBV. If we remember the circle and its four parts, what triggers HBV is solely the 'loss of honour or the protecting of honour.' In other words, even if a man loses his patriarchal authority or hierarchy, or if anything takes place that threatens patriarchal culture and tradition, these situations alone do not trigger HBV if they have no link to honour (*namus*, chastity, and *şeref*). The challenges to these values may cause varying degrees of violence, but in order to name a crime as HBV they must have a certain link to honour. Therefore, in the following sections, I analyse how individuals and society create this link and its patriarchal and traditional roots. I start by describing the term 'honour possessors.' This will help to explain how cultural and traditional norms have an effect on possessing honour. This analysis will also shed some light on the case analysis made in Chapter 6.

2. Honour causes problems before committing HBV

When the traditional Turkish concept of honour (as the first chapter describes) is considered, it reveals some of the major anxieties and problems in honour-based societies. These arise from the possessing and protecting of honour and their respective protagonists. Who has honour and who is responsible for protecting honour involve different agents. While men are the main possessors of honour, women carry a greater burden to protect it. Therefore, this section focuses on the problems of possessing and protecting honour, how this causes discrimination and inequality against women, and how this discrimination and inequality is supported by the patriarchy and hierarchy that were discussed in the previous chapter.

2.1 Possessing honour and its possessors

Possessing honour affects individuals, families, and societies. This shows the influence of a patriarchal social structure on conceptualising the value of honour. Under the influence of patriarchy and hierarchy, families and societies are strongly tightened up; honour remains in the middle so as to keep the gender imbalance, thereby securing male dominance and superiority.

While honour in a wider concept can be possessed in many different forms, in the hermeneutical circle of HBV it is, as we have seen, generally based on women's sexual behaviours and chastity.[1] In other words, honour is not a value that is considered by the community independently and individually but is rather attached to other values, such as chastity, modesty, and esteem. At this point,

1 Rachel A Ruane, 'Murder in the Name of Honor: Violence Against Women in Pakistan' (2000) 14 Emory International Law Review 1523, 1531–32.

another question arises, as to whether one is born with honour, chastity, *namus*, and *şeref*, or instead achieves them during a lifetime.[2]

First, the suggestion that everyone is born with honour is not sustainable, as it lacks relevant terms and subjects. It is commonly accepted that in Mediterranean and Middle Eastern societies, women do not have honour; instead, they have chastity, virginity, and *namus*.[3] It could thus be said that the link between honour and its related values is actually broken. Women can be the possessors of chastity, virginity, and modesty but not honour, meaning that they can possess several components of honour, but women do not ever equate to honour.[4] In these societies, women are born surrounded by honour-related values but not by honour, and they do not inherit these values from their families, either. As explained above, although women are not born with honour, they are responsible for maintaining their families' honour by protecting and preserving their chastity and virginity.[5]

Second, while the situation is slightly complex from the women's perspective, it is actually more complex from the men's side. In societies in which honour has a significant role to play, men are the main possessors of honour but not chastity, *namus*, or virginity. Although honour has a link to chastity and virginity, men's honour in this regard is dependent on their female kin's behaviour; in other words, the honour of men can be described as 'dependent honour.'[6] This dependence

2 For instance, it is claimed by Campbell that in Sarakatsani society, all Sarakatsani are born with honour into families of honour, with the exception of persons of certain families at the lowest level of the prestige hierarchy (John Kennedy Campbell, 'Honour and the Devil' in JG Peristiany (ed), *Honour and Shame: The Values of Mediterranean Societies* (London, Weidenfeld and Nicolson 1965) 144). Also, Maria Pia Di Bella claims that "every man was invested at his birth with a quota of honor deriving from his family and/or his lineage, since he was a part of the whole which bequeathed to him, among other things, his 'share' of this collective honor which it was his duty to protect and develop as individual" (Maria Pia Di Bella, 'Name, Blood and Miracles: The Claims to Renown in the Traditional Sicily' in JG Peristiany and Julian Pitt-Rivers (eds), *Honour and Grace in Anthropology* (Cambridge, Cambridge University Press 1992) 150).

3 Anton Blok, 'Rams and Billy-Goats: A Key to the Mediterranean Code of Honour' (1981) 16 Man, New Series 427, 438.

4 Ibid.; Pınar Ecevitoğlu, *Namus Töre ve İktidar: Kadının Çıplak Hayat Olarak Kuruluşu* (Ankara, Dipnot 2012) 279.

5 Julian Pitt-Rivers, 'Postscript: The Place of Grace in Anthropology' in JG Peristiany and Julian Pitt-Rivers (eds), *Honour and Grace in Anthropology* (Cambridge, Cambridge University Press 1992) 226.

6 Delenay also reflects that 'male honor is so inextricably tied to women' (David D Gilmore, 'Seeds of Honor, Fields of Shame' in *Honor and Shame and the Unity of the Mediterranean* (Washington, American Anthropological Association 1987) 36; see also 'Töre ve Namus Cinayetleri İle Kadınlara ve Çocuklara Yönelik Şiddetin Sebeplerinin Araştırılarak Alınması Gereken Önlemlerin Belirlenmesi Amacıyla Kurulan TBMM Araştırma Komisyonu Raporu' (Ankara, TC BaŞbakanlık Kadın Statüsü Genel Müdürlüğü 2006) <www.kadininstatusu.gov.tr/upload/kadininstatusu.gov.tr/mce/eski_site/Pdf/tbmmkom-bolum1.pdf> accessed 3 July 2019. See also Joanne Payton, 'Collective Crimes, Collective Victims: A Case Study of the Murder of Banaz Mahmod' in Mohammad Mazher Idriss and Tahir Abbas (eds), *Honour, Violence, Women and Islam* (Oxon, Routledge 2011) 69.

makes men the protectors of honour through the influence of patriarchy as well as from pressure by society.[7] In relation to this, women, to protect their kinsmen's honour, are expected to meet and fulfil all of society's requirements, to behave appropriately, and to be obedient and submissive.[8]

Possessing and sharing honour have dual aspects in Turkish societies. First, if a man is not married, he possesses honour through his kinwomen's behaviour. However, if he is married, then he also possesses honour through the behaviour of his wife and daughters. While possessing honour in general seems somewhat complex, the same complexity is not seen when *şeref* is considered. In other words, when honour is only related to *şeref*, the link between *şeref* and honour in terms of possession is direct. As already mentioned, *şeref* usually reflects reputation, dignity, esteem.[9] It is more related to men's behaviours, and so the possessors of *şeref* are usually men. In contrast to chastity and virginity, men are normally not born with *şeref*; it is a value for them to achieve and maintain.[10] *Şeref* in this sense has a masculine character, and it is a value that is strongly related to men and their masculinity.

Honour, within the hermeneutical circle of HBV, on the other hand, has a collective character;[11] families can possess honour collectively. As Ercevik Amado explains, not only individual men but also families and sometimes even societies are considered to be possessors of honour.[12] The link between the individual and families is the most crucial aspect of HBV, as the perpetrators of this violence feel themselves responsible for not merely their own honour and reputation but also that of their family. As we will see later on, this is why family members usually take an active role in persuading or even forcing male members to commit HBV. The criminal justice system in Turkey, unfortunately, realised the existence of these shadow/hidden family members very late and only started to prosecute them in 2004.

2.2 *Protecting honour and its problems*

When honour is possessed collectively, protecting it also has a collective character. However, there are differences in the roles collectivism plays in possession and protection respectively. Although women cannot be the possessors of honour,

7 Ghada Karmi, 'Women, Islam, and Patriarchalism' in Mai Yamani (ed), *Feminism and Islam: Legal and Literary Perspectives* (Reading, Garnet Publishing Limited 1996) 76.

8 Nazand Begikhani, Aisha K Gill, and Gill Hague, *Honour-Based Violence: Experiences and Counter-Strategies in Iraqi Kurdistan and the UK Kurdish Diaspora* (Surrey, Ashgate 2015) 8.

9 Clementine Van Eck, *Purified By Blood: Honour Killings Among Turks in the Netherlands* (Amsterdam, Amsterdam University Press 2003) 19–20.

10 Deniz Kandiyoti, 'Emancipated But Unliberated? Reflections on the Turkish Case' (1987) 13 Feminist Studies 317, 327.

11 Michael Boiger and others, 'Defending Honour, Keeping Face: Interpersonal Affordances of Anger and Shame in Turkey and Japan' (2014) Cognition & Emotion 1, 3–4.

12 Liz Ercevik Amado, 'Promoting Sexual Rights Through Human Rights Education: Experiences at Grassroots in Turkey' (2006) 17 Institute of Development Studies Bulletin 117, 119.

they will take an active part in protecting honour alongside men.[13] Their function as protectors is the key to guaranteeing family honour, as well as their kinsmen's honour, through their sexual and social behaviours; their public face is judged by society, and it proves that the honour of their families is well protected and maintained.[14]

Although women have the key role in protecting and maintaining family honour, they are not the only protectors. There is a significant and unequal difference between males and females in the protection of a family's honour. This is because women usually do not take an active role in protecting the family honour. As Ecevitoğlu highlights, they do it through their behaviour, and this is usually not direct but rather indirect action: avoiding sexual relationships before marriage, preserving chastity, and avoiding rumours and suspicion.[15] In contrast, men usually visibly take action to protect the family honour, and their actions can be applied to their kinswomen, keeping them suppressed and obedient. As discussed earlier, these actions remind society that men have a duty to protect the family's honour both internally and externally.[16]

Not only protecting honour but also maintaining it causes problems. The duty to actively maintain honour also falls mainly on the shoulders of men. As discussed earlier, a patriarchal social structure requires them to be responsible for keeping themselves and their families in a situation in which they enjoy a good reputation with a high level of prestige and are highly esteemed.[17] Men fulfil this duty by oppressing females, controlling their behaviour, and restricting their movements and their visibility in public. This shows that there are similarities between the actions of protecting the family honour from threat and those of maintaining it. In both situations, the main aim is having and keeping honour via applying physical or mental/emotional pressure on women.

3. What can tarnish honour?

Although the protection mechanism of honour is extremely strict in Turkish societies, there are some situations men cannot control or prevent, and in which they cannot interfere. The common ground of these situations is that they are all related to women's sexuality and their sexual behaviours.[18] Illicit sexual relation-

13 Blok (n 3) 438; Frank Henderson Stewart, *Honor* (California and London, The University of California Press 1994) 107.

14 Amani M Awwad, 'Gossip, Scandal, Shame, and Honour Killing: A Case for Social Constructionism and Hegemonic Discourse' (2002) 24 Social Thought & Research 39, 44.

15 Ecevitoğlu (n 4) 338.

16 Campbell (n 2) 146; John Davis, *People of the Mediterranean: An Essay in Comparative Social Anthropology* (London, Routledge and Kegan Paul 1977) 95.

17 Begikhani, Gill, and Hague (n 8) 28.

18 Esther Blum, Reashelle Braiden, and Tuula Heinonen, 'Service Delivery Considerations in Dealing with Honour-Based Violence' (2016) 48 Canadian Ethnic Studies 129, 130; Natasha Mulvihill and others, 'The Experience of Interactional Justice for Victims of

ships, seeking divorce, being raped, the spread of rumours, and being Western are some of the significant situations through which the honour of families is seriously tarnished. Sen provides a list of actions that bring dishonour; "associating with male friends, having a boyfriend, attending college or going to work without permission, violating dress codes, choosing one's own marriage partner, and so on" are some of the actions that bring dishonour.[19] Aysan Sev'er et al. also give some examples of dishonourable actions:

> Going to movies without approval, chaperon to kissing, holding hands, dating, or having intercourse with a man who is not one's culturally or legally sanctioned husband.[20]

The interviews conducted with the prisoners also revealed that the prominent situations that tarnish honour are sexual relationships before marriage and infidelity.[21]

This section mainly focuses Purna Sen's list: illicit sexual relationships, seeking divorce, being raped, gossiping about women's behaviour, and being Western.[22] It analyses why these situations have considerable effects on family honour, how they tarnish honour and bring dishonour, and how families and societies react to them.

3.1 Illicit sexual relationships

Women's sexual autonomy is controversial in traditional Turkey societies. A strict patriarchal family structure requires the submissiveness of women. Therefore, controlling women's sexuality is one of the visible actions taken to establish this submission. Women's sexual autonomy is controlled in various ways. The main way is to control her sexual activities before and after marriage using extreme pressure.[23]

The main question here is *what constitutes an illicit sexual relationship in a Turkish context?* In traditional Turkish societies, the only licit sexual relationship

---

"Honour"-Based Violence and Abuse Reporting to the Police in England and Wales' (2019) 29 Policing and Society: An International Journal of Research and Policy 640.

19 Purna Sen, 'Crimes of "Honour", Value and Meaning' in Lynn Welchman and Sara Hossain (eds), *'Honour': Crimes, Paradigms, and Violence Against Women* (London, Zed Books 2005) 47.

20 Aysan Sev'er and Gokcecicek Yurdakul, 'Culture of Honor, Culture of Change: A Feminist Analysis of Honor Killings Rural Turkey' (2001) 7 Violence Against Women 964, 965.

21 Please see Appendix 1.16.

22 See also R Khan, 'Attitudes Towards "Honor" Violence and Killings in Collectivist Cultures: Gender Differences in Middle Eastern, North African, South Asian (MENASA) and Turkish Populations' in JL Ireland, P Birch, and CA Ireland (eds), International Handbook in Aggression: Current Issues and Perspectives (Routledge 2018).

23 Pinar Ilkkaracan, 'Exploring the Context of Women's Sexuality in Eastern Turkey' in Pinar Ilkkaracan (ed), *Women and Sexuality in Muslim Societies* (Istanbul, Women for Women's Human Rights (WWHR) 2000) 10.

is between a husband and a wife. Sex out of wedlock, infidelity, and homosexuality are considered illicit by custom and tradition and trigger HBV. As seen in Appendix 2.2, 58% of the motives behind illicit sexual relationships are infidelity, extramarital affairs, pregnancy out of wedlock, delivering a baby out of wedlock, and eloping.

Perhaps the most common situation considered illicit in traditional Turkish societies is having a sexual relationship before marriage. As we saw in Chapter 2, failure to prove virginity on the wedding night can have fatal consequences for women. If defloration does not take place, the bride's family is immediately informed about the result and the bride is declared *namussuz*, which brings dishonour to her family. The second consequence of failure to prove virginity thus relates to the bride's family. It is usually alleged by the groom's family and even by the wider community that the bride's kinsmen cannot keep an eye on their women, are not able to raise their daughters in an appropriate way, and fail to exercise authority and control over their kinwomen.[24] Dishonouring the bride and her family are not the only consequences of this failure on the nuptial night; it can also result in the immediate dissolution of the marriage.[25]

Moreover, if loss of virginity causes pregnancy as well, it is not only the woman but also the baby that stands at the centre of the violence, as the baby is considered as evidence of shame.[26] For instance, the well-known Guldunya case drew much attention from both the national and international media. Prior to the murder, the victim appealed to the authorities that her life was in danger because of her pregnancy out of wedlock.[27] In another case in Turkey in 2010, a new-born baby delivered out of wedlock was strangled, buried, and covered by cement in West Turkey, Tekirdag.[28] In this case, the family council reached an agreement with a midwife to deliver the baby and then offered her some money to not register the baby. After the baby was born, the grandmother strangled her with a cloth, and the uncles buried the baby and covered her with cement in order to hide the illicit sexual relationship.[29] This is one of the rare examples of a mother's involvement in an honour killing case. In a similar situation, Sevim (one of the interviewees in this research) and her mother killed Sevim's new-born baby, who was delivered out of wedlock, because of fears concerning society's

24 Anahid Devartanian Kulwicki, 'The Practice of Honor Crimes: A Glimpse of Domestic Violence in the Arab World' (2002) 23 Issues in Mental Health Nursing 77, 86.

25 Interestingly, the Turkish Appeal Court decided in 2007 that virginity is a material fact of marriage, and not being a virgin on the wedding night results in the immediate dissolution of the marriage (Turkish Court of Appeal for the 2nd Circuit 2006/14694 E, 2007/2504 K, Date: 22.02.2007). This is clear evidence of how the State actually supports patriarchy and traditional social norms.

26 Rachel Aplin, 'Exploring the Role of Mothers in "Honour" Based Abuse Perpetration and the Impact on the Policing Response' (2017) 60 Women's Studies International Forum 1, 5.

27 Bakırköy 5th High Criminal Court 2006/303 E, 2007/458 K, Date: 12.11.2007.

28 Mehmet Yirun and Ferhat Akkun, '2 Gunluk Bebegi Bogup Betona Gomduler' *Istanbul, Hurriyet* (Istanbul, 2010) <www.hurriyet.com.tr/gundem/14439769.asp> accessed 24 January 2020.

29 Ibid.

rumours about Sevim. Sevim and her mother received 36 years of aggravated life imprisonment for intentional murder.[30]

3.2 Rape

Although rape is a form of sexual intercourse to which one of the parties does not consent, it is still commonly treated as a violation of family honour, and women who are the victims of rape are considered as the sources of this shame.[31] It is important here to ask why rape has the effect of tarnishing family honour and why women who are raped are treated badly and abused by their families as a result of violent sexual assault that has been done to them without their consent.

First of all, rape is a violation of a woman's bodily integrity, safety, and autonomy, and it is a demonstration of power over women's bodies.[32] In Turkish societies, it has collective effects.[33] It affects not only the victim but also their families; it is a violation of women's bodies but is also considered to be an attack on and violation of the morality of the family, society, and even the State.[34] More than this, it is agreed to be a violation of men's property;[35] because women are still considered the property of their families,[36] any attack on this 'property' makes a woman a 'used item,'[37] which brings shame and dishonour on the whole family.[38] While the attack comes externally and women do not have any capacity to consent to the sexual encounter, the responsibility for its fatal consequences is shared by victims and their families. Victims – who, as women, are the providers of their families' honour and dignity – are considered responsible to a high degree.[39] From the men's perspective, on the other hand, the situation has a slightly different nature. First, rape proves to wider society that the women of their family cannot protect their *namus*, and this is shameful for the whole family. Thus,

30 Interview with Sevim (Istanbul, 4 September 2012).

31 Niaz A Shah Kakakhel, 'Honour Killings Islamic and Human Rights Perspective' (2004) 55 Northern Ireland Legal Quarterly 78, 80.

32 Dorothy E Roberts, 'Rape, Violence, and Women's Autonomy' (1993) 69 Chicago-Kent Law Review 359.

33 Andrea Parrot and Nina Cummings, *Forsaken Females: The Global Brutalization of Women* (Oxford, Rowan & Littlefield Publishers, Inc 2006) 95.

34 Women for Women's Human Rights-New Ways, *Türk Ceza Kanunu'nda Cinsel Haklarımız Var* (Istanbul, Punto Baskı Çözümleri 2007) 6–7.

35 Mohammad Mazher Idriss and Tahir Abbas (eds), *Honour, Violence, Women and Islam* (Abington, Routledge 2011) 24.

36 Nancy Kaymar Stafford, 'Ending Honour Crimes in Sub-Saharan Africa: Looking at a Long Hard Death' in Mohammad Mazher Idriss and Tahir Abbas (eds), *Honour, Violence, Women, and Islam* (Oxon, Routledge 2011) 169. For an opposite view, see Lila Abu-Lughod, *Do Muslim Women Need Saving?* (Cambridge, MA, Harvard University Press 2013) 116.

37 Parrot and Cummings (n 33) 175. Susan Moller Okin, 'Is Multiculturalism Bad for Women?' in *Is Multiculturalism Bad for Women* (Princeton, Princeton University Press 2001) 15.

38 Anna Carline, 'Honour and Shame in Domestic Homicide: A Critical Analysis of the Provocation Defence' in Mohammad Mazher Idriss and Tahir Abbas (eds), *Honour, Violence, Women and Islam* (Oxon, Routledge 2011) 12.

39 Parrot and Cummings (n 33) 178.

women are, in fact, blamed for not protecting themselves and for allowing the perpetrators to steal their bodily integrity; therefore, they are named as shameful and disgraceful.[40] Second, it shows that men cannot protect their families from any external attack, and so are not able to fulfil their obligations to protect their female kin. This situation not only causes dishonour for the family but also damages the patriarchal structure of the family and men's masculine standing within it – a failure that is visible to all.

This is why, for instance, 14-year-old Nuran was killed by her father after she was kidnapped and raped,[41] which was considered shameful by her family. In that case, although the rapist was caught by the police and sentenced, this State punishment was not sufficient for the victim's family to regain their honour. Therefore, the family sought to enact its own punishment by committing an honour killing, a violent act which is approved not by the State but by society.[42] Like many other honour killing cases, in this case the family also believed that the victim was responsible for the incident and therefore she should be punished.[43] During the murder trial, the victim's father did not mention any regret but said he had cleaned his *namus*.[44]

3.3 Seeking divorce

Irrespective of the real causes of a divorce, society and families tend to blame women for it;[45] it is considered the women's fault, which has a negative effect on the family's honour and reputation.[46] Divorce in these societies proves the failure of the woman to fulfil her duties as a wife.[47] When she returns to her paternal family, she may not be treated well by her relatives. Both parents and brothers

40 Nadera Shalhoub-Kevorkian, 'Reexamining Femicide: Breaking the Silence and Crossing "Scientific" Borders' (2003) 28 Signs 581, 182.

41 Bakırköy 5th High Criminal Court 2009/260 E, 2009/317 K, Date: 16.10.2009.

42 More analysis regarding the conflict between State and society punishment will be made in Chapter 5 when dealing with legal pluralism in Turkey.

43 Mehmet Farac, a well-known Turkish journalist from Eastern Anatolia, has looked at rape incidents and how the honour of the families is cleansed with the blood of the rape victim. In one of the cases, he provides another example of the same problem. In 2006, a married woman from Van was raped several times by her neighbour when her husband was in another city. When the husband discovered the incident, the rapist offered him his 16-year-old daughter as a second wife in order to compensate for the rape, and the husband started to have sexual relations with the 16-year-old girl without her consent (Mehmet Farac, *Söyleyin Anama Ağlamasın* (Istanbul, Cumhuriyet Kitaplari 2007) 108–09). This case is important for showing that women not only are the subject of cleansing the honour of the victim's family but also are used as tools to compensate for their male kin's transgression and to prevent blood revenge.

44 Bakırköy 5th High Criminal Court 2009/260 E, 2009/317 K, Date: 16.10.2009.

45 Nooria Faizi, 'Domestic Violence in the Muslim Community' (2000) 10 Texas Journal of Women and the Law 209, 217.

46 Ibid. 218.

47 Maha AZ Yamani, *Polygamy and Law in Contemporary Saudi Arabia* (Reading, Ithaca 2008) 213–14.

may become stricter towards the divorced woman because of her misbehaviour as a result of her divorce and the subsequent tarnishing of her family's honour. Her brothers especially may become stricter and may not hesitate to use physical violence against her to discipline her. As Akpinar emphasises, she must from then on be very careful with her behaviour, as she can easily cause more damage to her family's honour and reputation.[48]

According to the Turkish Statistical Institution, although there has been an increased number of divorces in recent times,[49] it is still not acceptable for a woman to seek it in many parts of the Middle East. As Kardam mentions in her report, it is commonly accepted that if a woman attempts to leave her husband, she deserves to be punished.[50] Kardam refers to several interviews conducted with husbands and village women in rural areas of Turkey to show how such societies react when a woman looks for a divorce.[51] In one of the interviews, the village women stated that a woman who was killed by her son because she wanted a divorce deserved to be killed.[52] They added that she should have remained at her house and beside her husband, as her husband had the right either to treat her well or to beat her.[53] Either way, she should not have left her husband.[54] During an interview with a young village man from the Batman region in Turkey, he said:

> I definitely do not accept divorcing. Once we got married and I said 'she became my *namus* (honour),' I cannot think her lying under someone else. Either I will kill myself or her.[55]

From the husband's perspective, there are two important consequences from a wife who seeks a divorce. First, the divorce proves that the husband is not able to control his wife's behaviour, and therefore his wife is disobedient. This situation is considered a definite threat to his patriarchal authority as well as to his masculinity. Second, if the wife divorces him, she might have a sexual relationship with someone else, which may motivate HBV, as happened in the case of Salih, who murdered his ex-wife for having a relationship with someone else after the divorce.[56]

48 Aylin Akpinar, 'Honour/Shame Complex Revisited: Violence Against Women in the Migration Context' (2003) 26 Women's Studies International Forum 425, 427.

49 Turkish Statistical Institute's 2019 data available at 'Turkish Statistical Institute' <https://biruni.tuik.gov.tr/medas/?locale=tr> accessed 24 January 2020.

50 Filiz Kardam, 'Turkiyede'ki Namus Cinayetleri'nin Dinamikleri: Eylem Programi Icin Onerilen Sonuc Raporu' (UNDP and UNFPA 2005) 32 <www.undp.org.tr/traboutusdocvuments/namuscinayetleri.pdf> accessed 4 March 2019.

51 Ibid.

52 Ibid.

53 'Her husband could either treat her well or beat her' can be translated as 'kocası; ister sever, ister döver' in Turkish. This is a common phrase in Turkey and is used by both men and women in rural areas in order to demonstrate the full authority of husbands over their wives.

54 Kardam (n 50) 32.

55 Ibid. 18.

56 Interview with Salih (3 September 2012).

A woman seeking divorce affects not only the husband but also the wife's paternal family. Her behaviour is considered shameful because her disobedience proves that she has not been raised properly by her natal family. Onal interviewed a perpetrator of HBV in Turkey who killed his elder sister for returning to the paternal home because of the constant sexual and physical abuse she suffered.[57] One of the quotes from her interview clearly showed how families in such situations react when their female relatives leave their husbands' houses. The perpetrator said to her sister when she refused to return to her husband that, "Deserting your home has brought shame on us. What did you have to walk out for? What you have done will drag our good name through the mud."[58]

Furthermore, if a woman seeks a divorce because of another relationship she has engaged in, then this brings extreme shame to her natal family. In such situations, either her family or her husband usually applies violence to her to clean the shame from their families. As Appendix 2.2 shows, among the cases collected for this research, 14% consider infidelity to be a motive for honour killings.

3.4 Rumours and suspicion

Pitt-Rivers's most quoted sentence, "honour is the value of a person in his own eyes, but also in the eyes of his society," provides an excellent explanation of how someone's honour is related to society's judgement.[59] In Turkey, society has an important role in evaluating the honour and reputation of families by judging female behaviours. If rumours against a woman start, families usually take this situation seriously, impelling them to respond to the gossip immediately in order to protect their honour.[60] In many cases, unfortunately, the families' actions are then abusive and violent: not against the members of the society who started the rumours, but against their own blood relations.[61] In many cases, however, the honour of the families is threatened even before the gossip starts. In other words, even the suspected behaviours are taken as serious threats to the family honour.[62] Although those suspected behaviours are usually linked to women's sexuality and *namus*, this does not always mean that these women are actually involved in

57 Ayse Onal, *Honour Killing: Stories of Men Who Killed* (London, Saqi Books 2008) 75–99.

58 Ibid. 93.

59 Julian Pitt-Rivers, 'Honour and Social Status' in JG Peristiany (ed), *Honour and Shame: The Values of Mediterranean Societies* (London, Weidenfeld and Nicolson 1965) 21.

60 Aisha K Gill, 'Feminist Reflections on Researching So-Called "Honour" Killings' (2013) 21 Feminist Legal Studies 241, 248: Centre for Egyptian Women's Legal Assistance, 'Crimes of Honour as Violence Against Women in Egypt' in Lynn Welchman and Sara Hossain (eds), *'Honour': Crimes, Paradigms and Violence Against Women* (London, Zed Books 2005) 141.

61 Ibid.; Sercan Tokdemir, 'Honor Crimes in Turkey: Rethinking Honour Killings and Reconstructing the Community Using Restorative Justice System' (2013) 4 Law & Justice Review 257, 264.

62 Anna Grabolle-Celiker, *Kurdish Life in Contemporary Turkey: Migration, Gender and Ethnic Identity* (London, IB Tauris 2013) 188; Recep Dogan, 'The Dynamics of Honour Killings: Perpetrators' Experiences' (2016) 20 Homicide Studies 53, 61.

any sexual relationship.[63] For instance, in February 2007, a 16-year-old girl in Trabzon, northern Turkey, was shot by her father because she was coming home late; she was gossiped about and suspected of drinking alcohol, using drugs, and spending time with unrelated men.[64] During the trial, the father confessed that he was angry because of her misbehaviour; he felt ashamed, and his honour was affected.[65] Prior to the incident, the father had even taken his daughter for a virginity test.[66] On the day of the incident, the perpetrator claimed that he had tried to talk to his daughter first and asked her "why she was playing with her father's honour and why she ran away and stayed with other men."[67] According to the father's defence in court, the victim replied, "you cannot butt in on my life; I can do whatever I want."[68] Following these words, the perpetrator claimed that he had lost his control and shot his daughter dead. Although the perpetrator murdered his own daughter as a result of rumours, this case was not considered to be an honour killing by the Turkish criminal court.[69] A provocation defence was applied to the case, and the perpetrator received 17 years' imprisonment instead of aggravated life imprisonment.[70]

3.5 Challenging patriarchal authority

As Reddy argues, one of the reasons to commit HBV is to repair family honour that has been damaged as a result of behaviours that challenge patriarchal authority.[71] This argument, however, raises two important questions: How can a woman challenge patriarchal authority, and why does this challenge cause dishonour for the family? Within traditional patriarchal societies, if a woman tries to increase her autonomy, she challenges patriarchal authority. Any behaviour intended to increase women's autonomy, and which at the same time reduces men's superiority, capacity for oppression, or degree of control, is considered a serious challenge

63 Sally Engle Merry, *Gender Violence: A Cultural Perspective*, vol 3 (West Sussex, Wiley-Blackwell 2011) 268.
64 Trabzon 2nd High Criminal Court 2007/41 E, 2007/27 K, Date: 26.12.2007.
65 Ibid.
66 Ibid. 2. The medical report showed that the victim was still a virgin at the time of the virginity examination (ibid. 7).
67 Ibid.
68 Ibid.
69 This case is also important for showing how the Turkish criminal court conceptualises 'honour killings and customary killings.' Court records show that the murder took place because of the misbehaviour of the victim. The Court stated: "in other words the murder had not been committed as 'honour killings' or customary killings. Honour killings and customary killing are committed because of the incidents that the murdered was actually the victim of them and she was not able to prevent them (such as sexual assault)." This sentence is clear evidence that the criminal court accepts 'misbehaviour' as substantive cause for provocation. (I will examine the defence mechanism and provocation in honour killing cases further on.)
70 Ibid.
71 Rupa Reddy, 'Gender, Culture, and the Law: Approaches to Honour Crimes in the UK' (2008) 16 Feminist Legal Studies 305, 306.

to patriarchal authority as well as family honour. This challenge, however, can take different forms. First, a woman may challenge the oppression she suffers in her patriarchal family by starting to make her own decisions and by contravening her family's and/or community's norms.[72] This is perhaps the first step in a woman realising her agency and personal autonomy, a step I call 'the awakening step.' Women, at that point, realise and start to question their existence as a 'person' (self) which is separate from their families. They also start thinking about and analysing the patriarchal and hierarchal boundaries around them and try to find a way to escape from the oppression, and this is when the challenge starts. This situation is treated as a threat to the power of the patriarchal family, as it may result in loss of control over the woman. For instance, by seeking divorce or refusing arranged and forced marriages,[73] women show that they can make decisions against those of their families, and therefore they damage patriarchal authority as well as family honour.[74]

The second situation that can challenge the patriarchal family is an increase in a woman's sexual autonomy. This is even more dangerous to patriarchy than the first step; at that awakening step, women question their lack of autonomy in general, but in taking the second step they consider their sexual rights and freedom directly, which has a strong link to family honour. An unmarried woman in a traditional patriarchal family is expected to remain non-sexual and to abstain from any sexual activity before marriage.[75] Remaining non-sexual is the best way of protecting the patriarchal imbalance, and if a woman tries to explore her sexuality and increase her sexual autonomy, this threatens to unbalance patriarchy. Her actions can be taken as a serious danger to the whole family's reputation and honour, as both patriarchal authority and the ownership of the woman's body are threatened by the increase of sexual autonomy. For instance, having a boyfriend or simply talking to men who are not relatives can be taken as a serious challenge to patriarchal authority. One internationally famous honour killing case from

72 CIMEL/INTERRIGHTS, 'Roundtable on Strategies to Address "Crimes of Honour": Summary Report' (2001) Women Living Under Muslim Laws Occasional Paper 15.

73 Joanne Payton, 'For the Boys in the Family: An Investigation Into the Relationship Between "Honor"-Based Violence and Endogamy' (2017) 32 Journal of Interpersonal Violence 1332, 1336. Forced marriage in some situations is accepted as a form of honour protection mechanism. For more arguments on forced marriage as a form of HBV, please see Aisha Gill, 'Patriarchal Violence in the Name of Honour' (2006) 1 International Journal of Criminal Justice Sciences 1; Aisha K Gill and Sundari Anitha (eds), *Forced Marriage: Introducing a Social Justice and Human Rights Perspective* (London, Zed Books 2011).

74 Anne Phillips, 'Does the Body Make a Difference?' in Sumi Madhok, Anne Phillips, and Kalpana Wilson (eds), *Gender, Agency, and Coercion* (Hampshire, Palgrave Macmillan 2013) 145.

75 Sandeep Hunjan and Shelagh Towson, '"Virginity Is Everything": Sexuality in Context of Intimate Partner Violence in South Asian Community' *Body Evidence: Intimate Violence Against South Asian Women in America* (New Brunswick, Rutgers University Press 2007) 54; Lama Abu-Odeh, 'Crimes of Honour and Construction of Gender in Arab Societies' in Mai Yamani (ed), *Feminism and Islam: Legal and Literary Perspectives* (Reading, Garnet Publishing Limited 1996) 149.

Turkey shows exactly this situation. In 2010, a 16-year-old girl was buried alive by her father and grandfather in Adiyaman, Turkey.[76] According to the police reports, she was killed because she dishonoured her family by talking to boys.[77] Talking to unrelated men and how this can damage the honour of families is also the focus of Boon's attention in her work 'They Killed Her for Going Out With Boys.'[78] Boon starts her critical analysis of HBV with a well-known honour killing case in Turkey, when a 13-year-old girl was killed by her father with a kitchen knife in their bathroom. Prior to the incident, she had run away and had been talking to boys, both activities deemed unchaste and shameful.[79] Boon highlights that interacting with men outside of the family for any perceived or actual sexual reasons can be considered a threat to family honour.[80] And it is important to highlight the fact that any independent behaviour, whether linked to women's sexuality or not, can be treated as a challenge to patriarchal authority. A research study from Germany on HBV committed between 1996 and 2005 shows that 20 honour killings out of 78 had been committed because of the victims' desire for more independence.[81] To elope from the paternal house, to choose one's own spouse, and to get married without the consent of the father are some of the common situations that are considered challenges to patriarchal authority, because through them the woman seeks more independence and autonomy.

The third situation that is taken as a challenge to patriarchal authority and family honour is 'being too Western.' The concept of 'being too Western' is explained by Chesler:[82]

> being seen as too independent, not subservient enough, refusing to wear varieties of Islamic clothing (including forms of the veil), wanting an advanced education and a career, having non-Muslim (or non-Sikh or non-Hindu) friends or boyfriends, refusing to marry one's first cousin, wanting to choose one's own husband, choosing a socially "inferior" or non-Muslim (or non-Sikh or non-Hindu) husband; or leaving an abusive husband. There were statistically significant regional differences for this motive.[83]

76 Anadolu Ajansi, 'Medine Uzerine Atilan Olum Topragini Gordu' *Hurriyet* (Turkey, 2010) <www.hurriyet.com.tr/gundem/medine-uzerine-atilan-olum-topragini-gordu-13692511> accessed 25 June 2019; 'Teenage Girl Buried Alive in Turkey for Talking to Boys' *The Telegraph* (2010) <www.telegraph.co.uk/news/worldnews/europe/turkey/7161701/Teenage-girl-buried-alive-in-Turkey-for-talking-to-boys.html> accessed 25 June 2019.

77 Jonathan Head, 'Turkish Girl "buried Alive" in Family Garden' *BBC* (UK, 2010) <http://news.bbc.co.uk/1/hi/world/europe/8501181.stm> accessed 25 June 2019.

78 Rebecca Boon, 'They Killed Her for Going Out With Boys' (2006) 33 Hofstra Law Review 815.

79 Bakırköy 13th High Criminal Court 2007/526 E, 2007/17 K, Date: 20.11.2007.

80 Boon (n 78) 816–17.

81 Johannes Korge, 'Justice Slammed in Honor Killing Study' *Spiegel Online International* (Germany, 2011) <www.spiegel.de/international/germany/0,1518,777997,00.html> accessed 25 June 2019.

82 Phyllis Chesler, 'Worldwide Trends in Honor Killings' (2010) 17 The Middle East Quarterly 3.

83 Ibid.

In rural areas, where family lives are tied up with deep-rooted customs and traditions, or in the diaspora, where families are a minority culture, any behaviour that crosses the boundaries of the family can be considered a threat to patriarchal authority. This boundary crossing can take different forms, and being 'too Western' is one of them. For instance, not following the required dress code and adopting a more 'Western' style is one of the motives for VAW because it dishonours the family. Refusing the Islamic dress code and how doing so can cause VAW has been examined in the case of Nuran.[84] Onal also dealt with this case and conducted an interview with Nuran's attacker.[85] Before Nuran ran away from her home and was raped by a stranger, she had refused to put on the veil and wear strict Islamic dress. Her behaviour then led to serious physical and mental violence being inflicted on her.[86] She sustained severe physical injuries from being beaten, and she was not allowed to go out without a companion.[87] In fact, she decided to run away from home to stop the oppression and pressure, without taking into account the probability that her behaviour might have fatal consequences for her. Another case also stemmed from refusal to wear appropriate attire. A woman spoke to the Women's Foundation Centre in Batman to say that one girl was reported as falling from a window while she was cleaning. However, according to eyewitnesses, her family pushed her.[88] Prior to the incident, she had been forced by her family to wear the headscarf and withdraw from school.[89]

The phrase 'being Western' is also commonly used in Turkey to refer to being like people who live in Western cities with liberal, open-minded, and modern habits.[90] Families who migrated from the rural part of Turkey to the West become oppressive and try to control their female relatives from becoming 'city women,' i.e. from adopting Western styles or behaviours. It has been stated by UNICEF Turkey that changing social circumstances may have an effect on HBV.[91] When traditional boundaries are crossed and women become more Western, the pos-

84 For Nuran's case, please see the section 'Rape' in this chapter; Onal (n 57) 99–124.

85 Ibid.

86 Ibid. 109.

87 Ibid.

88 Cagla Pinar Tuncel, 'Recent Suicides By Women in Batman Raise Alarms' *Hurriyet Daily News* (Istanbul, 2011) <www.hurriyetdailynews.com/n.php?n=recent-women-suicides-in-batman-raise-alarms-2011-08-22> accessed 25 June 2019.

89 Ibid.

90 'City women' or 'women from the city' are common phrases used in Turkey to represent women who are independent, sociable, educated, employed, and self-confident, who do not follow the Islamic dress code, and who are sexually active (being sexually active in this context does not necessarily mean having sexual intercourse outside of marriage. Having a boyfriend, interacting with the opposite sex, and having a close relationship with boys (this might include just touching, kissing etc.) but remaining a virgin can also be considered as being sexually active in the Middle Eastern context). Lama Abu-Odeh discusses these types of sexuality in her essay by categorising women as 'sexy virgins' and 'virgins of love.' For more information, see Abu-Odeh (n 75) 172–73.

91 UNICEF, 'Honour Crimes and Forced Suicides' (UNICEF 2005) <www.unicef.org.tr/en/content/detail/74/honour-crimes-and-forced-suicides-2.html> accessed 25 June 2019.

sibility of violence increases.[92] Korteweg and Yurdakul also stress this concept of crossing boundaries.[93] The phrase 'bright boundaries' is used to explain the situation within immigrant communities in Germany and the Netherlands. According to them,

> bright boundaries imply that society is structured around a sharp 'distinction between insiders and outsiders' so that individual members of minority groups (but not groups in their entirety) can cross into majority society only if they give up part of their group identity and adopt some of the practices of majority society.[94]

One of the more well-known examples of crossing these boundaries and how it led to family punishment was the case of Hatun Sürücü in Germany. Hatun was killed by her family in 2005 because she adopted the Western lifestyle: She left her husband, took off her headscarf, and began an apprenticeship as an electrician.[95] Her tragic life story has recently been filmed as a documentary in Germany.[96] When an interviewer asked her brother what his sister did to deserve her own death, he replied, "lifestyle change."[97] Although the perpetrator confessed that he had made the worst mistake, her other brother still thinks that she committed a sin, and told the interviewer that: "I want Allah to forgive her sins."[98] This confession clearly proves two important assumptions about HBV. First, the whole family did not feel that they had done something wrong by committing homicide. Second, even though they may have killed her, they still believe that she is sinful, and that the homicide can only clean the shame from the family, not the sin she committed.

To this point, we have dealt with how honour causes problems, and in which situations honour is considered to be tarnished. Keeping these analyses in mind, the next section aims to analyse the consequences of loss of honour. This is important for showing the link between honour-tarnishing situations and HBV. As the following section underlines, even when honour is stained, this does not directly lead to HBV. Certain steps need to be passed to reach this final consequence:

92 Ibid.

93 Anna Korteweg and Gokce Yurdakul, 'Islam, Gender, Immigrant Integration: Boundary Drawing in Discourses on Honour Killing in the Netherlands and Germany' (2009) 32 Ethnic and Racial Studies 218, 220.

94 Ibid. 219.

95 Justus Leicht, 'Germany: The Murder of Hatun Sürücü and the Debate Over "Honour Killings"' *World Socialist Website* (2006) <www.wsws.org/articles/2006/may2006/germ-m17.shtml> accessed 25 June 2019.

96 Dogan Haber Ajansi, 'Namus Cinayeti Belgesel Oldu' *Dogan Haber Ajansi* (Istanbul, 2011) <http://haberler.com/namus-cinayeti-belgesel-oldu-2895983-haberi/> accessed 25 June 2019.

97 Barbara Hans, 'The Murder in Berlin: The Lost Honor of the Sürücü Family' *Spiegel Online International* (Germany, 2011) <www.spiegel.de/international/germany/0,1518,777109,00.html> accessed 25 June 2019.

98 Ibid.

shame; loss of prestige, reputation, and honour; and finally the use of violence. Therefore, the following section looks more precisely at the form, structure, and process of these steps and the situations that lead to HBV.

4. Consequences of loss of honour

When the honour of individuals or families is lost, this has various consequences. First of all, it brings severe shame on people and families; as this happens, families, and the male members of those families, lose their reputation, prestige, fame, and esteem. Following this, society expects individual male members of the families to cleanse themselves of that shame. If they do not, family members are usually excluded from their families and ostracised from society. The shame, loss of reputation and prestige, and social marginalisation then put pressure on families to remove the taint.[99] In order to do so and regain the family's honour, normally the only action taken by family members is violence.[100] This shows the circle in which loss of honour spins. And, without taking the necessary measures to enable members of families to break this circle, it is not possible to talk about restoring family honour. Therefore, the following sections specifically focus on loss of honour while considering these specific measures.

4.1 Shame

Shame is the first consequence that individuals and families face as a result of a female family member's behaviour that is deemed dishonourable, unacceptable, or inappropriate for society. When honour is lost, shame takes honour's place, and it stays as a black stain on families until it is cleansed.[101] According to Peristiany, honour and shame are polar concepts; he explains the relationship between honour and shame as "two poles of an evaluation."[102] Wikan, however, argues that honour and shame form a "contestable pair," and that it is not always possible to assert that they are binary concepts.[103] To support her argument, Wikan raises several issues. First, she states that, for some Mediterranean and Muslim people, shame is the predominant concern, not honour.[104] Second, she claims that it is not self-evident that shame and honour are binary opposites. She also argues that "honour is an aspect of person, whereas shame only applies to act."[105] These suggestions have been reviewed and commented on by Stewart;

99 Dogan (n 62) 64–65.
100 Ibid.
101 Tanella Boni, 'The Dignity of the Human Person: On the Integrity of the Body and Struggle for Recognition' (2007) 54 Diogenes 59.
102 JG Peristiany (ed), *Honour and Shame: The Values of Mediterranean Society* (London, Weidenfeld and Nicolson 1965) 9–10.
103 Unni Wikan, 'Shame and Honour: A Contestable Pair' (1984) 19 Man, New Series 635, 635–36.
104 Ibid.
105 Ibid. 636.

he accepts the idea that shame is dominant, but at the same time he claims that this dominance in Western societies is primarily lexical, as the word 'ashamed' is used more than 'honour' in daily life.[106] Apart from this, he finds Wikan's second claim indisputably correct, arguing that

> shame is generally looked on as an emotion, whereas honour is not usually regarded as an emotion, and emotion can scarcely be the exact opposite of something that is not emotion.[107]

In traditional Turkish societies, honour and shame usually are treated with the same level of concern. The amount of effort put into protecting and maintaining honour is usually equal to the amount of effort put into avoiding shame in these societies. As discussed earlier, although men and women shoulder different levels of responsibility for protecting honour and avoiding shame, what is common to both men and women is that, once honour is protected, shame is also avoided.

However, Wikan's argument about dominance can be applied to the situation of regaining honour and removing shame. This is because it is usually more difficult to remove shame from the family than to regain lost honour. Although the violent actions taken as a result of dishonour help families to regain their honour, these actions are not so effective at removing shame; even after the violence has taken place, shame remains.[108] For instance, in cases of adultery/infidelity in traditional Middle Eastern, Muslim, and even Mediterranean societies, the public expects that the deceived husband will commit homicide against his wife in order to regain his honour; this action is undertaken by the husband as a duty. Once this duty is fulfilled, he and his family will regain their honour, but removing the shame they suffer in the public eye takes longer.

Another point that should be highlighted here concerns the level of shame. In many traditional Turkish societies, although shame is one of the primary consequences of the loss of honour, the term may have different levels of severity. For instance, in the Turkish language shame can be translated as *utanç*, *ayıp*, and *ar*. *Ar* is usually used for severe shame that arises as a result of the unacceptable sexual behaviour of a woman.[109] For instance, *ar* can refer to adultery, illegitimate relationships, loss of virginity before marriage, or any situation that can lead to suspicion about the woman's virginity, such as having a boyfriend or being seen with non-family members etc. On the other hand, *ayıp* mostly denotes a less severe degree of shame. Dressing inappropriately; attracting attention in society; and disobeying daily basic customs, such as disrespecting the patriarchy, not practising religion properly, and behaving disrespectfully, are some of the

106 Stewart (n 13) 128–29.
107 Ibid.
108 JK Campbell, *Honour, Family and Patronage: A Study of Institutions and Moral Values in a Greek Mountain Community* (New edn, Oxford, Oxford University Press 1974) 271.
109 Ibid.

situations that can cause *ayıp*.[110] As we can see, the differences between *ar* and *ayıp* are not only about the level of shame but also concern the values that they represent. While *ar* represents sexual behaviour, *ayıp* refers to any behaviour that contravenes society's norms.

Utanç has a wider meaning than both *ayıp* and *ar*; it is used as lexically parallel to shame and includes the meanings of both *ayıp* and *ar*. Although the term *utanç* subsumes both sets of meanings, the possessors of *utanç* are usually women in the Turkish language. For instance, the well-known phrase '*utanç kaynaği*'[111] is mostly used for women. This phrase is also important for demonstrating the position of women in relation to shame; they are considered to be the root cause or source of shame in their families and societies, and because of that, as explained before, even when the visible sign of shame is cleansed from the family, it always remains at its source in the form of the woman who caused it.

Even though shame exists at different levels, the consequences of *ar* and *ayıp* are the same: dishonour, loss of esteem, bad reputation, and so on. Similarly, the level of pressure that society exerts on families and their male members is different. This is especially true in the process of regaining honour and removing shame. For example, if there is an instance of *ar*, it is believed that only severe, violent, retaliatory actions can cleanse the shame and regain the lost honour; these actions mostly result in homicide.[112] If there is *ayıp*, the actions are usually less violent and harmful but can still include beating, assault, or exclusion from society.[113] However, in some societies, even if only *ayıp* exists, families still feel the pressure from society to take severe actions in order to erase the shame. For instance, in one situation a 25-year-old woman was killed by her brother because her friend requested a song for her from a local radio station and her name was mentioned during its broadcast.

> The announcement of her name from the radio was considered a great disgrace for the family because the song was a love song which implied that she had a love affair in the eyes of the local people.[114]

Reading out a name on the radio might seem absolutely normal in many societies, but in strict patriarchal and extremely conservative societies, it is seen as *ayıp*

110 Ibid.

111 This phrase can be translated as 'sources of shame.'

112 Valerie Plant, 'Honour Killings and the Asylum Gender Gap' (2005) 15 Journal of Transnational Law & Policy 109, 112.

113 S Douki, F Nacef, and A Belhadj, 'Violence Against Women in Arab and Islamic Countries' (2003) 6 Archives of Women's Mental Health 165, 167; James Brandon and Salam Hafez, 'Crimes of the Community: Honour – Based Violence in the UK' (The Centre for Social Cohesion 2008) <http://www.civitas.org.uk/pdf/CrimesOfTheCommunity.pdf> accessed 06 February 2020.

114 NGO Country Report on Implementation of the CEDAW in Turkey, Prepared for Submission to the United Nations (UN) Committee for the Elimination of Discrimination Against Women at its Periodic Review of Turkey, 16th Session (New York, 1997), 10. <www.wwhr.org/yayin_2.php?detay=56> accessed 26 June 2019.

and shameful.[115] And even though in this example the level of shame might not be seen as reaching the severity of *ar*, society's pressure to remove the shame nevertheless operated at the same level it would have for *ar*.[116] This example takes us to the argument of Gill and Brah, who stress that it is quite easy to measure the level of shame through the action or actions that are taken to remedy it.[117]

4.2 Loss of prestige and reputation

Although shame is the leading consequence of loss of honour, it is not the only one. As a result of dishonour and shame, the other honour-related values are dramatically affected by its loss.[118] When a person loses his honour, he also loses his reputation, prestige, esteem, and fame in people's eyes.[119] In many societies, especially those in which men have dominant positions, loss of reputation and prestige can equate to loss of manhood, because it is believed that a man is not a man without prestige, good reputation, and honour.[120] More than this, it is not only individuals but also families that lose their reputation,[121] which proves that honour is not only an individual value but also a collective one.

4.3 Exclusion from family and society

The other consequence of losing honour is exclusion of the shameful person from her/his family and ostracising him/her and the family from society. This dramatic conclusion usually arises when there is a failure to regain honour or cleanse dishonour. The families are questioned about whether they have cleansed their shame or not; consequently, any action concerning the family's honour is usually witnessed by or disclosed to the community.[122] Otherwise, the social relations of these families with the rest of the community would be extremely limited.[123]

115 For similar discussion on the effect of social media, please see Ceren Günsoy and others, 'Would You Post That Picture and Let Your Dad See It? Culture, Honor, and Facebook' (2015) 45 European Journal of Social Psychology 323.

116 Ibid.

117 Aisha K Gill and Avtar Brah, 'Interrogating Cultural Narratives About "Honour"-Based Violence' (2014) 21 European Journal of Women's Studies 72, 74.

118 Nancy Lindisfarne, 'Variant Masculinities, Variant Virginities: Rethinking "Honour and Shame"' in Andrea Cornwall (ed), *Dislocating Masculinity: Comparative Ethnographies* (London, Routledge 2003) 85.

119 Campbell (n 2) 144.

120 To emphasise this situation, Unni Wikan uses the phrase 'a man must be a man' (Wikan (n 103) 646).

121 Tenzin Dorjee, Noorie Baig, and Stella Ting-Toomey, 'A Social Ecological Perspective on Understanding "Honour Killing": An Intercultural Moral Dilemma' (2013) 42 Journal of Intercultural Communication Research 1, 6.

122 Peristiany (n 102) 27.

123 Mohammad Mazher Idriss, 'Key Agent and Survivor Recommendations for Intervention in Honour-Based Violence in the UK' (2018) 42 International Journal of Comparative and

4.4 Physical violence

Apart from shame, loss of reputation and esteem, exclusion of the family, and ostracism from society, the last consequence of loss of honour is violence. Despite shame and other consequences of loss of honour, violence does not directly arise when honour is lost; it appears in the process of protecting honour or restoring it and cleansing the shame. The main reason to use violence is because violence is believed to be the best and sometimes only way of erasing shame from families and individuals.[124] For instance, Blok argues that "for men, the use of violence is the best way to obtain satisfaction for stained honour and to restore their reputation for manliness."[125] Blok's argument is worth examining for two reasons. First, his claim is gender-specific; according to him, men are most likely to use violence. However, society should also be considered as abettors from a criminal law perspective. The reason for this is because society's pressure on men to use violence is almost absolute. Second, Blok claims that violence is used to restore reputation and manliness. Although Blok's research is mostly limited to the region of Sicily, his claim can be applied to many other Mediterranean, Middle Eastern, and Muslim societies; in those societies men do have a dominant position and their masculinity and manliness have crucial importance in sustaining their honour and reputation.

Although violence can be applied in many different forms when family honour is lost, the most serious one is committing homicide against the 'shameful' relative, which will be dealt from the legal aspect in more detail in the following chapters. However, as well as honour killings, a high number of female suicides have strong links to family honour in Turkey. Batman, a small city in the Eastern Anatolia, has seen an alarmingly high number of suicides. Halis, a Turkish journalist, investigated female suicides in Batman in her 2001 book.[126] She investigated 45 suicides in Batman and analysed the official data provided by the Turkish government. Halis' book mainly focuses on the issue of female suicides as a result of severe oppression and the restrictions applied to women by their families. In her analysis, those women who attempt suicide are uneducated; are faced with severe patriarchal authority; are housewives; do not interact with society; and have lives that are considerably restricted and controlled by their families.[127] Kardam focused on the same problems faced by women in Batman, and she

Applied Criminal Justice 321, 323. This situation was highlighted by the prisoner participants of this research. Please see Appendix 1.7.

124 Dogan (n 62) 64–65; Mohammad Mazher Idriss, 'Not Domestic Violence or Cultural Tradition: Is Honour-Based Violence Distinct From Domestic Violence?' (2017) 39 Journal of Social Welfare and Family Law 3, 9.

125 Anton Blok, *Honour and Violence* (Cambridge, Polity Press 2001) 105.

126 Mujgan Halis, *Batman'da Kadınlar Ölüyor* (Istanbul, Metis Yayinlari 2011). See also Batman Barosu BaŞkanlığı, 'Batman'da YaŞanan İntihar Olayları İle İlgili AraŞtırma Raporu' (Batman, Batman Barosu BaŞkanlığı 2001) 15.

127 Halis (n 126) 88–89.

addressed how those problems trigger further restrictions on women's lives and how they cause women to commit suicide.[128]

Both analyses show that for women who live in Batman, suicide is considered a way of escaping from severe oppression, violence, and abuse. In most situations, women commit suicide when they cannot raise their voices against the patriarchal authorities. For instance, sometimes women find no way to save themselves from different types of forced marriages but to kill themselves.[129] Kadriye, Gulbahar, and Fatma are only three women who committed suicide because they could not find any other solution to avoiding forced marriage.[130] This again takes us to the arguments relating to women's autonomy in general, and problems of female agency in Turkey in particular. It is important to remember Phillips's argument in the context of agency under severe oppression, which highlights that even in such circumstances women's agency should be recognised[131] and women be allowed to realise that agency. The State has an important duty to consider 'classic patriarchy' (addressed previously by Kandiyoti)[132] and understand that for women living under the strong hegemonic forces of masculinity, patriarchy, and hierarchy (all examples of severe oppression, as pointed out by Phillips), not recognising their autonomy and agency can lead women to seek to end their lives. One could argue at this point that committing suicide involves some degree of agency and autonomy for these women, as it shows them exercising their free will. However, this argument is not supportable, as these suicides are not true exercises of free will and their autonomy, but show the desperation of being caught in an oppressive family trap without any escape. Thus, the State's role at this stage is not only to recognise women's agency and autonomy (which means pushing the patriarchal State approach to one side) but also to provide women with escape exits and inform them that such escape is available to use anytime. Then feminists may argue that in Turkey, although severe oppression of women still exists, there is nevertheless women's autonomy and agency.

128 Filiz Kardam, 'Namus Gerekcesiyle Oldurme Ya Da Kendi Canina Kiyma: Kadin Cinselligi Uzerinde Baskilarin Benzer Kosullarda Farkli Sonuclari Mi' *Hacettepe Universitesi Kadin Sorunlari ve Uygulama Merkezi* (Ankara, Hacettepe Universitesi Yayinlari 2003) <www.huksam.hacettepe.edu.tr/Turkce/SayfaDosya/namus_ger_oldurme.pdf> accessed 26 June 2019. See also Omer Muftuoglu, 'İntihar Olayları Üzerine Bir Değerlendirme: Doğu ve Güneydoğu Anadolu'daki Kadın İntihar Olayları Örneği' (2002) 2 Dinbilimleri Akiademik AraŞtırma Dergisi 143, 152–55.

129 Mahmut Tezcan, Turkiye'de Tore (Namus), *Cinayetleri: Sosyo Kulturel Antropolojik Yaklasim* (Ankara, Naturel 2003) 61–68.

130 Engin Ozturk, 'Intihari Seciyorlar' *Oz Diyarbakir* (Diyarbakir, 2010) <www.google.co.uk/search?q=Intihari+Seciyorlar%E2%80%99&aq=f&oq=Intihari+Seciyorlar%E2%80%99&aqs=chrome.0.57.1584j0&sourceid=chrome&ie=UTF-8#sclient=psy-ab&q=Intihari+Seciyorlar%E2%80%99+oz+diyarbakir&oq=Intihari+Seciyorlar%E2%80%99+oz+diyarbakir&gs_l=serp.3 . . . 4579.6945.0.7104.14.14.0.0.0.0.46.506.14.14.0 . . . 0.0 . . . 1c.1.11.psy-ab.rP3qr8Z1IaE&pbx=1&bav=on.2,or.r_qf.&bvm=bv.45645796,d.d2k&fp=51a2b47f571cda6f&biw=1310&bih=1031> accessed 25 June 2019.

131 Anne Phillips, *Gender and Culture* (Cambridge, Polity Press 2010) 11.

132 Deniz Kandiyoti, 'Bargaining With Patriarchy' (1988) 2 Gender and Society 274, 278.

Yet the State fails in its above-mentioned duties in many aspects. Although suicides are mostly attempted because women feel they have no choice but to end their lives, these actions are still considered to be non-criminal actions, and they are thought of by the authorities as women's free choice, which shows the State's lack of understanding of women and their situation. The State authorities turn a blind eye to the fact that the incidents are not always 'simple suicides.' Sometimes suicide is not just to escape; women are often forced to kill themselves in order to restore family honour, or their family members kill them and the crimes are reported as suicides.[133] In the first instance, as Kardam mentions, mothers feel primarily responsible for the moral behaviour of their children, and they feel guilty when their daughters bring shame on their families. Therefore, they try to persuade their daughters to commit suicide.[134] In one case, a girl was forced to kill herself because she was seen with a boy in public and rumours had spread across the village. The family felt that their honour had been tarnished, and they ordered her to kill herself. When she failed, they decided to kill her.[135] A similar scenario was seen in the famous Guldunya case. Prior to the incident, Guldunya had been told by her family to commit suicide, and she had been left in a room with a rope to hang herself.[136] In Kahramanmaras, Elif was also instructed to kill herself when her family found out that her cousin had raped her. Her mother and brother forced her to end her life, and her mother gave her a rope and her brother prepared the rope for her.[137] He also wrote the suicide letter on behalf of her sister.[138] Derya, from Batman, was also forced to commit suicide because she had fallen in love with a boy from her school. She was told that either she could commit suicide, or her family would kill her.

In the second type of scenario, families commit honour killings but report the incidents as suicides to the authorities. In these cases, the women are not forced to end their lives are actually killed by their families to restore family honour; suicide is used as justification in order to hide the homicide.[139] The fact that both

133 M Cengiz Yıldız, 'Türkiye'de Töre Baskısına Bağlı İntiharlar ve Töre Cinayetleri' (2008) 1 Sosyal Bilimler Enstitüsü Dergisi 209.

134 Filiz Kardam, 'The Dynamics of Honour Killings in Turkey: Prospects for Action' (Ankara, United Nations Population Fund 2005) 58 <www.unfpa.org/upload/lib_pub_file/676_filename_honourkillings.pdf> accessed 26 June 2019.

135 Remzi Kocoz, 'Aile İçi Şiddet, İntiharlar, Ensest İliŞkiler, Diğer Adıyla Töreseli, Yöresel Cinayetler' (2004) Cagin Polisi <www.caginpolisi.com.tr/39/33-34-35-36.htm#_ftn1> accessed 25 June 2019.

136 Cihan Ahmetbeyzade, 'Gendering Necropolitics: The Juridical-Political Sociality of Honour Killings in Turkey' (2008) 7 Journal of Human Rights 187, 197.

137 Yakin Ertürk, 'Birlesmis Milletler Kadinlara Karsi Siddet, Sebepleri ve Sonuclari Ozel Raportoru Yakin Ertürk'un Turkiye Ziyaretine Iliskin Raporu' (The United Nations Commission on Human Rights 2006) 199 <http://insanhaklarimerkezi.bilgi.edu.tr/Books/khuku/kadinlara_karsi_siddet/siddet_bm__ozel_raportoru_yakin_erturk_turkiye_ziyaretine_il.pdf> accessed 26 June 2019.

138 Salih Zeki İskender, *Öğreti ve Yargısal Kararlar Işığında Töre Saikiyle İnsan Öldürme Suçu (Namus Cinayetleri)* (Ankara, Yetkin 2011) 66.

139 Ertürk (n 137) 208.

types of situations still appear – forcing women to commit suicide or committing homicide and reporting it as a suicide – proves the lack of gender consciousness and acceptance of women's autonomy in Turkey; they have the same *mens rea*, or guilty mind. The guilty mind behind these actions is to cleanse the shame, restore family honour, and get rid of the shameful family member by ending her life. These actions are intended to end women's lives intentionally, and there is no free choice from the women's side, even to commit suicide; therefore, there is no female agency and no autonomy. Based on the above-mentioned examples, it is clear that suicides are forced upon women by their families, and the women are given no choice to live. It is not misleading to say that these so-called suicides are actually honour killings without prosecuted perpetrators. This is perhaps the most important point to make when distinguishing between honour killings and so-called suicides. Because women are forced to commit suicide, or actual murder is presented as a form of suicide, at first sight there is no defendant to accuse of a criminal act.

Furthermore, although so-called suicides bring about a particular result – death – and this result assuages the guilty mind of the whole family, because there is no perpetrator to accuse there is no proper link between so-called suicides and the *actus reus* of the death. Although almost all penal codes or existing criminal laws legislate that forcing someone to commit suicide is a criminal act, and that people who force or cause someone to commit suicide are also liable for murder, there is a problem of investigation and prosecution in Turkey. As United Nations special reporter Ertürk mentioned, there is a lack of "psychological autopsy" of suicide incidents.[140] In other words, the authorities fail to investigate the psychological roots of those suicides.[141] Because of this lack of investigation and failure to implement the laws sufficiently, the State has a significant role in allowing the perpetrators of so-called suicides remain without punishment. When the State fails to investigate such incidents carefully or to prosecute suspected family members, it proves its patriarchal attitudes to gender-based violence, allowing family members who have direct links to the deaths of women remain free and failing to seek justice for women whose lives end tragically.

5. Conclusion

This chapter has analysed the social environment in which HBV is committed in three stages: possessing honour, protecting honour, and losing honour. These stages have been explained by considering the first three parts of the hermeneutical circle of HBV: the concept of honour; patriarchy, hierarchy, and masculinity; and culture and traditions. By using the earlier discussions of these concepts, the chapter has revealed important distinctions between possessing and protecting honour within traditional Turkish societies.

140 Ibid. 209–10.
141 Ibid.

By considering the hermeneutical circle of HBV with our earlier discussions of its first three parts, the circle was used to interpret other directly related issues. Possessing honour, protecting it, and losing it are very much linked to how we interpret the first three parts of the circle. These interpretations lead us to further analyse possessing, protecting, and losing honour by remaining in the same interpretative circle. Without this circle, the analysis of possessing honour and its possessors would be different. When considering the Western interpretation of honour, one might easily assume that women and men both have honour and possess it in the same way, such as by being an honest person. This interpretation, however, is misleading when considering the hermeneutical circle of HBV. Therefore, this chapter analysed the social environment that pertains before HBV is committed by considering it within the circle of HBV.

The analysis of the environment that exists before HBV is committed started with the problem of possessing honour. It showed that, with the effect of 'classic patriarchy,' women play a significant role in the process of possessing honour. Although they are not considered the main possessors of honour, they are under the burden of being chaste, *namuslu*, and modest, which are seen as the main sources of their and their families' honour. Men, on the other hand, possess honour through the behaviour of their women, which makes their honour conditional.

The chapter also analysed the common situations that are considered threats to both individual and collective honour. By considering the earlier analysis on gender relations and 'classic patriarchy' in Turkey, it is clear that these threats are strongly linked to women's behaviours, especially their sexual autonomy. The chapter argued that the concept of 'sexual' that threatens honour should be considered very broadly when dealing with HBV in its hermeneutical circle. Many things, including dying hair, putting on makeup, or dressing stylishly, could be considered 'sexual' by families and societies, and if that 'sexuality' crosses the boundaries of social norms, then it also violates honour codes and threatens a family's reputation. As mentioned, although almost anything can be considered a motive for HBV, the data collected from the court cases during this research shows the most frequent motives.[142]

Once honour is tarnished, different consequences occur within society that trigger HBV: shame, loss of prestige and reputation, exclusion from society, and physical violence. Shame is the one consequence that immediately arises when honour is tarnished. The level of shame differs depending on the behaviour that damaged honour. Shame directly affects the reputation of the individual and their families, and the social pressure to cleanse this shame starts immediately. Although society sometimes directly expresses its reaction to the shame and loss of honour, the data of this research, shown in Appendix 1.7, suggests that the perpetrators also commit HBV in order to extricate themselves from these consequences even before they are expressed by society. Society's judgement is shaped

142 Please see Appendix 2.2.

by the level of shame with which individuals and families have been tainted. This level also determines the degree of physical violence that the individuals and families must exert in order to restore their honour. As the chapter has highlighted, and the following part will analyse, the most severe measure taken by families to restore honour is committing homicide against the woman responsible for this loss of honour. The perpetrators and the families, as Appendix 1.6 and 1.7 show, do not always commit honour killings because society tells them that this is the most appropriate way to cleanse their shame, but rather because they assume that society will expect that this level of violence needs to be done.

The chapter is designed as the concluding chapter to answer the first part of the book's question: ***How and under which conditions are honour killings committed in Turkey?*** Using the analysis provided from this part, the second part will deal with the legal problems surrounding the criminalisation and prosecution of honour killings in Turkey that hinder the securing of justice for the victims.

Bibliography

Abu-Lughod L, *Do Muslim Women Need Saving?* (Cambridge, MA, Harvard University Press 2013)

Abu-Odeh L, 'Crimes of Honour and Construction of Gender in Arab Societies' in Mai Yamani (ed), *Feminism and Islam: Legal and Literary Perspectives* (Reading, Garnet Publishing Limited 1996)

Ahmetbeyzade C, 'Gendering Necropolitics: The Juridical-Political Sociality of Honour Killings in Turkey' (2008) 7 Journal of Human Rights 187

Akpinar A, 'Honour/Shame Complex Revisited: Violence Against Women in the Migration Context' (2003) 26 Women's Studies International Forum 425

Anadolu Ajansi, 'Medine Uzerine Atilan Olum Topragini Gordu' *Hurriyet* (Turkey, 2010) <www.hurriyet.com.tr/gundem/medine-uzerine-atilan-olum-topragini-gordu-13692511> accessed 25 June 2019

Aplin R, 'Exploring the Role of Mothers in "Honour" Based Abuse Perpetration and the Impact on the Policing Response' (2017) 60 Women's Studies International Forum 1

Awwad AM, 'Gossip, Scandal, Shame, and Honour Killing: A Case for Social Constructionism and Hegemonic Discourse' (2002) 24 Social Thought & Research 39

Batman Barosu BaŞkanlığı, 'Batman'da YaŞanan İntihar Olayları İle İlgili AraŞtırma Raporu' (Batman, Batman Barosu BaŞkanlığı 2001)

Begikhani N, Gill AK and Hague G, *Honour-Based Violence: Experiences and Counter-Strategies in Iraqi Kurdistan and the UK Kurdish Diaspora* (Surrey, Ashgate 2015)

Blok A, 'Rams and Billy-Goats: A Key to the Mediterranean Code of Honour' (1981) 16 Man, New Series 427

———, *Honour and Violence* (Cambridge, Polity Press 2001)

Blum E, Braiden R and Heinonen T, 'Service Delivery Considerations in Dealing with Honour-Based Violence' (2016) 48 Canadian Ethnic Studies 129

Boiger M and others, 'Defending Honour, Keeping Face: Interpersonal Affordances of Anger and Shame in Turkey and Japan' (2014) Cognition & Emotion 1

Boni T, 'The Dignity of the Human Person: On the Integrity of the Body and Struggle for Recognition' (2007) 54 Diogenes 59

Boon R, 'They Killed Her for Going Out With Boys' (2006) 33 Hofstra Law Review 815

Brandon J and Hafez S, 'Crimes of the Community: Honour – Based Violence in the UK' (The Centre for Social Cohesion 2008) <http://www.civitas.org.uk/pdf/CrimesOfTheCommunity.pdf> accessed 06 February 2020

Campbell JK, 'Honour and the Devil' in JG Peristiany (ed), *Honour and Shame: The Values of Mediterranean Societies* (London, Weidenfeld and Nicolson 1965)

———, *Honour, Family and Patronage: A Study of Institutions and Moral Values in a Greek Mountain Community* (New Ed, Oxford, Oxford University Press 1974)

Carline A, 'Honour and Shame in Domestic Homicide: A Critical Analysis of the Provocation Defence' in Mohammad Mazher Idriss and Tahir Abbas (eds), *Honour, Violence, Women and Islam* (Oxon, Routledge 2011)

Centre for Egyptian Women's Legal Assistance, 'Crimes of Honour as Violence Against Women in Egypt' in Lynn Welchman and Sara Hossain (eds), *'Honour': Crimes, Paradigms and Violence Against Women* (London, Zed Books 2005)

Chesler P, 'Worldwide Trends in Honor Killings' (2010) 17 The Middle East Quarterly 3

CIMEL/INTERRIGHTS, 'Roundtable on Strategies to Address "Crimes of Honour": Summary Report' [2001] Women Living Under Muslim Laws Occasional Paper

Davis J, *People of the Mediterranean: An Essay in Comparative Social Anthropology* (London, Routledge and Kegan Paul 1977)

Di Bella MP, 'Name, Blood and Miracles: The Claims to Renown in the Traditional Sicily' in JG Peristiany and Julian Pitt-Rivers (eds), *Honour and Grace in Anthropology* (Cambridge, Cambridge University Press 1992)

Dogan Haber Ajansi, 'Namus Cinayeti Belgesel Oldu' *Dogan Haber Ajansi* (Istanbul, 2011) <http://haberler.com/namus-cinayeti-belgesel-oldu-2895983-haberi/> accessed 25 June 2019

Dogan R, 'The Dynamics of Honour Killings: Perpetrators' Experiences' (2016) 20 Homicide Studies 53

Dorjee T, Baig N and Ting-Toomey S, 'A Social Ecological Perspective on Understanding "Honour Killing": An Intercultural Moral Dilemma' (2013) 42 Journal of Intercultural Communication Research 1

Douki S, Nacef F and Belhadj A, 'Violence Against Women in Arab and Islamic Countries' (2003) 6 Archives of Women's Mental Health 165

Ecevitoğlu P, *Namus Töre ve İktidar: Kadının Çıplak Hayat Olarak Kuruluşu* (Ankara, Dipnot 2012)

Ercevik Amado L, 'Promoting Sexual Rights Through Human Rights Education: Experiences at Grassroots in Turkey' (2006) 17 Institute of Development Studies Bulletin 117

Ertürk Y, 'Birlesmis Milletler Kadinlara Karsi Siddet, Sebepleri ve Sonuclari Ozel Raportoru Yakin Ertürk'un Turkiye Ziyaretine Iliskin Raporu' (The United Nations Commission on Human Rights 2006) <http://insanhaklarimerkezi.bilgi.edu.tr/Books/khuku/kadinlara_karsi_siddet/siddet_bm__ozel_raportoru_yakin_erturk_turkiye_ziyaretine_il.pdf> accessed 26 June 2019

Faizi N, 'Domestic Violence in the Muslim Community' (2000) 10 Texas Journal of Women and the Law 209

Farac M, *Söyleyin Anama Ağlamasın* (Istanbul, Cumhuriyet Kitaplari 2007)
Gill A, 'Patriarchal Violence in the Name of Honour' (2006) 1 International Journal of Criminal Justice Sciences 1
Gill AK, 'Feminist Reflections on Researching So-Called "Honour" Killings' (2013) 21 Feminist Legal Studies 241
Gill AK and Anitha S (eds), *Forced Marriage: Introducing a Social Justice and Human Rights Perspective* (London, Zed Books 2011)
Gill AK and Brah A, 'Interrogating Cultural Narratives About "Honour"-Based Violence' (2014) 21 European Journal of Women's Studies 72
Gilmore DD, 'Seeds of Honor, Fields of Shame,' *Honor and Shame and the Unity of the Mediterranean* (Washington, American Anthropological Association 1987)
Grabolle-Celiker A, *Kurdish Life in Contemporary Turkey: Migration, Gender and Ethnic Identity* (London, IB Tauris 2013)
Günsoy C and others, 'Would You Post That Picture and Let Your Dad See It? Culture, Honor, and Facebook' (2015) 45 European Journal of Social Psychology 323
Halis M, *Batman'da Kadınlar Ölüyor* (Istanbul, Metis Yayinlari 2011)
Hans B, 'The Murder in Berlin: The Lost Honor of the Sürücü Family' *Spiegel Online International* (Germany, 2011) <www.spiegel.de/international/germany/0,1518,777109,00.html> accessed 25 June 2019
Head J, 'Turkish Girl "buried Alive" in Family Garden' *BBC* (UK, 2010) <http://news.bbc.co.uk/1/hi/world/europe/8501181.stm> accessed 25 June 2019
Hunjan S and Towson S, '"Virginity Is Everything": Sexuality in Context of Intimate Partner Violence in South Asian Community,' *Body Evidence: Intimate Violence Against South Asian Women in America* (New Brunswick, Rutgers University Press 2007)
Idriss MM, 'Not Domestic Violence or Cultural Tradition: Is Honour-Based Violence Distinct From Domestic Violence?' (2017) 39 Journal of Social Welfare and Family Law 3
———, 'Key Agent and Survivor Recommendations for Intervention in Honour-Based Violence in the UK' (2018) 42 International Journal of Comparative and Applied Criminal Justice 321
Idriss MM and Abbas T (eds), *Honour, Violence, Women and Islam* (Abington, Routledge 2011)
Ilkkaracan P, 'Exploring the Context of Women's Sexuality in Eastern Turkey' in Pinar Ilkkaracan (ed), *Women and Sexuality in Muslim Societies* (Istanbul, Women for Women's Human Rights (WWHR) 2000)
Interview with Salih (3 September 2012)
Interview with Sevim (Istanbul, 4 September 2012)
İskender SZ, *Öğreti ve Yargısal Kararlar Işığında Töre Saikiyle İnsan Öldürme Suçu (Namus Cinayetleri)* (Ankara, Yetkin 2011)
Kakakhel NAS, 'Honour Killings Islamic and Human Rights Perspective' (2004) 55 Northern Ireland Legal Quarterly 78
Kandiyoti D, 'Emancipated But Unliberated? Reflections on the Turkish Case' (1987) 13 Feminist Studies 317
———, 'Bargaining With Patriarchy' (1988) 2 Gender and Society 274
Kardam F, 'Namus Gerekcesiyle Oldurme Ya Da Kendi Canina Kiyma: Kadin Cinselligi Uzerinde Baskilarin Benzer Kosullarda Farkli Sonuclari Mi,' *Hacettepe Universitesi Kadin Sorunlari ve Uygulama Merkezi* (Ankara, Hacettepe Universitesi

Yayinlari 2003) <www.huksam.hacettepe.edu.tr/Turkce/SayfaDosya/namus_ger_oldurme.pdf> accessed 26 June 2019

———, 'The Dynamics of Honour Killings in Turkey: Prospects for Action' (Ankara, United Nations Population Fund 2005) <www.unfpa.org/upload/lib_pub_file/676_filename_honourkillings.pdf> accessed 26 June 2019

———, 'Turkiyede'ki Namus Cinayetleri'nin Dinamikleri: Eylem Programi Icin Onerilen Sonuc Raporu' (UNDP and UNFPA 2005) <www.undp.org.tr/traboutus docvuments/namuscinayetleri.pdf> accessed 4 March 2019

Karmi G, 'Women, Islam, and Patriarchalism' in Mai Yamani (ed), *Feminism and Islam: Legal and Literary Perspectives* (Reading, Garnet Publishing Limited 1996)

Kaymar Stafford N, 'Ending Honour Crimes in Sub-Saharan Africa: Looking at a Long Hard Death' in Mohammad Mazher Idriss and Tahir Abbas (eds), *Honour, Violence, Women, and Islam* (Oxon, Routledge 2011)

Khan R, 'Attitudes Towards "Honor" Violence and Killings in Collectivist Cultures: Gender Differences in Middle Eastern, North African, South Asian (MENASA) and Turkish Populations' in JL Ireland, P Birch and CA Ireland, *International Handbook in Aggression: Current Issues and Perspectives* (Routledge 2018)

Kocoz R, 'Aile İçi Şiddet, İntiharlar, Ensest İliŞkiler, Diğer Adıyla Töresel, Yöresel Cinayetler' (2004) Cagin Polisi <www.caginpolisi.com.tr/39/33-34-35-36.htm#_ftn1> accessed 25 June 2019

Korge J, 'Justice Slammed in Honor Killing Study' *Spiegel Online International* (Germany, 2011) <www.spiegel.de/international/germany/0,1518,777997,00.html> accessed 25 June 2019

Korteweg A and Yurdakul G, 'Islam, Gender, Immigrant Integration: Boundary Drawing in Discourses on Honour Killing in the Netherlands and Germany' (2009) 32 Ethnic and Racial Studies 218

Kulwicki AD, 'The Practice of Honor Crimes: A Glimpse of Domestic Violence In the Arab World' (2002) 23 Issues in Mental Health Nursing 77

Leicht J, 'Germany: The Murder of Hatun Sürücü and the Debate Over "Honour Killings"' *World Socialist Website* (2006) <www.wsws.org/articles/2006/may2006/germ-m17.shtml> accessed 25 June 2019

Lindisfarne N, 'Variant Masculinities, Variant Virginities: Rethinking "Honour and Shame"' in Andrea Cornwall (ed), *Dislocating Masculinity: Comparative Ethnographies* (London, Routledge 2003)

Merry SE, *Gender Violence: A Cultural Perspective*, vol 3 (West Sussex, Wiley-Blackwell 2011)

Muftuoglu O, 'İntihar Olayları Üzerine Bir Değerlendirme: Doğu ve Güneydoğu Anadolu'daki Kadın İntihar Olayları Örneği' (2002) 2 Dinbilimleri Akademik Araştırma Dergisi 143

Mulvihill N and others, 'The Experience of Interactional Justice for Victims of "Honour"-Based Violence and Abuse Reporting to the Police in England and Wales' (2019) 29 Policing and Society: An International Journal of Research and Policy 640

Okin SM, 'Is Multiculturalism Bad for Women?' in *Is Multiculturalism Bad for Women* (Princeton, Princeton University Press 2001)

Onal A, *Honour Killing: Stories of Men Who Killed* (London, Saqi Books 2008)

Ozturk E, 'Intihari Seciyorlar' *Oz Diyarbakir* (Diyarbakir, 2010) <www.google.co.uk/search?q=Intihari+Seciyorlar%E2%80%99&aq=f&oq=Intihari+Seciyorlar%E

2%80%99&aqs=chrome.0.57.1584j0&sourceid=chrome&ie=UTF-8#sclient=psy-ab&q=Intihari+Seciyorlar%E2%80%99+oz+diyarbakir&oq=Intihari+Seciyorlar%E2%80%99+oz+diyarbakir&gs_l=serp.3 . . . 4579.6945.0.7104.14.14.0.0.0.0.46.506.14.14.0 . . . 0.0 . . . 1c.1.11.psy-ab.rP3qr8Z1IaE&pbx=1&bav=on.2,or.r_qf.&bvm=bv.45645796,d.d2k&fp=51a2b47f571cda6f&biw=1310&bih=1031> accessed 25 June 2019

Parrot A and Cummings N, *Forsaken Females: The Global Brutalization of Women* (Oxford, Rowan & Littlefield Publishers, Inc 2006)

Payton J, 'Collective Crimes, Collective Victims: A Case Study of the Murder of Banaz Mahmod' in Mohammad Mazher Idriss and Tahir Abbas (eds), *Honour, Violence, Women and Islam* (Oxon, Routledge 2011)

———, 'For the Boys in the Family: An Investigation Into the Relationship Between "Honor"-Based Violence and Endogamy' (2017) 32 Journal of Interpersonal Violence 1332

Peristiany JG (ed), *Honour and Shame: The Values of Mediterranean Society* (London, Weidenfeld and Nicolson 1965)

Phillips A, *Gender and Culture* (Cambridge, Polity Press 2010)

———, 'Does the Body Make a Difference?' in Sumi Madhok, Anne Phillips and Kalpana Wilson (eds), *Gender, Agency, and Coercion* (Hampshire, Palgrave Macmillan 2013)

Pitt-Rivers J, 'Honour and Social Status' in JG Peristiany (ed), *Honour and Shame: The Values of Mediterranean Societies* (London, Weidenfeld and Nicolson 1965)

———, 'Postscript: The Place of Grace in Anthropology' in JG Peristiany and Julian Pitt-Rivers (eds), *Honour and Grace in Anthropology* (Cambridge, Cambridge University Press 1992)

Plant V, 'Honour Killings and the Asylum Gender Gap' (2005) 15 Journal of Transnational Law & Policy 109

Reddy R, 'Gender, Culture, and the Law: Approaches to Honour Crimes in the UK' (2008) 16 Feminist Legal Studies 305

Roberts DE, 'Rape, Violence, and Women's Autonomy' (1993) 69 Chicago-Kent Law Review 359

Ruane RA, 'Murder in the Name of Honor: Violence Against Women in Pakistan' (2000) 14 Emory International Law Review 1523

Sen P, 'Crimes of "Honour", Value and Meaning' in Lynn Welchman and Sara Hossain (eds), *'Honour': Crimes, Paradigms, and Violence Against Women* (London, Zed Books 2005)

Sev'er A and Yurdakul G, 'Culture of Honor, Culture of Change: A Feminist Analysis of Honor Killings Rural Turkey' (2001) 7 Violence Against Women 964

Shalhoub-Kevorkian N, 'Reexamining Femicide: Breaking the Silence and Crossing "Scientific" Borders' (2003) 28 Signs 581

Stewart FH, *Honor* (California & London, The University of California Press 1994)

'Teenage Girl Buried Alive in Turkey for Talking to Boys' *The Telegraph* (2010) <www.telegraph.co.uk/news/worldnews/europe/turkey/7161701/Teenage-girl-buried-alive-in-Turkey-for-talking-to-boys.html> accessed 25 June 2019

Tezcan M, *Turkiye'de Tore (Namus) Cinayetleri: Sosyo Kulturel Antropolojik Yaklasim* (Ankara, Naturel 2003)

Tokdemir S, 'Honor Crimes in Turkey: Rethinking Honour Killings and Reconstructing the Community Using Restorative Justice System' (2013) 4 Law & Justice Review 257

'Töre ve Namus Cinayetleri İle Kadınlara ve Çocuklara Yönelik Şiddetin Sebeplerinin Araştırılarak Alınması Gereken Önlemlerin Belirlenmesi Amacıyla Kurulan TBMM Araştırma Komisyonu Raporu' (Ankara, TC BaŞbakanlık Kadın Statüsü Genel Müdürlüğü 2006) <www.kadininstatusu.gov.tr/upload/kadininstatusu.gov.tr/mce/eski_site/Pdf/tbmmkom-bolum1.pdf> accessed 3 July 2019

Tuncel CP, 'Recent Suicides By Women in Batman Raise Alarms' *Hurriyet Daily News* (Istanbul, 2011) <www.hurriyetdailynews.com/n.php?n=recent-women-suicides-in-batman-raise-alarms-2011-08-22> accessed 25 June 2019

'Turkish Statistical Institute' <https://biruni.tuik.gov.tr/medas/?locale=tr> accessed 25 June 2019

UNICEF, 'Honour Crimes and Forced Suicides' (UNICEF 2005) <www.unicef.org.tr/en/content/detail/74/honour-crimes-and-forced-suicides-2.html> accessed 25 June 2019

Van Eck C, *Purified By Blood: Honour Killings Among Turks in the Netherlands* (Amsterdam, Amsterdam University Press 2003)

Wikan, U, 'Shame and Honour: A Contestable Pair' (1984) 19 Man, New Series 635

Women for Women's Human Rights-New Ways, *Türk Ceza Kanunu'nda Cinsel Haklarımız Var* (Istanbul, Punto Baskı Çözümleri 2007)

Yamani MAZ, *Polygamy and Law in Contemporary Saudi Arabia* (Reading, Ithaca 2008)

Yirun M and Akkun F, '2 Gunluk Bebegi Bogup Betona Gomduler' *Istanbul, Hurriyet* (Istanbul, 2010) <www.hurriyet.com.tr/gundem/14439769.asp> accessed 19 June 2019

Yıldız MC, 'Türkiye'de Töre Baskısına Bağlı İntiharlar ve Töre Cinayetleri' (2008) 1 Sosyal Bilimler Enstitüsü Dergisi 209

Part II

Honour killings and legal challenges

5 Honour killings and Turkish customary law

1. Introduction

The first four chapters (Part I) were designed to conceptualise honour and HBV and provide the necessary groundwork for understanding under what conditions and motivations and how and why honour crimes are committed in Turkey. Following this analysis, Chapters 5 and 6 (Part II) specifically aim to analyse how the Turkish Penal Code deals with honour killings.

In Part II, I will again make use of the hermeneutical circle of HBV. The hermeneutical circle of HBV sets out the relationship between honour and HBV; the last part of the circle relates this cluster of concepts to law. In order to analyse and interpret the hermeneutical circle of HBV, it is crucial to consider the law, because this not only shows society's approach to this type of violence but also allows for a detailed evaluation of the State's response to HBV. However, with problems such as HBV, which are related to society in such complex ways, it is important to consider not only State law but also non-State forms that include 'law-like' norms or 'law-like' dispute resolution mechanisms/institutions. Alongside State law, we must also consider other forms of norms/orders accepted and applied by society. One technique that allows us to look at a wider phenomenon than State law is the concept of legal pluralism. As we will see later on, there are different interpretations and formulations of legal pluralism in the literature. My aim is not to repeat all this established scholarship, but rather to link it to the particular context of HBV. This chapter provides some introductory analysis on legal pluralism in general, and legal pluralism in Turkey in the particular context of HBV, to address the key issues. Following this, the chapter shows to what extent HBV contradicts State law and to what extent the State actually condones it by considering Turkish customary laws.

2. Effects of legal pluralism in the context of HBV

According to Engle Merry, legal pluralism, in a very broad sense, means "more than one legal order in a social field";[1] further, she argues, "every society is

1 Sally Engle Merry, 'Legal Pluralism' (1988) 22 Law & Society Review 869, 878–79.

legally plural."[2] Similarly, Griffiths argues that "although legal centralism is the myth, legal pluralism is the fact."[3] Taking this fact into consideration, however, leads us to ask: How can society be legally plural? Griffiths prefers to define pluralism very broadly, as "the presence in a social field of more than one legal order," and he divides it into strong and weak legal pluralism.[4] Hooker also provides a broad definition, as a "situation in which two or more laws interact."[5] Woodman, on the other hand, took these broad definitions one step further, dividing legal pluralism in two categories: State law pluralism and deep legal pluralism:[6]

> State law pluralism refers to the two bodies of norms within the law of a state and deep legal pluralism consists of instances in which the elements are, respectively, the law of the State, and normative orders not directly associated with the State.[7]

The division between State and non-State legal pluralism is important when dealing with HBV, especially in Turkey. As will be discussed later on, this division will help us to analyse the State's approach to HBV. Although in Turkey State law aims to create legal solutions for HBV, there are other factors that hinder justice. Customs and traditions, and especially the strong patriarchal social structure, stand at the centre of this judicial journey.

The aim of this section is to analyse what role customs and traditions have in Turkey when dealing with HBV. However, before analysing them specifically, we need to consider the different forms of legal pluralism. As mentioned above, although legal pluralism is divided between State law, legal pluralism/deep legal pluralism by Woodman[8] and between strong/weak legal pluralism by Griffiths,[9] the situation in practice is usually more complex than this. In order to shed some light on this complexity, Miranda Forsyth provides a typology that explains relationships between State and non-State jurisdictions, focusing on the situations in more than 20 countries.[10] Forsyth's typology includes seven different models, and she provides a general overview of these relationships as follows:

2 Ibid. 869.
3 John Griffiths, 'What Is Legal Pluralism?' (1986) 24 Journal of Legal Pluralism and Unofficial Law 1, 4.
4 Ibid. 1, 5.
5 MB Hooker, *Legal Pluralism: An Introduction to Colonial and Neo-Colonial Laws* (Oxford, Oxford University Press 1975) 6.
6 Gordon R Woodman, 'The Idea of Legal Pluralism' in Baudouin Dupret and others (eds), *Legal Pluralism in the Arab World* (The Netherlands, Kluwer Law International 1999) 7.
7 Ibid. 5. These different definitions will be used later on when analysing legal pluralism in Turkey.
8 Ibid.
9 Griffiths (n 3) 5.
10 Miranda Forsyth, 'A Typology of Relationships Between State and Non-State Justice Systems' (2007) 56 Journal of Legal Pluralism 67, 68–70.

1 There are various relationships
2 It is assumed that a State justice system is important and will always exist
3 The relationship is related to Woodman's institutional pluralism,[11] which includes recognising different "structures, institutions and processes of other legal systems"
4 More than one model may exist in the same country
5 A "uniform relationship" between State and non-State justice systems is not necessary[12]

These seven modules of legal pluralism show both the State and deep legal pluralism that Woodman[13] describes and the strong and weak legal pluralism introduced by Griffiths.[14] Models 4, 5, 6, and 7 are examples of State pluralism, where two bodies of norms exist within a state. Model 1 reflects the deep legal pluralism that there is no direct association between State law and the normative order. Although Models 2 and 3 seem to be in the categories of neither State legal pluralism nor deep legal pluralism, they do seem closer to deep legal pluralism

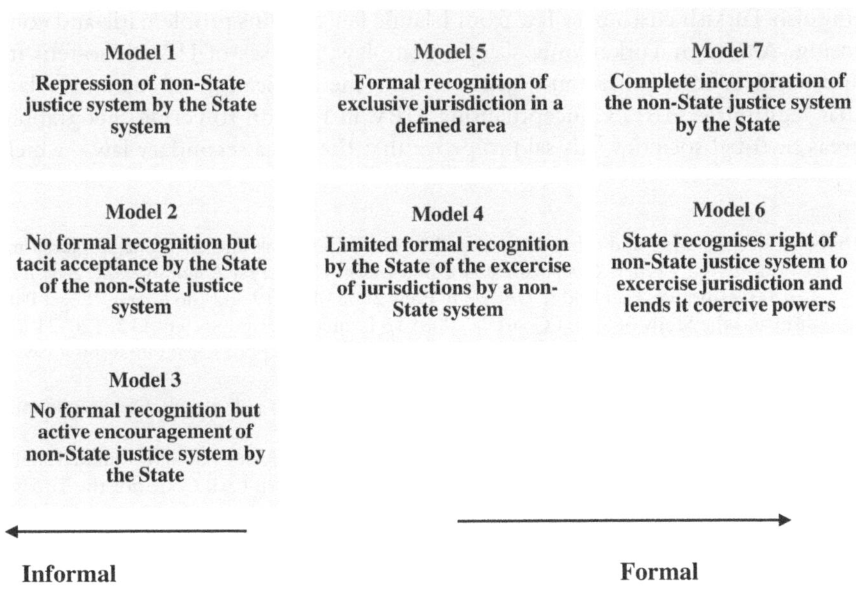

Diagram 5.1 Miranda Forsyth's typology of legal pluralism[15]

11 Gordon R Woodman, 'The Possibilities of Co-Existence of Religious Laws with Other Laws' in Petersen Hanne, Rubya Mehdi, and Reenberg Sand (eds), *Law and Religion in Multicultural Societies* (Copenhagen, DJØF Publishing Copenhagen 2008) 33–35.
12 Forsyth (n 10) 70–72.
13 Woodman (n 6) 7.
14 Griffiths (n 3) 5–14.
15 Ibid. 70.

in their implicit acceptance of non-State norms. From Griffiths's perspective, because weak legal pluralism requires hierarchy within State law (which he also describes as another form of legal centralism), all other models, except for Models 6 and 7, can be considered examples of weak legal pluralism.[16] Since Griffiths's strong legal pluralism is based on the assumption that pluralism is a product of social science that contains the arguments of the plurality of legal orders that exist in all societies, all the above-mentioned models can be treated as falling within the category of strong legal pluralism as well.[17]

Accepting the assumption that legal pluralism exists in all societies in different forms, it is important to determine which of Forsyth's models may be used to best describe the situation in Turkey. Although, as Örücü argues, there is no official recognition of legal pluralism in Turkey,[18] it is impossible, as discussed below, to reach a definite conclusion that the State forbids other laws, like customary law. The evidence of this is the first section of the Turkish Civil Code, which allows the State to apply customary law in specific circumstances.[19] Only religious legal norms are constitutionally forbidden, because of the State's secular formation.[20] However, the extent to which it is possible to distinguish Turkish customary law from Islamic law remains problematic and confusing. Although Turkey only accepts State law, in cases of HBV it softens its approach, as seen below, and tacitly accepts the application of customary law that legitimises HBV. Conceptualising HBV in relation to certain geographic areas or tribal societies,[21] is said to prove that there is a secondary law – which

16 For a deep analysis and arguments related to Griffiths's weak and strong legal pluralism, see also Menski Werner, *Comparative Law in a Global Context the Legal Systems of Asia and Africa* (Cambridge, Cambridge University Press 2006) 113–19 and Ido Sharar, 'Legal Pluralism and the Study of Sharia Courts' (2008) 15 Islamic Law and Society 112, 120–21.

17 Brian Z Tamanaha, 'The Folly of the "Social Scientific" Concept of Legal Pluralism" (1993) 20 Journal of Law and Society 192, 203.

18 Esin Örücü, 'Diverse Cultures and Official Laws: Multiculturalism and Euroscepticism?' (2010) 6 Utrecht Law Review 75, 82.

19 Not only the Turkish Civil Code but also the Turkish Commercial Code allows limited application of Turkish customary law. However, neither the Turkish Civil Code nor the Turkish Commercial Code provides any definition or explanation of the meaning of customary law; Bethany A Corbin, 'Between Saviors and Savages: The Effect of Turkey's Revised Penal Code on the Transformation of Honor Killings Into Honor Suicides and Why Community Discourse Is Necessary for Honor Crime Eradication' (2014) 29 Emory International Law Review 277, 306–07.

20 The Constitution of the Turkish Republic, Number: 2709, Year: 1982, Section: 2. <www.tbmm.gov.tr/anayasa/anayasa_2011.pdf> accessed 15 January 2019.

21 Derya Bayir, 'Representation of the Kurds by the Turkish Judiciary' (2013) 35 Human Rights Quarterly 116, 137–39. Derya Bayir, along with Vahap Coskun and Recep Dogan, ('Mardin Olayi Tore Degil Katliam' (2009) Anlayis, available at <https://www.academia.edu/26156599/Mardin_Olay%C4%B1_T%C3%B6re_De%C4%9Fil_Katliam> accessed 15 January 2019]) and Turkan Yalcin Sancar ('Kadinlar, Toreler, ve Otekiler' (2008) Radikal <www.radikal.com.tr/ek_haber.php?ek=r2&haberno=8090> accessed 15 January 2019), critically argues that HBV is conceptualised as a 'Kurdish minorities problem.' In contrast, Fındıkçı suggests that honour killings (*töre cinayeti*) are distinctly related to the Kurds' social

is considered as having supreme legal force by the tribes – within the country.[22] It is argued that the State considers this secondary or tribal law system the law of 'others,'[23] and the judgements made in respect to such cases show that this customary/tribal law within the State is accepted either because of the patriarchal attitude of the whole State/the legislators, or to show that minorities are barbarian and backwards.[24] This leads us to Forsyth's second model of legal pluralism,[25] which posits that there is "no formal recognition but tacit acceptance by the State or the non-State justice system."[26] In this model, Forsyth claims that the State 'turns a blind eye' to and tacitly allows the non-State justice system to apply its own rules and procedures to specific situations.[27] As discussed below, by following this approach, the State hinders justice for victims of HBV. What the State should follow, instead, is the first model,[28] which suppresses the non-State justice system in the context of HBV, not only to provide justice for the victims but also to eliminate this form of violence; and it should follow this approach both in its laws and in practice.

3. Legal pluralism in Turkey

3.1 Turkish customary law: customary law or just customs?

It is impossible to talk about a society without inherited culture, customs, and traditions, and Weber makes the distinction between these terms. According to Weber,

> if an orientation toward social action occurs regularly, it will be called 'usage' (Brauch) insofar as the probability of its existence within a group is based on nothing but actual practice. A usage will be called a 'custom' (Sitte) if the practice is based upon long standing.[29]

Although 'usage' and 'custom' are based on regularity, custom requires long-lasting usage within society. Weber takes his arguments on customs one step further, adding that they are only valid if they are demanded by society. However, this demand should occur only as a result of free will, and this creates the difference between 'law' and 'custom,' as 'law' has an enforcing character whereas 'custom' emerges

---

life and the culture that shapes this life. Aydın Fındıkçı, *Töre Cinayetleri Kürt Kültürünün Bir Parçası Mı: Arama Sonuçları* (Ankara, İmaj Yayınları 2010) 189.

22 Bayir (n 21) 121.

23 Ibid.

24 Ibid.

25 Forsyth (n 10) 75–79.

26 Ibid. 70.

27 Ibid. 75.

28 Ibid. 73–75.

29 Max Weber, *Economy and Society: An Outline of Interpretive Sociology* (Guenther Roth and Claus Wittich eds, Berkley, University of California Press 1978) 29.

naturally.[30] Weber distinguishes between not only usage and custom but also custom, customary law, and convention. Weber's interpretation of convention[31] and customary law has great importance for analysing the concept of HBV within the context of Turkish culture, tradition, and custom. From Weber's perspective,

> convention exists wherever a certain conduct is sought to be induced without, however, any coercion, physical or psychological, and at least, under normal circumstances, without any direct reaction other than the expression of approval or disapproval on the part of those persons who constitute the environment of the actor.[32]

Coercion here is the key concept in Weber's thought to differentiate between customary law and convention. While convention does not include any coercion, customary law includes a certain degree of enforcement. An example of such enforcement within the context of HBV can be seen when honour is lost. As discussed previously, in Chapter 4, when honour is lost, customs and traditions require certain actions to be taken in order to restore it.

One of the crucial questions at this stage is: When does custom become customary law?[33] In other words, what is the line between custom and customary law, and where does convention stand when dealing with customary law? In light of Weber's interpretation of customs, customary law, and convention, Isiktac explains the relationship between custom and customary law.[34] Although Isiktac agrees that both usage and custom have deep-rooted history, what makes custom differ from usage is the expectation or the requirement of following it by succeeding generations.[35] These requirements or expectations also create the difference between habits and customs.[36] While habits can be changed or abandoned easily, this is not the case for customs. Another difference is that, while habits or usage can be bad, it is accepted by societies that customs are always good and beneficial for society; they reflect the *sine qua non* of society.[37]

30 Ibid.
31 Convention in this context can be represented by the word '*tore*' in Turkish. 'Töre cinayeti' is commonly used to mean honour killing in Turkish literature, and even the Turkish Penal Code refers to this type of violence as 'tore.' However, in daily language the word 'tore' can be translated into English as 'custom,' and this can lead to misinterpretation of the term.
32 Weber (n 29) 319.
33 Benda-Beckham joins this argument by interpreting the term 'folk law,' which is commonly used to mean customary law in the literature. According to Benda-Beckham, "the concept of folk law is often appropriate where knowledge of law and procedures is largely shared by most people and not entrusted to specialized experts." Franz von Benda-Beckmann, 'Who Is Afraid of Legal Pluralism?' (2002) 42 Journal of Legal Pluralism 37, 49.
34 Yasemin Isiktac, *Hukukun Kaynagi Olarak Orf ve Adet Hukuku* (Istanbul, Filiz Kitabevi 2009).
35 Ibid. 28.
36 Ibid.
37 Ibid. 34.

Another important question that follows on from these concerns when customs become norms, and what is needed to consider customs as social norms. As mentioned above, coercion and enforcement are the key concepts for customs to become norms. If community members feel pressure on themselves to follow customs, then customs/traditions become norms. And if these customary norms are systematically used over the years, and if not following them has serious consequences, that means they are customary laws. When looking at the principles of customary law in Turkey, Isiktac argues that there are three elements: continuality (material element), enforcement (moral element), and State support.[38] Enforcement has great importance in a Turkish customary law context. It does not require individual belief for customs to be applied and followed, but it does require collective belief,[39] especially in the context of honour.

3.2 Customary law v State law

Although there are societies where customary law and State law exist at the same time, there are significant differences between the two institutions. These differences, however, vary from one society to another. In the Turkish context, the first difference is that while State law is written and based on the codified law, customary law is mainly unwritten and passes from one generation to another. Urfa Salnamesi, which was written by the Governor of Urfa in 1927, is one of the important documents to set out customary law in that region in written format.[40] Although the document was written as a yearbook and is not legally binding, it shows important evidence of how customary law in the Urfa region to do with honour is patriarchal and has denied women's autonomy and agency. Fuad Bey states that

> a girl who belongs to a tribe falls in love with a man and elopes, both the girl and the man are condemned to death by her parents or guardians (extended family members are meant here). Even if they get married, nothing will be given to the girl's family as bride prize. If there is no peace between the families, the rules that are applied to the murderers will be applied to whom the girl runs away.[41]
>
> If a married woman runs away with a man, both of them have to continue their lives somewhere far from their hometowns. The woman's relatives and husband will follow the man closely who has eloped with the married woman. The right to kill both the man and the woman remains.[42]

38 Ibid. 42–47.
39 Ibid. 45.
40 Fuad Bey, 'Urfa Salnamesi' <www.sanliurfahbr.com/463-urfada-asiretlerin-tarihi.html> accessed 28 June 2019.
41 Ibid. section 12.
42 Ibid. section 13.

Going back to the discussions relating to customary law, one can argue that, because the customary law of Turkey is not primarily written down, it has been – and could still be – open to changes and amendments over the years. This assumption, however, does not reflect the reality in traditional Turkish societies when we examine the facts in more detail. Although there have been some changes over the years in the context of customary law, this law is still strictly attached to its roots, especially for situations that relate to family and private lives. The other reason for the stability of the customary law of Turkey is the relationship between religious norms and customary law. Since most of Turkish customary law is based on religious norms, and a specific interpretation of Islam, it is not easy to amend it or change those rules in society.

Another difference between customary law and State law is that, while Turkish State law was created for the whole of society, and it adopted mainly Western laws, customary law was created for different purposes. There is one important distinction to highlight here. First, the roots of Turkish State law and customary law are quite different. Turkish State law can, at least in part, be traced back to the Ottoman Empire's legal systems, and specifically the Kemalist movement, which aimed to create one law for the whole society, but this movement did not actually require the full integration of the law or its adaptation to society. Despite establishing a notionally democratic state, it has been argued by some scholars that the Kemalist movement itself was not actually particularly democratic.[43] Customary law, on the other hand, has been created by society itself over the years. It requires full integration into and acceptance by society in order to be considered customary law, and because of this characteristic, in many situations customary law is much stricter than State law in terms of enforcement within conservative societies. Furthermore, while State law binds every citizen, and there is only one law for all, customary law can change from one region to another, from one community to another.

As mentioned above, Isiktac indicates that one of the necessities for the perpetuation of customary law is State support.[44] If the full support of the State is required for the existence and enforcement of customary law, it is difficult to talk about a separate customary law system within a society, as in this case customary law has already become a part of State law. What Isiktac argues, however, is the possibility of losing the binding character of customary law by removing State law support, as the only binding law in the country is State law.[45] It could be argued that in Turkey only those situations that contravene State law should face punishment, yet this is not the case for the customary law. If there is any customary law infringement in society, unless it is also a contravention of State

43 Donald Everett Webster, *The Turkey of Ataturk: Social Process in the Turkish Reformation* (Philadelphia, The American Academy of Political and Social Science 1939) 109; Ersin Kalaycioglu, *Turkish Dynamics: Bridge Across Troubled Lands* (New York, Palgrave Macmillan 2005) 46.

44 Isiktac (n 34) 67.

45 Ibid.

law, the State does not usually interfere and impose sanctions. Yet, although this discussion sheds light on a small part of the situation in the country, it leaves the bigger picture in darkness. Therefore, the following section aims to explain the customary law of Turkey as it relates to HBV and the conflict between the State and customary law.

3.3 Customary law relating to HBV and the State's approach

It is not easy to make a clear-cut division between traditional norms and religious norms in the Turkish context, as they are usually interwoven. Therefore, not only because of the previous analysis of customary law, but also because of the difficulty of separating those norms from each other, I prefer using 'customary law' for both religious and traditional norms in Turkey.

It is not only the roots of customary law of Turkey but also the enforcement bodies of this law and the consequences of not following the customary law which need more analysis. The existence of customary law in Turkey depends upon society's commitment to it. However, the question is: How and why are members of the community strictly bound by this 'unwritten law'? The most obvious answer to this question perhaps becomes clearer if we relate it to Kandiyoti's 'classic patriarchy' discussion.[46] Customary law is seen as the most powerful mechanism to maintain and protect the patriarchal society structure. Customary law, in that sense, not only supports patriarchy and hierarchy but also maintains women's subordination by denying their autonomy and agency.[47] Although contemporary Turkish society shows some evidence that it has begun to improve women's agency, it is undeniable that customs and traditions are still interpreted in ways that subordinate women.[48]

As mentioned in previous chapters, in order to be a member of a community, people (especially men) feel great pressure to follow customary law. The strictest customary law enforcement can be seen within tribal societies. The tribal or religious leaders of these societies take significant roles in applying customary law, making sure it is followed properly, transferring this law to the next generations, or punishing those who do not follow the customary law. Although the feudal system has been dissolving in Turkey, those leaders can still be considered as the most powerful figures in some parts of the country, predominantly in the east and south-east. Their power is even considered superior to the State's power.[49]

46 Deniz Kandiyoti, 'Bargaining With Patriarchy' (1988) 2 Gender and Society 274, 278.

47 Pratiksha Baxi, Shirin M Rai, and Shaheen Sardar Ali, 'Legacies of Common Law: "Crimes of Honour" in India and Pakistan' (2006) 27 Third World Quarterly 1239.

48 Mehmet Farac, *Söyleyin Anama Ağlamasın* (Istanbul, Cumhuriyet Kitaplari 2007) 114–24. See also Feride Acar and Gulbanu Altunok, 'The "Politics of Intimate" at the Intersection of Neo-Liberalism and Neo-Conservatism in Contemporary Turkey' (2013) 41 Women's Studies International Forum 14, 14–15–16.

49 Hasan Emir Aktas, 'Authority Perception of the Groups Which Maintain Customs of Blood Feud and Honor Killing' (2015) 13 CBÜ Soyal Bilimler Dergisi 35, 42–43.

If we remember the family structure explained in Chapter 3, a similar structure is also seen in relation to customary laws and their application. In these societies, a strict hierarchy applies; tribal or religious leaders stand at the top of the hierarchy. Below them are their close family members. Other community members are placed at the bottom of the hierarchy and are dependent on the tribal/religious leaders; however, they may advance their positions as they get older.[50] As a result, a man situated at the bottom of the hierarchal structure feels great pressure to follow customary law and obey his leader. This is the only way for him to remain in society. As we have seen in the previous chapters, being honourable is one of the conditions necessary for living in society, and customary law requires positive actions to be taken either to protect or to restore honour. Failure to take action on either will result in a man being ostracised.[51]

While a man will mainly behave automatically in ways required to protect his family honour, without visible external pressure from society, the actions taken to restore family honour will differ from person to person. Enforcement of customary law in cases of restoring family honour creates these differences. It is not possible, as a result, to generalise about how enforcement is applied by society to individuals, but there are common situations that are applied to the majority of HBV incidents. Because honour and shame are shared collectively by family members,[52] family or tribal councils, for instance, have significant roles to play in committing HBV by enforcing customary laws that allow and support this type of violence.[53] The leader, who rules over the council[54] and is usually the oldest man[55] in the tribe/family,[56] is at the top of the hierarchy within the community. When an ordinary man faces a situation that has had the effect of tarnishing his honour, he either receives a call from the council or applies to the council by himself to cleanse the 'shame.' In both situations,

50 Aysan Sev'er and Gokcecicek Yurdakul, 'Culture of Honor, Culture of Change: A Feminist Analysis of Honor Killings Rural Turkey' (2001) 7 Violence Against Women 964, 965.

51 Mehmet Farac, *Töre Kıskacında Kadın* (Istanbul, Günizi Yayıncılık 2006) 62.

52 Nicole L Asquith, 'Honour, Violence and Heteronormativity' (2015) 4 Crime Justice Journal 73, 76.

53 Vildan Yirmibesoglu, *Töre ve Namus Gerekçesiyle İşlenen Cinayetler: Toprağa Düşen Sevdalar* (Istanbul, Hurriyet 2007) 104.

54 Mahmut Tezcan, *Turkiye'de Tore (Namus) Cinayetleri: Sosyo Kulturel Antropolojik Yaklasim* (Ankara, Naturel 2003) 23.

55 I should mention here that the council comprises mainly men (Sev'er and Yurdakul (n 51) 965.): As Ince et al. highlight, occasionally we witness the oldest female members of the family taking part during these councils; they do not do so to protect other women's lives but to support the patriarchal customary law applications (Hilal Onur Ince, Aysun Yarali, and Dogancan Ozsel, 'Customary Killings in Turkey and Turkish Modernization' (2009) 45 Middle Eastern Studies 537, 548); Payton (n 305) 75; Leyla Pervizat, 'Lack of Due Diligence: Judgements of Crimes of Honour in Turkey' in Mohammad Mazher Idriss and Tahir Abbas (eds), *Honour, Violence, Women and Islam* (Abington, Routledge 2011) 143; Nicole Pope, *Honor Killings in the Twenty-First Century* (New York, Palgrave Macmillan 2012) 50.

56 Nicole Pope, 'Namus Cinayetleri: Ataerkil Denetim Araclari' in *Namus Adina Siddet: Kuramsal ve Siyasal Yaklasimlar* (Istanbul, Istanbul Bilgi Universitesi Yayinlari 2006) 115.

the members of these feudal councils, as Farac argues, act as the decision makers and decide what measures are to be taken, and by whom.[57] Either applying to the council or taking action to cleanse the shame without waiting for the council meeting are accepted as reputable ways out for an ordinary man, as they prove his intention to remove the shame by applying the customary law related to family honour.

At this stage, it is important to analyse the State's response to the council mechanism, as it creates the structure within which the State conceptualises honour killings. For instance, if a person takes action without waiting for the council's decision, there is a presumption by the State authorities that an honour killing is a 'passion killing' because of the immediacy of the action taken by the perpetrator(s), which may be accepted as the result of provocation and loss of self-control.[58] For instance, the following decision made by the Turkish Appeal Court in one case shows how passion killing is framed and separated from honour killing.

> What is meant by honour killing is that: murdering women in order to protect their families' honour and dignity. The victim was killed because she rejected the marriage proposal, as she was in love with someone else, and there is no intention to protect the family's honour and dignity here.[59]

However, while the majority of the judges applied provocation to this case and considered the murder to be not a form of HBV, Judge Iskender mentioned that

> the defendant's action, without any doubt, was love, passion, and jealousy killing. In general, 'passion' can be described as emotionally focusing on one target. The defendant's only motive was to gain the possession of someone who did not respond his love and when the victim loved someone else, this was considered as dishonourable by the defendant. Therefore, the action which focused on the victim's body and gender and which had a feeling of fanatically possessing her should be considered as honour killing.[60]

57 Farac (n 49) 54–55. See also Nazand Begikhani, Aisha K Gill, and Gill Hague, *Honour-Based Violence: Experiences and Counter-Strategies in Iraqi Kurdistan and the UK Kurdish Diaspora* (Surrey, Ashgate 2015) 55, 62.

58 The preamble of the Turkish Penal Code s. 82 clearly indicates that in order to consider these crimes honour killings (the law identifies them as 'customary killings'), there must be no element that can be considered provocation. The judges of the Turkish Appeal Court also do not tend to adjudicate the murders as honour killings if there is an element of jealousy (Salih Zeki İskender, *Öğreti ve Yargısal Kararlar Işığında Töre Saikiyle İnsan Öldürme Suçu (Namus Cinayetleri)* (Ankara, Yetkin 2011) 79.

59 Department No:1 of the Criminal Appeal Court 2008/5953 E, 2009/1075 K, Date: 04.03.2009. Aydin Fındıkçı also supported the idea of separating passion and honour killings because of the sudden loss of control in passion killings and premeditation in honour killings. Fındıkçı (n 21) 105–06.

60 Department No:1 of the Criminal Appeal Court 2008/5953 E, 2009/1075 K, Date: 04.03.2009. Not only Judge Iskender but also some of the literature considers passion killing

Unfortunately, because only a majority decision is accepted by the Appeal Court, Judge Iskender's comments were not considered during this judgement.[61]

After providing brief information about the enforcement of customary law and the State's response to customary councils, the last part of this section focuses on how the family council mechanism works in Turkey. When looking at the nature of the councils, it is possible to say that community members consider these councils as judicial authorities.[62] Their decisions are binding and final. Therefore, the council in this context is considered to be an enforcing body with its own power to apply traditional rules/customary law, and the members of society feel great pressure on them to obey council decisions. Because of this, and in contradiction with Elakkary et al.,[63] who argue that HBV is a form of 'self-administered justice' applied by community members, practicing customary law is usually considered to be the result of applying the decisions of council or society or meeting society's expectations. It is also important to highlight here that councils only gather to take action to restore family honour, not to protect it. They meet to decide the most suitable way to cleanse shame. Although Tezcan suggests that the family gathers to decide not whether the murder should be committed or not but rather who should commit it,[64] this is not the case in many situations. The council assembles not to decide whether the woman who is accused of bringing shame is guilty or not, but rather what measures should be taken and who should apply these measures.[65] The woman in such cases (and, in some situations, the man as well) is, *inter alia*, considered to be guilty and responsible for dishonouring her family, her community, and her society.

This is why the council, although it seems to be a form of judicial trial because of its setting, is far from offering a fair trial. When a family council gathers, it first of all discusses what actions should be taken against the woman in order to restore family honour. Despite Tezcan's analysis, the council considers not only murder but also other options, such as forcing the woman to marry, to commit suicide, to have an abortion, to murder the new-born baby, or to suffer severe domestic violence.[66] As we have seen, these actions have two functions; they

---

as a form of honour killing (Pinar Ilkkaracan, 'How Adultery Almost Derailed Turkey's Aspiration to Join the European Union' *Deconstructing Sexuality in the Middle East* (Aldershot, Ashgate 2008) 53; Mazhar Bağlı and Ertan Özensel, *Türkiye'de Töre ve Namus Cinayetleri: Töre ve Namus Cinayetleri İşleyen Kişiler Üzerine Sosyolojik Bir Araştırma* (Istanbul, Destek Yayınevi 2011) 55–59.

61 I will come back to Judge Iskender's opinions about honour killings and passion killings in the following chapter.

62 Tezcan (n 55) 23.

63 Sally Elakkary and others, 'Honour Crimes: Review and Proposed Definition' (2014) 10 Forensic Science, Medicine and Pathology 76, 77.

64 Tezcan (n 55) 19–20.

65 Farac (n 49) 114–24; Yirmibesoglu (n 54) 59.

66 Tezcan (n 55); 'Töre ve Namus Cinayetleri İle Kadınlara ve Çocuklara Yönelik Şiddetin Sebeplerinin Araştırılarak Alınması Gereken Önlemlerin Belirlenmesi Amacıyla Kurulan TBMM Araştırma Komisyonu Raporu' (Ankara, TC Başbakanlık Kadın Statüsü Genel Müdürlüğü

punish the 'shameful' woman and they restore family honour. However, at this stage, although punishing the woman restores the honour, the actions the council takes now become subject to the State's punishment. Whereas the council considers the woman to be guilty, from the State's perspective she becomes the victim of HBV. More than this, while the council is the body for enforcing punishment through customary law, the members of the council themselves become the target of the State for committing HBV.[67]

In addition, the council decides who will take action against the 'shameful' woman. Although the research and statistics show that the council usually nominates the youngest member of the family, this is not the case for every situation.[68] There are, of course, many reasons to choose the young members of the family. One obvious reason is the economic difficulties that the family may face if its older members spend many years in prison, because older family members have more responsibilities for keeping the family financially stable. Therefore, the council nominates younger family members who have less responsibility.[69] The other reason to nominate the younger members, especially underage males, is to reduce the severity of the State's punishment. However, because the State has become aware of this situation and realised the motives behind choosing underage boys to commit the crimes, it has taken extra measures to include other family members in the punishment process.[70] Apart from that, State law becomes a barrier to applying customary law. When State law softens its patriarchal attitude and distances itself from customary law, it can begin to be considered as exacting punishment on those who follow customary law. LaVaque-Manty's suggestion that "law should not punish where it cannot help, that is, where a stronger social custom overrides its regulatory force" (which is related to the conflict between duelling and State law) summarises

2006) 111 <www.kadininstatusu.gov.tr/upload/kadininstatusu.gov.tr/mce/eski_site/Pdf/tbmmkom-bolum1.pdf> accessed 3 July 2019; Filiz Kardam, 'The Dynamics of Honour Killings in Turkey: Prospects for Action' (Ankara, United Nations Population Fund 2005) 64 <www.unfpa.org/upload/lib_pub_file/676_filename_honourkillings.pdf> accessed 26 June 2019.

67 Mark Cooney, 'Death By Family: Honor Violence as Punishment' (2014) 16 Punishment & Society 406, 407.

68 According to the report and the statistics provided by the Directorate General on the Status of Women, 22% of honour killing defendants are between the age of 19 and 25, 18% are between 26 and 30, and 9% are younger than 18 ('Töre ve Namus Cinayetleri İle Kadınlara ve Çocuklara Yönelik Şiddetin Sebeplerinin Araştırılarak Alınması Gereken Önlemlerin Belirlenmesi Amacıyla Kurulan TBMM Araştırma Komisyonu Raporu' (n 67) 117); 'T.C Mardin Valiliği İl İnsan Hakları Raporu: Töre ve Namus Cinayetleri Raporu' <http://mardin.gov.tr/online/insanhaklari/tore.asp> accessed 6 April 2013; Tezcan (n 434) 19; Bağlı and Özensel (n 61), 95, 196.

69 Anna Korteweg, '"Honour Killing" in the Immigration Context: Multiculturalism and the Racialization of Violence Against Women' (2014) Politikon: South African Journal of Political Studies 183, 9.

70 The Turkish Penal Code s.37–41 clearly regulates participation in crime and also covers HBV. Not only the code but also case law typically includes members of councils as abettors or perpetrators.

perfectly how members of society feel about situations related to honour, and this can also be applied to the feudal and patriarchal society structures that we see in Turkey.[71]

4. Conclusion

The second part of this book aimed to analyse the legal challenges relating to HBV in Turkey. The analysis of these legal challenges requires a consideration of not only the State law but also the customary law applied in Turkey. This dual consideration, however, leads us to consider legal pluralism and the relationship between customary and State law in Turkey. Therefore, the beginning of this chapter provided some brief introductory information about the arguments related to legal pluralism in the literature. I specifically followed Miranda Forsyth's model of legal pluralism, not only to show different forms of legal pluralism but also to analyse the existing types of legal pluralism in Turkey. Since customary law in Turkey is one source of legal pluralism, I analysed what customary law includes and how traditions and customs are considered to be 'law,' not by the State but by society. During the analysis, I referred to earlier discussions of family structure, patriarchy, and hierarchy in order to create the necessary link between customary law and its application. This context is important for my further discussions on honour killings and State law but is not the only evidence of certain customary laws that deny women's autonomy and agency. The next chapter will show how these customary laws can be used as a defence in some honour killing cases, especially when the perpetrators allege that they were influenced by society or provoked by influential members of it.

As this chapter has briefly highlighted, it is not only community members but also, in some cases, the State who tacitly accept/encourage the application of patriarchal customs and traditions, which reminds us of Forsyth's Model 3.[72] However, the State also uses these customary law enforcements to 'other' certain ethnic groups and communities and to address them as backwards and uncivilised; this can also be considered as evidence of tacit acceptance of customary law in Turkey in a negative way. Taking these early analyses into an account, the State's approach to customary law in Turkey will be analysed in more detail in the next chapter when we look at specific honour killing cases.

Bibliography

Acar F and Altunok G, 'The "Politics of Intimate" at the Intersection of Neo-Liberalism and Neo-Conservatism in Contemporary Turkey' (2013) 41 Women's Studies International Forum 14

71 Mika LaVaque-Manty, 'Dueling for Equality: Masculine Honor and the Modern Politics of Dignity' (2006) 34 Political Theory 715, 722.

72 Forsyth (n 10) 70, 79–83.

Aktas HE, 'Authority Perception of the Groups Which Maintain Customs of Blood Feud and Honor Killing' (2015) 13 CBÜ Soyal Bilimler Dergisi 35

Asquith NL, 'Honour, Violence and Heteronormativity' (2015) 4 Crime Justice Journal 73

Bağlı M and Özensel E, *Türkiye'de Töre ve Namus Cinayetleri: Töre ve Namus Cinayetleri İşleyen Kişiler Üzerine Sosyolojik Bir Araştırma* (Istanbul, Destek Yayınevi 2011)

Baxi P, Rai SM and Ali SS, 'Legacies of Common Law: "Crimes of Honour" in India and Pakistan' (2006) 27 Third World Quarterly 1239

Bayir D, 'Representation of the Kurds by the Turkish Judiciary' (2013) 35 Human Rights Quarterly 116

Begikhani N, Gill AK and Hague G, *Honour-Based Violence: Experiences and Counter-Strategies in Iraqi Kurdistan and the UK Kurdish Diaspora* (Surrey, Ashgate 2015)

Benda-Beckmann F von, 'Who Is Afraid of Legal Pluralism?' (2002) 42 Journal of Legal Pluralism 37

Bey F, 'Urfa Salnamesi' <www.sanliurfahbr.com/463-urfada-asiretlerin-tarihi.html> accessed 28 June 2019

Cooney M, 'Death By Family: Honor Violence as Punishment' (2014) 16 Punishment & Society 406

Corbin BA, 'Between Saviors and Savages: The Effect of Turkey's Revised Penal Code on the Transformation of Honor Killings Into Honor Suicides and Why Community Discourse Is Necessary for Honor Crime Eradication' (2014) 29 Emory International Law Review 277

Elakkary S and others, 'Honour Crimes: Review and Proposed Definition' (2014) 10 Forensic Science, Medicine and Pathology 76

Ersöz T, *İlköğretim 5. Sınıf Sosyal Bilgiler Öğretmen Kılavuz Kitabı* (Ankara, Pasifik Yayınları 2011)

Farac M, *Töre Kıskacında Kadın* (Istanbul, Günizi Yayıncılık 2006)

———, *Söyleyin Anama Ağlamasın* (Istanbul, Cumhuriyet Kitaplari 2007)

Fındıkçı A, *Töre Cinayetleri Kürt Kültürünün Bir Parçası Mı: Arama Sonuçları* (Ankara, İmaj Yayınları 2010)

Forsyth, Miranda, 'A Typology of Relationships Between State and Non-State Justice Systems' (2007) 56 Journal of Legal Pluralism 67

Griffiths J, 'What Is Legal Pluralism?' (1986) 24 Journal of Legal Pluralism and Unofficial Law 1

Hooker MB, *Legal Pluralism: An Introduction to Colonial and Neo-Colonial Laws* (Oxford, Oxford University Press 1975)

Ilkkaracan P, 'How Adultery Almost Derailed Turkey's Aspiration to Join the European Union' in Pinar Ilkkaracan (ed), *Deconstructing Sexuality in the Middle East* (Aldershot, Ashgate 2008)

Ince HO, Yarali A and Ozsel D, 'Customary Killings in Turkey and Turkish Modernization' (2009) 45 Middle Eastern Studies 537

Isiktac Y, *Hukukun Kaynagi Olarak Orf ve Adet Hukuku* (Istanbul, Filiz Kitabevi 2009)

İskender SZ, *Öğreti ve Yargısal Kararlar Işığında Töre Saikiyle İnsan Öldürme Suçu (Namus Cinayetleri)* (Ankara, Yetkin 2011)

Kalaycioglu E, *Turkish Dynamics: Bridge Across Troubled Lands* (New York, Palgrave Macmillan 2005)

Kandiyoti D, 'Bargaining With Patriarchy' (1988) 2 Gender and Society 274

Kardam F, 'The Dynamics of Honour Killings in Turkey: Prospects for Action' (Ankara, United Nations Population Fund 2005) <www.unfpa.org/upload/lib_pub_file/676_filename_honourkillings.pdf> accessed 26 June 2019

Korteweg A, '"Honour Killing" in the Immigration Context: Multiculturalism and the Racialization of Violence Against Women' (2014) Politikon: South African Journal of Political Studies 183

LaVaque-Manty M, 'Dueling for Equality: Masculine Honor and the Modern Politics of Dignity' (2006) 34 Political Theory 715

Lewis B, 'Developments in Turkey' (1951) 27 International Affairs (Royal Institute of International Affairs) 320

Merry SE, 'Legal Pluralism' (1988) 22 Law & Society Review 869

'Mardin Olayi Tore Degil Katliam' (2009) Anlayis <https://www.academia.edu/26156599/Mardin_Olay%C4%B1_T%C3%B6re_De%C4%9Fil_Katliam> accessed 15 January 2019

Örücü E, 'Diverse Cultures and Official Laws: Multiculturalism and Euroscepticism?' (2010) 6 Utrecht Law Review 75

Payton J, 'Collective Crimes, Collective Victims: A Case Study of the Murder of Banaz Mahmod' in Mohammad Mazher Idriss and Tahir Abbas (eds), *Honour, Violence, Women and Islam* (Oxon, Routledge 2011)

Pervizat L, 'Lack of Due Diligence: Judgements of Crimes of Honour in Turkey' in Mohammad Mazher Idriss and Tahir Abbas (eds), *Honour, Violence, Women and Islam* (Abington, Routledge 2011)

Pope N, 'Namus Cinayetleri: Ataerkil Denetim Araclari' in *Namus Adina Siddet: Kuramsal ve Siyasal Yaklasimlar* (Istanbul, Istanbul Bilgi Universitesi Yayinlari 2006)

———, *Honor Killings in the Twenty-First Century* (New York, Palgrave Macmillan 2012)

Sev'er A and Yurdakul G, 'Culture of Honor, Culture of Change: A Feminist Analysis of Honor Killings Rural Turkey' (2001) 7 Violence Against Women 964

Sharar I, 'Legal Pluralism and the Study of Sharia Courts' (2008) 15 Islamic Law and Society 112

Tamanaha BZ, 'The Folly of the "Social Scientific" Concept of Legal Pluralism' (1993) 20 Journal of Law and Society 192

'T.C Mardin Valiliği İl İnsan Hakları Raporu: Töre ve Namus Cinayetleri Raporu' <http://mardin.gov.tr/online/insanhaklari/tore.asp> accessed 6 April 2013

Tezcan M, *Turkiye'de Tore (Namus) Cinayetleri: Sosyo Kulturel Antropolojik Yaklasim* (Ankara, Naturel 2003)

'Töre ve Namus Cinayetleri İle Kadınlara ve Çocuklara Yönelik Şiddetin Sebeplerinin Araştırılarak Alınması Gereken Önlemlerin Belirlenmesi Amacıyla Kurulan TBMM Araştırma Komisyonu Raporu' (Ankara, TC Başbakanlık Kadın Statüsü Genel Müdürlüğü 2006) <www.kadininstatusu.gov.tr/upload/kadininstatusu.gov.tr/mce/eski_site/Pdf/tbmmkom-bolum1.pdf> accessed 3 July 2019

Turkan Yalcin Sancar, 'Kadinlar, Toreler, ve Otekiler' (2008) Radikal <www.radikal.com.tr/ek_haber.php?ek=r2&haberno=8090> accessed 15 January 2019

Weber M, *Economy and Society: An Outline of Interpretive Sociology* (Guenther Roth and Claus Wittich eds, Berkley, University of California Press 1978)

Webster DE, *The Turkey of Ataturk: Social Process in the Turkish Reformation* (Philadelphia, The American Academy of Political and Social Science 1939)

Werner M, *Comparative Law in a Global Context the Legal Systems of Asia and Africa* (Cambridge, Cambridge University Press 2006)

Woodman GR, 'The Idea of Legal Pluralism' in Baudouin Dupret and others (eds), *Legal Pluralism in the Arab World* (The Netherlands, Kluwer Law International 1999)

———, 'The Possibilities of Co-Existence of Religious Laws with Other Laws' in Petersen Hanne, Rubya Mehdi and Reenberg Sand (eds), *Law and Religion in Multicultural Societies* (Copenhagen, DJØF Publishing Copenhagen 2008)

Yirmibesoglu V, *Töre ve Namus Gerekçesiyle İşlenen Cinayetler: Toprağa Düşen Sevdalar* (Istanbul, Hurriyet 2007)

6 Honour killings

The Turkish Penal Code and the criminal justice system

1. Introduction

Prior to this chapter, I have dealt with the concepts of honour and HBV within traditional Turkish communities in Turkey. In this chapter, I would like to focus mainly on honour killings and the Turkish Penal Code.

Although there have been a large number of legal and political achievements to prevent VAW in general and HBV in particular, there is still HBV in Turkey. This chapter focuses on legal doctrine in order to answer one of the fundamental questions of this book: *How does the Turkish Penal Code deal with honour killings?* A critical evaluation of Turkish criminal law relevant to HBV requires an analysis of the law as a whole as well as its relation to society. While analysing this relation, my earlier analysis of the hermeneutical circle of HBV will be used.

First, the chapter analyses the Turkish Penal Code and how it is applied to honour killing cases. It critically examines not only the substantive law but also the law-making process, and how this process causes problems for the criminalisation of honour killings and provides justice for the victims. Second, the chapter addresses problems relating to law enforcement. Several arguments are considered to analyse the judiciary process in Turkey, set out in two subsections. In the first section, the actors in the judiciary process are analysed in detail to see if there is any bias. Some of the questions addressed include how evidence in the cases is collected; how the prosecutors and judges conceptualise and criminalise honour killings; and how long the judgements take. The second section analyses and provides an overview of the punishments that are applied to honour killing offenders in Turkey. Finally, in light of the situation within the judiciary, the chapter analyses problems of sentencing. This third part specifically focuses on the punishment mechanisms, seeking to answer whether the punishment of killings satisfies the general aims of punishment or not.

From a wider criminology perspective, there are several aims behind punishing perpetrators. These aims are stated by Walker as deterring others, educating and satisfying others, elimination and incapacitation, and correction.[1] Therefore, the

1 Nigel Walker, *Why Punish?: Theories of Punishment Reassessed* (Oxford, Oxford University Press 1991).

purpose of this chapter is to analyse how, why, and to what extent the State manages to fulfil those aims while criminalising honour killings. In order to make an accurate analysis, I will give some examples from the interviews that I conducted with the perpetrators of honour killings. These will provide some details about the lives of prisoners and whether their prison sentence affects their understanding of honour killings. In sum, this section analyses whether the punishment they receive has an impact on making them feel remorse or not. In order to support the data analysis and the arguments, the existing literature relating to HBV perpetrators is used.[2] This will determine the adequacy or inadequacy of legal punishment intended to change society's approach to honour killings.

2. State law: causing problems or creating solutions?

As mentioned previously, the aim of this first section is to analyse the Turkish Penal Code and how it is applied to honour killing cases. This section focuses on descriptive legal information about the law, and how the law itself is problematic and even gendered, as mentioned by Warrick,[3] in the way it conceptualises and criminalises honour killings. The section also analyses the implementation of the current law by specifically focusing on criminal court cases and judges' opinions in order to provide their legal reasoning.

2.1 The Turkish Penal Code and gender consciousness

The late 1990s witnessed important legal developments on gender equality in Turkey: Amendments to the Turkish Civil and Penal Codes and significant changes to the Turkish Constitution were the major ones. However, these developments were neither coincidental nor due to a growing gender consciousness in Turkey; they were mainly for political reasons and to follow up the European Union (EU) *acquis*[4] as Turkey became a candidate for the EU in 1999. During the same period in which the Turkish Civil Code was amended, the Turkish Penal Code also started to be re-drafted. Professor Celikel was appointed as an independent member for the Ministry of Justice during the period of drafting the new Penal Code in the early 2000s.[5] Her contribution was highly important for

2 Ayse Onal, *Honour Killing: Stories of Men Who Killed* (London, Saqi Books 2008) 362; Mazhar Bağlı and Ertan Özensel, *Türkiye'de Töre ve Namus Cinayetleri: Töre ve Namus Cinayetleri İşleyen Kişiler Üzerine Sosyolojik Bir Araştırma* (Istanbul, Destek Yayınevi 2011); Recep Dogan, 'Honour Killings in Turkey; Culture, Subjectivism, and Provocation' (Keele University 2010).

3 Catherine Warrick, 'The Vanishing Victim: Criminal Law and Gender in Jordan' (2005) 39 Law & Society Review 315, 318–19.

4 Meltem Müftüler-Bac, 'Gender Equality in Turkey' (Directorate General for Internal Policies, European Parliament 2012) 5 <www.europarl.europa.eu/document/activities/cont/201204/20120424ATT43808/20120424ATT43808EN.pdf> accessed 10 August 2019.

5 Feride Acar and others, 'Issue Histories Turkey: Series of Timelines of Policy Debates' (Institute for Human Sciences (IWM) 2007) <www.quing.eu/files/results/ih_turkey.pdf> accessed 10 August 2019.

imposing gender consciousness during this process. However, when the Justice and Development Party (AKP) came into power in 2002, the commission created by the AKP prepared a new draft, and most of Celikel's suggestions relating to women and gender were not taken into account and gender consciousness was ignored.[6]

This was the final straw for women's NGOs and activists, including the Women's Platform on the Turkish Penal Code. Although the Platform was established in the early stages of the drafting period, its members were not very active in the beginning. However, they started to raise their voices after the AKP government created the new draft.[7] First, they criticised the draft; they were strongly against the definition part of the draft, which used 'virginity' as the base for the division between the terms 'women' and 'girls.'[8] This was considered by the Platform as a continuation of state patriarchy and displayed ignorance of women's bodily integrity. Therefore, the Platform denounced the AKP draft as a 'macho draft.'[9] Under pressure from the Platform and NGOs, the government was forced to remove this discriminatory definition from its draft.[10]

The Platform went on to insist on changing the definition of sexual assault and rape from 'crimes against society/crimes against public morality and family' to 'crimes against individuals/crimes against inviolability of sexual integrity.'[11] This was an important step to break up the State's patriarchal approach, because by considering rape and sexual assault as crimes against society and public morality, the State equated victims and others directly affected by the crimes with wider society, and thus positioned the sexual crimes

6 Pinar Ilkkaracan, 'Reforming the Penal Code in Turkey: The Campaign for the Reform of the Turkish Penal Code from a Gender Perspective' (2007) Institute of Development Studies Bulletin 1, 13.

7 Burcu Özdemir, 'The Role of the EU in Turkey's Legislative Reforms for Eliminating Violence Against Women: A Bottom-Up Approach' (2014) 16 Journal of Balkan and Near Eastern Studies 119, 128.

8 Women for Women's Human Rights–New Ways, 'Gender Discrimination in the Turkish Penal Code Draft Law: An Analysis of the Draft Law From a Gender Perspective and Proposed Amendments by the Women's Platform on the Penal Code' (Istanbul, WWHR 2003). For the same division in general, see Gul Ozyegin, 'Virginal Facades: Sexual Freedom and Guilt Among Young Turkish Women' 16 European Journal of Women's Studies 103, 104.

9 Ilkkaracan (n 6) 17. For an evaluation of the draft code's definition section, see also Erhan Buken and Nuket Ornek Buken, 'Evaluation of the Turkish Penal Code Draft Bill From a Women's Viewpoint' (2005) 4 Journal of International Society Fort the History of Islamic Medicine (ISHIM) 4–5 <http://ishim.net/ishimj/jishim4_7_8/Vol4No7/EDITORIAL.htm> accessed 10 August 2019.

10 The AKP's commission was forced to remove not only the definition but also the articles relating to abduction, which allowed for different degrees of punishment depending on whether or not the victim was a virgin. If the victim was a virgin, the commission would accept this as an aggravated factor, as, according to the commission, the consequences of rape of a virgin are more serious than the sexual assault of a non-virgin (i.e. a woman). (Women for Women's Human Rights-New Ways (n 8); Buken and Ornek Buken (n 9) 11–12.

11 Pinar Ilkkaracan and Liz Ercevik Amado, 'Legal Reforms on Violence Against Women in Turkey: Best Practices' in Moha Ennaji and Fatima Sadiqi (eds), *Gender and Violence in the Middle East* (Oxon, Routledge 2011) 195.

as attacks on public morality, not individual bodily integrity. This approach implicitly supported the patriarchal ideology that women and their sexualities belong to their families and societies, providing clear evidence of how the State links women's sexuality and bodily integrity with public morality and showing how the law in Turkey was far from 'gender neutral.'[12] Therefore, changing the definition of these crimes would not only break up the patriarchal approach of the State but also exclude moral values and honour/*namus* from the concept of rape/sexual assault. However, although this picture was promising, showing a breakup of the State's patriarchal approach, it is important to analyse whether the same approach was also seen when honour killings were criminalised. Therefore, the following section looks at the Turkish Penal Code in the context of honour killings.

2.2 Honour killings and the Turkish Penal Code

Now, for the first time in its history, the Turkish Penal Code addresses customary killing as an aggravated factor in s.82 and forbids the application of a provocation defence if there was no unjust action caused by the victim. I will discuss this issue in depth to analyse whether this new ruling was sufficient for responding to feminist requirements. My main focus, however, will be on conceptualising honour killing, and how its conceptualisation brought injustice to the victims of this crime.

2.2.1 Overview of section 82 of the Turkish Penal Code

Section 82 of the Turkish Penal Code regulates aggravated factors for homicide, which are *numerus clausus*.

If the homicide is committed:

a Deliberately
b Ferociously or brutally
c By fire, flood, destruction, dousing, or bombing, or by using nuclear, biological, or chemical weapons
d Against a descendant or an ascendant, or a spouse or a sibling
e Against a child or someone who cannot protect him/herself mentally or physically
f Against a pregnant woman
g By virtue of public duty
h In order to conceal a crime or to destroy the evidences or to facilitate committing the crime
i With the motive of blood feud
j With the motive of custom[13]

12 Shaheen Sardar Ali, 'Overlapping Discursive Terrains of Culture, Law and Women's Rights' in *Scratching the Surface: Democracy, Traditions, Gender* (Lahore, Heinrich Böll Foundation 2007) 80.
13 This section is usually referred to as 82/1-k instead of 82/1-j in the literature, a convention followed in this work.

The penalty shall be aggravated life imprisonment instead of life imprisonment.

What is striking about this section is that there is no specific reference to honour or reputation. Determining how this section is applied to honour killing cases takes us to section 'j,' which regulates the motive of custom.

The State deliberately avoids mentioning honour in the Penal Code, and preferring to use the term 'custom' instead. That was the main source of initial conflict between the State and feminist activists, as well as the Platform, during the discussions regarding honour killings.[14]

The conflict arose from two different factors:

- Definition of 'customary killing'
- Distinction between 'customary killing' and 'honour killing'

The following section analyses these conflicted issues and how the State and the legal authorities dealt with them.

2.2.1.1 DEFINITION OF CUSTOMARY KILLING

Although s.82 of the Penal Code mentioned 'customary killing,' it did not provide any definition of the phrase. Even in the Penal Code's preamble, the State did not give any information about what constituted 'customary killing.' This resulted, as Iskender mentioned, in infringement of the general principle of criminal law, ***nullum crimen sine lege***, as the State regulated aggravated punishment using the requirement of specific motive but failed to define what this specific motive was.[15]

Because the State did not provide a definition, a gap was left for the literature and the courts to fill. However, this approach did not provide justice for the victims; instead, as will be discussed in the following sections, it gave freedom to judges to create case law that sometimes favoured the perpetrators. Moreover, it caused instability within the criminal law system in Turkey because it gave rise to several different definitions and interpretations. When we analyse the definitions of 'customary killings' alongside the literature and the courts' decisions, several issues arise.

In the literature, there are two approaches to conceptualising customary killings:

- Separating customary killing from honour killings
- Merging customary killings and honour killings

14 Derya Demirler and Pınar Gümüş, 'TURKISH Değişirken . . .' (2004) 7 BÜ'de Kadın Gündemi; Pinar Ilkkaracan 'How Adultery Almost Derailed Turkey's Aspiration to Join the European Union' in Pinar Ilkkaracan (ed), *Deconstructing Sexuality in the Middle East* (Aldershot, Ashgate 2008) 52–54; Hande Eslen-Ziya, 'Türk Ceza Kanunu Değişiminde Kadın Aktivistler: Bir Lobicilik Hikayesi' (2012) 15 Sosyoloji Araştırmaları Dergisi 120, 142; Senem Öner, 'Namus: Woman as "Translation"' (2018) 8 Trakya Üniversitesi Edebiyat Fakültesi Dergisi 110, 111; Derya Tekin, 'Victims of Law: The Efficiency of Turkish Penal System on Honour Killings' (2012) Strategic Outlook.

15 Salih Zeki İskender, *Öğreti ve Yargısal Kararlar Işığında Töre Saikiyle İnsan Öldürme Suçu (Namus Cinayetleri)* (Ankara, Yetkin 2011) 103–04.

In the first approach, it is evident from the literature that some academics and community members preferred separating customary killings from honour killings.[16] Their distinctions were based on family council decisions and on the distinction between family honour and individual honour. For instance, Fındıkçı argues that customary killings are an aspect of feudalism and require family decisions, which make them collective acts; they are intended to restore family honour, whereas an honour killing is an individual act that does not require any family involvement.[17] Although Fındıkçı states that an honour killing can be committed as a form of customary killing, his understanding of honour and customary killing lies in the distinction between individual and family honour, and it seems as if restoring individual honour is more tolerated. Similar to Fındıkçı's argument, a study conducted by Kardam showed that community members address customary killings by referring to family council decisions, whereas they consider honour killings to be individual acts.[18] This distinction is also used by some courts, which will be analysed below.

The second approach, which is based on not separating customary and honour killings, mainly reflects the feminist interpretations that this book also strongly supports.[19] Their main argument is that if the notion of customary killing is considered in quite a narrow sense, by only accepting family involvement and feudalism, other forms of homicides that are committed for the sake of honour without family involvement will receive less punishment.

The courts and the State, on the other hand, have been following these different approaches to address and explain customary killing – approaches that have made the situation even worse for victims. The State's failure to provide a consensus definition and conceptualisation not only causes confusion within

16 Ihsan Cetin, 'Defining Recent Femicide in Modern Turkey: Revolt Killing' (2015) 16 Journal of International Women's Studies 346, 347–49; Aydın Fındıkçı, *Töre Cinayetleri Kürt Kültürünün Bir Parçası Mı: Arama Sonuçları* (Ankara, İmaj Yayınları 2010) 106; İskender (n 15) 50–53; Hilal Onur Ince, Aysun Yarali, and Dogancan Ozsel, 'Customary Killings in Turkey and Turkish Modernization' (2009) 45 Middle Eastern Studies 537, 538; Deniz Erdem, 'Political Reforms in Turkey and EU Membership: Honor Killings and Kurdish Language Rights' (Master of Arts, Sabanci University 2008) 54; Serap Akcaoglu Saydim, 'Medyada Tore ve Namus Cinayetlerinin Yansimalari, Veliler ve Ogrenciler Uzerindeki Etkileri' (Milli Egitim Bakanligi Egitim Arastirma ve Gelistirme Dairesi Baskanligi 2008) 9–12; Bağlı and Özensel (n 2); Filiz Kardam, 'The Dynamics of Honour Killings in Turkey: Prospects for Action' (Ankara, United Nations Population Fund 2005) 62 <www.unfpa.org/upload/lib_pub_file/676_filename_honourkillings.pdf> accessed 26 June 2019.

17 Fındıkçı (n 16) 109–16. For family decisions, see also 'Töre ve Namus Cinayetleri İle Kadınlara ve Çocuklara Yönelik Şiddetin Sebeplerinin Araştırılarak Alınması Gereken Önlemlerin Belirlenmesi Amacıyla Kurulan TBMM Araştırma Komisyonu Raporu' (Ankara, TC Başbakanlık Kadın Statüsü Genel Müdürlüğü 2006) 156 <www.kadininstatusu.gov.tr/upload/kadininstatusu.gov.tr/mce/eski_site/Pdf/tbmmkom-bolum1.pdf> accessed 3 July 2019. (Aydin Durdu).

18 Kardam (n 16) 62.

19 'Töre ve Namus Cinayetleri İle Kadınlara ve Çocuklara Yönelik Şiddetin Sebeplerinin Araştırılarak Alınması Gereken Önlemlerin Belirlenmesi Amacıyla Kurulan TBMM Araştırma Komisyonu Raporu' (n 17) 176. (Av. Senay Sarihan); Demirler and Gümüş (n 14).

the judiciary, but, as seen below, also supports the patriarchal social structure, allowing judges to interpret the law by considering customs and traditions. It is useful to analyse how the State and the courts define 'customary killing' and how these definitions affect the trials. The following four sections address different definitional problems arising from the State's failure to provide a definition for 'customary killing.'

a. Definitions that address customary killing within the concept of family councils' decisions

As mentioned earlier, the lack of legal definition of 'customary killing' in s.82 of the Penal Code created a gap to be filled by the judges. One of the problematic ways of filling this gap was the decision to look for a specific situation to use to conceptualise customary killing. The existence of family council decisions was considered necessary by courts in the early period of the new Penal Code. The Appeal Court's decision in 2007 was to create case law for First Degree Courts by drawing on 'family council decisions' as integral to implementing s.82/1-k. During a case in which the defendant murdered his pregnant sister, the Appeal Court decided that, because there was a lack of evidence proving that there had been a family decision to kill the victim, there had been no 'customary killing' in this situation. Therefore, s.82/1-k should not be applied.[20]

This decision was problematic because it exposed the difficulties in proving family decisions and pre-plan in practice. In situations where underage boys are prosecuted for homicide, the courts can readily reach a decision that the family is behind the murder, because of the age of the offender.[21] However, in cases where the perpetrator is over 18, it is hard to prove this. No family member will appear in court to confess that they had decided and planned to murder the victim; it is also very unlikely that family members will appear in court and confess to the existence of a family council, much less its decision-making process, thereby putting other family members and themselves in a position to be prosecuted. The data collected from the prisoners also showed that, the perpetrators intend to mention that the crime was a sudden decision and not a premeditated murder.[22] That is why scholars and activists criticised this decision heavily.[23] Oral, a well-known journalist, criticised the Appeal Court in her column for being ignorant of the concepts of 'honour' and 'honour killings.'[24] Oral even alleged that the Court's decision would encourage committing of more honour killings.[25] For similar reasons, one of the Appeal Court judges, Iskender, indicated that the Court's decision was unacceptable

20 Department No:1 of the Criminal Appeal Court 2007/6700 E, 2008/1986 K, Date: 14.03.2008.

21 Diyarbakir 3rd High Criminal Court 2011/250 E, 2012/116 K, Date: 15.03.2012.

22 Please see Appendix 1.2.

23 Bağlı and Özensel (n 2) 62.

24 Zeynep Oral, 'Bu Yargıtay Japonya'da Mı Yaşıyor?' (*Zeynep Oral*, 2008) <www.zeyneporal.com/yazilar/2008/0808030.html> accessed 18 August 2019.

25 Ibid.

and that it should change its attitude, otherwise this would allow accessories and abettors to murder to remain unpunished.[26] Also, the CEDAW Shadow Report prepared by the Federation of Women association in Turkey raised this issue and demonstrated that it was a problem that would prevent the elimination of honour killings.[27]

After the Appeal Court's above-mentioned decision to involve family council decisions in First Degree Courts led to a separation between customary and honour killings when considering family decisions. For instance, during the trial of Aysel, who was murdered by her former brother-in-law for getting married after her divorce, the Criminal Court stated that 'customary killings' are usually committed because of a breach of 'customs,' and that they are usually committed by a family member in order to fulfil the family's decision.[28] However, when this ruling was appealed in 2009, the Appeal Court changed its approach to family council decisions.[29]

The Appeal Court's new approach was necessary and pertinent in order to eliminate injustice for honour killing victims. Later on, the Appeal Court significantly changed its attitude to 'family decisions.' In seven decisions between 2009 and 2010, the Court of Appeal ruled that although in some cases family decisions could be seen as triggers causing perpetrators to commit the crimes, the existence of 'family decisions' alone is not a sufficient criterion for considering the crime a 'customary killing,' thereby allowing the application of s.82/1-k.[30] However, it is important to note that changing the Appeal Court's attitude on 'family decisions' took some time. While in one ruling, in 2007, the Appeal Court sought out the family's decision, with only one vote opposing this approach,[31] it was only from 2009 that it ruled that family decisions

26 <http://arsiv.sabah.com.tr/2008/08/28/haber,03F74A003F2A4E5FB385FB030F9118BA.html> accessed 18 August 2019.

27 Federation of Women Associations of Turkey, 'CEDAW SHADOW REPORT OF TURKEY 46th SESSION' (Ankara, Federation of Women Associations of Turkey 2010) 9 <http://www2.ohchr.org/english/bodies/cedaw/docs/ngos/FWAT_Turkey46.pdf> accessed 17 June 2019. See also WWHR, 'Shadow NGO Report on Turkey's Sixth Periodic Report to the Committee on the Elimination of Discrimination against Women' (WWHR 2010) 3 <http://www2.ohchr.org/english/bodies/cedaw/docs/ngos/WPTPC_Turkey46.pdf> accessed 17 June 2019.

28 Izmir 6th High Criminal Court 2007/359 E, 2009/52 K, Date: 30.3.2009.

29 Department No:1 of the Criminal Appeal Court 2009/10191 E, 2010/6617 K, Date: 13.10.2010.

30 Department No:1 of the Criminal Appeal Court 2009/10191 E, 2009/293, Date: 30.01.2009; Department No:1 of the Criminal Appeal Court 2009/2339 E, 2009/1039 K, Date: 03.03.2009; Department No:1 of the Criminal Appeal Court 2009/6048 E, 2009/1937 K, Date: 08.04.2009; Department No:1 of the Criminal Appeal Court 2009/2357 E, 2010/414 K, Date: 27.01.2010; Department No:1 of the Criminal Appeal Court 2010/2637 E, 2010/7269 K, Date: 08.11.2010; Department No:1 of the Criminal Appeal Court 2010/1509 E, 2010/7851 K, Date: 08.12.2010; Department No:1 of the Criminal Appeal Court 2010/7469 E, 2011/3272 K, Date: 23.05.2011.

31 Department No:1 of the Criminal Appeal Court 2007/2927 E, 2007/8501 K, Date: 19.11.2007.

were not compulsorily applied s.82/1-k.[32] The Assembly of the Criminal Chambers, which is the highest criminal court in Turkey, then approved in 2010 that the First Degree and Appeal Courts should not only seek 'family decisions' to apply s.82/1-k.[33] Yet, although the decision was made five years after the Penal Code had been amended, it was still an important step for criminalising honour crimes. This precedent now binds the courts to have a broader understanding of customary killings, while compelling them to avoid restricting their decisions based on the existence of family decisions. For instance, Erzurum High Criminal Court followed this precedent by stating that 'family decisions' are not necessarily applicable to s.82/1-k.[34] And Manisa High Criminal Court also abided by this decision by ruling that following 'traditional and/or customary rituals' is sufficient to apply s.82/1-k, and a family decision is not necessary if these rituals are proved sufficient.[35] Although the Assembly of the Criminal Chambers changed its attitudes positively and influenced the First Degree Courts to follow it, it is evident that there are still some First Degree Courts that apply the 'customary killing' motive because of family council decisions.[36]

b. Definitions that consider customary killings and honour killings separately

Apart from the courts' earlier approach, considering the family councils' decisions as necessary to distinguish between customary and honour killings, there were further problems related to this separation in general. As analysed in more detail below, the distinction significantly reduced the number of cases considered to fall under s.82/1-k; this allowed offenders to offer a provocation defence.

The Court decisions that specifically reflected the difference between customary and honour killing addressed the following points:

- Customary killings are premeditated, whereas honour killings are usually committed as a result of loss of control/provocation.[37]
- Customary killings are collective crimes that aim to restore 'family honour', whereas honour killings are individual crimes that aim to restore 'personal honour;[38] customary killings are committed as a result of expectations from

32 Department No:1 of the Criminal Appeal Court 2009/10191 E, 2009/293, Date: 30.01.2009; Department No:1 of the Criminal Appeal Court 2009/6048 E, 2009/1039 K, Date: 03.03.2009.

33 Assembly of the Criminal Chambers 2010/111 E, 2010/32606 K, Date: 11.05.2010.

34 Erzurum 3rd High Criminal Court, 2008/157 E, 2011/86 K, Date: 18.05.2011.

35 In that decision, the perpetrator asked the victim to have a bath before he murdered her, which was accepted as a customary ritual by the Court (Manisa 2nd High Criminal Court 2011/246 E, 2012/153 K, Date 14.05.2012).

36 Batman 2nd High Criminal Court 2015/343 E, 2017/171 K, Date: 21.06.2017.

37 Bursa 4th High Criminal Court 2009/333 E, 2009/350 K, Date: 20.11.2009; Bakırköy 6th High Criminal Court 2006/170 E, 2009/221 K, Date: 16.07.2009.

38 Kayseri 1st High Criminal Court 2009/233 E, 2009/287 K, Date: 02.09.2009; Izmir 6th High Criminal Court 2007/359 E, 2009/52 K, Date: 30.03.2009; Tarsus High Criminal

society to punish the victim in such a way because of behaviour by the victim that is deemed as unacceptable by the society.[39]

- Customary killings are committed for revenge, whereas honour killings are committed as a result of a wrong that was caused by the victim.[40]

Two of the Assembly of the Criminal Chambers decisions are particularly important to highlight the difference between 'customary killing' and 'honour killing.' The Court's decisions in these cases indicated that the State separated 'customary killing' from 'honour killing' for specific purposes.[41] According to the Court, the State did not aim to include 'honour killings' within s.82 because it preferred to criminalise honour killings that were only committed for the sake of 'custom' within this section. The Court continued by saying that if 'honour and customary killings' were combined and used interchangeably, this would be a form of analogy, which is not permitted by criminal law.[42] The Appeal Court also followed the Assembly of the Criminal Chambers' decision and stated that a subjective meaning of 'honour,' which is based on personal jealousy, unrequited love, or inability to control a person should not be considered within s.82/1-k. Otherwise, this would be against *nullum crimen sine lege* and the prohibition against analogy within criminal law.[43]

In respect to the decisions of the Assembly of the Criminal Chambers, although the Court tried to separate 'customary killings' from 'honour killings' in relation to the prohibition against analogy within criminal law, from the feminist perspective it seemed that the Court was adopting a patriarchal attitude towards VAW. Not addressing crimes committed for the sake of personal honour as an aggravated factor clearly showed that the Court tacitly approved of applying less severe punishments to these crimes. And if we remember the difficulties of proving the existence of the desire to restore collective honour, rather than personal honour,

---

Court 2010/117 E, 2010/245 K, Date: 03.08.2010; Department No:1 of the Criminal Appeal Court 2012/3659 E, 2012/9331 K, Date: 12.12.2012; Bakırköy 15th High Criminal Court 2009/116 E, 2009/217 K, Date: 13.05.2011; Assembly of the Criminal Chambers 2012/1-76 E, 2012/258 K, Date: 26.06.2012.

39 Department No:1 of the Criminal Appeal Court 2014/4124 E, 2014/4693 K, Date: 22.10.2014.

40 Kayseri 1st High Criminal Court 2009/233 E, 2009/287 K, Date: 02.09.2009. This approach is no longer adopted by the courts.

41 Assembly of the Criminal Chambers 2011/1–52 E, 2011/180 K, Date: 12.07.2011; Assembly of the Criminal Chambers 2012/1–76 E, 2012/258 K, Date: 26.06.2012; Assembly of the Criminal Chambers 2013/1–355 E, 2013/456 K, Date: 19.11.2013.

42 Ibid.

43 Department No:1 of the Criminal Appeal Court 2012/3659 E, 2012/9331 K, Date: 12.12.2012; Department No:1 of the Criminal Appeal Court 2013/2120 E, 2013/5542 K, Date: 07.10.2013; Department No:1 of the Criminal Appeal Court 2011/7167 E, 2013/3268 K, Date: 18.04.2013; Department No:1 of the Criminal Appeal Court 2013/2789 E, 2014/184 K, Date: 22.01.2014; Department No:1 of the Criminal Appeal Court 2015/2328 E, 2015/4272 K, Date: 02/07/2015; Department No:1 of the Criminal Appeal Court 2015/1374 E, 2015/5380 K, Date: 10.11.2015.

in these cases, the Assembly of the Criminal Chambers' approach is clearly biased against victims. This is because, without considering the social mechanisms that treat women as the sources of honour for families as well as for individual men, the judges not only ignore feminist arguments about women's lack of autonomy and agency but also tacitly support the patriarchal social structure by limiting the criminalisation of honour killing. Moreover, if a narrow interpretation is applied to the meaning of 'customary killing,' this results in excluding crimes committed as 'passion killings' from s.82/1-k.

Appeal Court Judge Iskender criticised the exclusion of 'honour killings' committed as a form of 'passion killing' when applying s.82/1-k, and he used his vote to oppose the Appeal Court judges' decision in 2009.[44] The judge gave his opinion that passion killings should be considered under s.82/1-k, as such killings include the concept of ownership over women's bodies; he considered that this concept of ownership rightly falls within the scope of s.82/1-k.[45]

If we remember the three points addressed regarding the separation of customary killing and honour killing, we once again realise that there is a problem with conceptualising customary killings. This issue was explained by Department No:1 of the Criminal Appeal Court Judge Muzaffer Ozdemir during his interview. Ozdemir explained that

> absence of the definition of customary killings causes some confusion for the courts. Because of this absence we have witnessed different definitions, even within the same courts. For instance, in the Appeal Court (because we have two different panels) sometimes each panel reached different conclusions on the meaning of customary killing.[46]

However, Judge Ozdemir continued by saying that the Appeal Court prefers to interpret customary killings very narrowly. According to this approach, honour and customary killings are separate crimes, and the meaning of customary killings should not be broadened. According to this attitude, honour killings are subjective while customary killings are objective and represent common culture and common beliefs in society.[47] Ozdemir added that broadening the definition of customary killing to include honour killings would be a breach of the prohibition against analogy and would have a negative effect on Turkey's reputation in the international arena. If customary killings also encompass honour killings, and s.82/1-k is applied to honour killings, it would seem to outsiders as if the

44 Department No:1 of the Criminal Appeal Court 2008/5953 E, 2009/1075 K, Date: 05.03.2009; Department No:1 of the Criminal Appeal Court 2008/6646 E, 2009/1558 K, Date: 25.03.2009; Department No:1 of the Criminal Appeal Court 2008/9651 E, 2009/4794 K, Date: 15.07.2009.

45 Ibid. For the opposite argument, please see Pınar Ecevitoğlu, *Namus Töre ve İktidar: Kadının Çıplak Hayat Olarak Kuruluşu* (Ankara, Dipnot 2012) 373.

46 Interview with Muzaffer Ozdemir (Ankara, 8 July 2013).

47 Ibid.

number of customary killings in Turkey is very high,[48] whereas if honour killing cases are excluded from customary killings, the majority of the cases will not be dealt with under s.82/1-k and so a considerable sentence reduction will be applied to offenders.

As mentioned earlier, feminists such as Ilkkaracan[49] and Demirler and Gümüş[50] raised their concerns about separating honour from customary killings. The Appeal Court's ensuing decision to separate these terms reduced the hopes of a decrease in the number of honour killings in Turkey. By narrowing the concept of customary killings, the courts would now only target specific traditions/customs, and any murder committed in the name of honour (without proof of involvement of any tribe, family, or so-called tradition) would receive less punishment.

In terms of this book, I agree with the Appeal Court's approach in one way. It is also true that some honour killings are committed in the name of so-called tradition, custom, and even religion, but they are also committed for personal honour and to protect or restore patriarchy or masculinity. As I discussed in Chapter 4, not all HBV is committed for the sake of family honour. When we remember the common motives of HBV – illicit sexual relationship, rape, seeking divorce, rumours, and challenging patriarchal authority – these motives do not always correspond with certain customary norms, but are often strongly associated with patriarchy and hegemonic masculinity, which creates its boundaries by restricting women's autonomy. It is not understandable, then, why the Appeal Court considers restoring collective honour as an aggravated factor while accepting personal honour as a mitigating factor. If we remember the discussion on possessing honour, men possess honour first for themselves and then for their families. If there is any danger to honour, first the individual honour and then the family honour is tarnished. A man may commit HBV in order to save his honour and then to cleanse his family's honour. Although there are some situations in which the family involvement occurs immediately, it is usually individuals who feel themselves responsible for the whole family. Therefore, in practice there is not much difference between committing honour killings for personal reasons or to restore family honour, because the motives are the same: punishing women who tarnish the honour of individuals and families through their (usually sexual) misconduct, because they are the source of both personal and collective honour.

c. Definitions that consider honour killings and customary killings interchangeably

Courts, State publications, and the literature reveal that on many occasions 'honour killings' and 'customary killings' are used interchangeably, as if they have the same meaning, often separated only by '/' or by using brackets to mention 'honour killing.' For instance, Tezcan and Iskender prefer to use brackets when addressing this type of violence, referring to "customary

48 Ibid.
49 Ilkkaracan (n 14) 52–54.
50 Demirler and Gümüş (n 14).

killing (honour killing)" in their publications.[51] On the other hand, scholars like Centel,[52] Acar et al.,[53] and Ertürk[54] prefer to only use the term 'honour killing,' not 'customary killing,' when considering this form of violence more broadly.

The State's approach is particularly important at this stage. As the examples show, the State's intention is to use 'honour killings' and 'customary killings' interchangeably in some of its important documents. For instance, the Prime Ministry Directorate of Women's Status is one of the leading institutions that addresses honour and customary killings interchangeably. The Status's publication[55] is based on intensive research on the reasons for this form of violence in Turkey and considers it as 'customary/HBV.'[56] However, when the report is read in more detail, it is obvious that its claim to treat 'honour and custom-based violence' together remains unfulfilled. This is because the report explains that if individual honour is taken into account and the crime is committed under pressure from the community, then this is not customary killing; it is honour killing.[57] Again, the State here follows the approach of separating customary killings from honour killings based on collective and individual honour. Another report, prepared by the Human Rights Presidency in Turkey, preferred to use 'honour killings' and 'customary killings' together. This is clever wording, as in doing so the report avoided defining the terms but combined them (but not interchangeably) in addressing a specific type of violence.[58] However, this approach cannot be accepted as widening the concept of customary killings.

Courts' decisions also have particular importance in revealing the attitudes of judges to HBV. When the Appeal Court's decisions are analysed, we realise that the Court also intends to use 'customary' and 'honour' killings interchangeably by using brackets. However, this does not necessarily mean that the Court considers honour killings under s.82/1-k. For instance, in one case, in which the perpetrator murdered his sister because of rumours about her lifestyle, the Appeal Court held that the crime committed was a 'customary killing,' referring to the need to 'restore honour' in brackets.[59] Similarly, in other decisions the Court has often

51 Mahmut Tezcan, *Turkiye'de Tore (Namus) Cinayetleri: Sosyo Kulturel Antropolojik Yaklasim* (Ankara, Naturel 2003); İskender (n 15).

52 Nur Centel, 'Yeni Turk Ceza Yasasi ve Kadin' (2005) 44 Polis Dergisi 1, 11–12.

53 Acar and others (n 5) 57–58.

54 Yakin Ertürk, 'Turkiye Raporu' (Ankara, Human Rights Joint Platform 2007) 11–12 <www.ihop.org.tr/dosya/YE/yeturkiyerapor.pdf> accessed 17 August 2019.

55 'Töre ve Namus Cinayetleri İle Kadınlara ve Çocuklara Yönelik Şiddetin Sebeplerinin Araştırılarak Alınması Gereken Önlemlerin Belirlenmesi Amacıyla Kurulan TBMM Araştırma Komisyonu Raporu' (n 17).

56 Ibid. 108.

57 Ibid. 111.

58 Hasan Tahsin Fendoğlu, 'Insan Hakları Başkanlığı 2007 Töre ve Namus Cinayetleri Raporu' (TC Başbakanlık İnsan Hakları Başkanlığı 2008).

59 Department No:1 of the Criminal Appeal Court 2008/359 E, 2009/3640 K, Date: 17.06.2009. Similarly, see also Department No:1 of the Criminal Appeal Court 2011/5057 E, 2012/3350 K, Date: 30.04.2012.

linked 'custom (restore honour)' together to adjudge the crime.[60] What needs to be understood from these decisions is that if restoring honour is a part of custom, then it needs to be dealt with in s.82/1-k. Again, the definition of custom is left to the judges, which may cause further complications within the judiciary.

The Appeal Court uses not only brackets but also '/'[61] or 'and'[62] between custom and honour, treating them interchangeably and thereby creating more

60 Department No:1 of the Criminal Appeal Court 2008/5009 E, 2009/5002 K, Date: 22.07.2009; Department No:1 of the Criminal Appeal Court 2008/6528 E, 2009/3761 K, Date: 23.06.2009; Department No:1 of the Criminal Appeal Court 2008/6782 E, 2010/4691 K, Date: 22.06.2010; Department No:1 of the Criminal Appeal Court 2008/8385 E, 2009/3412 K, Date: 11.06.2009; Department No:1 of the Criminal Appeal Court 2008/8615 E, 2009/6878 K, Date: 11.11.2009; Department No:1 of the Criminal Appeal Court 2008/9038 E, 2009/3764 K, Date: 23.06.2009; Department No:1 of the Criminal Appeal Court 2008/9234 E, 2009/4140 K, Date: 02.07.2009; Department No:1 of the Criminal Appeal Court 2008/9435 E, 2009/4468 K, Date: 09.07.2009; Department No:1 of the Criminal Appeal Court 2008/9934 E, 2009/4994 K, Date: 23.07.2009; Department No:1 of the Criminal Appeal Court 2008/10847 E, 2009/6194 K, Date: 21.10.2009; Department No:1 of the Criminal Appeal Court 2009/190 E, 2009/6887 K, Date: 11.11.2009; Department No:1 of the Criminal Appeal Court 2009/270 E, 2009/6891 K, Date: 11.11.2009; Department No:1 of the Criminal Appeal Court 2009/2674 E, 2011/4286 K, Date: 05.07.2011; Department No:1 of the Criminal Appeal Court 2009/6163 E, 2009/6188 K, Date: 21.10.2009; Department No:1 of the Criminal Appeal Court 2009/6772 E, 2010/3058 K, Date: 29.04.2010; Department No:1 of the Criminal Appeal Court 2009/7465 E, 2010/5325 K, Date: 07.07.2010; Department No:1 of the Criminal Appeal Court 2009/10191 E, 2010/6617 K, Date: 13.10.2010; Department No:1 of the Criminal Appeal Court 2010/1509 E, 2010/7851 K, Date: 08.12.2010; Department No:1 of the Criminal Appeal Court 2010/3190 E, 2010/8043 K, Date: 14.12.2010; Department No:1 of the Criminal Appeal Court 2010/3722 E, 2012/2270 K, Date: 28.03.2012; Department No:1 of the Criminal Appeal Court 2010/4407 E, 2011/695 K, Date: 15.02.2011; Department No:1 of the Criminal Appeal Court 2010/5426 E, 2011/1760 K, Date: 23.03.2011; Department No:1 of the Criminal Appeal Court 2010/6241 E, 2011/3025 K, Date: 11.05.2011; Department No:1 of the Criminal Appeal Court 2011/1811 E, 2011/2444 K, Date: 20.04.2011; Department No:1 of the Criminal Appeal Court 2011/2467 E, 2011/6863 K, Date: 17.11.2011; Department No:1 of the Criminal Appeal Court 2011/4322 E, 2012/3639 K, Date: 07.05.2012; Department No:1 of the Criminal Appeal Court 2011/5149 E, 2011/6551 K, Date: 02.11.2011.

61 Department No:1 of the Criminal Appeal Court 2008/5953 E, 2009/1075 K, Date: 04.03.2009; Department No:1 of the Criminal Appeal Court 2008/7373 E, 2009/2154 K, Date: 15.04.2009; Department No:1 of the Criminal Appeal Court 2008/8227 E, 2009/3039 K, Date: 27.05.2009; Department No:1 of the Criminal Appeal Court 2009/2858 E, 2011/1787 K, Date: 23.03.2011; Department No:1 of the Criminal Appeal Court 2009/8192 E, 2010/7538 K, Date: 24.11.2010; Department No:1 of the Criminal Appeal Court 2009/840 E, 2010/3970 K, Date: 03.06.2010; Department No:1 of the Criminal Appeal Court 2010/2637 E, 2010/7269 K, Date: 08.11.2010; Department No:1 of the Criminal Appeal Court 2010/4522 E, 2011/1511 K, Date: 15.03.2011; Department No:1 of the Criminal Appeal Court 2010/5786 E, 2011/1972 K, Date: 01.04.2011; Department No:1 of the Criminal Appeal Court 2010/7496 E, 2011/3277 K, Date: 23.05.2011; Department No:1 of the Criminal Appeal Court 2011/2688 E, 2011/2667 K, Date: 27.04.2011.

62 Department No:1 of the Criminal Appeal Court 2008/8055 E, 2009/3527 K, Date: 16.06.2009. Department No:1 of the Criminal Appeal Court 2008/8285 E, 2010/7220

confusion. For instance, in 2011 the Appeal Court mentioned that the First Degree Court should consider s.82/1-k, as it is understood from that the defendant murdered his underage daughter in order to 'restore custom/honour.'[63] In another case, the Appeal Court approved the First Degree Court's decision and stated that the crime was committed for both honour and custom.[64] The use of 'and' between these terms is problematic, as it does not actually show that the Court intended to use these terms interchangeably; the use of 'and' tells us that the Court still considered 'customary killing' and 'honour killing' as two different terms. In recent cases, however, the Appeal Court has preferred to use the term 'customary killing' without mentioning 'honour killing.'[65] For instance, in 2013 the Appeal Court only used the term 'customary killing' in a case in which the defendant murdered a man who had eloped with his wife.[66] This was perhaps because the Court preferred using 'customary killing,' which is already in the Penal Code, in order to avoid confusion, probably for the same reason the Assembly of the Criminal Chambers prefers using the term 'customary killing' but not 'honour killing' in its decisions.[67] However, as mentioned earlier, following this approach limits the definition of honour killing to certain circumstances, such as when customs put pressure on families to commit honour killings or legitimise VAW as a result of breaching social norms.

d. Definitions that consider honour killing as a form of customary killing

Apart from the above-mentioned approaches, the literature also tends to treat 'honour killing' as a form of 'customary killing.' For instance, Bağlı and Özensel consider

---

K, Date: 04.11.2010; Department No:1 of the Criminal Appeal Court 2009/2357 E, 2010/414 K, Date: 28.01.2010; Department No:1 of the Criminal Appeal Court 2009/4558 E, 2009/6033 K, Date: 19.10.2009; Department No:1 of the Criminal Appeal Court 2012/1475 E, 2012/4900 K, Date: 13.06.2012,

63 Department No:1 of the Criminal Appeal Court 2011/2688 E, 2011/2667 K, Date: 27.04.2011.

64 Department No:1 of the Criminal Appeal Court 2009/2357 E, 2010/414 K, Date: 28.01.2010.

65 Department No:1 of the Criminal Appeal Court 2010/4303 E, 2010/6578 K, Date: 12.10.2010; Department No:1 of the Criminal Appeal Court 2012/838 E, 2012/3806 K, Date: 10.05.2012; Department No:1 of the Criminal Appeal Court 2012/1116 E, 2012/4037 K, Date: 21.05.2012; Department No:1 of the Criminal Appeal Court 2012/838 E, 2012/3806 K, Date: 10.05.2012; Department No:1 of the Criminal Appeal Court 2012/3490 E, 2013/665 K, Date: 31.01.2013; Department No:1 of the Criminal Appeal Court 2013/372 E, 2013/3427 K, Date: 30.04.2013.

66 Department No:1 of the Criminal Appeal Court 2013/372 E, 2013/3427 K, Date: 30.04.2013.

67 Assembly of the Criminal Chambers 2010/111 E, 2010/32606 K, Date: 11.05.2010; Assembly of the Criminal Chambers 2011/18 E, 2011/1–10 K, Date: 01.02.2011; Assembly of the Criminal Chambers 2011/1–52 E, 2011/180 K, Date: 12.07.2011; Assembly of the Criminal Chambers 2011/1–138 E, 2011/130 K, Date: 14.06.2011.

honour killing as a sub-category of customary killing.[68] A report prepared by the General Directorate of Security Affairs addresses honour killing the same way.[69] The report considers customary killing as a main category and honour killings as a sub-category. According to this report, there are other types of incidents, such as blood feuds, bride exchanges, intra-family disputes, sexual assaults, illicit relationships, and rape, which can be considered under the umbrella of custom.[70] Although the report shows that honour killings take up the biggest portion, with 29%, other forms of customary violence which occur in high numbers, such as illicit sexual relationships, intra-family disputes, and blood feuds,[71] are separated into sub-categories, and the report tends to consider them as different types of violence that are committed under the influence of custom. However, when the sub-categories assigned by the report are clearly analysed, all actually include the motive of honour, which makes the sub-categorisation process useless and unnecessarily confusing.

It is evident that the courts also consider honour killing as a form of customary killing, but they usually rule that not all honour killings are customary killings.[72] The Appeal Court, for instance, stated in one of its decisions that not all honour killings are forms of customary killings (*töre cinayeti*), providing definitions of both crimes.[73] According to this case, honour killings might be considered a subcategory of customary killings in certain situations, like following a certain custom, becoming reputable after committing the crime, or vice versa.[74] The Court continued by stating that if a crime is committed because of 'subjective honour,' jealousy, being sexually rejected, or losing authority, this is not enough to identify it as a form of customary killing.[75] With this approach, although the Court tried to clarify the meaning of customary killings and honour killings, and although it considered only certain types of honour killings as forms of customary killing, it gave the judges the opportunity to apply general provocation defences and reduce the sentences considerably.

The Appeal Court's approach was based on a precedent created by the Assembly of the Criminal Chambers in 2010. The Assembly of the Criminal Chambers

68 Bağlı and Özensel (n 2) 55–59.

69 'Emniyet Genel Müdürlüğü Asayiş Dairesi Başkanlığı Töre ve Namus Cinayetleri Raporu' (Emniyet Genel Müdürlüğü Asayiş Dairesi Başkanlığı 2006) 1.

70 Ibid.

71 Ibid. 2.

72 Department No:1 of the Criminal Appeal Court 2012/3659 E, 2012/9331 K, Date: 12.12.2012; Department No:1 of the Criminal Appeal Court 2012/4767 E, 2013/1774 K, Date: 06.03.2013.

73 Department No:1 of the Criminal Appeal Court 2012/3659 E, 2012/9331 K, Date: 12.12.2012.

74 Ibid.

75 Ibid. For similar cases see also Department No:1 of the Criminal Appeal Court 2014/2849 E, 2014/4347 K, Date: 01.10.2014; Department No:1 of the Criminal Appeal Court 2014/1719 E, 2014/2733 K, Date: 29.04.2014.

stated that customary killings cover honour killings only in certain circumstances (without mentioning which circumstances); it also ruled that not all honour killings should be considered to be customary killings.[76] In this way, the courts included the concept of honour in 'customary killings,' but without broadening the meaning of customary killings. Although this was a significant move in the criminalisation of honour killing, it was still far from satisfying for feminists and activists, especially given the possible application of a provocation defence.

e. Definitions of customary killings that target specific groups

Lastly, the courts define customary killings by targeting specific groups and regions in Turkey. This approach is considered to be biased and discriminatory by many scholars, as the Kurdish community and their regions are used to define custom and customary killing.[77] There is a tendency to consider HBV committed within these communities and regions as 'customary killings,' whereas in other regions and communities HBV is usually considered as 'honour killing' or 'passion killing.' This classification has serious consequences for the criminalisation of HBV. As I discussed, if the crime is considered to be a 'customary killing,' s.82/1-k is applied, with the prohibition of using a general defence. However, if it is considered an honour killing or passion killing, a general provocation defence is applicable to the case, and this has a significant effect on the punishment.

Scholars have criticised the State's policies against minority groups, especially against the Kurds. For instance, as mentioned in the previous chapter, Bayir not only questions the representation of the Kurds in HBV cases but also alleges that the State has a biased approach against the Kurds by analysing civil and criminal cases.[78] According to Bayir, Kurds are represented in the courts as 'Eastern' and the place where they live or to which they originally belong is referred to as 'the region.'[79] Bayir continues by stating that this classification creates division between the Turks and the Kurds and represents the Kurds as "uncivilized" with "cruel customs and practices."[80] Kogacioglu also highlights how conceptualising customary killing is stereotyped in Turkey as a 'Kurdish phenomenon'[81] and claims that treating honour killings as a 'Kurdish

76 Assembly of the Criminal Chambers 2010/111 E, 2010/32606 K, Date: 11.05.2010.

77 Yakın Ertürk, 'Towards a Post-Patriarchal Gender Order: Confronting the Universality and Particularity of Violence Against Women' (2009) 46 Sociologisk Forskning 61, 66; Bethany A Corbin, 'Between Saviors and Savages: The Effect of Turkey's Revised Penal Code on the Transformation of Honor Killings Into Honor Suicides and Why Community Discourse Is Necessary for Honor Crime Eradication' (2014) 29 Emory International Law Review 277, 296–99.

78 Derya Bayir, 'Representation of the Kurds by the Turkish Judiciary' (2013) 35 Human Rights Quarterly 116, 137–42.

79 Ibid. 138.

80 Ibid. A stereotypical image of Kurds was criticised by Ergin, who underlined that Kurds are usually considered as 'other' because of their facial hair and physical characteristics and are named as 'ignorant and uncultured' in relation to HBV. Murat Ergin, 'The Racialization of Kurdish Identity in Turkey' (2014) 37 Ethnic and Racial Studies 322, 330, 332.

81 Dicle Kogacioglu, 'Gelenek Söylemleri ve Iktidarın Doğallaşması: Namus Cinayetleri Örneği' (2007) 3 Kültür ve Siyasette Feminist Yaklaşımlar 1, 5–6; Dicle Kogacioglu, 'Knowledge,

phenomenon' is a form of "ethnicization of the tradition."[82] Similarly, Pervizat highlights that the authorities intend to consider honour killing as a specific form of violence that is only applied in eastern and south-eastern Turkey.[83] Pervizat continues that through this approach the authorities try to emphasise that "backward Kurds are killing their women," whereas the rest of the country does not have that problem.[84]

Some scholars also claim that 'customary killings' are a Kurdish problem and that they are committed either in eastern and south-eastern Turkey or in other places where the Kurds have migrated. For instance, Fındıkçı questions in his work whether customary killings are part of Kurdish culture or not.[85] Fındıkçı reaches the conclusion that customary killings are not only part of Kurdish culture but are also part of Kurdish unwritten law; according to him, they reflect a Kurdish problem, and saying so does not demonstrate a racist approach.[86] Similarly, two well-known journalists, Özkök and Aktan, address 'customary killings' as a Kurdish problem.[87] Özkök mentioned in his column that the

> majority of the customary killings are committed amongst people from the East and Southern East. This is a fact and expressing a fact does not mean to be racist.[88]

Aktan took this argument one step further, indicating that customary killings are based on a tribal social structure and that this structure is only seen among Kurds.[89]

Yet this approach is problematic in many ways. First, although the authors mentioned that their observations are unquestionably factual, and that stating them cannot be considered 'racist,' they can easily be seen as 'othering' the Kurdish community and, as Grabolle-Celiker mentions, discrediting Kurdish

---

Practice, and Political Community: The Making of the "Custom" in Turkey' (2011) 22 A Journal of Feminist Cultural Studies 172, 184.

82 Dicle Kogacioglu, 'The Tradition Effect: Framing Honor Crimes in Turkey' (2004) 15 A Journal of Feminist Cultural Studies 118, 130.

83 Leyla Pervizat, 'Lack of Due Diligence: Judgements of Crimes of Honour in Turkey' in Mohammad Mazher Idriss and Tahir Abbas (eds), *Honour, Violence, Women and Islam* (Abington, Routledge 2011) 144.

84 Ibid. Similar criticisms were made by Gill and Brah regarding Asian communities living in the UK. According to Gill and Brah, HBV is associated with minorities in the UK, and minority groups are targeted as "uncivilized and backwards." Aisha K Gill and Avtar Brah, 'Interrogating Cultural Narratives About "Honour"-Based Violence' (2014) 21 European Journal of Women's Studies 72, 73.

85 Fındıkçı (n 16) 116–20.

86 Ibid. 116.

87 Ertuğrul Özkök, 'O "ırkçı" Benim' *Hurriyet* (Istanbul, 26 September 2006) <www.hurriyet.com.tr/yazarlar/5148997.asp?yazarid=10> accessed 22 August 2019; Gunduz Aktan, 'Aşiret Düzeni' *Radikal* (Istanbul, 4 November 2006) <www.radikal.com.tr/yazarlar/gunduz_aktan/asiret_duzeni-796489> accessed 22 August 2019.

88 Özkök (n 87).

89 Aktan (n 87).

culture.[90] As Pervizat mentions, by addressing this issue as a case of 'Kurds are killing their women,'[91] scholars also denigrate this minority group as a whole. Following this approach not only supports the othering approach of some scholars but also raises concerns about the issue of the relationship between culture and honour killings and how this relationship is interpreted. As discussed at the beginning of this book, during the process of analysing the hermeneutical circle of HBV, the interpretation of culture – and especially the Western interpretation of minority culture – can cause misunderstandings of the whole concept of HBV by disregarding certain groups in order to identify this violence.[92] Also, linking customary killings to tribal society and customary law, excluding other types of HBV that are not part of the custom, means that the term 'customary killing' does not cover honour killing, as WWHR mentioned in their shadow report submitted to the CEDAW Committee.[93]

At this stage, it is important to analyse the State's approach to this type of classification. Official documents, such as a report prepared by the General Directorate of Security Affairs, provide statistics based on perpetrators' birthplace. A copy of the statistics can be seen in Table 6.1.[94]

Although the statistics show that the majority of perpetrators were actually born in the eastern part of Anatolia, this does not mean that HBV is predominantly committed in that region. The same report confirms that most HBV is committed in western Turkey, not eastern.[95] Another report, prepared by the Prime Ministry Directorate of Women's Status, addresses the fact that "in some regions of Turkey murders are committed based on customs."[96] The wording of

90 Anna Grabolle-Celiker, *Kurdish Life in Contemporary Turkey: Migration, Gender and Ethnic Identity* (London, IB Tauris 2013) 182.

91 Pervizat (n 83) 144.

92 For discussions on the relationship between minority group culture and arguments related to the Western interpretation of it, please see P Fournier, 'The Ghettoisation of Difference in Canada: "Rape by Culture" and the Danger of a "Cultural Defence" in Criminal Law Trials' (2002) 29 Manitoba Law Journal 1, 7; Inderpal Grewal, 'Outsourcing Patriarchy' (2013) 15 International Feminist Journal of Politics 1, 3–8; Leti Volpp, 'Blaming Culture for Bad Behavior' (2000) 12 Yale Journal of Law & the Humanities 89, 96; Dorota A Gozdecka, Selan A Ercan, and Magdalena Kmak, 'From Multiculturalism to Post-Multiculturalism: Trends and Paradoxes' (2014) 50 Journal of Sociology 51, 54; Janet Batsleer and others, 'Domestic Violence and Minoritisation: Supporting Women to Independence' (Women's Studies Research Centre, the Manchester Metropolitan University 2002) 94–95 <e-space.mmu.ac.uk/e-space/bitstream/2173/ . . . /978-0-954155-01-8.pdf> accessed 8 July 2019.

93 Women for Women's Human Rights–New Ways (n 8).

94 'Emniyet Genel Müdürlüğü Asayiş Dairesi Başkanlığı Töre ve Namus Cinayetleri Raporu' (n 69) 10.

95 Ibid. 3. A more recent report prepared by the Prime Ministry Human Rights Commission also provides similar statistics (Fendoğlu (n 58) 6.)

96 'Töre ve Namus Cinayetleri İle Kadınlara ve Çocuklara Yönelik Şiddetin Sebeplerinin Araştırılarak Alınması Gereken Önlemlerin Belirlenmesi Amacıyla Kurulan TBMM Araştırma Komisyonu Raporu' (n 17) 111.

Table 6.1 The birthplace of perpetrators between 2000 and 2005 (Emniyet Genel Müdürlüğü Asayiş Dairesi Başkanlığı Töre ve Namus Cinayetleri Raporu)

Region	*Number of defendants*
Marmara (Marmara region)	121
Ege (Aegean region)	172
Akdeniz (Mediterranean region)	175
Ic Anadolu (Central Anatolia region)	243
Karadeniz (Black Sea region)	160
Dogu Anadolu (East Anatolia region)	325
Guneydogu Anadolu (South-east Anatolia region)	388
TOTAL	1584

this statement means that there are some regions in Turkey in which customary killings are not committed, and this wording can be easily accepted as biased.

When the situation is as complicated as it is in the State's official documents, we also need to consider the court records to analyse the judiciary's approach to this issue. In one decision, the First Degree Court referred to the victim's and the perpetrator's places of origin, Saosan and Agri respectively, and the customs of those places, to conceptualise the crime.[97] Van 1st Degree Criminal Court, in another decision, defined 'customary killing' with reference to 'some regions' and a 'tribal community structure.'[98] This approach was also used by other first-degree courts to distinguish between customary and honour killings, implying that customary killings are only committed in some regions.[99] Manisa High Criminal Court, in one of its cases, adopted a similarly discriminatory approach by expressing the view that "the offender and the victim are from the East Anatolian Region where customary killings are seen in high proportion."[100] When comparing the two regions of Manisa and East Anatolia (Manisa belongs to the Aegean region and is located in West Turkey), the Court's explanation easily leads to the conclusion that customary killings are not committed in Manisa but are committed predominantly in 'another region.'

The approach of the Assembly of the Criminal Chambers, as the highest criminal court, is highly important because its decisions create a precedent for the Appeal and First Degree Courts. The Chambers tend not to refer to customary killings directly, preferring the definition provided by the Turkish Language

97 Agri High Criminal Court 2007/215 E, 2008/191 K, Date: 24.06.2008.

98 Van 1st High Criminal Court 2007/139 E, 2009/3 K, Date: 09.01.2009.

99 Izmir 6th High Criminal Court 2007/359 E, 2009/52 K, Date: 30.03.2009 and Duzce High Criminal Court 2008/29 E, 2009/208 K, Date: 27.08.2009; Tarsus High Criminal Court 2010/117 E, 2010/245 K, Date: 03.08.2010; Bakırköy 15th High Criminal Court 2009/116 E, 2011/217 K, Date: 13.05.2011; Sanliurfa 2nd High Criminal Court 2011/224 E, 2011/215 K, Date: 23.09.2011.

100 Manisa 2nd High Criminal Court, 2011/246 E, 2012/153, Date: 14.05.2012.

Association,[101] which is also a State institution. According to this institution, customary killings (*töre cinayeti*) involve

> murdering young girls and women, in some regions, by the decision of their family and again by their own family member due to their disobedience to the traditional concept, honour killing.[102]

Although the definition covers 'honour killing' as well and uses it interchangeably, the first part identifies customary killings with 'some regions.' The interpretation of this wording is that customary killings are not committed across Turkey but only in certain areas. The Assembly of the Criminal Chambers not only uses the Turkish Language Association's definition but also treats this type of killing as tribal.[103] Similarly, the First Degree Courts followed this approach and used the Turkish Language Association's definition of 'customary killing' in their judgements.[104] The othering approach of the courts and the State reminds us again of the concept of Orientalism, and specifically Said's question about Orientalism: "what right have you to take up to these airs of superiority with regard to people whom you choose to call Oriental?"[105] As the above-mentioned othering approach shows, the State and the courts also follow this ideology by referring to the othered region as 'the East' and its people as 'Easterns' In this approach, we do not witness Said's Orientalism, but we do recognise a form of internal Orientalism, or perhaps Orientalism within Orientalism – what Poyraz identifies as "inward orientalism," which is created as a result of classifying one's own people.[106]

The previous sections have shown that there is no definitional consensus on 'customary' and 'honour' killing in Turkey. This not only results in confusion and instability within the judiciary but also allows judges to interpret the crimes while supporting patriarchal attitudes that hinder justice for victims. When we remember the second part of this book's question – *How does the Turkish Penal Code deal with honour killings?* – the lack of definition and the ensuing confusion

101 Assembly of the Criminal Chambers 2011/1–138 E, 2011/130 K, Date: 14.06.2011; Assembly of the Criminal Chambers 2011/1–52 E, 2011/180 K, Date: 20.09.2011; Assembly of the Criminal Chambers 2012/1–76 E, 2012/258 K, Date: 03.07.2012.

102 The original definition is 'Bazı bölgelerde geleneksel anlayışlara uymama sebebiyle genellikle genç kız veya kadınların ailesinin kararıyla yine aileden biri tarafindan öldürülmesi, namus cinayeti' <www.tdk.gov.tr/index.php?option=com_gts&arama=gts&guid=TDK.GTS.52174e01c49880.09247367>accessed 23 August 2019.

103 Assembly of the Criminal Chambers 2010/111 E, 2010/32606 K, Date: 15.10.2010; Assembly of the Criminal Chambers 2011/1–52 E, 2011/180 K, Date: 20.09.2011.

104 Izmir 6th High Criminal Court 2007/359 E, 2009/52 K, Date: 30.03.2009; Tarsus High Criminal Court 2010/117 E, 2010/245 K, Date: 03.08.2010; Duzce High Criminal Court 2008/29 E, 2009/208 K, Date: 27.08.2009; Bakırköy 15th High Criminal Court 2009/116 E, 2011/217 K, Date: 13.05.2011.

105 Edward W Said, *Orientalism* (London, Penguin Books 2003) 31.

106 Serdar Poyraz, 'Thinking About Turkish Modernization: Cemil Meriç N Turkish Language, Culture, and Intellectuals' (2006) 26 Comparative Studies of South Asia, Africa, and the Middle East 434, 441.

this caused shows that the current law related to honour killings is insufficient to tackle this type of violence and that the conceptualisation of honour killings should be made carefully, considering the victims, not the social norms and rules that allow VAW to be perpetrated in the name of honour.

After analysing the definitions of customary killings from different perspectives and addressing the problems related to this approach, the next section aims to further analyse how the Turkish legal system deals with honour killings, specifically considering the defence mechanism that is applied to honour killing cases.

2.2.2 Defence mechanism and honour killings

The most controversial defence that is applied to honour killing cases is the defence of provocation. The provocation defence, as stated under s.29 of the Turkish Penal Code, has various elements. The Code states:

> A person committing an offense with effect of anger or asperity caused by the unjust act is sentenced to imprisonment from eighteen years to twenty-four years instead of aggravated life imprisonment, and to imprisonment from twelve years to eighteen years instead of life imprisonment. In other cases, the punishment is abated from one-fourth up to three thirds.

According to this section, the elements of provocation are:

- There should be an action (said or done) that is provocative
- This action should be unjust
- This provocative unjust action should be caused by the victim
- This provocative and unjust action should cause anger or asperity for the perpetrator
- The crime should be committed with the effect of this anger or asperity

The second and the last elements have particular importance for honour killing cases. The preamble of s.29 specifically mentions that the main reason for seeking to prove that an 'unjust action' has taken place is to prevent a perpetrator from using this defence for the murders committed under s.82/1-k. The preamble of the section explains that the perpetrator shall not benefit from an unjust provocation defence if the unjust action was caused because of an offence committed against the victim previously.[107] In order to make this explanation clearer, the preamble provides a specific example: If a father/brother murders his daughter/sister because she was raped or sexually assaulted, the unjust provocation defence shall not be available to those perpetrators. The example clearly excludes unjust provocation in the case of sexual assault and rape; yet the other types of motive remain unclear. In order to eliminate this lack of clarity, the

107 Preamble s.29.

preamble explains what 'unjust action' means: action that is not approved by law.[108] However, while the preamble is intended to provide a path for judges to determine whether an action can be deemed unjust, it actually causes more complication in practice.

The complexity starts with the wording 'not approved,' which the preamble uses instead of 'forbidden by law.' The problem here is that it is quite unclear what it is meant by 'not approved': specifically, who will decide, and according to which criteria it will be decided, that the action is not approved by law. This takes us directly to the judges, who have the power to create precedents. In the literature, it has been argued that the judges should consider the law as a whole when considering the issue of 'not approved by law.'[109] Following this subjective approach, judges would consider not only the written but also the unwritten law, as well as the social values prominent within society.[110] However, some academics have criticised this approach, arguing that judges should consider the action based on objective elements, and that prominent social values should be excluded from that consideration.[111]

It is my argument that in order to eliminate the possibility of admitting an unjust provocation defence in honour killing cases, judges should follow the second approach, as the first approach can easily result in fatal consequences and injustice for the victims. If subjective criteria are considered and social values are taken into account, then all the motives behind honour killings might be considered as 'unjust' by the judges. As Demren Donmez argues, this would be incompatible with the scope of the Penal Code and might lead to a reduction in the punishment of honour killing.[112] Following a subjective approach and considering the law as a whole, including the unwritten law, would also mean accepting the customary laws that permit VAW in the name of honour. As discussed in the previous chapter, allowing this form of customary law interpretation favours perpetrators and patriarchal society at the expense of victims.

Apart from the wording of 'not approved by law,' the preamble is also problematic in how it addresses honour killing cases. The preamble states that honour killings are murders that are committed by relatives within families.[113] Therefore,

108 Ibid.

109 Mahmut Koca and Ilhan Uzulmez, *Turk Ceza Hukuku Genel Hukumler* (Ankara, Seckin 2008) 276–77.

110 Ibid. 277; Mehmet Emin Artuk, Ahmet Gokcen, and Ahmet Caner Yenidunya, *Ceza Hukuku Genel Hukumler I* (2nd edn, Ankara, Adalet Yayinevi 2006) 688; Nur Centel, Hamide Zafer, and Ozlem Cakmut, *Turk Ceza Hukukuna Giris* (6th edn, Istanbul, Beta 2010) 432–33.

111 Bahri Ozturk and Mustafa R Erdem, *Uygulamali Ceza Hukuku ve Guvenlik Tedbirleri Hukuku* (11th edn, Ankara, Seckin 2011) 283; Burcu Demren Donmez, 'Ceza Sorumlulugunu Azaltan Bir Neden Olarak Haksiz Tahrik' (2013) 71 Istanbul Universitesi Hukuk Fakultesi Mecmuasi 267, 280; Centel, Zafer, and Cakmut (n 111) 433.

112 Demren Donmez (n 112) 280.

113 The same approach was also followed by Bekir Bozdag (a member of parliament) during the discussion of s. 29 of the Penal Code. The speech is available at <www.tbmm.gov.tr/develop/owa/tutanak_b_sd.birlesim_baslangic?P4=12465&P5=B&page1=52&page2=52> accessed 10 September 2019.

according to this explanation, any murder that is committed in the name of honour by an unrelated offender could benefit from the unjust provocation defence. For instance, if a man murders his ex-wife for being in a relationship after his divorce, he could benefit from section 29, because the victim and the perpetrator would no longer be relatives (assuming the marriage was not already between relatives) after the divorce was settled. Moreover, if a man murders his wife in a marriage that is customary/religious but not registered, for the sake of honour, he is eligible to raise an unjust provocation defence, as they would not be relatives according to the law. As Goztepe argues, because honour killing perpetrators are not always relatives, the preamble's approach at this point works for the benefit of many perpetrators and should be abandoned.[114] At this stage, then, it is crucial to focus on the practice of offering such a defence and how judges deal with complex situations such as these in cases.

Although the Penal Code provides an explanation of the meaning of 'unjust provocation,' the courts also prefer to provide their own definition. For instance, Duzce High Criminal Court, Gaziantep 2nd High Criminal Court, Kayseri 2nd High Criminal Court, and Kirsehir High Criminal Court are some of the first-degree courts that follow this approach during trials. Kirsehir and Gaziantep High Criminal Courts tend to follow the subjective approach to explaining unjust provocation. For instance, Kirsehir High Criminal Court stated in one of its decisions that actions that are against custom/tradition and regional moral values are also unjust.[115] In this case, the Court considered the perpetrator's social situation and education and the size of the town (in this case, a small town where people knew each other well, and where gossip might spread quickly) where the crime was committed when it considered 'unjust provocation.'[116] Similarly, Gaziantep High Criminal Court stated that "according to the regional customs and traditions Hafize's elope to Hikmet is an action that causes unjust provocation."[117] Duzce and Kayseri High Criminal Courts, on the other hand, followed the objective approach when explaining unjust provocation.[118] This shows that there is still no consensus within the First Degree Courts regarding the explanation of unjust provocation.

While the situation is inconsistent among the First Degree Courts, the Appeal Court offers a more promising picture. It usually prefers the safe approach while explaining 'unjust provocation'; it refers to the Penal Code and its preamble and

114 Ece Goztepe, 'Namus Cinayetlerinin Hukuki Boyutu: Yeni Turk Ceza Kanunu'nun Bir Degerlendirmesi' (2005) 59 Turkiye Barolar Birligi Dergisi 29, 44.

115 Kirsehir High Criminal Court 2007/54 E, 2007/68 K, Date: 17.05.2007. The Court continued to say that, even if the action contravenes custom and tradition, if it is lawful it should not be considered unjust. See also Department No:1 of the Criminal Appeal Court 2014/4124 E, 2014/4693 K, Date: 22.10.2014.

116 Ibid.

117 Gaziantep 2nd High Criminal Court 2008/275 E, 2008/318 K, Date: 11.11.2008. Because the crime was committed in 1992, both the abolished Penal Code and the provocation defence were applied to this case.

118 Duzce High Criminal Court 2008/29 E, 2009/208 K, Date: 27.08.2009; Kayseri 2nd High Criminal Court 2007/32 E, 2007/181 K, Date: 29.05.2007.

avoids using secondary sources.[119] The Assembly of the Criminal Chambers, on the other hand, refers not only to the Penal Code and its preamble but also to the literature,[120] which may cause further complication.

2.2.2.1 APPLICATION OF PROVOCATION DEFENCE IN HONOUR KILLING CASES

While the definitions of 'unjust' and 'not approved by law' are blurred in both the Penal Code and its preamble, it is important to analyse how the judges interpret these phrases in cases. The below cases show that neither the First Degree Courts nor the Appeal Court are in agreement about which situations are accepted as triggers for unjust provocation. Probably the only consensus that the courts have reached is on the matter of infidelity.

Although adultery was abolished as a crime in the Turkish Penal Code, infidelity is still considered to be a strong source of provocation in Turkish criminal law. This is because even if infidelity is no longer a criminal action, it is considered by civil law to be strong justification for divorce. Therefore, the criminal courts treat infidelity as an action that is 'not approved by law.'[121] For instance, suspecting or discovering a spouse's extra-marital relationship has been considered a legitimate motive for unjust provocation by many First Degree Courts and the Appeal Court.[122] In one case, in which the perpetrator murdered his wife because of a suspected relationship with his friend, Adana 2nd High Criminal Court decided that the victim's behaviour had caused unjust provocation and that s.29 should therefore be applied.[123]

It is important to highlight that it is not only husbands who are considered within the context of unjust provocation in cases of infidelity, but also other family members, such as brothers, sons, and uncles. In one case, in which a woman was murdered by her sons and brother-in-law for having an affair, Gaziantep 2nd

119 Department No:1 of the Criminal Appeal Court 2011/2467 E, 2011/6863 K, Date: 17.11.2011; Department No:1 of the Criminal Appeal Court 2012/838 E, 2012/3806 K, 10.05.2012.

120 Assembly of the Criminal Chambers 2011/1–138 E, 2011/130 K, Date: 14.06.2011.

121 "Even if the defendant discovered his ex-wife's infidelity during their marriage after their divorce, because of the social environment that he belongs to and his cultural background, it should be accepted that he committed the crime under the unjust provocation." (Aksaray High Criminal Court 2006/367 E, 2008/14 K, Date: 05.02.2008).

122 It is important to highlight here that the courts consider fidelity to be an obligation only between legally married spouses. Both the first instance and the Appeal Courts exclude *imam nikahi* (religious marriages) from offering the defence of unjust provocation in the case of infidelity. (Duzce High Criminal Court 2008/29 E, 2009/208 K, Date: 27.08.2009; Department No:1 of the Criminal Appeal Court 2005/1329 E, 2006/587 K, Date: 10.03.2006; Department No:1 of the Criminal Appeal Court 2010/2637 E, 2010/7269 K, Date: 08.11.2010; Department No:1 of the Criminal Appeal Court 2008/8615 E, 2009/6878 K, Date: 11.11.2009; Assembly of the Criminal Chambers 2013–1/665 E, 2014/66 K, Date: 11.02.2014).

123 Adana 2nd High Criminal Code 2007/36 E, 2008/167 K, Date: 29.05.2008.

High Criminal Court applied an unjust provocation defence for the perpetrators.[124] The Court held that:

> With considering the social environment where the perpetrators and the victim live and their cultural environment, the Court reached the decision that the crime was committed under the unjust provocation.[125]

In a similar case, Adiyaman High Criminal Court applied an unjust provocation defence to a perpetrator who murdered his mother because of her relationship out of wedlock, which was discovered by members of the community.[126]

These decisions are problematic in two ways. First, the courts followed the approach of extending the fidelity obligation from spouses to the whole family by including sons and uncles as the beneficiaries of an unjust provocation defence. This shows us that the courts still consider women's sexual activities out of wedlock as the concern of not only their husbands but also the whole family, which reminds us of the collective male ownership of women's bodies we witness in classic patriarchal societies. Yet, although the Turkish Civil Code accepts infidelity as grounds for divorce and compensation for the spouse, this is not the case for other family members. Why, then, are those family members able to ask for an unjust provocation defence during criminal cases? The only explanation can be the continuing patriarchal approach of judges and prosecutors who believe that women's bodies belong to their families. Another problematic point is that in these two decisions, the courts adopted the subjective approach while deciding on unjust provocation by considering the society to which the perpetrators belong and that society's cultural norms.[127] This proves that judges do not always consider the situation from the perspective of the victims, or view women's autonomy as their human right, but look through the eyes of society, which allows them to reach a patriarchal interpretation.

Recognising the inequality and lack of gender consciousness in such cases, Adana High Criminal Court decided in 2012 that infidelity could only be considered as a defence of unjust provocation between spouses. Therefore, when Ahmet murdered his mother's lover after discovering their relationship, this was not considered a provocation defence as there was no fidelity obligation between mothers and sons.[128] This was an important decision for feminists and activists, who could see that patriarchal domination within the judiciary had, however imperceptibly, begun to crack.

124 Gaziantep 2nd High Criminal Court 2007/396 E, 2008/177 K, Date: 01.05.2008.
125 Ibid.
126 Adiyaman 1st High Criminal Court 2007/17 E, 2007/177 K, Date: 13.11.2008.
127 Ibid; Gaziantep 2nd High Criminal Court 2007/396 E, 2008/177 K, Date: 01.05.2008.
128 Adana 1st High Criminal Court 2011/182 E, 2012/91 K, Date: 02.03.2012.

The courts consider the fidelity obligation not only between spouses, but also between ex-husbands and wives. In several decisions, the courts accepted an unjust provocation defence for an ex-husband when his ex-wife started another relationship after she had obtained a divorce. For instance, Aysel was injured and her lover murdered in Izmir because she started a relationship with another man after she got divorced. Izmir 6th Criminal Court followed a very strict patriarchal approach that denied women's autonomy and bodily integrity.[129] The facts that the Court considered as the reasons for unjust provocation were:

- Aysel started a new relationship with someone right after she divorced
- Aysel took her five children and moved to be with her lover
- Aysel got married to her lover with a religious ceremony
- Aysel's lover was already married under Civil Law

None of the above-mentioned situations were approved by society.

In another case, the Court stated that:

> We cannot ignore the culture and traditions of the society we live in, the family structure and its values. It is not acceptable for a woman, who was divorced and had three children, to live with someone without valid marriage (nikah), to leave their children for that, and to start working in a pub.[130] Therefore, it is understood that, the defendant committed the crime with the unjust provocation caused by the victim.[131]

These decisions remind us why the feminist campaigns on sexual autonomy began in Turkey, and why they are never-ending. These decisions, in a way, support the patriarchal ideology that sees women's bodies as subject of ownership, and that this ownership is obtained by husbands through marriage.[132] If we remember our earlier discussion relating to how marriages are considered to be contracts that give husbands right of ownership over their wives' bodies, we should also remember that this ownership is usually considered 'permanent' for the husbands. Even when the couple is divorced, the husband assumes that he still owns his ex-wife's body, because he still believes that his *namus* is dependent on her sexual behaviours.

What we also see from these decisions is that the courts implicitly accept the patriarchal belief that divorced women should act within the boundaries of social norms, and because their ex-husbands are still their children's fathers, ex-husbands

129 Izmir 6th High Criminal Court 2007/359 E, 2009/52 K, Date: 30.03.2009.

130 'Pub' in the Turkish context refers to a place that serves alcohol, mainly to men, and it is considered shameful for a woman to work in or to enter pubs.

131 Denizli 1st High Criminal Court 2006/289 E, 2007/74 K, Date: 20.02.2007.

132 Danielle Hoyek, Rafif Rida Sidawi, and Amira Abou Mrad, 'Murders of Women in Lebanon: Crimes of Honour Between Reality and The Law' in Lynn Welchman and Sara Hossain (eds), *'Honour': Crimes, Paradigms, and Violence Against Women* (London, Zed Books Ltd 2005) 113.

are still responsible in society for their ex-wives' behaviours. This hegemonic ideology was also supported by one of the prisoners whom I interviewed in 2012. Salih murdered his ex-wife for being in a relationship with someone else after their divorce. Salih mentioned that:

> I warned her that she could not drift apart even if we divorced because she was my children's mother. If she got married with dignity after our divorce, this (murder) would not happen. But, it was impossible to accept what she did.[133]

Although the First Degree Courts still follow the patriarchal approach and tend to apply unjust provocation in cases of infidelity, one court case underlines the importance of the meaning of infidelity and its scope. Manisa 2nd High Criminal Court stated that infidelity should be considered as limited to a sexual relationship.[134] The Court underlined that although s.185 of the Civil Code requires fidelity within marriage, this does not include restricting the spouses' lives. According to the Court, infidelity does not cover:

- Talking to someone who is not a family member
- Having male friends
- Talking on the internet
- Going out alone
- Going to a cinema or a café[135]

Manisa 2nd High Criminal Court instead highlighted that

> if the above mentioned situations are considered as infidelity, then it means that the courts approved the patriarchal ideology of the society that treats women as if they belong to their male relatives or families and allowing so-called traditional practices that requires punishing females for being 'dishonourable.'[136]

Although this decision was criticised previously in this book for being biased against Kurds, it was still an important decision for showing gender consciousness. As mentioned in Chapter 2, feminists in Turkey are very much concerned with not only individual but also state patriarchy, and they hope now that if the courts follow this approach then state patriarchy will be damaged; and, in the long term, this will have a top-down effect on individual patriarchy.

While the First Degree Courts' approach still provides some evidence of the patriarchal ideology of the judges, it is also necessary to consider the Appeal

133 Interview with Salih (3 September 2012).
134 Manisa 2nd High Criminal Court 2011/246 E, 2012/153 K, Date: 14.05.2012.
135 Ibid.
136 Ibid.

Court's decisions. The Appeal Court is almost unswerving in its belief that infidelity should be considered as unjust provocation in murder cases. It has stated in many decisions that spouses are under an obligation to be faithful in marriage according to s.185 of the Turkish Civil Code, and that if a murder is committed against a spouse because of his/her infidelity, then the First Degree Courts should consider an unjust provocation defence.[137] However, it should be underlined that the Appeal Court mainly considers infidelity as an unjust provocation defence only for spouses, not for other family members.[138] For instance, in 2010 it decided that the unjust provocation defence was not applicable to a perpetrator who murdered his sister because of her infidelity.[139] This is a promising picture, showing that the Court considers the obligation of fidelity as quite narrowly applicable.

While society still follows the strong patriarchal approach and considers women to be the property of men, the above-mentioned examples show that the State's approach has been changing in favour of victims, albeit at a snail's pace. Although the State has started to limit its acceptance of an unjust provocation defence in cases of infidelity, allowing spouses to benefit from this defence still causes huge problems within the judiciary, with the result that many honour killing cases are adjudicated in favour of offenders because of their spouses' infidelity allegations. This means that courts turn a blind eye to honour killing cases and do not apply section 82/1-k, with its opportunity for harsher punishment.

Apart from infidelity, the Penal Courts also consider other situations as motives for unjust provocation. For instance, in 2008 Bakırköy 5th High Criminal Court stated during the trial that Nuran's murder by her family, which took place because she had run away from home and was raped after she left home, should not be considered as a motive for unjust provocation, as there had been no provocative action caused by the victim when she run away from home and was raped.[140] However, during the same year, Gaziantep 2nd High Criminal Code accepted an unjust provocation defence for a perpetrator who murdered his daughter for eloping.[141] In applying this unjust provocation defence, the Court considered

137 Department No:1 of the Criminal Appeal Court, 2013/372 E, 2013/3427 K, Date: 30.04.2013; Department No:1 of the Criminal Appeal Court 2012/3769 E, 2012/8528 K, Date: 21.11.2012; Department No:1 of the Criminal Appeal Court 2009/248 E, 2009/3297 K, Date: 08.06.2009.

138 Department No:1 of the Criminal Appeal Court 2010/4522 E, 2011/1511 K, Date: 15.03.2011; Department No:1 of the Criminal Appeal Court 2010//5426 E, 2011/1760 K, Date: 23.03.2011; Department No:1 of the Criminal Appeal Court 2008/248 E, 2009/3287 K, Date: 08.06.2009.

139 Department No:1 of the Criminal Appeal Court 2009/8804 E, 2010/4214 K, Date: 07.06.2010. For similar situation see also Department No:1 of the Criminal Appeal Court 2010/5426 E, 2011/1760 K, Date: 23.03.2011. Department No:1 of the Criminal Appeal Court 2014/923 E, 2014/3551 K, Date: 17.06.2014. (One member of the panel provided a disentail vote and said that the fidelity obligation should be considered only between the spouses.)

140 Bakırköy 5th High Criminal Court 2007/269 E, 2008/27 K, Date: 04.02.2008.

141 Gaziantep 2nd High Criminal Court 2008/275 E, 2008/318 K, Date: 11.11.2008.

the social environment in which the perpetrator lived and the cultural and traditional norms followed by his society.[142] In this decision, the Court unfortunately demonstrated tacit acceptance of the cultural norms that allow VAW in the name of family honour by applying a subjective interpretation considering social and cultural norms when reaching its decision.

Although some courts still tend to follow the approach of taking cultural and traditional norms and customs into account during trials, the majority of recent cases have shown that this patriarchal attitude has been softened. The courts have started to consider having sexual relationships out of wedlock as a right of women and as exercising their freedom of choice. For instance, in 2006 Elbistan High Criminal Court stated that the victim's choice to have a relationship with a married man should not be accepted as an unjust provocation of her brother, as the victim was an adult who was responsible for her own actions and choices.[143]

The Appeal Court also considers not applying an unjust provocation defence in cases where the victims are killed because of their relationships and behaviours. For instance, in 2009 the Appeal Court held that:

> The victim was only responsible for her own decisions; she has no responsibility towards her brother. Therefore, her relationship should not be considered as unjust provocation for the perpetrator.[144]

In this approach, the Appeal Court not only showed that it has developed gender consciousness but also proved that the ideology of women's bodies belonging to their families has started to dissolve in the eyes of the State. However, the same thing cannot be said for society yet. Up-rooting this deep-lying patriarchal ideology from society will take longer.

This section has analysed the criminalisation of honour killings and how this is interpreted by the State and the judiciary. As discussed, the conceptualisation of honour killings is confusing, and there is almost no consensus between State

142 Ibid.

143 Elbistan High Criminal Court 2006/201 E, 2006/322 K, Date: 19.12.2006. For a similar approach, see Ankara 3rd High Criminal Court 2004/545 E, 2005/235 K, Date: 11.11.2005; Odemis High Criminal Court 2010/172 E, 2011/78 K, Date: 15.03.2011; Kayseri 2nd High Criminal Court 2011/177 E, 2011/212 K, Date: 30.06.2011; Igdir High Criminal Court 2011/34 E, 2011/69 K, Date: 05.05.2011.

144 Department No:1 of the Criminal Appeal Court 2008/359 E, 2009/3640 K, Date: 17.06.2009. For a similar approach, see also Department No:1 of the Criminal Appeal Court 2008/6048 E, 2009/1039 K, Date: 03.03.2009; Department No:1 of the Criminal Appeal Court 2008/7373 E, 2009/2154 K, Date: 15.04.2009; Department No:1 of the Criminal Appeal Court 2009/270 E, 2009/6891 K, Date: 11.11.2009; Department No:1 of the Criminal Appeal Court 2009/2674 E, 2011/4286 K, Date: 05.07.2011; Department No:1 of the Criminal Appeal Court 2009/2965 E, 2009/1533 K, Date: 24.03.2009; Department No:1 of the Criminal Appeal Court 2009/8192 E, 2010/7538 K, Date: 24.11.2010; Department No:1 of the Criminal Appeal Court 2009/9808 E, 2010/4917 K, Date: 01.07.2010; Department No:1 of the Criminal Appeal Court 2012/3659 E, 2012/9331 K, Date: 12.12.2012.

authorities as to what causes injustice for the victims of this crime. The section has shown that although there has been some improvement in gender consciousness in the various honour killings cases in Turkey, there is still strong evidence that a patriarchal interpretation of the law is often applied that supports not the victims but rather the perpetrators. The next section looks at whether the patriarchal approach of State authorities is still evidenced within the criminal justice system in Turkey by considering different stages of the justice system.

3. The criminal justice system and honour killings

After analysing the laws and how they are applied during honour killing cases, it is also necessary to highlight how these killings stand under the Turkish criminal justice system in order to examine whether the State follows a patriarchal and traditional approach that allows all forms of VAW. To do this, this section starts by analysing the detention and custodial period. Following this, evidence collection, prosecution, trial, and, finally, sentencing will be explained to give the whole picture of the criminal justice system. Each section highlights different problems that hinder justice for honour killing victims. As discussed below, they show not only the patriarchal approach but also a lack of gender consciousness and a lack of necessary conditions to deter the crime and eliminate honour killings.

3.1 Denunciation, detention, and the police's approach to honour killings

As in many other jurisdictions, in Turkey the criminal procedure usually starts with either the police or the gendarme's involvement.[145] The police or the gendarmes either discover incidents by themselves or start the investigation after a report or accusation. Starting an investigation into suspected honour killing cases, however, usually has its own character, which is different to many other crimes.

If the motives and reasons for committing HBV are remembered, the perpetrators usually commit this crime either to protect or to restore family honour.[146] Therefore, committing an honour killing is considered a duty, usually by families to regain their reputation, and because of that, as Farac argues, sometimes crimes have been traditionally committed in public for quick honour restoration.[147] For instance, the murder of Rabia, which led to huge media attention, is one of the

145 According to the Jandarma Teşkilat, Görev ve Yetkileri Kanunu section 10, a gendarme is on duty where police forces are not located (Law No: 2803, Date enforced 10.03.1983, available at <www.mevzuat.gov.tr/MevzuatMetin/1.5.2803.pdf> accessed 7 September 2019). Gendarmes are mainly located in small villages.

146 Musa Öztürk and Mehmet Ali Demirdağ, 'Namusu/Nu Kanla Temizleyenler: Mardin Cezaevi'nde Namus Davası Nedeniyle Yatan Mahkumlar Üzerine Bir Araştırma' (2013) 7 Sosyal Politika Calışmaları 117, 122–24.

147 Mehmet Farac, *Töre Kıskacında Kadın* (Istanbul, Günizi Yayıncılık 2006) 49–64.

well-known honour killings that took place in public.[148] Rabia was hit by a tractor driven by her cousins, in order to punish her for the shame she had brought to her family for being in a sexual relationship out of wedlock.[149] Even though she screamed for help, people in the centre of the village pretended not to see or hear anything. This was similar to the case of Hatice, a young woman murdered by her husband in a public park because of her infidelity.[150]

Following public or non-public murders, the perpetrators usually prefer either to call the police or give themselves up to the police. As with public murder, even in private murders, the perpetrators believe that in this way they have fulfilled their duty, shame has been cleansed, and honour has been restored. It is quite common for the perpetrators to admit, 'I did it for honour'[151] when they first call the police or give themselves up. More than 66% of the prison participants of this research also supported this argument by declaring that they gave themselves up to the police.[152] The important question here is: Although the perpetrators believe that customary law should be obeyed and that the judgement of society is very important, why do they give themselves up to the police, state representatives who have no direct link to society or to customary law? First, perpetrators are aware that what they have done is a criminal act (42% of the prisoners interviewed for this research declared that they were guilty),[153] despite their belief that they have fulfilled a duty approved by the community.[154] Although perpetrators usually believe that honour killing should not be criminalised and that the State should be blamed for severely punishing them, they still think that if the State puts them in prison for what they have done, then they will serve their sentence with their heads held high.[155] Second, the perpetrators believe that the police are on their side, which means that the police/gendarmes will consider the incident by taking customary law and tradition into account.

Let us have a close look at the second issue, in which the perpetrators believe that the police are on their side. Despite the fact that a large number of people within society do not really trust and do not have a good relationship with the police forces in Turkey,[156] when it comes to honour killing cases, they consider

148 Ibid.; Aysan Sev'er and Gokcecicek Yurdakul, 'Culture of Honor, Culture of Change: A Feminist Analysis of Honor Killings Rural Turkey' (2001) 7 Violence Against Women 964, 981; Amand Kirti, Prateek Kumar, and Rachana Yadav, 'The Face of Honour Based Crimes: Global Concerns and Solutions' (2011) 6 International Journal of Criminal Justice Sciences 343, 350.
149 Farac (n 148) 53–54.
150 Sanliurfa 1st High Criminal Court 2005/178 E, 2005/200 K, Date: 04.10.2005.
151 It is translated as '*Namusum için öldürdüm.*' This is a sentence that is very commonly used by perpetrators after committing honour killings. Pervizat (n 83) 147.
152 Please see Appendix 1.5.
153 Please see Appendix 1.9.
154 Pervizat (n 83) 147.
155 Ibid.
156 M Emin İnal, Esen Gürbüz and Mehmet Peşmen, 'Halkın Polis Güçlerine ve Polis Hizmetlerine Bakış Açısı Üzerine Bir Araştırma: Niğde Örneği' (2006) 39 Amme İdaresi

police officers from the point of view of the perpetrators. There are several reasons for this. From the perspective of the victims and the NGOs, the common belief is that the police still follow strict patriarchal attitudes and support cultural norms and traditions in society.[157] Not only in the case of HBV but also in the case of any form of domestic violence, the police are still thought to support the perpetrators rather than the victims by following strict patriarchal gender role divisions.[158] For instance, according to a survey conducted by Ünal et al., a large number of domestic violence victims reported that the police officers treated them badly, and that they were not referred to the appropriate social services by the police.[159] It is also quite well known that in many domestic violence incidents, police officers try to convince victims to return their homes, or they call families to collect their female relatives from the police station.[160] In many cases, the police do not consider victim complaints seriously; they tolerate the violence[161] and act as mediators between victims and families.[162] The police's biased

---

Dergisi 71, 79–80, 86; Abdullah Yılmaz and M Kemal Demirci, 'Polis-Halk İlişkilerini Vatandaşların Değerlendirmeleri Üzerine Bir Araştırma' (2004) 11 Dumlupınar Üniversitesi Sosyal Bilimler Dergisi 83. For the police's disproportionate use of force, please see Esra Ercan Bilgiç and Zehra Kafkaslı, 'Gencim, Özgürlükçüyüm, Ne İstiyorum?' (Istanbul, İstanbul Bilgi Üniversitesi 2013) <www.bilgiyay.com/Content/files/DIRENGEZI.pdf> accessed 14 August 2019; Human Rights Watch, '"He Loves You, He Beats You": Family Violence in Turkey and Access to Protection' (New York, Human Rights Watch 2011) <www.hrw.org/sites/default/files/reports/turkey0511webwcover.pdf> accessed 10 April 2019.

157 Elif Gazioğlu, 'Kadın Cinayetleri: Kavramsallaştırma ve Sorunlu Yaklaşımlar' (2013) 7 Sosyal Politika Calışmaları 89, 90; Kardam (n 16) 33; Jorgen Lovdal, 'The Trial of Kerem Cakan: The Turkish Judiciary and Honour Killings' (Kurdish Human Rights Project, Vakad, The Norwegian Bar Association 2011) 11, 14; Aylin Akpinar, 'Honour/Shame Complex Revisited: Violence Against Women in the Migration Context' (2003) 26 Women's Studies International Forum 425, 428.

158 Aysan Sever, 'In the Name of Fathers: Honour Killings and Some Examples from South Eastern Turkey' (2005) 30 Atlantis: Women's Studies Journal 129, 132.

159 Süheyla Ünal and others, 'Aile İçi Şiddet Mağdurlarının Polise Başvurularında Polise Uygun Davranış Modellerinin Kazandırılması' (2011) <http://suconleme.org/wp-content/uploads/2013/02/18-Aile-%C4%B0%C3%A7i-%C5%9Eiddet-Ma%C4%9Fdurlar%C4%B1n%C4%B1n-Polise-Ba%C5%9Fvurular%C4%B1nda-Polise-Uygun-Davran%C4%B1%C5%9F.pdf> accessed 14 September 2019.

160 Gülseren Ülker, 'Kadın Hareketinin Türkiye'de Kadına Yönelik Şiddet İle İlgili Mücadele Deneyimi "Anadolu'nun Orta Yerinde Şiddete Karşı Kadınlar Elele"' in *1. Kadın Sağlığı Kongresi: 'Kadına Yönelik Şiddet'* (Ankara, UNFPA 2008) <www.ttb.org.tr/kutuphane/kadinsaglikikong.pdf?ref=herseybedava.info#page=50> accessed 14 September 2013; Human Rights Watch (n 157) 36.

161 Tutku Ayhan, 'Protecting the Woman or the Family? Contradiction Between the Law and Its Practice in Violence Against Woman Cases in Turkey' (2017) 5 Marmara University Journal of Political Science 137; Bülent Günal, 'Devletin Koruyamayıp Ölümün Kucağına Attığı Kadınların Hikayeleri' *Habertürk* (İstanbul, 25 February 2011) <www.haberturk.com/yasam/haber/604679-devletin-koruyamayip-olumun-kucagina-attigi-kadinlarin-hikayeleri> accessed 14 September 2019.

162 *Opuz v Turkey* [2010] 50 EHRR 28; Gökçesu Özgül, 'Türkiye'de Kadın Cinayetleri Gerçeği ve Durdurmak İçin Çözüm Yolları' in *Değişen Dünyada Biyoetik* (Istanbul, Türkiye Biyoetik Derneği Yayını 2012) 160.

and discriminatory approach to domestic violence has been asserted not only by national sources but also by the ECtHR, during the *Opuz v Turkey* case,[163] when the ECtHR reached the decision that there had been a violation of article 3 of the European Convention on Human Rights as a result of the State authorities' failure to protect the victim from violence.[164]

More than this, in some situations how police officers behave might suggest that they support the perpetrators. Onal, for instance, discovered during one of her interviews with a perpetrator that the police had been very kind to him and that he had been treated well by police officers.[165] Like many other honour killing perpetrators, he was considered a 'victim of fate.'[166] Similarly, in an interview with a journalist who witnessed an interrogation of an honour killing case, Kardam highlights that the police officers offered the perpetrator some tea and a cigarette and congratulated him during the interrogation.[167] Of course, it is not possible to generalise from these two examples that all police officers are on the side of offenders, but such incidents still provide us with some evidence of their biased behaviour.

The police/gendarmes are not only accused of being patriarchal and following cultural and traditional norms, they are also blamed for not collecting evidence properly or not investigating incidents thoroughly enough in cases of HBV. This is particularly so when the incidents are reported as accidents or when murders are reported as suicides.[168] For instance, in Diyarbakir, Aysel's death was reported as a suicide and no further investigation was carried out by the police.[169] However, Aysel's mother applied to the local NGO, KAMER, and requested some help to convince the police and the prosecutors that it was an honour killing.[170] Unfortunately, due to lack of evidence, the authorities closed the case.[171]

Although perpetrators and their families tend to confess to the murder, sometimes they prefer to keep it secret in order to escape punishment. Different reasons can be offered for this particular behaviour. One is that, as will be explained below, the punishments have increased considerably for honour killings, and this may be having a deterrent effect on perpetrators.[172] Another reason is that the perpetrators and their families believe that they have done something right and necessary, and therefore do not deserve any State punishment for their actions.[173] As discussed earlier, because of the strong traditional patriarchal ideology that is supported by so-called customs, the consequences of loss of honour need to be

163 *Opuz v Turkey* [2010] 50 EHRR 28.
164 *Opuz v Turkey* [2009] European Court of Human Rights 33401/02.
165 Onal (n 2) 94.
166 Ibid.
167 Kardam (n 16) 33.
168 Interview with Elcioglu Tulay, 'KAMER, Mardin' (17 July 2012).
169 Interview with Nilufer Yilmaz, 'KAMER, Diyarbakir' (28 June 2012).
170 Ibid.
171 Ibid.
172 Ibid.
173 Pervizat (n 83) 147.

removed by taking positive action if the family is to remain in society. That is why perpetrators, families, and societies as a whole believe that killing should be done according to society's norms.

For instance, during the interview with Kemal, who murdered his sister for becoming pregnant out of wedlock, he mentioned that although committing murder was his decision, he felt society's pressure on him to commit this crime, as it was his duty to cleanse the dishonour and it was what needed to be done.[174] He continued to say that, after the murder, everybody supported him.[175] When he was asked what would happen if he had not killed his sister, he mentioned that:

> Shame would remain, my family and the society would ostracize me, I would not be able to look at anyone's face, and someone else would kill her anyway.[176]

His statement supports our earlier discussion on the serious consequences of loss of honour for individuals and for their families. Offenders feel not only that they should cleanse the shame, but also that this is the only way to eliminate the serious consequences of loss of honour that society imposes.

If we remember the book's main question – *How and under which conditions are honour killings committed in Turkey, and how does the Turkish Penal Code deal with them?* – we realise in this section that not only law makers, judges, and prosecutors but also police officers play important roles as state actors in responding to honour killings. This section has shown that these actors unfortunately fail to provide justice for victims, and this situation has been approved by the ECtHR, as discussed above.

3.2 Prosecutors and the bill of indictment in the context of honour killings

Apart from the attitude of the police/gendarmes, it is also important to focus on how prosecutors and judges deal with honour killings in order to explore whether the patriarchal attitudes of these state actors persist and have even become institutionalised and entrenched over time. To do this, this section analyses the prosecutors' attitudes to investigating such incidents. It has been argued, similar to the situation with police and gendarmes, that the prosecutors' approach to honour killing cases are sometimes biased and demonstrate patriarchal and customary attitudes. Aylin, from an NGO called VAKAD, highlighted this issue during our interview:

> At the end of the day prosecutors and judges are members of this society. If they do not have gender consciousness and if they have a traditional

174 Interview with Kemal (7 September 2012).
175 Ibid.
176 Ibid.

backgrounds, usually, they cannot break this traditional identity and reach their professional identity.[177]

Another problem related to the prosecution of cases is that the investigation and preparation of the bill of indictment typically takes too long.[178] The Turkish Criminal Procedural Code[179] does not include any section relating to the time period within which prosecutors should conclude the bill of indictment, and obviously the nature of the cases means that the time frame for collecting evidence is crucial. However, regarding the cases collected for this research, it took several months to submit the bill of indictment to the courts.

Furthermore, when the bill of indictment is submitted to the courts to start the trials, the content of the indictment is also often problematic, demonstrating a lack of awareness of honour killings within the Turkish Prosecution Service. The majority of the cases covered in this research show that the prosecutors usually considered the cases as murder, premeditated murder, or murder of a close family member, but not honour killings (*töre cinayeti*). As Appendix 2.5 shows, the percentage of cases treated as customary killings remains 26%. For instance, in one case the prosecutor considered the case as premeditated murder when the perpetrator had killed his sister and her lover for eloping.[180] The prosecutor stated that the murder was premeditated, but there was no reference to honour killing.[181] Nonetheless, despite the fact that the prosecutor presented the case as just a premeditated murder, the Court took honour killing into account and sentenced the perpetrator accordingly.[182] In another case, however, the Court followed the prosecutor's lead and treated the case as murder rather than honour killing.[183] Unfortunately, as will be discussed below, this attitude leads to injustice for honour killing victims and shows how judges, as well as prosecutors, neglect gender consciousness. Of course, it is not possible to reach the conclusion that all judges and prosecutors strictly follow a patriarchal attitude, considering cases as simple murder rather than honour killing, but to some extent it shows that the situation is still far from desirable for women in Turkey.

3.3 Judges and trials in the context of honour killings

While the attitudes of prosecutors usually seem biased, unfortunately the situation is even more serious when it comes to the judges. The first criticism that can be made about judges actually links to the arguments raised in the previous

177 Interview with Aylin Celik, 'Van Kadin Dernegi (VAKAD), Van' (26 June 2012); Vildan Yirmibesoglu, *Töre ve Namus Gerekçesiyle İşlenen Cinayetler: Toprağa Düşen Sevdalar* (Istanbul, Hurriyet 2007) 162.
178 Human Rights Watch (n 157) 34.
179 Law No: 5274, Enforcement Date: 1 June 2005.
180 Agri High Criminal Court 2007/215 E, 2008/191 K, Date: 24.06.2008.
181 Ibid.
182 Ibid.
183 Van 2nd High Criminal Court 2009/361 E, 2013/108 K, Date: 19.03.2013.

section. Although some judges insist on considering certain cases as honour killings irrespective of prosecutors' statements, some of them still follow the prosecutors' arguments. And so, as mentioned above, a large number of murder cases that include certain elements of honour killings are still not considered as honour killings by judges. Unfortunately, the consequences of this are serious. If a case is considered under sections 81 or 82 (except 82/1-k), then judges are able to apply a general provocation defence to the cases. However, if the case is considered as an 'honour killing,' there is a legal restriction on applying this defence. Although there is no difference between the subsections of section 82 in terms of the sentence that the perpetrators receive, there is an important difference in the application of a provocation defence, and this does affect the length of the sentence. Let me draw a clearer picture and what the main concern is with the following examples.[184]

Example 1

A and B are brothers. A catches his mother, C, at D's workplace. C's hair and clothes are untidy, as are D's. D tries to zip up his trousers when A catches them. A tells this to B. A and B take their guns and run to D's workplace. They both fire; C and D die.[185]

During this (actual) case, the prosecutor and the Court considered the incident within the framework of section 81 of the Penal Code, which regulates ordinary murder. The Court sentenced A and B to life imprisonment; however, the judge applied section 29 (provocation defence), considering that the crime had been committed because of the illicit sexual relationship between the perpetrators' mother and another man, and the sentence was reduced to 12 years.[186]

Example 2

H and R are married. R runs away with I, and H discovers the elopement. H and his brothers, Y and E, decide to kill R, throw R in the sea, and report it as a suicide. By the seaside, R tells the three that she is also having a relationship with O,

184 Please see section 29 of the Turkish Penal Code in Appendix 3.

185 Kayseri 1st High Criminal Court 2007/146 E, 2007/328 K, Date: 23.11.2007.

186 Ibid. Because A was under age when the crime was committed, his sentence was reduced to six years. For similar examples of how article 81 is used instead of honour killing and how the unjust provocation defence is applied, please see Adana 2nd High Criminal Court 2008/432 E, 2009/162 K, Date: 30.04.2009; Bursa 4th High Criminal Court 2009/333 E, 2009/350 K, Date: 20.11.2009; Gaziantep 2nd High Criminal Court 2007/396 E, 2008/177 K, Date: 01.05.2008; Kastamonu High Criminal Court 2009/28 E, 2009/167 K, Date: 30.07.2009; Mardin 2nd High Criminal Court 2006/80 E, 2006/350 K, Date: 20.06.2006; Seydisehir High Criminal Court 2008/461 E, 2008/485 K, Date: 25.04.2008; Sanliurfa 1st High Criminal Court 2005/276 E, 2006/250 K, Date: 06.06.2006. For similar decisions that did not consider the mother's extramarital relationship as a form of customary killing, please see Department No:1 of the Criminal Appeal Court 2014/1502 E, 2014/3859 K, Date: 15.09.2014; Department No:1 of the Criminal Appeal Court 2014/4124 E, 2014/4693 K, Date: 22.10.2014; Department No:1 of the Criminal Appeal Court 2018/3283 E, 2018/4629 K, Date: 13.11.2018.

who is another of H's brothers; she tells them this hoping to avoid being killed. H, Y, and E return home with R and call O to come over. When O arrives, H and E stab O and R to death while Y stands guard at the front door.[187]

In this case, the Court considered s.82/1-d (murder of close family members) and sentenced the perpetrators to aggravated life imprisonment. Then, the Court applied s.29 (unjust provocation defence), considering R's confession that she was having a sexual relationship with I and O. Based on s.29, the Court reduced the sentence by two-thirds.[188] The Appeal Court, however, decided that the case should have been considered under s.82/1-k (honour killing) rather than s.82/1-d, and it reversed the judgement.[189]

These two examples show us that if judges do not consider murders as honour killings, then they are allowed to reduce the sentence given out to perpetrators considerably. From a feminist perspective, this makes us consider, first, the lack of gender consciousness among judges, and, second, the lack of understanding of the concept of honour killings and, perhaps, the holding of patriarchal attitudes. These examples not only show us the judges' attitudes but also tell us that sometimes the Appeal Court overrules judgements and request the First Degree Courts to apply s.82/1-k and not s.29.[190] Although the Court of Appeal's attitude is encouraging and has the effect of pushing the First Degree Courts judges to consider cases without ruling out the possibility of honour killing, it is still far from meeting the expectations of feminists in practice. The reason for this is the *prohibition of the reformation in peius* under Turkish Criminal Procedure Law. Section 307/4 of the Turkish Criminal Procedure Code[191] states that:

> If the motion of appeal on law was filed only by the accused, or by the Office of Public Prosecution on his favour, or by individuals mentioned in Article 262, then the punishment included in the new judgment cannot be more severe than the previous judgment.[192]

187 Kocaeli 1st High Criminal Court 2007/195 E, 2007/341 K, Date: 18.10.2007.

188 Ibid. For similar cases, please see Bakırköy 3rd High Criminal Court 2011/310 E, 2012/137 K, Date: 25.04.2012; Bakırköy 14th High Criminal Court 2007/219 E, 2009/132 K, Date: 14.05.2009; Diyarbakir 1st High Criminal Court 2011/207 E, 2012/280 K, Date: 17.05.2012; Kozan High Criminal Court 2007/282 E, 2008/30 K, Date: 24.01.2008; Kirsehir High Criminal Court 2007/54 E, 2007/68 K, Date: 17.05.2007; Osmaniye 1st High Criminal Court 2007/153 E, 2009/228 K, Date: 03.12.2009; Sanliurfa 1st High Criminal Court 2005/178 E, 2005/200 K, Date: 04.10.2005.

189 Department No:1 of the Criminal Appeal Court 2008/5009 E, 2009/5002 K, Date: 22.07.2009.

190 Ibid. The Court of Appeal also reversed the judgement in the first example mentioned above (Department No:1 of the Criminal Appeal Court 2008/7373 E, 2009/2154 K, Date: 15.04.2009). For similar Court of Appeal decisions, please see Department No:1 of the Criminal Appeal Court 2009/8192 E, 2010/7538 K, Date: 24.11.2010; Department No:1 of the Criminal Appeal Court 2008/59 E, 2009/5002 K, Date: 22.07.2009; Department No:1 of the Criminal Appeal Court 2010/3722 E, 2012/2270 K, Date: 28.03.2012.

191 Law No: 5271, Date of Acceptance: 04.12.2004, Enforcement Date: 1 June 2005.

192 Feridun Yenisey, *Turkish Criminal Procedure Code* (Istanbul, Beta 2009) 308–10.

According to this section, if the above-mentioned persons appeal the First Degree Court's decision, and even if the Appeal Court decides that the First Degree Courts should have applied other sections that would result in more severe punishment, this decision does not have any *reformation in peius* effect against the perpetrator. This is exactly what happened in the previous examples. Although the Appeal Court stated in those decisions that the First Degree Courts should have applied s.82/1-k instead of sections 81 and 82/1-a-I, this did not have any effect on the length of the sentence that the First Degree Courts had previously decided.[193] All the defences, especially s.29 (unjust provocation defence) and the reduction in sentence of up to two-thirds based on this section, are still biased in favour of the perpetrators. This is why, even if the Appeal Court reverses a judgment because of not applying s.82/1-k, this does not provide any practical benefit for the rights of the victims.[194]

Another problem related to the judges and the trials is evidence collection and length of the trials. According to the s.192 of the Turkish Criminal Procedure Code, judges are entitled to collect evidence by themselves; however, it is likely that they will tend to rely on evidence that has been collected by police officers and prosecutors in order to save time during the judicial process. Calling witnesses has particular importance at this stage. Because of the characteristics of honour killing cases (that the victims and perpetrators are mostly relatives), witness statements usually become useless during the trials. Although the witnesses testify under oath, their testimonies are often biased and designed to help the perpetrator go free or to receive less punishment. Even if the witnesses are non-relatives, their testimonies might be biased through fear of social pressure if they testify against the perpetrators.

Apart from witnesses, the length of the trials is also problematic, not only for honour killing cases but also for other criminal cases. According to the records, some honour killing cases took more than ten years to reach a decision, such as one of the cases held by the Gaziantep High Criminal Court.[195] The chronological judgement procedure for this case is as follows:

193 Department No:1 of the Criminal Appeal Court 2008/59 E, 2009/5002 K, Date: 22.07.2009; Department No:1 of the Criminal Appeal Court 2008/7373 E, 2009/2154 K, Date: 15.04.2009. For more decisions on *prohibition of the reformation in peius*, please also see Department No:1 of the Criminal Appeal Court Appeal Court 2008/59 E, 2009/5002 K, Date: 22.07.2009; Department No:1 of the Criminal Appeal Court 2009/8804 E, 2010/4214 K, Date: 07.06.2010; Department No:1 of the Criminal Appeal Court 2009/8192 E, 2010/7538 K, Date: 24.11.2010; Department No:1 of the Criminal Appeal Court 2010/3722 E, 2012/2270 K, Date: 28.03.2012; Department No:1 of the Criminal Appeal Court 2010/4522 E, 2011/1511 K, Date: 15.03.2011.

194 However, it has an effect on the points of the First Degree Courts' judges who carry out the judgement. The more the judges' decisions are reversed by the Appeal Court, the less chance they have to promote them (Decision No: 282/1 of the Supreme Council of Judges and Public Prosecutors, Date: 30.09.2011, Section: 6).

195 Gaziantep 2nd High Criminal Court 2008/275 E, 2008/318 K, Date: 11.11.2008.

- The crime was committed in 1992
- The bill of indictment was prepared after seven years in 1999
- The trial started at the First Degree Courts in 1999
- The First Degree Courts reached its decision in 2002[196]
- The Appeal Court approved the First Degree Court's decision in 2003[197]
- The Prosecution Office requested a new judgement based on the amended Penal Code in 2004
- The First Degree Courts reached its decision in 2005[198]
- The Appeal Court reversed the judgement in 2008[199]
- The First Degree Courts complied with the remittitur in 2008
- The First Degree Courts reached its final decision in 2008[200]

Such a long time to conclude one case could easily result in a loss of trust in the judiciary in Turkey, as after all these years one can lose hope in a fair judgement and non-biased decisions.

Beyond all of the above-mentioned situations, sometimes the attitudes of the judges and the judgement process also prove that victims of honour killings (especially if they are women) are not represented sufficiently during the trials. Because the crime is usually committed within families, family members usually prefer to hire lawyers to represent the perpetrators but not the victims. If that happens, the courts will appoint lawyers from the Bar Association, and in such cases, there is a possibility that the appointed lawyer will have no expertise in honour killing cases or may have the sorts of patriarchal attitudes that support VAW. Because of this, feminist groups and NGOs always ask to participate in proceedings in order to protect victims' rights, to express them, and to eliminate any possible patriarchal interpretation of the law during the case. However, in most cases they are refused. For instance, in the case of Eylem Pesen and Guldunya Toren, the courts denied VAKAD[201] and Gokkusagi's[202] request to participate with applying s.237 of the Criminal Procedure Code.[203]

196 Ibid.

197 Department No:1 of the Criminal Appeal Court 2003/968 E, 2003/1333 K, Date: 10.06.2003.

198 Gaziantep 2nd High Criminal Court 1999/287 E, 2002/323 K, Date: 10.10.2002.

199 Department No:1 of the Criminal Appeal Court 2008/1345 E, 2008/3877 K, Date: 17.04.2008.

200 Gaziantep 2nd High Criminal Court 2008/275 E, 2008/318 K, Date: 11.11.2008.

201 Van 2nd High Criminal Court 2009/361 E, 2013/108 K, Date: 19.03.2013. However, the same court accepted the participation of the Ministry of Family and Social Policies during the case.

202 Bakırköy 5th High Criminal Court 2006/303 E, 2007/458 K, Date: 12.11.2007.

203 Please see Appendix 3 for the full text of this section. The NGOs and sometimes even the Ministry of Family and Social Policies are considered not to be damaged by the crime and are refused the opportunity to participate in these cases.

As we have seen from the above, many of the trial procedures and occasional attitudes of judges are problematic during honour killing cases. The problem starts with defining the crime itself. After this problem with conceptualisation, structural and procedural problems arise. The length of some of the trials and how the evidence is collected usually lead to injustice for the victims, and even sometimes for the perpetrator. These procedural problems provide evidence of judicial problems in Turkey. Not allowing NGOs to participate in trials, on the other hand, shows not only the procedural problems we have in Turkey but also the lack of gender consciousness within the judiciary. These problems altogether affect the courts' decisions and the sentences that perpetrators receive. Therefore, the next section aims to underpin the problems relating to sentencing and punishment for perpetrators of honour killing in Turkey.

4. Sentencing and punishment for honour killing perpetrators in Turkey

After the analysis of the laws and the criminal justice system in Turkey, this section aims to critically analyse the law on criminal execution in Turkey within the context of honour killings. Analysing punishments and the sentences will be the last element to show us how the Turkish legal system deals with honour killings and whether the State sufficiently deters honour killings by applying punishments through sentencing.

The section will first shed light on the main aim of punishment, considering the issue using different theories of criminology. Following this, I will turn to specific examples from both the literature and the empirical work of the research to provide a better framework for conceptualising the current situation for honour killing prisoners in Turkey. Finally, the section will cover the responses of community members to current punishment options, allowing me to examine the success of the Turkish criminal execution process regarding honour killings.

4.1 Aims of punishment, deterrence, and honour killings

4.1.1 Degree of punishment and deterrence in the context of honour killings

Nagin and Wilkstöm argue that the degree or severity of punishment and its deterrent effect are directly proportional.[204] In other words, when punishment is severe, its deterrent effect will be more successful both for society and for offenders.

204 Daniel S Nagin, 'Deterrence and Incapacitation' in Michael Tonry (ed), *The Handbook of Crime and Punishment* (Oxford, Oxford University Press 1998) 347; Per-Olof H Wilkstöm, 'Deterrence and Deterrence Experiences: Preventing Crime Through the Threat of Punishment' in Shlomo Giora Shoham, Ori Beck and Martin Kett (eds), *International Handbook of Penology and Criminal Justice* (Boca Raton, CRC Press 2008) 350.

When we consider Turkish criminal law within the context of honour killing punishments, however, we unfortunately realise that the degree or severity of punishments does not always have the desired level of deterrence either individually or generally.[205] As discussed below in more detail, social norms and pressure play a significant role in diminishing this desired effect.

The Turkish Penal Code recommends the heaviest punishment for the perpetrators of customary killings without consideration of an unjust provocation defence: aggravated life imprisonment. However, as discussed and argued in the previous section, although the State demands the heaviest punishment in theory, in practice the majority of perpetrators receive lenient punishments because of a patriarchal conceptualisation of the crime on the part of the prosecutors and judges. More than this, even when courts apply s.82/1-k to the cases, sentencing may still be reduced based on s.62 of the Penal Code,[206] which allows judges to consider matters of discretionary mitigation.[207] This section provides strong discretionary power to judges to use in favour of perpetrators of honour killing. As Appendix 2.6 shows, almost all cases receive sentence reduction from the courts. Given that the punishment will most likely be reduced as a result of the application of either s.81, 82/1-a-h, 29, or s.62, despite the aggravated life imprisonment sentence stated in the Penal Code, it is difficult to talk about successful deterrence, as these reductions eradicate 'fear of the consequences'[208] and undermine the belief that 'you cannot get away with it.'[209] Furthermore, prisoners are also aware that the State frequently applies either pardon or amnesty to such crimes.[210] Dolu et al. address this situation, calling it a loss of balance of proportionality between the crime and the punishment, as prisoners are aware of the fact that they will receive either a pardon or amnesty during their sentencing.[211] This can easily encourage members of society to commit honour killings with less fear.

205 Fifty per cent of the prisoners interviewed for this research declared that if they had known the sentence they would receive for their crime, they would not have chosen to commit them, which shows some level deterrence affect for the participants.

206 See Appendices 2.1, 2.6.

207 Adana 4th High Criminal Court 2011/259 E, 2011/256 K, Date: 07.07.2011; Agri High Criminal Court 2007/215 E, 2008/191 K, Date: 24.06.2008; Ankara 3rd High Criminal Court 2004/545 E, 2005/235 K, Date: 11.11.2005; Bakırköy 5th High Criminal Court 2009/260 E, 2009/317 K, Date: 16.10.2009; Bakırköy 15th High Criminal Court 2009/116 E, 2011/217 K, Date: 13.05.2011; Istanbul 1st High Criminal Court 2011/70 E, 2012/106 K, Date: 16.04.2012; Sanliurfa 1st High Criminal Court 2008/235 E, 2008/310 K, Date: 13.10.2009; Sanliurfa 2nd High Criminal Court 2008/147 E, 2010/396 K, Date: 28.12.2010; Van 1st High Criminal Court 2010/291 E, 2011/267 K, Date: 27.04.2011.

208 Wilkstöm (n 205) 349–50.

209 Gary F Jensen, 'Crime Doesn't Pay: Correlates of a Shared Misunderstanding' (1969) 17 Social Problems 189.

210 Osman Dolu, Hasan Büker, and Şener Uludağ, 'Türk Ceza Adalet Sisteminin Caydırıcılık Kapasitesine İlişkin Eleştirel Bir Değerlendirme' (2012) 61 AUHFD 69, 83–84.

211 Ibid. 83.

4.1.2 Social punishment v State punishment: failure of deterrence

The deterrent effect fails in Turkey in cases of honour killings not only because of the belief that judges are willing to reduce sentences with power given them by the State, based on s.62, but also because there is a conflict between social and State punishment of honour killings. In the previous chapter, we dealt with how society considers the State's role when honour killing offenders are punished heavily.

The main difference between punishment by society and the State is that social punishment occurs when someone fails to fulfil his duty to restore or protect his/his family's honour. In other words, social punishment is only applied when honour killings are *not* committed as expected and required by the community. State punishment, on the other hand, occurs when someone actually *commits* honour killings. And when we compare the actual punishments applied by society and by the State, we also realise that the deterrent effect of social punishment is greater than the deterrent effect of State punishment.

Diagram 6.1 provides a hypothetical model of the various consequences of committing/not committing honour killings from both State and society perspectives.

The diagram shows that the social effects of not committing honour killings are more serious than the State's punishments for committing them. If we remember our previous discussions of the consequences of loss of honour, not committing honour killings will put the individuals in the position of being shameful, leading to loss of their prestige or that of their family's and being excluded from society. Therefore, it is not surprising that some of the prisoner participants in the fieldwork clearly expressed the belief that the severity or length of the punishment does not prevent or reduce the number of honour killings. The following quotes also show what the offenders think of the punishment and the deterrent effect.

> I know the laws. Even if I knew I would get this punishment, I would do the same. This is a matter of honour.[212]
>
> I did not commit a crime.[213]
>
> This is what needs to be done, I would do the same thing again. I had society's pressure on me.[214]
>
> I think I would do the same thing again because we have grown up like this. Honour is a very sensitive issue for my society. Punishment does not deter. It is a matter of family upbringing.[215]

212 Interview with Kenan (7 September 2012).
213 Interview with Ali (3 September 2012).
214 Interview with Kemal (7 September 2012) (n 175).
215 Interview with Murat (2 November 2012).

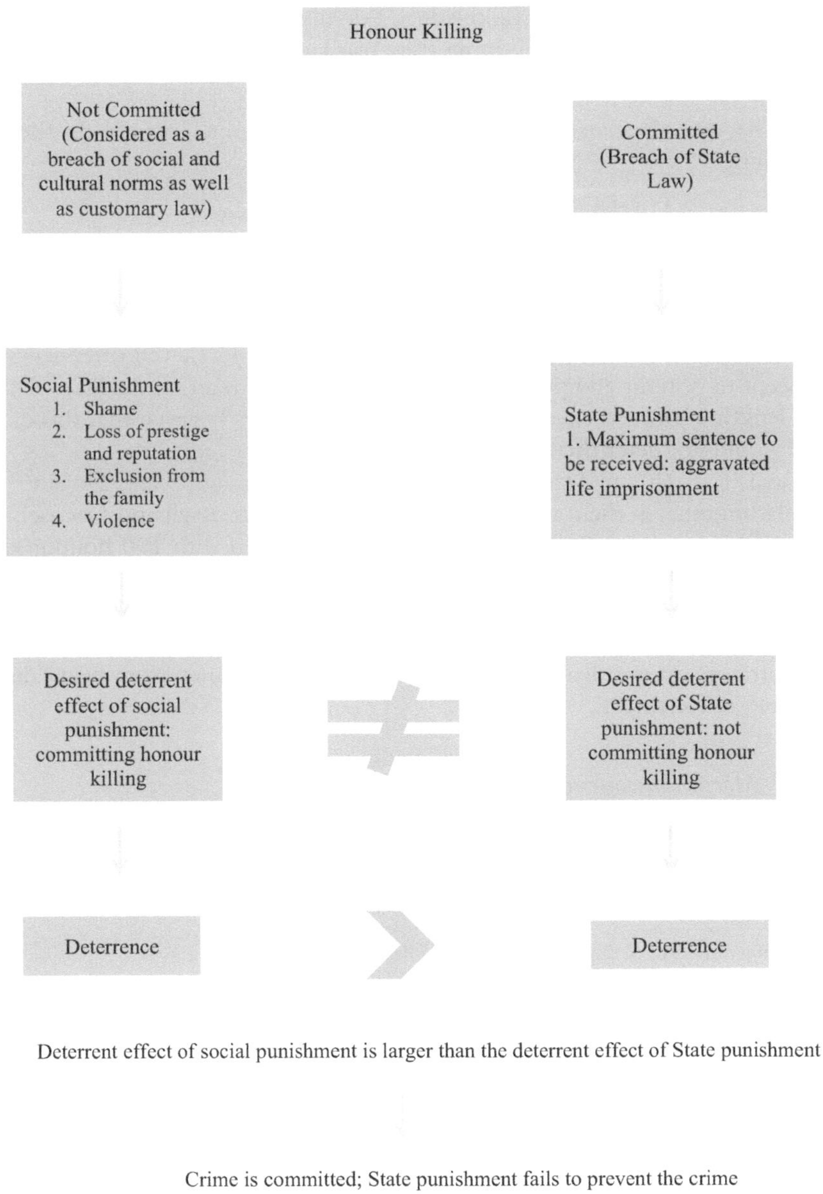

Diagram 6.1 Social punishment v State punishment

> Killing for honour is about mentality. If you have that mentality nothing can stop you.[216]
>
> My family forced me to do that. I was told that honour is my honour so I should do that. Killing was my duty. I do not think length of the punishment would prevent me committing this. You know, honour is very important in our society.[217]
>
> That was what needs to be done. I do not regret. I would do the same thing.[218]
>
> At the end of the day this is honour. She should die.[219]
>
> I do not believe punishment prevents this murder. Even if I got death penalty I would do the same thing.[220]

As we can see, the main concern expressed by the interviewed offenders is the concept of honour and punishment by society rather than by the State. Despite the length of the sentence they received, the offenders believed that this did not and would not deter them.[221]

Onal,[222] Bağlı and Özensel,[223] Ozturk and Demirdağ,[224] and Dogan[225] had similar findings in their empirical work with offenders. Bağlı and Özensel highlight in their empirical research, which was conducted with 190 honour killing perpetrators, that 48.4% believed that increasing punishments for honour killings would not have any effect on reducing the crimes.[226] Dogan also provided some evidence of society's pressure on committing honour crimes, showing how the perpetrators believe that honour killings will 'deter' women from being dishonourable and shameful.[227]

4.1.3 Moral consequences of State punishment

Foucault explains in his famous *Discipline and Punish: The Birth of the Prison* that the two aims of prisons are punishing and disciplining wrongdoers.[228] Through

216 Interview with Mahmut (3 September 2012).
217 Interview with Gokhan (3 September 2012).
218 Interview with Ufuk (2 November 2012).
219 Interview with Baris (3 September 2012).
220 Interview with Salih (3 September 2012) (n 134).
221 Please see Appendix 1.13.
222 Onal (n 2) 164.
223 Bağlı and Özensel (n 2).
224 Öztürk and Demirdağ (n 147) 130.
225 Dogan (n 2).
226 Bağlı and Özensel (n 2) 106, 209.
227 Dogan (n 3), 157.
228 Michel Foucault, *Discipline & Punish: The Birth of the Prison* (New York, Vintage Books 1995).

'deprivation of liberty,'[229] prisons not only deter offenders from committing a crime again in the future but also make them regret what they have done.[230] Apart from deprivation of liberty, 'deprivation of goods and services, deprivation of autonomy, the loss of heterosexual relationships, deprivation of security'[231] also affect the psychology of the prisoners in terms of feeling guilty or not. Guilty feelings or regret are the desired states that punishment would like to reach; it then prevents offenders from re-offending and leads to moral rehabilitation. It is quite common for prisoners, after a certain time spent in prison, to feel guilt and remorse for what they have done, and even to feel ashamed.[232] According to the experimental research conducted by Mandel and Dhami, shame and guilt have significant differences, as blame is more related to guilt than to shame.[233] Furthermore, they argue that, in terms of rehabilitating prisoners, feeling guilty is more productive than feeling ashamed.[234] Tangney et al. conducted similar research, and they separated shame and guilt when analysing the feelings of prisoners.[235] They argue that the outcomes of feeling shame and guilt are different; while guilt leads prisoners to "confess, apologize, and repair," shame usually has the result that "people feel physically, psychologically, and socially diminished."[236] If we remember our earlier discussions relating to the consequences of loss of honour, shame is one of the motives of honour killings. Given this is the case, it is quite difficult to expect that honour killing offenders will feel ashamed after committing the crime, as they have committed it specifically so as to cleanse themselves of shame.

Although some honour killing perpetrators experience guilt and remorse[237] and even mention regret, it is difficult to reach the general conclusion that they feel ashamed as well. For instance, 66% of the prisoners interviewed for this research mentioned regret, but none of them specifically said they felt ashamed as well.[238] In order to be ashamed, someone needs to feel that they have done something wrong/not approved by society. In the case of honour killings, as discussed earlier in this research, society and families support, and even sometimes pressure the individual to commit, this crime. It is not the committing but the *failure* to commit honour killing that is shameful in this context.

229 Ibid. 232.
230 CL Ten, *Crime, Guilt, and Punishment* (Oxford, Clarendon Press 1987) 14.
231 G Sykes, *The Society of Captives* (Princeton, Princeton University Press 1971) 65–77.
232 David R Mandel and Mandeep K Dhami, '"What I Did" Versus "What I Might Have Done": Effect of Factual Versus Counterfactual Thinking on Blame, Guilt, and Shame' (2005) 41 Journal of Experimental Social Psychology 627, 628.
233 Ibid.
234 Ibid. 632.
235 June P Tangney and others, 'Assessing Jail Inmates' Proneness to Shame and Guilt: Feeling Bad About the Behaviour or the Self?' (2011) 38 Criminal Justice and Behaviour 710, 711.
236 Ibid. See also June P Tangney, Jeffrey Stuewing, and Logaina Hafez, 'Shame, Guilt, and Remorse: Implications for Offender Populations' (2011) 22 The Journal of Forensic Psychiatry & Psychology 706.
237 Recep Dogan, 'The Dynamics of Honour Killings: Perpetrators' Experiences' (2016) 20 Homicide Studies 53, 19–21. Please see Appendix 1.6.
238 Please see Appendix 1.6.

When considering honour killings, it is not only society and family but also the prison environment that prevent offenders from feeling guilty and ashamed, because this environment supports and even encourages honour killings. For the perpetrator to feel ashamed, both the inside and outside environment would have to blame him/her for the crime committed and make the perpetrator feel that the crime is disgraceful. However, we realise that this is not the case for honour killings. As analysed below, the evidence shows that prison life in Turkey prevents prisoners from feeling ashamed if they commit honour killings because a large number of offenders still have no regrets, and do not feel guilty, even if they spend a long time in prison.[239] In order to understand the possible reasons for this psychology, we need to focus on the environment in which prisoners serve their sentences.

According to the Turkish Criminal Execution Code s.9, offenders who are sentenced for murder stay in high security prisons and are supposed to be confined with a maximum of three cellmates. The doors of the cells are kept closed during the day, and prisoners supposedly have limited access to the corridors and very restricted communications with other prisoners from different cells.[240] However, in reality, because the number of prisons in Turkey is not sufficient to accommodate all prisoners, they usually stay in cells with 10–12 other inmates.[241] Usually, prisoners are located based on their crimes, and so they share their cells with people who have committed similar offences. This situation can easily raise questions about whether inmates can ever properly embark on a rehabilitation process and begin to feel guilty and ashamed. As mentioned previously, honour killing perpetrators are usually considered 'victims of fate,' and so their status in a cell is higher than that of other inmates.[242] This is because the dignity and prestige of an inmate are based on the crime he/she has committed. If he/she has committed a sexual offence, child abuse, or a petty crime, he/she is considered shameful. However, if someone has committed a crime for the sake of honour, he/she is considered an honourable and respected person in the eyes of the other inmates, a status which is also described as 'heroic' by Gill and Brah.[243] The fieldwork I conducted during also supported this hypothesis. Some of the prisoners informed me

239 Bağlı and Özensel (n 16) 209; Öztürk and Demirdağ (n 147) 125; Minoo Alinia, *Honor and Violence Against Women in Iraqi Kurdistan* (New York, Palgrave Macmillan 2013) 49.

240 Section 9 of the Turkish Criminal Execution Code.

241 According to the statistics provided by TurkStat, there are 371 prisons in Turkey and they accommodated almost 140,000 prisoners as of 2011. (TurkStat, 'Prison Statistics' (Ankara, Turkish Statistical Institute 2011) 3889 1–2). For instance, a report provided by the IHD shows that while the capacity of the Batman M Type Closed Prison was 362, the prison accommodated 571 prisoners in 2010. (Nihat Ekinci, Osman Künteş, and Tahir İmret, 'Batman M Tipi Kapalı Cezaevi İnceleme Raporu' (Batman, İnsan Hakları Derneği (IHD) 2010) <https://www.ihd.org.tr/batman-m-tipi-kapali-cezaevi-inceleme-raporu/> accessed 8 February 2020).

242 Sylvia Maier, 'Honor Killings and the Cultural Defense in Germany' in Marie-Claire Foblets and Alison Dundes Renteln (eds), *Multicultural Jurisprudence: Comparative Perspectives on the Cultural Defense* (Oxford, Hart Publishing 2009) 235.

243 Gill and Brah (n 84) 75.

that their fellow inmates respected them.[244] The following quotes give examples of this:

> Both my inmates and the staff respect me. They think I had to do that, they think this is a matter of honour. Staff and the managers love me.[245]
>
> The inmates respect me, they support me.[246]
>
> Honour killing perpetrators hold the upper hand over others.[247]
>
> When you first enter the prison, it is important to be there because of a honour killing, they respect.[248]

Work by Onal,[249] Ozturk and Demirdağ,[250] and Bağlı and Özensel[251] also provides strong evidence to support this hypothesis. For instance, the interviews conducted by Bağlı and Özensel show that only three interviewees out of the 190 mentioned that their fellow prisoners behaved badly towards them because of honour killing.[252]

These situations reinforce the idea of the prison subculture[253] in a negative way and show that it prevents rehabilitation and feelings of guilt and regret about what prisoners have done to be incarcerated.[254] In other words, the attitudes of the inmates and the staff in prison usually prevent individual deterrence for honour killing prisoners. The continual support, encouragement, and respect from the inmates – and even sometimes from the prison staff – have the effect of stopping them from feeling guilty and therefore preventing the desired deterrent effect of the prison sentence.

5. Conclusion

This chapter has analysed the last part of the hermeneutical circle of HBV and answered the following question: *Why are current Turkish laws not sufficient to*

244 Please see Appendix 1.10.
245 Interview with Kenan (7 September 2012) (n 213).
246 Interview with Kemal (7 September 2012) (n 693); Interview with Murat (2 November 2012) (n 216); Interview with Ibrahim (3 September 2012); Interview with Baris (3 September 2012) (n 220).
247 Interview with Ufuk (2 November 2012) (n 219).
248 Interview with Salih (3 September 2012) (n 134).
249 Onal (n 2) 70.
250 Öztürk and Demirdağ (n 147) 127–28.
251 Bağlı and Özensel (n 2) 211.
252 Ibid.
253 For more information about prison subculture theory, please see Thomas G Blomberg and Karol Lucken, *American Penology: A History of Control* (2nd edn, New York, Transaction Publishers 2010); Sykes (n 232); Tim Newburn, *Criminology* (2nd edn, London, Routledge 2013) 199–207.
254 Zahir Kızmaz, 'Cezaevinin Ve Hapsetmenin Suçu Engellemedeki Etkisi' (2007) 17 Dumlupınar Üniversitesi Sosyal Bilimler Dergisi 44, 51–57.

prevent and decrease honour killings? In order to answer this question, the chapter was divided into three main sections: the Turkish Penal Code, the Turkish criminal justice system, and sentencing honour killings. This division was necessary to break down problematic issues into the different stages of the judicial process regarding honour killings in Turkey.

The first part, which mainly discussed the Turkish Penal Code and s.82, relating to homicide and the provocation defence, showed that there are certain issues that the law fails to address during the process of criminalising honour killings. The foremost problem that we analysed is the tendency to conceptualise honour killing by addressing it as 'customary killing,' without explaining what customary killing means. Because of this confusion, judges have licence to play in the grey areas of the law and easily apply a patriarchal interpretation of custom and honour when they deal with cases. As we have seen, this approach is not in favour of the victims, but instead strongly supports the society's patriarchy. This shows us how honour, patriarchy, culture/traditions, and the law are linked to each other in the circle of HBV. Apart from this confusing conceptualisation of honour killings, application of the defence article is also problematic in Turkey. As discussed, the courts usually avoid considering cases under s.82/1-k of the Penal Code, which prohibits a provocation defence. This again has serious consequences for victims of honour killings because it leads to sentence reductions for offenders.

The second part, which analysed the criminal justice system relating to honour killings, showed some evidence of how the different stages of the criminal justice system is gender biased when dealing with honour killings. Not only the judges and the prosecutors but also some police officers support so-called customs and traditions of society and stand by perpetrators and their patriarchal ideology. It is sad for not only feminists but also all women that this research provides evidence of deep-rooted 'classic patriarchy' in Turkey.

This dark picture of the law and the criminal justice system offered a sprinkle of hope for the victims, but the punishment mechanism of honour killings almost covers this hope with a heavy blanket. As the research shows, while reduction in the sentences encourages the perpetrators, their lives in prison also remove all of the possible deterrent effects that the sentencing might have. Sentence reduction is very much linked to the problems of conceptualising the crime and applying a patriarchal interpretation to honour killing cases. It is also related to the lack of gender consciousness within the judiciary, with a supporting patriarchal attitude to the committing of so-called honour killings. Prison life and how it reduces the deterrent effect is also directly related to deep-rooted patriarchal values within society. Turkey is not perhaps the only country where the perpetrators of honour killings are still considered heroes[255] and 'victims of fate,' not only by their cellmates but also by members of society and even, sometimes, by State representatives. That is why I consider this situation as a heavy blanket thrown over honour killing. Without removing this blanket, no matter how the laws are amended to

255 Alinia (n 240) 70.

show greater gender consciousness, these crimes are very unlikely to be reduced and eliminated.

Bibliography

Acar F and others, 'Issue Histories Turkey: Series of Timelines of Policy Debates' (Institute for Human Sciences (IWM) 2007) <www.quing.eu/files/results/ih_turkey.pdf> accessed 10 August 2019

Akcaoglu Saydim S, 'Medyada Tore ve Namus Cinayetlerinin Yansimalari, Veliler ve Ogrenciler Uzerindeki Etkileri' (Milli Egitim Bakanligi Egitim Arastirma ve Gelistirme Dairesi Baskanligi 2008)

Akpinar A, 'Honour/Shame Complex Revisited: Violence Against Women in the Migration Context' (2003) 26 Women's Studies International Forum 425

Aktan G, 'Aşiret Düzeni' *Radikal* (Istanbul, 4 November 2006) <www.radikal.com.tr/yazarlar/gunduz_aktan/asiret_duzeni-796489> accessed 22 August 2019

Ali SS, 'Overlapping Discursive Terrains of Culture, Law and Women's Rights' in *Scratching the Surface: Democracy, Traditions, Gender* (Lahore, Heinrich Böll Foundation 2007)

Alinia M, *Honor and Violence Against Women in Iraqi Kurdistan* (New York, Palgrave Macmillan 2013)

Artuk ME, Gokcen A and Yenidunya AC, *Ceza Hukuku Genel Hukumler I* (2nd edn, Ankara, Adalet Yayinevi 2006)

Ayhan T, 'Protecting the Woman or the Family? Contradiction Between the Law and Its Practice in Violence Against Woman Cases in Turkey' (2017) 5 Marmara University Journal of Political Science 137

Bağlı M and Özensel E, *Türkiye'de Töre ve Namus Cinayetleri: Töre ve Namus Cinayetleri İşleyen Kişiler Üzerine Sosyolojik Bir Araştırma* (Istanbul, Destek Yayınevi 2011)

Batsleer J and others, 'Domestic Violence and Minoritisation: Supporting Women to Independence' (Women's Studies Research Centre, the Manchester Metropolitan University 2002) <e-space.mmu.ac.uk/e-space/bitstream/2173/ . . . /978-0-954155-01-8.pdf> accessed 8 July 2019

Bayir, D, 'Representation of the Kurds by the Turkish Judiciary' (2013) 35 Human Rights Quarterly 116

Blomberg TG and Lucken K, *American Penology: A History of Control* (2nd edn, New York, Transaction Publishers 2010)

Buken E and Ornek Buken N, 'Evaluation of the Turkish Penal Code Draft Bill From a Women's Viewpoint' (2005) 4 Journal of International Society Fort the History of Islamic Medicine (ISHIM) <http://ishim.net/ishimj/jishim4_7_8/Vol4No7/EDITORIAL.htm> accessed 10 August 2019

Centel N, 'Yeni Turk Ceza Yasasi ve Kadin' (2005) 44 Polis Dergisi 1

Centel N, Zafer H and Cakmut O, *Turk Ceza Hukukuna Giris* (6th edn, Istanbul, Beta 2010)

Cetin I, 'Defining Recent Femicide in Modern Turkey: Revolt Killing' (2015) 16 Journal of International Women's Studies 346

Corbin BA, 'Between Saviors and Savages: The Effect of Turkey's Revised Penal Code on the Transformation of Honor Killings Into Honor Suicides and Why Community Discourse Is Necessary for Honor Crime Eradication' (2014) 29 Emory International Law Review 277

Demirler D and Gümüş P, 'TCK Değişirken . . .' (2004) 7 BÜ'de Kadın Gündemi

Demren Donmez B, 'Ceza Sorumlulugunu Azaltan Bir Neden Olarak Haksiz Tahrik' (2013) 71 Istanbul Universitesi Hukuk Fakultesi Mecmuasi 267

Dogan R, 'Honour Killings in Turkey; Culture, Subjectivism, and Provocation' (Keele University 2010)

———, 'The Dynamics of Honour Killings: Perpetrators' Experiences' (2016) 20 Homicide Studies 53

Dolu O, Büker H and Uludağ Ş, 'Türk Ceza Adalet Sisteminin Caydırıcılık Kapasitesine İlişkin Eleştirel Bir Değerlendirme' (2012) 61 AUHFD 69

Ecevitoğlu P, *Namus Töre ve İktidar: Kadının Çıplak Hayat Olarak Kuruluşu* (Ankara, Dipnot 2012)

Ekinci N, Künteş O and İmret T, 'Batman M Tipi Kapalı Cezaevi İnceleme Raporu' (Batman, İnsan Hakları Derneği (IHD) 2010) <https://www.ihd.org.tr/batman-m-tipi-kapali-cezaevi-inceleme-raporu/> accessed 8 February 2020

'Emniyet Genel Müdürlüğü Asayiş Dairesi Başkanlığı Töre ve Namus Cinayetleri Raporu' (Emniyet Genel Müdürlüğü Asayiş Dairesi Başkanlığı 2006)

Ercan Bilgiç E and Kafkaslı Z, 'Gencim, Özgürlükçüyüm, Ne İstiyorum?' (Istanbul, İstanbul Bilgi Üniversitesi 2013) <www.bilgiyay.com/Content/files/DIRENGEZI.pdf> accessed 14 August 2019

Erdem D, 'Political Reforms in Turkey and EU Membership: Honor Killings and Kurdish Language Rights' (Master of Arts, Sabanci University 2008)

Ergin M, 'The Racialization of Kurdish Identity in Turkey' (2014) 37 Ethnic and Racial Studies 322

Ertürk Y, 'Turkiye Raporu' (Ankara, Human Rights Joint Platform 2007) <www.ihop.org.tr/dosya/YE/yeturkiyerapor.pdf> accessed 17 August 2019

———, 'Towards a Post-Patriarchal Gender Order: Confronting the Universality and Particularity of Violence Against Women' (2009) 46 Sociologisk Forskning 61

Eslen-Ziya H, 'Türk Ceza Kanunu Değişiminde Kadın Aktivistler: Bir Lobicilik Hikayesi' (2012) 15 Sosyoloji Araştırmaları Dergisi 120

Farac M, *Töre Kıskacında Kadın* (Istanbul, Günizi Yayıncılık 2006)

Federation of Women Associations of Turkey, 'CEDAW Shadow Report of Turkey 46th Session' (Ankara, Federation of Women Associations of Turkey 2010) <http://www2.ohchr.org/english/bodies/cedaw/docs/ngos/FWAT_Turkey46.pdf> accessed 17 June 2019

Fendoğlu HT, 'Insan Hakları Başkanlığı 2007 Töre ve Namus Cinayetleri Raporu' (TC Başbakanlık İnsan Hakları Başkanlığı 2008)

Fındıkçı A, *Töre Cinayetleri Kürt Kültürünün Bir Parçası Mı: Arama Sonuçları* (Ankara, İmaj Yayınları 2010)

Foucault M, *Discipline & Punish: The Birth of the Prison* (New York, Vintage Books 1995)

Fournier P, 'The Ghettoisation of Difference in Canada: "Rape by Culture" and the Danger of a "Cultural Defence" in Criminal Law Trials' (2002) 29 Manitoba Law Journal 1

Gazioğlu E, 'Kadın Cinayetleri: Kavramsallaştırma ve Sorunlu Yaklaşımlar' (2013) 7 Sosyal Politika Calışmaları 89

Gill AK and Brah A, 'Interrogating Cultural Narratives About "Honour"-Based Violence' (2014) 21 European Journal of Women's Studies 72

Gozdecka DA, Ercan SA and Kmak M, 'From Multiculturalism to Post-Multi culturalism: Trends and Paradoxes' (2014) 50 Journal of Sociology 51

Goztepe E, 'Namus Cinayetlerinin Hukuki Boyutu: Yeni Turk Ceza Kanunu'nun Bir Degerlendirmesi' (2005) 59 Turkiye Barolar Birligi Dergisi 29

Grabolle-Celiker A, *Kurdish Life in Contemporary Turkey: Migration, Gender and Ethnic Identity* (London, IB Tauris 2013)

Grewal I, 'Outsourcing Patriarchy' (2013) 15 International Feminist Journal of Politics 1

Günal B, 'Devletin Koruyamayıp Ölümün Kucağına Attığı Kadınların Hikayeleri' *Habertürk* (İstanbul, 25 February 2011) <www.haberturk.com/yasam/haber/604679-devletin-koruyamayip-olumun-kucagina-attigi-kadinlarin-hikayeleri> accessed 14 September 2019

Hoyek D, Sidawi RR and Mrad AA, 'Murders of Women in Lebanon: Crimes of Honour Between Reality and The Law' in Lynn Welchman and Sara Hossain (eds), *'Honour': Crimes, Paradigms, and Violence Against Women* (London, Zed Books Ltd 2005)

Human Rights Watch, '"He Loves You, He Beats You": Family Violence in Turkey and Access to Protection' (New York, Human Rights Watch 2011) <www.hrw.org/sites/default/files/reports/turkey0511webwcover.pdf> accessed 10 April 2019

Ilkkaracan P, 'Reforming the Penal Code in Turkey: The Campaign for the Reform of the Turkish Penal Code from a Gender Perspective' (2007) Institute of Development Studies Bulletin 1

———, 'How Adultery Almost Derailed Turkey's Aspiration to Join the European Union' in Pinar Ilkkaracan (ed), *Deconstructing Sexuality in the Middle East* (Aldershot, Ashgate 2008)

Ilkkaracan P and Ercevik Amado L, 'Legal Reforms on Violence Against Women in Turkey: Best Practices' in Moha Ennaji and Fatima Sadiqi (eds), *Gender and Violence in the Middle East* (Oxon, Routledge 2011)

İnal ME, Gürbüz E and Peşmen M, 'Halkın Polis Güçlerine ve Polis Hizmetlerine Bakış Açısı Üzerine Bir Araştırma: Niğde Örneği' (2006) 39 Amme İdaresi Dergisi 71

Ince HO, Yarali A and Ozsel D, 'Customary Killings in Turkey and Turkish Modernization' (2009) 45 Middle Eastern Studies 537

Interview with Ali (3 September 2012)

Interview with Baris (3 September 2012)

Interview with Aylin Celik, 'Van Kadin Dernegi (VAKAD), Van' (26 June 2012)

Interview with Gokhan (3 September 2012)

Interview with Ibrahim (3 September 2012)

Interview with Kemal (7 September 2012)

Interview with Kenan (7 September 2012)

Interview with Mahmut (3 September 2012)

Interview with Murat (2 November 2012)

Interview with Muzaffer Ozdemir (Ankara, 8 July 2013)

Interview with Salih (3 September 2012)

Interview with Elcioglu Tulay, 'KAMER, Mardin' (17 July 2012)

Interview with Ufuk (2 November 2012)

Interview with Nilufer Yilmaz, 'KAMER, Diyarbakir' (28 June 2012)

İskender SZ, *Öğreti ve Yargısal Kararlar Işığında Töre Saikiyle İnsan Öldürme Suçu (Namus Cinayetleri)* (Ankara, Yetkin 2011)

Jensen GF, 'Crime Doesn't Pay: Correlates of a Shared Misunderstanding' (1969) 17 Social Problems 189

Kardam F, 'The Dynamics of Honour Killings in Turkey: Prospects for Action' (Ankara, United Nations Population Fund 2005) <www.unfpa.org/upload/lib_pub_file/676_filename_honourkillings.pdf> accessed 26 June 2019

Kirti A, Kumar P and Yadav R, 'The Face of Honour Based Crimes: Global Concerns and Solutions' (2011) 6 International Journal of Criminal Justice Sciences 343

Kızmaz Z, 'Cezaevinin Ve Hapsetmenin Suçu Engellemedeki Etkisi' (2007) 17 Dumlupınar Üniversitesi Sosyal Bilimler Dergisi 44

Koca M and Uzulmez I, *Turk Ceza Hukuku Genel Hukumler* (Ankara, Seckin 2008)

Kogacioglu D, 'The Tradition Effect: Framing Honor Crimes in Turkey' (2004) 15 A Journal of Feminist Cultural Studies 118

———, 'Gelenek Söylemleri ve Iktidarın Doğallaşması: Namus Cinayetleri Örneği' (2007) 3 Kültür ve Siyasette Feminist Yaklaşımlar 1

———, 'Knowledge, Practice, and Political Community: The Making of the "Custom" in Turkey' (2011) 22 A Journal of Feminist Cultural Studies 172

Lovdal J, 'The Trial of Kerem Cakan: The Turkish Judiciary and Honour Killings' (Kurdish Human Rights Project, Vakad, The Norwegian Bar Association 2011)

Maier S, 'Honor Killings and the Cultural Defense in Germany' in Marie-Claire Foblets and Alison Dundes Renteln (eds), *Multicultural Jurisprudence: Comparative Perspectives on the Cultural Defense* (Oxford, Hart Publishing 2009)

Mandel DR and Dhami MK, '"What I Did" versus "What I Might Have Done": Effect of Factual versus Counterfactual Thinking on Blame, Guilt, and Shame' (2005) 41 Journal of Experimental Social Psychology 627

Müftüler-Bac M, 'Gender Equality in Turkey' (Directorate General For Internal Policies, European Parliament 2012) <www.europarl.europa.eu/document/activities/cont/201204/20120424ATT43808/20120424ATT43808EN.pdf> accessed 10 August 2019

Nagin DS, 'Deterrence and Incapacitation' in Michael Tonry (ed), *The Handbook of Crime and Punishment* (Oxford, Oxford University Press 1998)

Newburn T, *Criminology* (2nd edn, London, Routledge 2013)

Onal A, *Honour Killing: Stories of Men Who Killed* (London, Saqi Books 2008)

Öner S, 'Namus: Woman as "Translation"' (2018) 8 Trakya Üniversitesi Edebiyat Fakültesi Dergisi 110

Opuz v Turkey [2009] European Court of Human Rights 33401/02

Oral Z, 'Bu Yargıtay Japonya'da Mı Yaşıyor?' (*Zeynep Oral*, 2008) <www.zeyneporal.com/yazilar/2008/0808030.html> accessed 18 August 2019

Özdemir B, 'The Role of the EU in Turkey's Legislative Reforms for Eliminating Violence Against Women: A Bottom-Up Approach' (2014) 16 Journal of Balkan and Near Eastern Studies 119

Özgül G, 'Türkiye'de Kadın Cinayetleri Gerçeği ve Durdurmak İçin Çözüm Yolları' in *Değişen Dünyada Biyoetik* (Istanbul, Türkiye Biyoetik Derneği Yayını 2012)

Özkök E, 'O "ırkçı" Benim' *Hurriyet* (Istanbul, 26 September 2006) <www.hurriyet.com.tr/yazarlar/5148997.asp?yazarid=10> accessed 22 August 2019

Ozturk B and Erdem M.R., *Uygulamali Ceza Hukuku ve Guvenlik Tedbirleri Hukuku* (11th edn, Ankara, Seckin 2011)

Öztürk M and Demirdağ MA, 'Namusu/Nu Kanla Temizleyenler: Mardin Cezaevi'nde Namus Davası Nedeniyle Yatan Mahkumlar Üzerine Bir Araştırma' (2013) 7 Sosyal Politika Calışmaları 117

Ozyegin G, 'Virginal Facades: Sexual Freedom and Guilt Among Young Turkish Women' 16 European Journal of Women's Studies 103

Pervizat L, 'Lack of Due Diligence: Judgements of Crimes of Honour in Turkey' in Mohammad Mazher Idriss and Tahir Abbas (eds), *Honour, Violence, Women and Islam* (Abington, Routledge 2011)

Poyraz S, 'Thinking About Turkish Modernization: Cemil Meriç n Turkish Language, Culture, and Intellectuals' (2006) 26 Comparative Studies of South Asia, Africa, and the Middle East 434

Said EW, *Orientalism* (London, Penguin Books 2003)

Sev'er A, 'In the Name of Fathers: Honour Killings and Some Examples from South Eastern Turkey' (2005) 30 Atlantis: Women's Studies Journal 129

Sev'er A and Yurdakul G, 'Culture of Honor, Culture of Change: A Feminist Analysis of Honor Killings Rural Turkey' (2001) 7 Violence Against Women 964

Sykes G, *The Society of Captives* (Princeton, Princeton University Press 1971)

Tangney JP and others, 'Assessing Jail Inmates' Proneness To Shame and Guilt: Feeling Bad About the Behaviour or the Self?' (2011) 38 Criminal Justice and Behaviour 710

Tangney JP, Stuewing J and Hafez L, 'Shame, Guilt, and Remorse: Implications for Offender Populations' (2011) 22 The Journal of Forensic Psychiatry & Psychology 706

Tekin D, 'Victims of Law: The Efficiency of Turkish Penal System on Honour Killings' (2012) Strategic Outlook

Ten CL, *Crime, Guilt, and Punishment* (Oxford, Clarendon Press 1987)

Tezcan M, *Turkiye'de Tore (Namus) Cinayetleri: Sosyo Kulturel Antropolojik Yaklasim* (Ankara, Naturel 2003)

'Töre ve Namus Cinayetleri İle Kadınlara ve Çocuklara Yönelik Şiddetin Sebeplerinin Araştırılarak Alınması Gereken Önlemlerin Belirlenmesi Amacıyla Kurulan TBMM Araştırma Komisyonu Raporu' (Ankara, TC Başbakanlık Kadın Statüsü Genel Müdürlüğü2006)<www.kadininstatusu.gov.tr/upload/kadininstatusu.gov.tr/mce/eski_site/Pdf/tbmmkom-bolum1.pdf> accessed 3 July 2019

TurkStat, 'Prison Statistics' (Ankara, Turkish Statistical Institute 2011) 3889

Ülker G, 'Kadın Hareketinin Türkiye'de Kadına Yönelik Şiddet İle İlgili Mücadele Deneyimi "Anadolu'nun Orta Yerinde Şiddete Karşı Kadınlar Elele",' in *1. Kadın Sağlığı Kongresi: 'Kadına Yönelik Şiddet'* (Ankara, UNFPA 2008) <www.ttb.org.tr/kutuphane/kadinsaglikikong.pdf?ref=herseybedava.info#page=50> accessed 14 September 2013

Ünal S and others, 'Aile İçi Şiddet Mağdurlarının Polise Başvurularında Polise Uygun Davranış Modellerinin Kazandırılması' (2011) <http://suconleme.org/wp-content/uploads/2013/02/18-Aile-%C4%B0%C3%A7i-%C5%9Eiddet-Ma%C4%9Fdurlar%C4%B1n%C4%B1n-Polise-Ba%C5%9Fvurular%C4%B1nda-Polise-Uygun-Davran%C4%B1%C5%9F.pdf> accessed 14 September 2019

Volpp L, 'Blaming Culture for Bad Behavior' (2000) 12 Yale Journal of Law & the Humanities 89

Walker N, *Why Punish?: Theories of Punishment Reassessed* (Oxford, Oxford University Press 1991)

Warrick C, 'The Vanishing Victim: Criminal Law and Gender in Jordan' (2005) 39 Law & Society Review 315

Wilkstöm P-OH, 'Deterrence and Deterrence Experiences: Preventing Crime Through the Threat of Punishment' in Shlomo Giora Shoham, Ori Beck and Martin Kett (eds), *International Handbook of Penology and Criminal Justice* (Boca Raton, CRC Press 2008)

Women for Women's Human Rights-New Ways, 'Gender Discrimination in the Turkish Penal Code Draft Law: An Analysis of the Draft Law From a Gender Perspective and Proposed Amendments by the Women's Platform on the Penal Code' (Istanbul, WWHR 2003) accessed 10 August 2019

———, 'Shadow NGO Report on Turkey's Fourth and Fifth Combined Periodic Report to the Committee on the Elimination of Discrimination Against Women' (2005) <https://cssplatform.org/wp-content/uploads/2018/02/Shadow-NGO-Report-on-Turkey%E2%80%99s-Fourth-and-Fifth-combined-Periodic-Report-to-the-Committee-on-the-Elimination-of-Discrimination-against-Women.pdf> accessed 8 February 2020

WWHR, 'Shadow NGO Report on Turkey's Sixth Periodic Report to the Committee on the Elimination of Discrimination against Women' (WWHR 2010) <http://www2.ohchr.org/english/bodies/cedaw/docs/ngos/WPTPC_Turkey46.pdf> accessed 17 June 2019

Yenisey F, *Turkish Criminal Procedure Code* (Istanbul, Beta 2009)

Yirmibesoglu V, *Töre ve Namus Gerekçesiyle İşlenen Cinayetler: Toprağa Düşen Sevdalar* (Istanbul, Hurriyet 2007)

Yılmaz A and Demirci MK, 'Polis-Halk İlişkilerini Vatandaşların Değerlendirmeleri Üzerine Bir Araştırma' (2004) 11 Dumlupınar Üniversitesi Sosyal Bilimler Dergisi 83

7 Concluding remarks, implications, and recommendations

1. Concluding remarks and implications

This book aimed to provide a comprehensive analysis of HBV by considering it as a form of gender-based violence committed with a so-called honour motivation. The main question driving this book is: *How and under which conditions are honour killings committed in Turkey, and how does the Turkish Penal Code deal with them?* Based on this question, the book has focused on three important issues, which have also created the main themes: conceptualisation of honour and HBV; criminalisation of honour killings; and the criminal justice system in Turkey regarding honour killings. These three issues are strongly linked to each other in the process of tackling honour killings in Turkey, and they have helped to understand two variables of this research: the motivations behind honour killings and the State's legal response to these crimes.

By considering the main research question and these variables, the research has explored two tentative hypotheses:

- *Since women's honour is considered as equivalent to the honour of the family and society, violence against women in the name of honour is legitimised by society.*
- *Although there have been considerable developments in the Turkish legal system in terms of recognition of gender equality, the existing Penal Code is still insufficient in deterring and denouncing honour killings.*

Each chapter tackled the themes, variables, and hypotheses from different aspects. Part I (Chapters 1, 2, 3, and 4) analysed the conceptualisation of honour and social honour codes and how they are shaped by other cultural values – *inter alia* patriarchy, masculinity, hierarchy, and sexuality – to create a system which conditions the level of violence in the name of honour that can be used by individuals, and the consequences of using or not using this type of violence in society. The analysis in this section allowed me to answer the first part of the book's question.

Part II (Chapters 5 and 6) primarily addressed the relationship between law and honour killings by specifically addressing State and non-State legal orders in Turkey. By considering these legal orders, the research provided intensive analysis of the concept of legal pluralism in Turkey in the context of HBV, which is one of the original contributions of this work. Moreover, by analysing the Penal Code, its interpretation, and its enforcement using primary sources (case records and interviews), the book not only makes an original contribution to the subject but also demonstrates the continuing failures of the existing law and its enforcement when tackling honour killings.

In order to answer the main question of this book, the study has adopted a hermeneutic and feminist methodology as a framework for analysis. Hermeneutics, as a mode for interpretation of human conduct, has been used as a theoretical approach to refine the conceptual interpretation of honour and HBV. By creating a 'hermeneutical circle' of HBV, the research aimed to keep the reader within a defined circle so as not to misinterpret the meaning of honour and HBV. As the further discussions during this book showed, my ultimate intention was not 'exoticising' honour killings, as Fernandez warns against; nor was I trying to suggest that because honour killing is committed in Turkey, the country and the people who live there are uncivilised and barbaric, and that therefore the West is a much better place for women.[1] Yet, although I considered honour within its own hermeneutical circle, I do not justify this violent practice in the eyes of the West. During this research, my intention has been to shift the approach to HBV away from its predominant focus on Islam[2] and onto a more complex analysis, which examines patriarchy as well as deep-rooted cultures and traditions as forces that legitimise HBV.

The hermeneutical circle of HBV was divided in four main sections in this research in order to show the link between different concepts: honour, patriarchy/hierarchy/masculinity, culture/tradition, and law. The clockwise circle started with the conceptualisation of honour, which is also the first chapter of this book. The second part then addressed the concept of patriarchy/hierarchy/masculinity as values that shape the concept of honour. The third part highlighted the existing cultures and traditions that shape not only the concept of honour but also gender relations in Turkey. Analysis of these three parts paved the way to answering the first part of the research question. The last part, however, focused on the law as a whole alongside a consideration of the earlier discussions.

Apart from the hermeneutical method, the book adopted a specific feminist approach and methodology during the process of analysing the concepts of honour, HBV, and its criminalisation. Feminist interpretations of autonomy, agency, sexuality, and gender relations were used not only to highlight some serious problems during the process of conceptualising honour but also to prove how the State itself is patriarchal and far from gender neutral. After careful consideration of the feminist movements, I was able not only to keep the reader within the principled hermeneutical circle but also to eliminate any possible 'Orientalist' approach. However, the analysis of the different Turkish feminist movements

1 Sonya Fernandez, 'The Crusade Over the Bodies of Women' (2009) 43 Patterns of Prejudice 269, 271, 280.

2 This is also the main argument that Fernandez developed: Ibid. 271–72.

also showed that even these movements and theories are sometimes problematic because of their regional character. As Chapter 3 highlighted clearly, Islamic feminist movements in Turkey have been quite unable to answer this research question, as their main concern is providing equal rights for conservative Muslim women within the wider community rather than fighting for women's autonomy and sexual rights in general. Analysing different feminist movements in Turkey also shows that there is no collaboration or consensus between different groups when tackling gender issues in general. Since each group has its own agenda, not being able to come together to tackle HBV may easily reduce the pressure on the State and wider community to change their patriarchal attitudes towards women and amend the laws accordingly.

By using both hermeneutical and feminist theories, the first chapter of this book analysed the concept of honour. It reflected on the fact that the term 'honour' is complex and needs careful interpretation when analysed in the context of HBV. Also, the analysis showed that the meaning of honour differs from the Western concept if we consider it only within the hermeneutical circle of HBV. Honour has different sub-categories: *namus*; chastity; *şeref*. Although there are commonalities for these categories, their meanings are slightly different. While *şeref* is usually connected to men, *namus* and chastity mainly relate to women. The common ground of these categories, however, mainly concerns women's sexuality and autonomy, which also reminds us of the intersubjective meaning of honour. Different than the concept of honour in the Western world, honour in the hermeneutical circle of HBV is conceptualised through women's sexualities. This conceptualisation shows that honour in the hermeneutical circle of HBV is a gendered value. As the further analysis provided by this research showed when dealing with the fieldwork data from both Turkey and the UK, not only individuals but also State actors follow this gendered approach. This approach is the foundation that creates injustice for the victims of HBV in every aspect of the criminal justice system. As the court case analyses reveal, conceptualising the term honour through its strong link to women's sexuality sometimes creates a patriarchal interpretation of the term, which shows that women's sexual autonomy may be problematic in society, and this in turn triggers and provokes men to commit HBV.

However, this work critically analysed this approach by using the feminist interpretation that it is not women's sexuality and autonomy that are problematic but rather the ideologies of hegemonic patriarchy, hierarchy, and masculinity. What has been revealed during this research is that women's sexuality and autonomy would not be considered problematic if they were not conceptualised within patriarchal social values. Since the roots of patriarchy, hierarchy, and masculinity are so deep and strong, the best way of addressing them in this book was to use Kandiyoti's 'classic patriarchy'[3] interpretation. By using the concept of classic patriarchy in Chapter 3 and the concept of honour in Chapter 2, it became

3 Deniz Kandiyoti, 'Bargaining With Patriarchy' (1988) 2 Gender and Society 274, 278.

clear that there have been some problematic relationships created between these terms in Turkey, and this became one of the main issues that the research question dealt with. As mentioned above, by conceptualising honour using patriarchal values, society creates a gendered understanding of women's sexuality. Because honour is described using the terms *namus* and chastity, which show a direct link to sexuality, women's sexual activities are always considered dangerous, with the potential power to destroy honour. Based on this patriarchal gendered understanding, it is assumed that women's sexuality belongs to men; it needs to be controlled, monitored, and protected, and this approach eliminates the personal autonomy of women.

More than this, and considering the analysis in Chapters 2 and 3 as a whole, it can be said that honour within the framework of the hermeneutical circle of HBV is not only an individual but also a collective value. The degree of its importance ripples out from individuals to societies. Again, this is significantly different from the Western concept of honour, where an individualistic interpretation is foremost in importance. This examination of collective and individual honour will hopefully provide a useful base for further research on the concept of honour in general.

Investigating how honour is a motive for committing HBV also led us to consider a patriarchal interpretation. This problematic interpretation affects individuals, especially the potential female victims, in the process of possessing and protecting honour. Because honour depends on women's sexual conduct, this places women at the centre of protecting and maintaining it. While women are not considered to be the main possessors of honour, they are overwhelmed with the heavy burden of protecting and maintaining it; if they fail, they need to restore it – often by giving their lives. This is again rather difficult to understand when the Western ideology of honour is considered. A Western ideology may unable to comprehend the chain of causation that leads someone to commit HBV. Again, this makes us consider hermeneutics and interpret the chain of causation by always considering the concepts of ownership, patriarchy, and denial of personal autonomy. When men, as the owners of not only females but also of women's sexual autonomies, encounter any female sexual misconduct, this is deemed not only a betrayal of their masculine authority but also a failure to control their property. In the context of the hermeneutical circle, a person who creates this unacceptable situation for these men should be punished with her life.

This fatal consequence is an example of where honour stands in their society. Boiger et al. argue that honour not only carries its own value but also affects how society values the individual and the family.[4] As Boiger et al. state, "a person does not have more honour than granted by others,"[5] and that makes the judgement of society so important. When honour is used as the key concept to judge the value of individuals and families, then, as Pitt-River argues, how society sees

4 Michael Boiger and others, 'Defending Honour, Keeping Face: Interpersonal Affordances of Anger and Shame in Turkey and Japan' (2014) Cognition & Emotion 1, 2–3.
5 Ibid. 3.

someone shapes how s/he exists within that society.[6] Therefore, loss of honour is equal to the loss of prestige and reputation within society, which needs immediate action to restore it. As Chapter 4 discussed in detail, these actions to restore honour are usually violent, and, again, gender biased. Like many countries where HBV is recorded, women become the main targets of this violence with the assumption that they bring dishonour with their inappropriate behaviours.

As the case record analysis of this research demonstrated, it is not only the members of society who follow this gendered honour possession and protection approach but also the judges. Although it is impossible to generalise about all of the courts in Turkey, it is evident that courts play a significant role in supporting patriarchal society's gendered interpretation in two ways: by conceptualising honour killings and by reducing sentences by applying a provocation defence. This also shows how the State is still patriarchal in Turkey.

While the first part of this book analysed how and under what conditions honour killings are committed in Turkey, the second part mainly focused on the legal aspect of the problem. State law's approach to this type of violence and how it tackles it has put questions in people's minds. In order to analyse whether criminal law in Turkey has reached the desired level for tackling this violence or not, for this research it was crucial to consider the law as a whole by including State and non-State laws in Turkey. Although Turkey follows a one-law-for-all approach, this does not mean that non-State legal norms do not exist. As analysed in Chapter 5, using Forsyth's typology of legal pluralism, certain customary laws and norms have significant influence within Turkish society and are sometimes even considered to be above State law. Customary law that relates to women's sexuality and honour is considered to be not only the social norm but also a 'law' that needs to be obeyed and enforced by members of society. The prisoner interviews for this research showed that when State law and customary law conflict, customary law prevails over State law if it relates to honour within the hermeneutical circle of HBV. This is an important legal understanding that provides some information about how State laws can lose their hierarchal authority over non-State norms. This situation is one of the most serious challenges to tackling HBV in Turkey and shows that dealing with State law and its implementation per se is insufficient. The research clearly showed that problems relating to State law and its implementation are only the tip of the iceberg, and focusing on them when dealing with HBV prevents us from seeing the bigger picture. While State law and its implementation may change and improve quickly and successfully under pressure from both women activists and external bodies, it is difficult to say the same for the non-State legal orders, as they have strong and deep roots that are created by an ossified patriarchal ideology. Therefore, further research and action are needed to determine how to tackle non-State patriarchal laws in an HBV context.

6 Julian Pitt-Rivers, 'Honour and Social Status' in JG Peristiany (ed), *Honour and Shame: The Values of Mediterranean Societies* (London, Weidenfeld and Nicolson 1965) 21.

Apart from the conflict between State law and customary law, the research revealed that the criminal law of Turkey raises serious problems when dealing with honour killings. As the research analysed in Chapter 6, the problems have different aspects:

- Drafting and applying the Penal Code
- Criminal justice process
- Failure of deterrence

These problems indicate that Turkish criminal law fails to tackle honour killings in every aspect of the judiciary and shows strong evidence of State patriarchy. The first problem that the research highlighted concerned the definitional gap for the term 'customary killing' and the inconsistency caused because of this. As Chapter 6 analysed, the State deliberately prefers using the term 'customary killing' rather than 'honour killing' in the Penal Code, while failing to provide any firm definition of customary killing. Indeed, as the cases collected for this research showed, the courts interpret the term and provide five separate definitions, which causes even more complications within the judiciary. These interpretations are usually far from giving gender recognition. Although there is some evidence of intent to limit social norms in some cases, especially in the context of infidelity, women's sexualities are still tied up with patriarchal honour codes, which affects whether judges consider cases within section 82/1-k or not. Since the majority of cases in this research show that judges still tend to accept social norms that blame women for provoking men to commit the crimes through their – the women's – misbehaviour, we again realise how non-State norms influence the enforcement of the Penal Code. As discussed in this research, this influence is clearly witnessed when the sentences are decided. Although customary killings are supposedly subject to aggravated life imprisonment in Turkey after the amendments of the Turkish Penal Code in 2004, as Appendix 2.6 shows, the majority of defendants benefit from the provocation defence. The judges frame the women's role as performing 'provocative' actions that lead men to commit honour killings; in this way, the judges take into consideration the existing cultural and traditional norms in society. As discussed earlier, because these norms are patriarchal and consider women's sexuality to be dangerous, it is not surprising that none of the prisoners in this research blamed society for pushing them to commit this crime, but instead blamed women's sexual misconduct. Although the amended Penal Code regulated customary killings with aggravated life imprisonment sentence, which shows a certain degree of paradigm shift from the previous Penal Code towards sanction of honour killings, without adopting a gender-neutral approach, those amendments remain only on paper – not much in practice.

The gendered approach that I identify in my fieldwork suggests that drafting legal solutions to deep-rooted cultural problems like honour killings will not be effective without gender-neutral applications of these rules. This book demonstrates the process through which State actors, especially judges and prosecutors, fail to tackle this problem by leaving their 'classic patriarchal' approach to one side and providing justice for the victims.

In relation to the discussion of the Turkish criminal justice system, another problematic issue that needs urgent attention is the failure of punishments' deterrent effect. As discussed previously, although the State advocates for aggravated life imprisonment for customary killings, by applying considerable sentence reduction to this crime, the State fails to deter not only the offenders but also the wider community. The failure of deterrence is also witnessed during the imprisonment period in Turkey. As the prisoners' interviews for this research prove, the living conditions for offenders are far from making them feel guilt or remorse. As Onal highlights, the prisoners are considered to be 'victims of fate'[7] when they commit honour killings, and this gives them higher status among fellow inmates. The interviewees highlighted not only the inmates, but also the State actors, including police officers and prison staff played a significant role in eliminating the desired deterrent effect. Their supportive attitudes towards the offenders directly affect the deterrence procedures. The families of the offenders, as well as the wider community, also support the offenders for the crimes they commit. When considering all these circumstances, it is not surprising that the current life imprisonment sentence for honour killing perpetrators does not have the desired deterrent effect to eliminate this crime. From this picture, we once again realise that the harshness of the punishments will not be sufficient to eliminate honour killings in Turkey unless the patriarchal understanding of honour is changed.

2. Recommendations for policy

The book reveals several policy recommendations that need to be considered in both the short and long term. First of all, as discussed in this work, although feminist movements and activism have a significant role to play in imposing policy change in Turkey, the ethnic, religious, and ideological polarisation of these two sides constitute a serious impediment to tackling HBV. Turkey has recently witnessed some examples of collaboration with different women's movements in order to tackle VAW, but the area still needs a lot more effort to confront the problem more seriously. Also, the same united approach should be witnessed in the international arena when providing regional reports about the situation in Turkey by representing all ethnic, religious, and ideological groups.

Since women's NGOs have significant importance in the region for providing information about problems that women experience in general, and HBV in particular, they urgently need regional and international funding to continue their work. The pilot study conducted with several NGOs for this research revealed that although the NGOs have great potential to reach women and raise their voices, lack of funding prevents them from continuing to support women and

7 Ayse Onal, *Honour Killing: Stories of Men Who Killed* (London, Saqi Books 2008) 94.

influence policy makers. Although the EU Turkey report 2015[8] suggested that politicians and the government have a duty to provide equality and assure the implementation of legislation, this should put more pressure on Turkey to tackle VAW in general and HBV in particular.

Apart from the problems relating to feminist movements, the research also addressed serious problems with the criminalisation of honour killing in the Turkish Penal Code. As analysed in depth, the lack of definition of honour killing causes serious injustice for victims. By allowing this gap in the law, judges have significantly failed to frame the concept of honour killing, and without any doubt, this has resulted in the patriarchal interpretation of many cases. The State should urgently consider filling this gap in the current Penal Code. Since Turkey is a signatory country of the CEDAW and the Istanbul Convention, it is under an obligation to take all necessary measures to tackle VAW in general and HBV in particular.[9] In this sense, a clear definition of HBV and honour killings is not only a necessity to provide better judgements but also an international obligation for Turkey. When considering representation of women within the Parliament, this will raise a number of challenges. Therefore, as mentioned earlier, pressure from NGOs and activists has an important role to drive policy change in a progressive direction.

Changing the law and including a definition are only parts of the solution. The State should adopt a gender-neutral approach to defining the crime. It needs to carefully design the definitional framework and should eliminate any possible interpretation that may result in lenient punishments for crimes that are committed with a so-called honour motive. Provocation and loss of self-control should not be considered when the motivation behind the crime is honour prevention or honour restoration. The courts should carefully consider the distinction between honour motivation and provocation. This, again, requires judges to distance themselves from a patriarchal interpretation. However, as the research demonstrates, this distancing has not reached the desired level in Turkey. Probably the most useful way they can ensure that they distance themselves from any patriarchal interpretation is by allowing the NGOs and other women organisations to participate during the trials, which is also another area in which legal reforms should be done urgently.

The book also revealed that there is a lack of specific and general deterrence in the case of honour killings. The research participants were almost in total agreement that the length of prison sentences set out in the Penal Code has no deterrent effect on society or on offenders. This failure of deterrence needs immediate attention from the State. The State should consider the factors that

8 European Commission, Commission Staff Working Document Turkey 2015 Report, SWD (2015) 216 final.

9 Convention on the Elimination of All Forms of Discrimination Against Women CEDAW) (United Nations, Treaty Series, vol. 1249, p. 13) (entered into force 3 September 1981), Council of Europe Convention on Preventing and Combating Violence Against Women and Domestic Violence (Istanbul Convention) (CETS No.210) (entered into force 1 August 2014).

reduce the deterrent effect and take measures to tackle this. I am not suggesting that harsher punishments or recommending any forms of corporal and/or capital punishment will increase the deterrent effect. However, the attitudes of police officers, judges, prosecutors, and prison staff have considerable effect on reducing the deterrent effect. As mentioned by the prisoners during this research, these actors have significant parts to play in eliminating the remorse, guilt, and self-judgement of the prisoners. This serious picture shows the necessity of training and other forms of education for professionals. Training and education need to be carried out by the State and NGOs collectively.

Training and education for professionals in the judiciary process, however, is only one part of the solution. Wider education campaigns and public awareness activities should be carried out in Turkey. As discussed, because HBV has very strong cultural and traditional roots in society, educational campaigns should target these roots. Socially influential figures, i.e. imams, community representatives, tribal leaders, and other notables, should be the main targets for this education campaign because of their potential to influence the wider community. While changing laws and closing legal loopholes could be short-term solutions, education and changing attitudes are long-term ones and need continuing commitment.

3. Recommendations for further research

The book has analysed ***how and under which conditions honour killings are committed in Turkey, and how the Turkish Penal Code deals with them*** from a socio-legal perspective. It has used both primary and secondary data to provide an answer to the question, and the findings may have some implications for further research.

First of all, although a protection mechanism that has been applied by Turkey in order to eliminate HBV in Turkey has been excluded from this research, the findings presented from the court cases and prison interviews may lead to further research on how to improve this mechanism.

Second, as discussed in detail during the second part of this book, the gendered attitude of the criminal justice system is still evident in Turkey. The evidence provided in Chapter 6 can be used as a basis for further research into both civil and criminal procedures.

Third, the book has provided an in-depth analysis of the concepts of honour and HBV, and the analysis may be used for further research in this area, not only in Turkey but also in other regions to provide some comparison. This comparison will create different hermeneutical circles, allowing us to compare and contrast them at an academic level.

Fourth, the book, like similar research conducted in this area, has included interviews with prisoners of honour killings. The data was used to compare findings with the existing literature. These findings, which have all reached similar conclusions, could, I suggest, be used to conduct further research: not with the prisoners as they serve their sentences, but with those who have completed them and returned to society. This will make a new contribution to the existing literature and allow us to analyse whether the deterrent effect is sufficient or not.

Bibliography

Boiger M and others, 'Defending Honour, Keeping Face: Interpersonal Affordances of Anger and Shame in Turkey and Japan' (2014) Cognition & Emotion 1

Fernandez S, 'The Crusade Over the Bodies of Women' (2009) 43 Patterns of Prejudice 269

Kandiyoti D, 'Bargaining With Patriarchy' (1988) 2 Gender and Society 274

Onal A, *Honour Killing: Stories of Men Who Killed* (London, Saqi Books 2008)

Pitt-Rivers J, 'Honour and Social Status' in JG Peristiany (ed), *Honour and Shame: The Values of Mediterranean Societies* (London, Weldenfeld and Nicolson 1965)

Appendices

Appendix 1
Prison interviews

1.1 Profile of prisoners interviewed

Name–age–gender	*Interview date*	*Education*	*Employment*	*Offence*	*Victim*	*Motive*	*Time served (years)*
Ali (56) (male)	03.09.2012	Primary school	Stallholder	Murder	Daughter	Extramarital relationship	4/Life imprisonment
Baris (33) (male)	03.09.2012	Literate	Waiter	Murder	Wife	Extramarital relationship	1/Not declared
Gokhan (21) (male)	03.09.2012	Secondary school	Stallholder	Murder	Sister	Extramarital relationship	4/20
Ibrahim (63) (male)	03.09.2012	Primary school	Restaurant owner	Attempt to murder	Wife	Denying husband's authority	1/Not declared
Kemal (34) (male)	07.09.2012	Secondary school	Waiter	Murder	Sister	Pregnancy out of wedlock	8/Life imprisonment
Kenan (64) (male)	07.09.2012	Primary school	Shop owner	Murder	Daughter	Extramarital relationship	6/36
Mahmut (41) (male)	03.09.2012	Secondary school	Buyer	Murder	Wife	Jealousy	1/Not declared
Murat (30) (male)	02.09.2012	High school	Security guard	Murder	Wife	Infidelity	4/25
Omer (35) (male)	03.09.2012	Undergraduate	IT support officer	Murder	Wife	Infidelity	1/Not declared
Salih (41) (male)	03.09.2012	Not declared	Marketing manager	Murder	Ex-wife	Being in a relationship	2/15
Sevim (32) (female)	04.09.2012	Primary school	Unemployed	Murder	Infant	Birth out of wedlock	4/36
Ufuk (30) (male)	02.11.2012	Secondary school	Truck driver	Murder	Wife	Extramarital relationship	3/17

1.2 How did you decide to commit this offence?

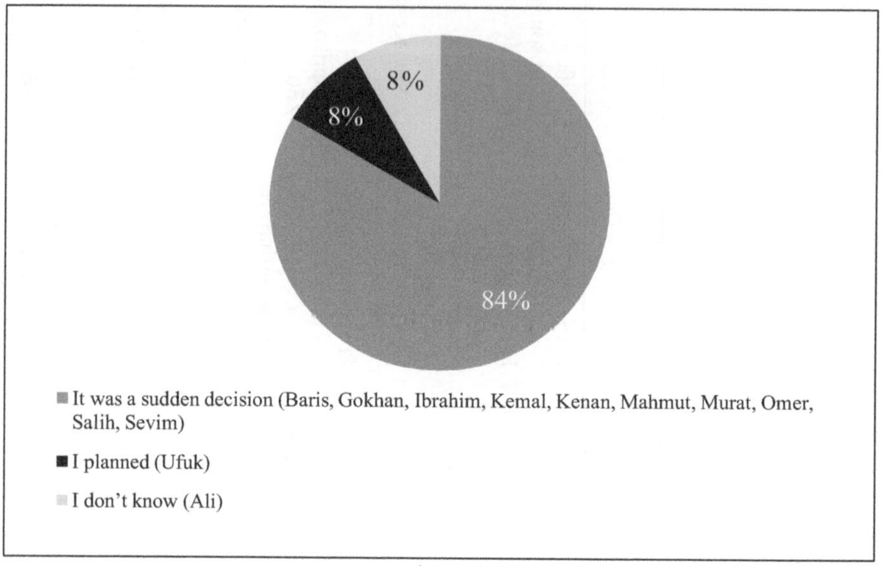

1.3 How did your family react after the incident?

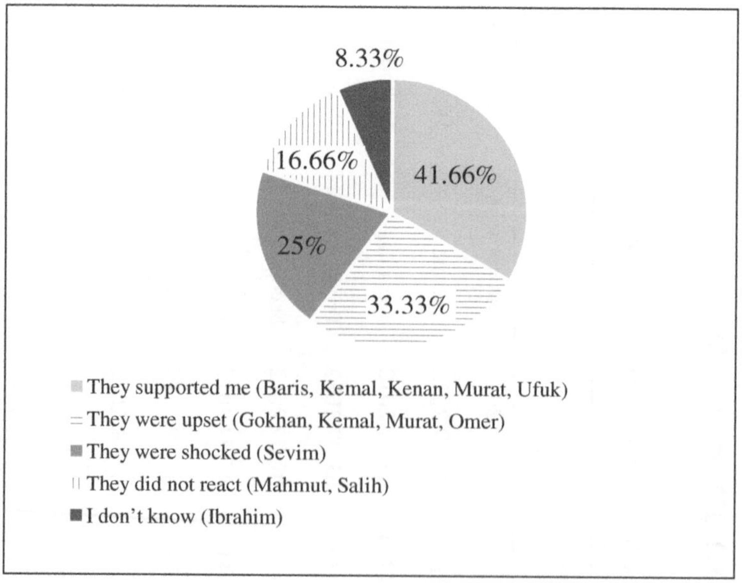

1.4 How did society react after the incident?

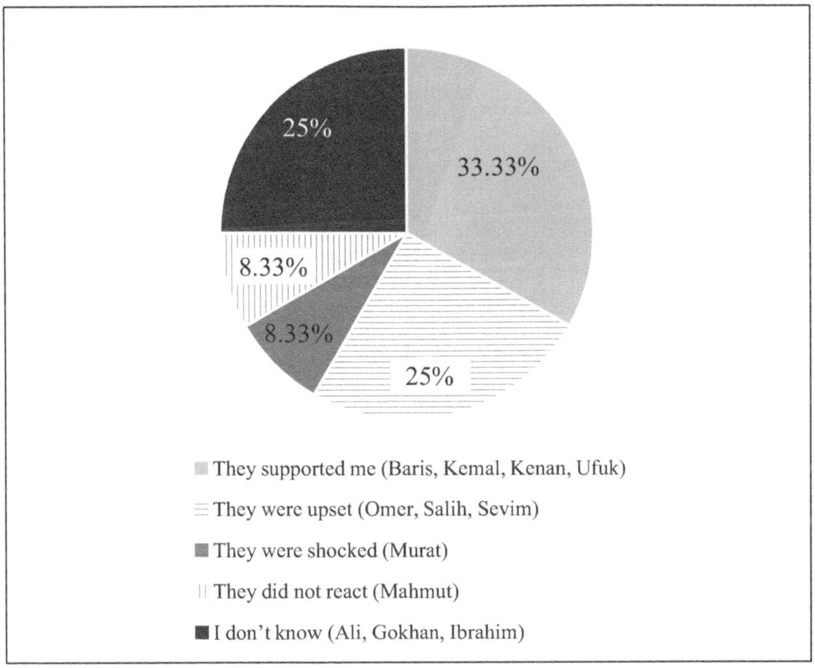

1.5 How did the criminal investigation start?

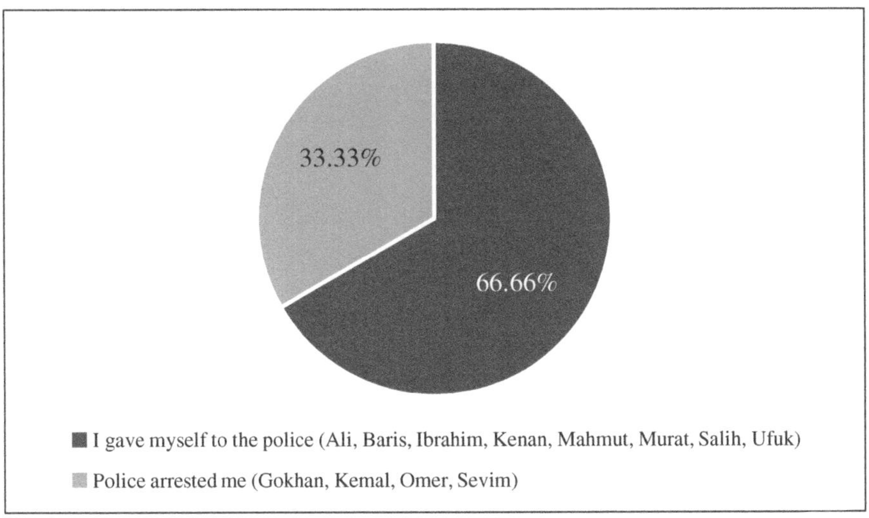

1.6 How do you feel about the incident?

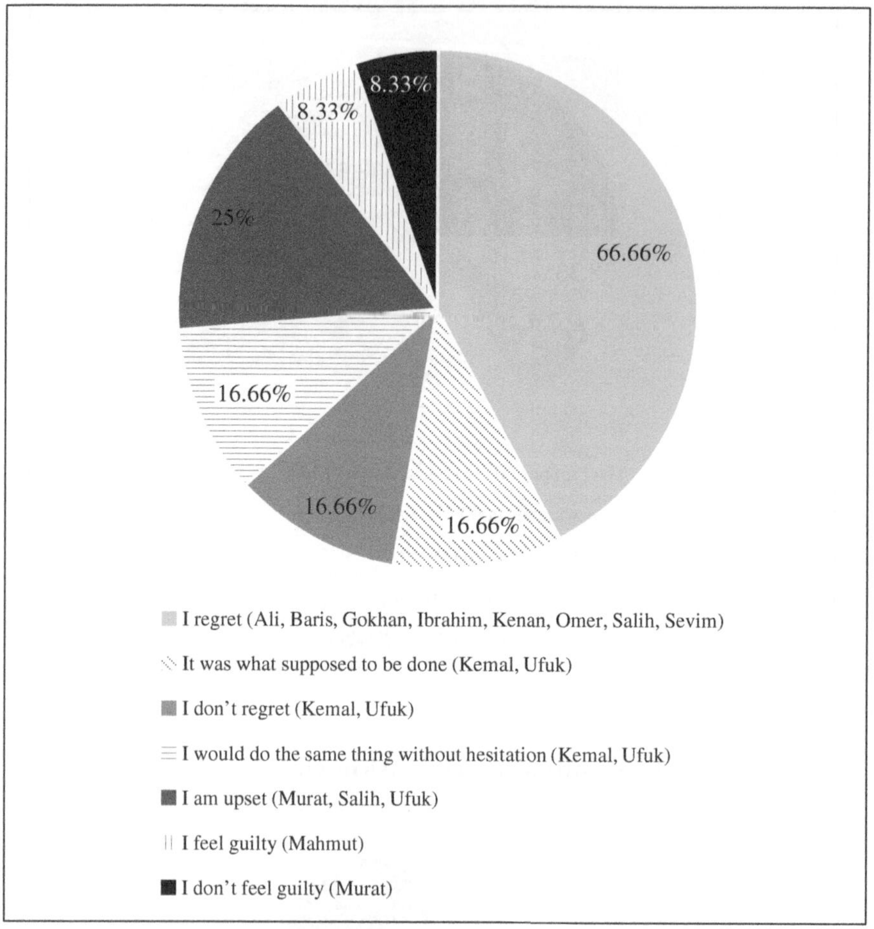

1.7 What would happen if you did not commit this crime?

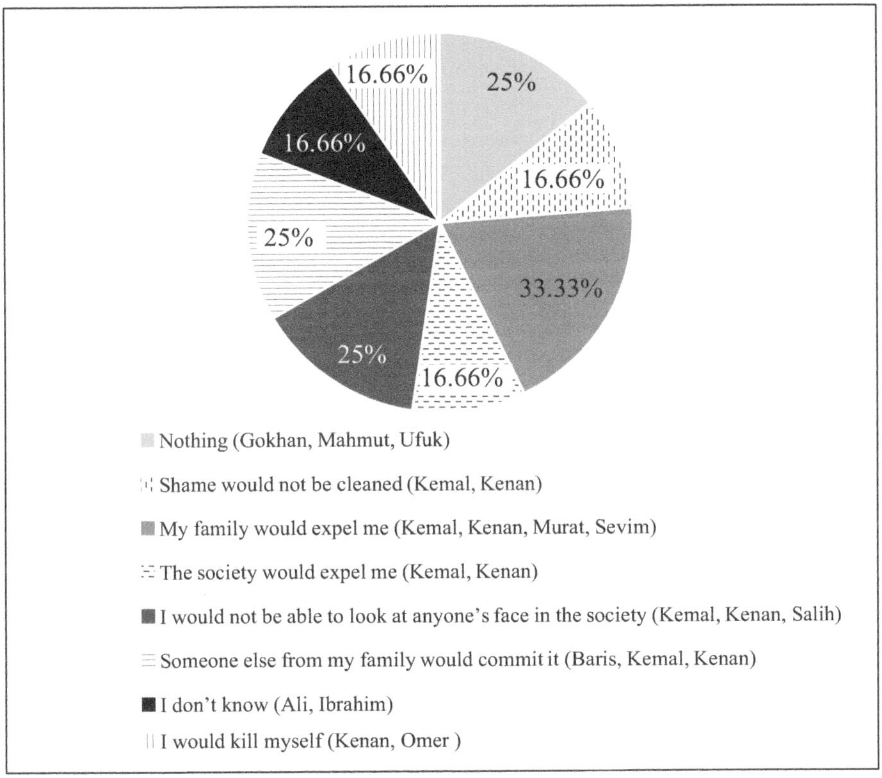

1.8 Do you think you had a fair trial?

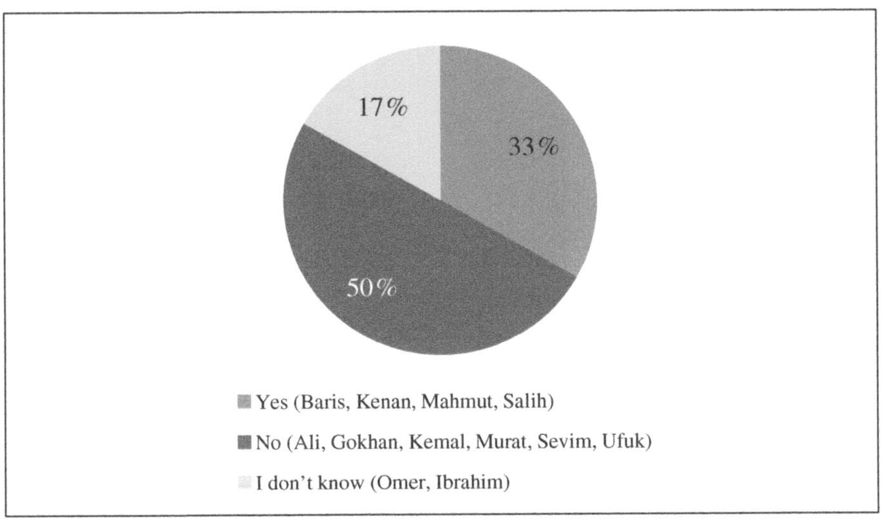

1.9 What do you think about your sentence?

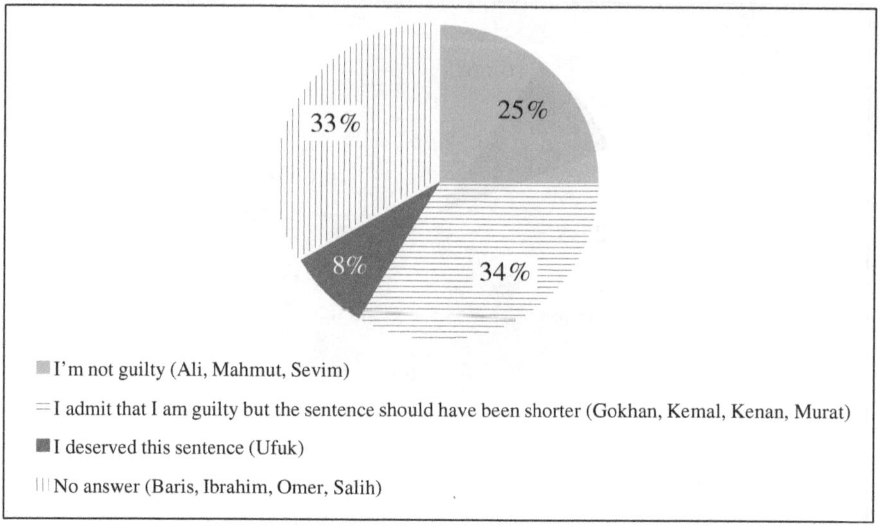

1.10 How are your relationships with other inmates?

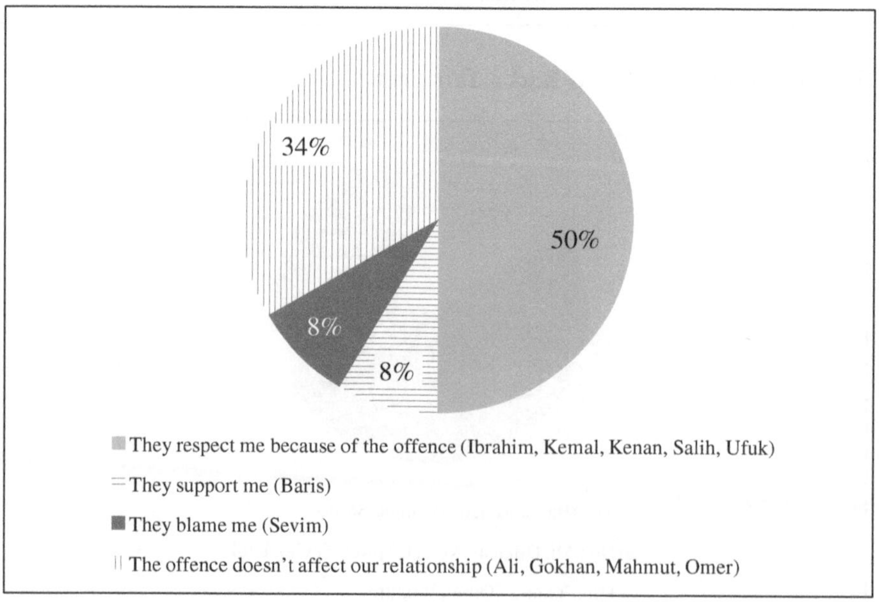

1.11 How are your relationships with members of your family since the incident?

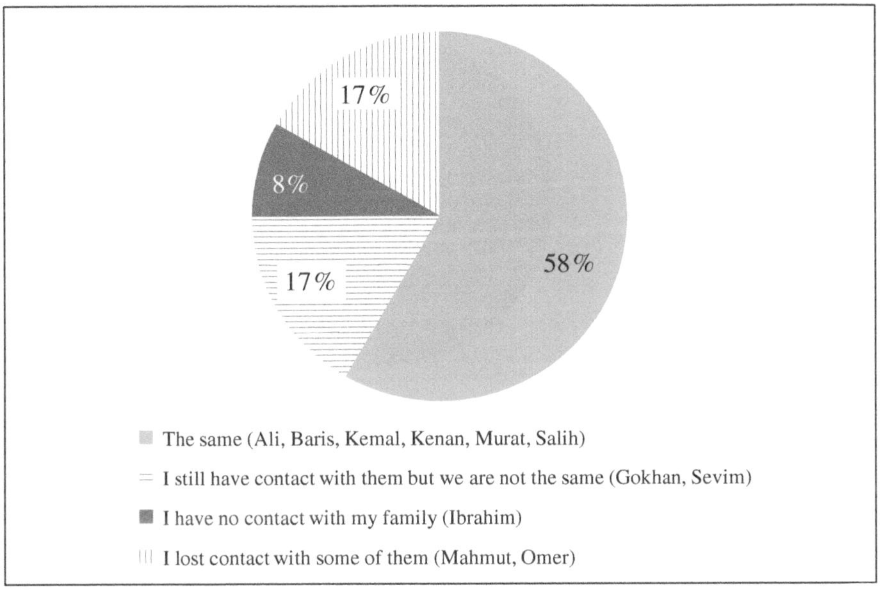

1.12 Where will you live after your sentence?

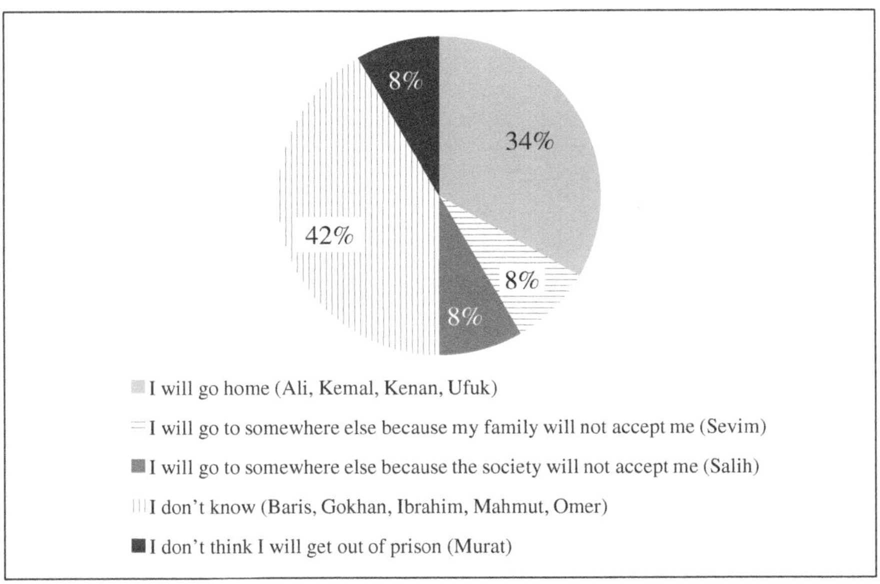

1.13 Do you think that the number of honour crimes will be reduced by increasing the severity of punishment?

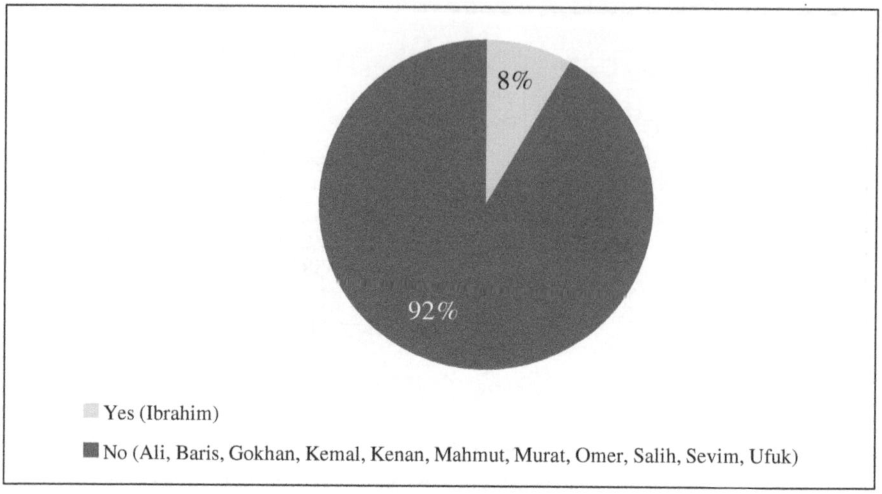

1.14 Had you known the sentence you would receive for your crime, would you still have chosen to commit it?

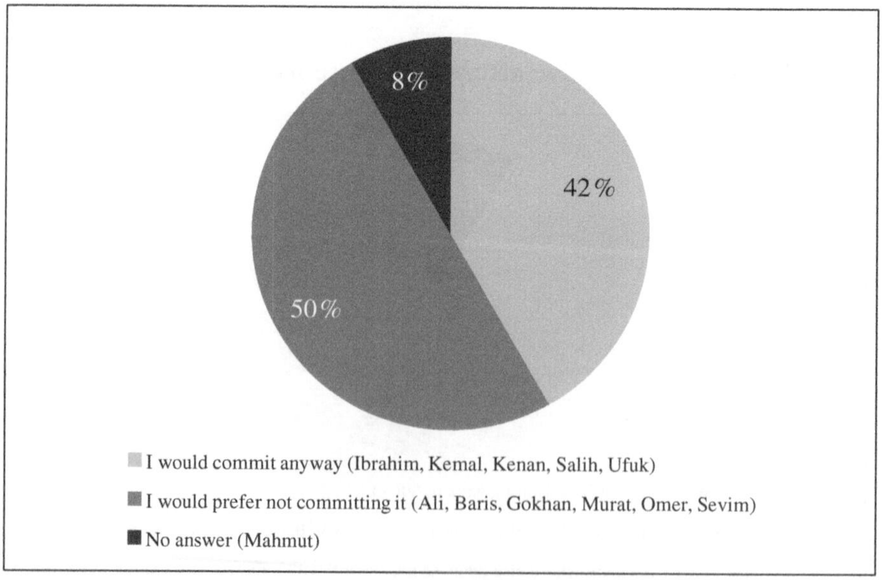

1.15 What is the source of honour?

Name	*Religion*	*Family*	*Custom*	*Tradition*
Ali	×	×		
Baris	×			
Gokhan			×	
Ibrahim	×			×
Kemal	×		×	
Kenan	×	×	×	
Mahmut				
Murat	×	×	×	×
Omer		×		
Salih			×	
Sevim	×			
Ufuk	×	×		

1.16 What can tarnish honour?

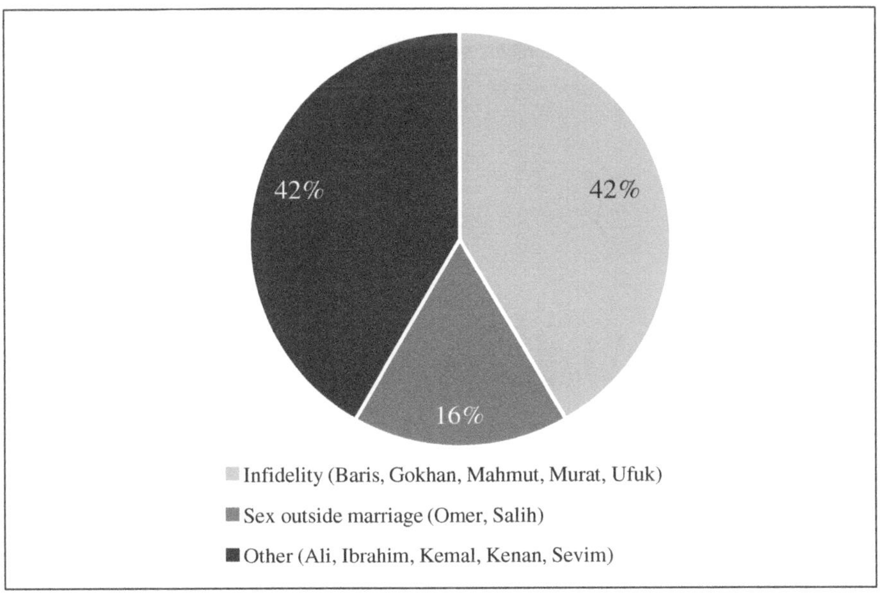

1.17 Is murder the only solution if honour is tarnished?

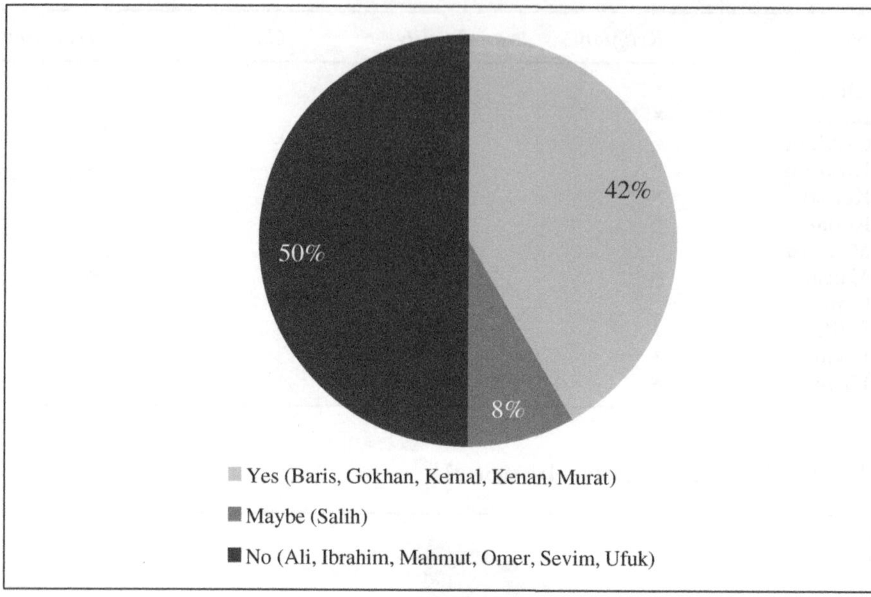

Appendix 2
First instance court cases

2.1 Overview of the court cases

	Court	*Defendant (male/female)*	*Victim (male/female)*	*Defendant–victim relationship*	*Offence*	*Motive*	*Year of offence*	*Sentence*
1	Adana 1st High Criminal Court 2005/144 E, 2008/82 K, Date: 10.03.2008	KY (M) MY (M)	MY (M) AK (F)	KY, MY–MY: non-acquaintance KY–AK: brother–sister-in-law MY–AK: divorced couple	Murder (S.81)	MY's marriage to MY's former wife	2005	KY–MY: life imprisonment reduced to 8 years 4 months imprisonment with application of s.39, s.62 KY–AK: life imprisonment reduced to 5 years imprisonment with application of s.35, s.39, s.62 MY: missing
2	Adana 1st High Criminal Court 2009/131 E, 2009/600 K, Date: 28.12.2009	ID (F)	MD (F)	Mother–daughter	Murder (s.82)	MD's extramarital relationship with a married man and rumours about it	2009	Aggravated life imprisonment reduced to 20 years imprisonment with application of s.29, s.62

(*Continued*)

(Continued)

	Court	*Defendant (male/female)*	*Victim (male/female)*	*Defendant–victim relationship*	*Offence*	*Motive*	*Year of offence*	*Sentence*
3	Adana 1st High Criminal Court 2011/182 E, 2012/91 K, Date: 02.03.2012	IB (M) CB (M) DAC (M)	MK (M)	Acquaintance	Murder (s.81, S.82)	MK's relationship with DAC's mother	2011	DAC: aggravated life imprisonment reduced to life imprisonment with application of s.62 IB: life imprisonment reduced to 10 years 10 months imprisonment with application of s.31, s.62 CB: life imprisonment reduced to 6 years 8 months imprisonment with application of s.39, s.31, s.62
4	Adana 2nd High Criminal Court 2007/36 E, 2008/167 K, Date: 29.05.2008	CU (M) OU (M)	AO (M) AU (F)	CU–AU: brother–sister-in-law OU–AU: married OU–AO: friends CU–AO: non-acquaintance	Premeditated murder (s.82)	AO and AU's extramarital relationship	2006	OU, CU: aggravated life imprisonment reduced to 20 years imprisonment with application of s.29, s.62
5	Adana 2nd High Criminal Court 2008/432 E, 2009/162 K, Date: 30.04.2009	VKC (M)	CMC (M)	distant relative	Murder (S.81)	Eloping with VKC's sister	2008	Life imprisonment reduced to 25 years imprisonment with application of s.62

6	Adana 3rd High Criminal Court 2011/391 E, 2012/243 K, Date: 11.06.2012	MU (M)	EU (F)	Married but separated	Murder (s.82)	Infidelity, reprobate	2011	Aggravated life imprisonment reduced to 17 years 6 months imprisonment with application of s.29, s.62
7	Adana 4th High Criminal Court 2007/85 E, 2008/241 K, Date: 08.07.2008	AB (M) AO (M)	NO (M)	Non-acquaintance	Murder (s.82)	Eloping with AO's daughter and refusing to marry her		AO: acquitted AB: aggravated life imprisonment reduced to life imprisonment with application of s. 62
8	Adana 4th High Criminal Court 2011/259 E, 2011/256 K, Date: 07.07.2011	AB (M) MB (M)	GB (F)	MB–GB: husband–wife AB–GB: brothers-in-law	Premeditated murder (s.82)	Dressing against the family's approval	2009	MB: acquitted AB: aggravated life imprisonment reduced to life imprisonment with application of s.62
9	Adiyaman 1st High Criminal Court 2007/17 E, 2008/177 K, Date: 13.11.2008	RY (M) SY (M) AY (M) YE (M) FY (M) HY (M) YY (M) ME (M)	RE (F)	ME–RE: son–mother RY–RE: grandson–grandmother) FY, YY, YE, SY, HY, RE: distanced relatives AY–RE: brother–sister	Murder (s.82)	Rumours about being in a relationship with several men	2006	RY, SY, AY, YE, FY, HY, YY: acquitted ME: aggravated life imprisonment reduced to 13 years 4 months imprisonment with application of s.29, s.31, s.62

(*Continued*)

(Continued)

	Court	*Defendant (male/ female)*	*Victim (male/ female)*	*Defendant–victim relationship*	*Offence*	*Motive*	*Year of offence*	*Sentence*
10	Adiyaman 1st High Criminal Court 2007/114 E, 2007/242 K, Date: 24.07.2007	SY (M)	MK (M)	Non-acquaintance	Murder (s.81)	Eloping with SY's sister	1995	Life imprisonment reduced to 12 years six months imprisonment with application of s.29, s.62
11	Agri High Criminal Court 2007/215 E, 2008/191 K, Date: 24.06.2008	YA (M)	OA (M) AT (F)	YA–OA: brothers YA–AT: non-acquaintance	Customary killing (s.82)	Eloping	2007	Aggravated life imprisonment reduced to life imprisonment with application of s.62
12	Aksaray High Criminal Court 2006/367 E, 2008/14 K, Date: 05.02.2008	SC (M)	ET (F)	Divorced couple	Murder (s.81)	ET's engagement	2006	Life imprisonment reduced to 11 years 8 months imprisonment with application of s.35, s.62
13	Akhisar High Criminal Court 2001/80 E, 2001/192 K, Date: 18.10.2001	HA (M)	HK (M) SA (F)	HA–SA: married HA–HK: non-acquaintance	Murder (abolished Penal Code s.462)	Relationship between HK and SA and rumours about it	2001	Life imprisonment reduced by half with application of (abolished Penal Code s. 51)

14	Ankara 3rd High Criminal Court 2004/545 E, 2005/232 K, Date: 11.11.2005	BY (M)	GY (F)	Son–mother	Murder (s.82)	Rumours about GY's chastity	2004	Aggravated life imprisonment reduced to life imprisonment with application of s.62
15	Ankara 9th High Criminal Court 2009/88 E, 2009/186 K, Date: 23.06.2009	SC (M)	MK (M)	Non-acquaintance	Murder (s.81)	Being seen with SC's sister	2009	Life imprisonment reduced to 25 years imprisonment with application of s.62
16	Bafra High Criminal Court 2009/132 E, 2010/43 K, Date: 12.02.2010	AA(M)(1) AA (M) (2) FA (M) NA (M) SA (M) RE (M)	AA (M)	Acquaintance	Murder (s.81)	Being in a relationship with AA (1)'s wife	2009	AA (1): life imprisonment reduced to 10 years imprisonment with application of s.29 and s.62 AA (2), FA: life imprisonment reduced to 3 years 4 months imprisonment with application of s.29, s.39/1, s.62 NA, SA, RE: acquitted
17	Bakırköy 3rd High Criminal Court 2011/310 E, 2012/137 K, Date: 25.04.2012	SG (M)	EG (M)	Husband–wife	Murder (s.82)	Infidelity	2011	Aggravated life imprisonment reduced to 20 years imprisonment with application of s.29, s.62

(*Continued*)

(Continued)

	Court	Defendant (male/female)	Victim (male/female)	Defendant–victim relationship	Offence	Motive	Year of offence	Sentence
18	Bakırköy 5th High Criminal Court 2010/435 E, 2011/64 K, Date: 14.03.2011	MT (M)	HT (M)	MT–HT: brothers)	Murder (s.81)	Infidelity	2007	Life imprisonment reduced to 15 years with application of s.29 and s.62
19	Bakırköy 5th High Criminal Court 2009/260 E, 2009/317 K, Date: 16.10.2009 2007/269 E, 2008/27 K, Date: 04.02.2008	MHH (M) MAH (M) SK (M) AH (M) HH (M) MM (M)	NH (F)	MHH–NH: father–daughter HH–NH: brother–sister MAH/MM–NH: uncle–niece AH–NH: cousins SK–NH: distance relative)	Customary killing (c.82)	Eloping, being raped	2004	MHH, MAH, SK: aggravated life imprisonment reduced to life imprisonment with application of s.62 AH: 6 months imprisonment (s.281) reduced to 5 months imprisonment with application of s.62
20	Bakırköy 5th High Criminal Court 2006/303 E, 2007/458 K, Date: 12.11.2007	MT (M) IT (M) FT (M)	GT (F)	IT/FT–GT: brothers–sister MT: uncle–niece	Premeditated murder (abolished Penal Code s.450)	Pregnancy out of wedlock	2004	MT: acquitted IT: aggravated life imprisonment reduced to life imprisonment with application of s.62 FT: aggravated life imprisonment reduced to 18 years imprisonment with application of s.31/3, s.62

21	Bakırköy 6th High Criminal Court 2006/170 E, 2009/221 K, Date: 16.07.2009	EB (M) AB (M)	IK (M)	Acquaintance	Premeditated murder (s.82)	Pregnancy out of wedlock	2006	EB: case separation AB: aggravated life imprisonment reduced to life imprisonment with application of s.62
22	Bakırköy 6th High Criminal Court 2008/76 E, 2009/207 K, Date: 06.07.2009	OO (M) SS (M) SA (M)	NS (F)	SS–NS: brother–sister SA–NS: uncle–niece OO–NS: non-acquaintance	Customary killing (s.82)	Eloping from forced marriage	2008	OO: separation of the case SS, SA: aggravated life imprisonment
23	Bakırköy 7th High Criminal Court 2006/246 E, 2008/170 K, Date: 11.04.2008	UK1 (M) UK2 (M)	AK (F)	Distance relatives	Murder (s.81)	Reprobate, rumours about prostitution	2006	Life imprisonment reduced to 12 years imprisonment with application of s.29, s.62
24	Bakırköy 8th High Criminal Court 2009/229 E, 2012/329 K, Date: 05.07.2012	MK (M)	FK (F)	Husband–wife	Murder (s.82)	Infidelity	2009	Aggravated life imprisonment reduced to life imprisonment with application of s. 62

(*Continued*)

(Continued)

	Court	Defendant (male/female)	Victim (male/female)	Defendant–victim relationship	Offence	Motive	Year of offence	Sentence
25	Bakırköy 13th High Criminal Court 2007/526 E, 2007/17 K, Date: 20.11.2007	SK (M)	DK (F)	Father–daughter	Murder (s.82)	Eloping, being in a relationship with several men	2001	Aggravated life imprisonment reduced to 20 years imprisonment with application of s.29, s.62
26	Bakırköy 13th High Criminal Court 2009/183 E, 2010/96 K, Date: 04.05.2010	MT (M)	ST(F) GE (M)	MT–ST: husband–wife MT–GE: non-acquaintance	Murder (s.81, s.82)	Infidelity	2008	MT–ST: aggravated life imprisonment reduced to 15 years imprisonment with application of s.29, s.62 MT–GE: life imprisonment reduced to 10 years imprisonment with application of s.29, s.62
27	Bakırköy 14th High Criminal Court 2007/219 E, 2009/132 K, Date: 14.05.2009	CK (M)	LK (F)	Brother–sister	Attempt to murder (s.82)	Having sexual relationship (prostitution)	2003	Aggravated life imprisonment reduced to 3 years 4 months imprisonment with application of s.29, s.35, s.62
28	Bakırköy 14 High Criminal Court 2010/179 E, 2012/462 K, Date: 20.12.2012	YS (M)	TM (F)	Divorced couple	Murder (s.81)	TM's relationship after divorce	2010	Life imprisonment reduced to 15 years imprisonment with application of s.29, s.62

29	Bakırköy 15th High Criminal Court 2009/116 E, 2011/217 K, Date: 13.05.2011	HS(M) MS(M) RS(M) OA (M) YS (M) AS(M) OS(M) TK (M) SS(M)	NA (F)	OK–NA: husband–wife HS–NA: father–daughter OS–NA: brother–sister MS, RS, YS: distance relative TK: family friend SS–NA: cousins AS–NA: uncle–niece	Customary killing (s.82)	Infidelity	2008	AS: closed (death) SS, TK, YS, RS, MS: acquitted OS: aggravated life imprisonment reduced to 20 years imprisonment with application of s.31/2, s.62 HS, OK: aggravated life imprisonment
30	Badırma High Criminal Court 2009/181 E, 2010/141 K, Date: 29.09.2010	DT (F)	ST (F) New-born baby	Mother-daughter	Murder (s.83/3)	Delivering a baby out of wedlock	2009	20 years imprisonment reduced to 16 years 8 months with application of s.62/1
31	Batman High Criminal Court 2011/222 E, 2011/236 K, Date: 23.06.2011	MSK (M)	MG (M)	Non-acquaintance	Premeditated murder (s.82)	Eloping with the defendant's niece	2009	Aggravated life imprisonment reduced to 15 years imprisonment with application of s.29, s.62
32	Batman 2nd High Criminal Court 2015/343 E, 2017/171 K, Date: 21.06.2017	GD (M)	HD (F)	Cousins	Customary killing (s.82/1-k)	Family council decision to kill the victim as a result of rape	2012	Aggravated life imprisonment

(*Continued*)

(Continued)

	Court	Defendant (male/female)	Victim (male/female)	Defendant–victim relationship	Offence	Motive	Year of offence	Sentence
33	Bursa 4th High Criminal Court 2008/184 E, 2008/289 K, Date: 17.10.2008	DO (M)	HA (F)	Father–daughter	Murder (s.82)	Having extramarital relationship	2006	Life imprisonment
34	Bursa 4th High Criminal Court 2009/333 E, 2009/350 K, Date: 20.11.2009	HY (M)	AC (M)	Acquaintance	Murder (s.81)	Being in a relationship with HY's mother	2006	Life imprisonment reduced to 16 years imprisonment with application of s.29
35	Denizli 1st High Criminal Court 2006/289 E, 2007/74 K, Date: 20.02.2007	SB (M)	AB (F)	Brother–sister	Premeditated murder (s.82)	Working in a pub and having a relationship after divorce	2006	Aggravated life imprisonment reduced to 16 years 8 months with application of s.29, s.62
36	Diyarbakir Juvenile Court 2006/29 E, 206/333 K, Date: 20.10.2006	AT (M) RD (M)	NK (F) FD (M)	RD–FD: brothers AT–NK: brothers-in-law	Customary killing (s.82)	Infidelity	2005	RD: aggravated life imprisonment reduced to 10 years imprisonment with application of s.31, s.62 AT: aggravated life imprisonment reduced to 5 years imprisonment with application of s.35/2, s.31/2, s.62

37	Diyarbakir 1st High Criminal Court 2011/140 E, 2011/192 K, Date: 10.05.2011	RM (M) BM (M) MM (M)	MZM (M)	In-laws	Premeditated murder (s.82)	Sending the wife back to her family for not being a virgin on the wedding night	2006	BM, RM, MM: aggravated life imprisonment reduced to life imprisonment with application of s.62
38	Diyarbakir 1st High Criminal Court 2011/207 E, 2012/280 K, Date: 17.05.2012	HS (M) BS (M) FG (M) MTS (M) TS (M) CS (M) SS (M)	CS (F)	HS–CS: husband–wife FG–CS: brother–sister BS–CS: brothers-in-law TS–CS: distance relative MTS–CS: cousins CS–CS: uncle–niece SS–CS: uncle–niece	Customary killing (s.82)	Infidelity	2010	FG, SS, BS, MTS, TS, CS: acquitted HS: aggravated life imprisonment reduced to 20 years imprisonment with application of s.29, s.62
39	Diyarbakir 1st High Criminal Court 2011/147 E, 2012/259 K, Date: 08.05.2012	HY(M) YY(M)	MZK (M)	Non-acquaintance	Customary killing (s.82)	Having a sexual relationship with YY's wife	2010	HY, YY: aggravated life imprisonment reduced to life imprisonment with application of s.62
40	Diyarbakir 1st High Criminal Court 2010/350 E, 2012/66 K, Date: 07.02.2012	YG (M)	SG(F)	Brother–sister	Customary killing (s.82)	Eloping – prostitution– working at a pub	2010	Aggravated life imprisonment reduced to life imprisonment with application of s. 62

(*Continued*)

(Continued)

	Court	*Defendant (male/ female)*	*Victim (male/ female)*	*Defendant–victim relationship*	*Offence*	*Motive*	*Year of offence*	*Sentence*
41	Diyarbakir 1st High Criminal Court 2010/247 E, 2010/397 K, Date: 23.09.2010	CT (M) ST (M) HT (M) RT (M) MT (M) ST (F) IT (M)	AT (F)	ST–AT: husband–wife ST–AT: sisters-in-law IT–AT: father-in-law CT–AT: brothers-in-law MT–AT: brothers-in-law HT–AT: brother–sister RT–AT: brother–sister	Customary killing (s.82)	Infidelity	2010	IT, CT, MT, HT, RT, ST: acquitted ST: aggravated life imprisonment reduced to 20 years imprisonment with application of s.29, s.62
42	Diyarbakir 1st High Criminal Court 2010/279 E, 2010/522 K, Date: 28.12.2010	HT (M) IT (M) BG (M) AG (M) MG (M) IG (M) OT (M) MST (M)	GG (F)	OT–GG: spouse MG–GG: brother–sister HT, IT, MST: brother-in-law, cousin BG–GG: distance relative AG–GG: distance relative IG–GG: uncle–niece	Customary killing (s.82)	Rumours about infidelity	2006	ST, OT: aggravated life imprisonment reduced to life imprisonment with application of s.62 HT, BG: aggravated life imprisonment reduced to 16 years 8 months imprisonment with application of s.39, s.62 AG, MG, IG, IT: aggravated life imprisonment reduced to 15 years imprisonment with application of s.39, s.62

43	Diyarbakir 1st High Criminal Court 2006/437 E, 2009/115 K, Date: 26.03.2009	RT(M) MT(M) MT(F) MT (M)	FD (M) NK(F)	RT, MT, MT-NK: in-laws RT, MT, MT, FD: non-acquaintance	Customary killing (s.82)	Sexual relationship out of wedlock	2005	MK(F), MK(M): acquitted MT, RT: aggravated life imprisonment reduced to 7 years 6 months imprisonment with application of s.35/2, s.39, s.29
44	Diyarbakir 1st High Criminal Court 2006/228 E, 2007/174 K, Date: 20.03.2007	RM (M) BM (M) MM (M) SM (M) NA (M)	MZM (M)	Distanced relatives	Premeditated murder (s. 82)	MZM's allegation on RM and BM's sister was not a virgin during the wedding night which results immediate divorce	2006	SM, NA: acquitted RM, BM, MM: aggravated life imprisonment reduced to 12 years 6 months with application of s.39, s.62
45	Diyarbakir 1st High Criminal Court 2004/6 E, 2006/376 K, Date: 21.12.2006	NO (M)	NY (F)	Boyfriend–girlfriend	Murder furiously and brutally (s.82)	Infidelity	2003	Aggravated life imprisonment reduced to life imprisonment with application of s.62
46	Diyarbakir 2nd High Criminal Court 2009/379 E, 2010/617 K, Date: 01.12.2010	HK (M) MK (M)	TK (F)	MK–TK: father–daughter HK–TK: boyfriend–girlfriend	Murder (s.81)	Infidelity	2008	MK: acquitted HK: life imprisonment reduced to 15 years imprisonment with application of s.31/3

(*Continued*)

(Continued)

	Court	*Defendant (male/ female)*	*Victim (male/ female)*	*Defendant–victim relationship*	*Offence*	*Motive*	*Year of offence*	*Sentence*
47	Diyarbakir 2nd High Criminal Court 2005/255 E, 2005/308 K, Date: 16.12.2005	HT (M) HT (F) MT (M) IT (M)	GT (F)	HT, HT–GT: parents-daughter IT, MT–GT: brothers–sister	Premeditated murder (s.82)	Sexual relationship out of wedlock	2003	HT, IT: acquitted HT(M): aggravated life imprisonment reduced to 20 years imprisonment with application of s.29, s.62 MT: aggravated life imprisonment reduced to 6 years 8 months imprisonment with application of s.29, s.31/3, s.62
48	Diyarbakir 3rd High Criminal Court 2011/250 E, 2012/116 K, Date: 15.03.2012	MY (M) MY (M)	BY (F)	MY–BY: father-in-law–daughter-in-law MY–BY: brother–sister-in-law	Customary killing (s.82)	Infidelity	2010	MY: aggravated life imprisonment MY: aggravated life imprisonment reduced to 15 years imprisonment with application of s.31/2 (being a minor)
49	Duzce High Criminal Court 2008/29 E, 2009/208 K, Date: 27.08.2009	NB (M) FB (M)	AK (F)	NB–AK: religiously married couple FB–AK: mother–son-in-law	Premeditated murder (s.82)	Eloping and infidelity	2007	FB, NB: aggravated life imprisonment reduced to life imprisonment with application of s.62

50	Elazig 1st High Criminal Court 2006/184 E, 2007/470 K, Date: 13.12.2007	YK (M) SK 1 (M) SK 2 (M)	ID (M)	Acquaintance	Attempt to murder (s. 456)	Breach of engagement with SK (1)'s sister	2004	SK (1), SK (2), YK: 2 years imprisonment reduced to 1 year 12 months imprisonment with application of s.457/1, 457/2, 463
51	Elbistan High Criminal Court 2008/36 E, 2009/138 K, Date: 16.06.2009	SO (M) ZO (M) AO (M) CA (M) CA2 (M)	MO (F)	SO/ZO–MO: brother–sister AO–MO: father-daughter CA/CA2–MO: uncle–niece	Customary killing (s.82/1-k)	Divorcing twice, living alone, being in an extramarital relationship, rumours about the chastity of MO	2007	SO: aggravated life imprisonment ZO, AO, CA, CA2: acquitted
52	Elbistan High Criminal Court 2006/201 E, 206/322 K, Date: 19.12.2006	MD (M)	ED (F)	Brother–sister	Attempt to murder (s.82)	Eloping to a married man	2006	Aggravated life imprisonment reduced to 10 years 10 months imprisonment with application of s.35/2, 62/1
53	Erzurum 3rd High Criminal Court 2008/157 E, 2011/86 K, Date: 18.05.2011	MEG (M) YG (M) AO (M) GG (M) MG (M) SG (M)	YG (M)	Non-acquaintance	Customary killing (s.82)	Having a sexual relationship with SG's minor sister	2008	SG: aggravated life imprisonment reduced to 19 years 2 months imprisonment with application of s.31, s.62 MEG, GG, MG, AO: acquitted

(*Continued*)

(Continued)

	Court	Defendant (male/female)	Victim (male/female)	Defendant–victim relationship	Offence	Motive	Year of offence	Sentence
54	Gaziantep 1st High Criminal Court 2010/259 E, 2012/214 K, Date: 25.04.2012	RK (M) MK (M)	CK (F) MK (M)	RK–CK: brother–sister MK–CK: cousins RK/MK–MK: cousins	Customary killing (s.82)	Rumours about being friends with prostitutes	2010	RK, MK: aggravated life imprisonment reduced to life imprisonment with application of s.62
55	Gaziantep 2nd High Criminal Court 2011/408 E, 2012/30 K, Date: 24.01.2012	FC (M)	RC (M)	Brothers	Murder (82)	Homosexuality	2011	Aggravated life imprisonment reduced to life imprisonment with application of s.62
56	Gaziantep 2nd High Criminal Court 2010/108 E, 2010/377 K, Date: 29.06.2010	VD (M)	ND (F)	Nephew–aunt	Premeditated murder (s.82)	Extramarital relationships and rumours	2009	Aggravated life imprisonment reduced to life imprisonment with application of s.62
57	Gaziantep 2nd High Criminal Court 2008/275 E, 2008/318 K, Date: 11.11.2008	MAK (M)	HM (M) HK (F)	MAK–HM: employer–employee MAK–HM: father–daughter	Premeditated murder (s.82)	Abducting MAK's daughter	1992	Aggravated life imprisonment reduced to 15 years imprisonment with application of s.29, s.62

58	Gaziantep 2nd High Criminal Court 2007/396 E, 2008/177 K, Date: 01.05.2008	MEA (M) MA (M)	MYH (M)	Non-acquaintance	Murder (s.81)	Having sexual relationship with defendants' sister	2007	MEA: life imprisonment reduced to 10 years imprisonment with application of s.29, s.62 MA: life imprisonment reduced to 8 years 4 months imprisonment with application of s.39, 62
59	Gaziantep 2nd High Criminal Court 1999/287 E, 2002/323 K, Date: 10.10.2002	MAK (M) FK (M) MK (M) HK (M)	HM (M) HK (F)	MAK–HK: father–daughter MAK–HM: non-acquaintance	Premeditated murder (abolished code s. 450)	Eloping	1992	FK, MK, HK: acquitted MAK: aggravated life imprisonment reduced to 30 years imprisonment
60	Gaziantep 3rd High Criminal Court 2006/130E, 2007/159 K, Date: 12.04.2007	SD (M)	ED (F)	Brother–sister	Premeditated murder (abolished Penal Code s.450)	Eloping	2003	Aggravated life imprisonment reduced to life imprisonment with application of s.59
61	Hatay High Criminal Court 2008/363 E, 2009/27 K, Date: 29.01.2009	MI (M) AI (M) HI (M)	AI (F)	MI–AI: father–daughter AI–AI: uncle–niece HI–AI: brother–sister	Premeditated murder (s.82)	Eloping	2008	AI: acquitted MI, HI: aggravated life imprisonment reduced to life imprisonment with application of s.62

(*Continued*)

(Continued)

	Court	*Defendant (male/ female)*	*Victim (male/ female)*	*Defendant–victim relationship*	*Offence*	*Motive*	*Year of offence*	*Sentence*
62	Igdır High Criminal Court 2011/34 E, 2011/69 K, Date: 05.05.2011	HS (M) CS (M)	SS (M)	Non-acquaintance	Customary killing (s.81, s.82)	HS and CS's sister's eloping	2011	CS: life imprisonment reduced to 12 years 6 months with application of s.21, 2.62, s.53 HS: life imprisonment reduced to 5 years 15 months with application of s.21, s.39, s.62, s.53
63	Istanbul 1st High Criminal Court 2011/70 E, 2012/106 K, Date: 16.04.2012	GO (M)	ZV (F) SV (M)	GO–SV: brother-in-law GO–ZV–brother–sister	Customary killing (s.82)	Getting married to someone from a different religion	2010	Aggravated life imprisonment reduced to life imprisonment with application of s.62
64	Istanbul 2nd High Criminal Court 2009/118 E, 2009/213 K, Date: 07.07.2009	SA (M) SA2(M) AA (M)	MT (M)	No-acquaintance	Customary killing (s.81, s.82)	Being in a relationship with defendants' married sister	2005	SA2, AK: life imprisonment reduced to 25 years imprisonment wit application of s.29, s.62 SA: life imprisonment reduced to 8 years 4 months imprisonment with application of s.39, s.29, s.62

65	Istanbul 3rd High Criminal Court 2000/205 E, 2001/131 K, Date: 10.05.2001	IS (M) ES (M) AS (M)	MS (F)	IS, ES, AS–MS (brothers–sister)	Customary killing (abolished Penal Code s. 449)	Eloping	2000	IS: aggravated life imprisonment reduced to 12 years and 6 months imprisonment with application of s.51/2, s.59/2 ES: aggravated life imprisonment reduced to 8 years 4 months imprisonment with application of s.51/2, s.55/3, s.59/2 AS: aggravated life imprisonment reduced to 4 years 5 months 10 days imprisonment with application of s.51/2, s.65/3, s.59/2
66	Izmir 6th High Criminal Court 2007/359 E, 2009/52 K, Date: 30.03.2009	NC (M) MC (M)	MD (M)	Non-acquaintance	Murder (S.81)	MD's relationship with NC's former wife and MC's former sister-in-law	2007	NC: acquitted MC: life imprisonment reduced to 15 years imprisonment with application of s.29, s.62
67	Karabuk High Criminal Court 2006/122 E, 2008/13 K, Date: 05.02.2008	IB (M)	BK (M)	Non-acquaintance	Murder (s.81)	Being in a relationship with IB's sister and rumours about it	2006	Life imprisonment reduced to 25 years imprisonment with application of s.62

(*Continued*)

(Continued)

	Court	Defendant (male/ female)	Victim (male/ female)	Defendant–victim relationship	Offence	Motive	Year of offence	Sentence
68	Karsiyaka 2nd High Criminal Court 2005/91 E, 2007/406 K, Date: 20.11.2007	VS (M) ZS (M)	AB (M)	Non-acquaintance	Premeditated murder (s.82)	Rumours about AB's relationship with VS and ZS's brother's wife	2005	ZS: acquitted VS: aggravated life imprisonment reduced to 20 years imprisonment with application of s.29, s.62
69	Kartal 2nd High Criminal Court 2007/372 E, 2008/116 K, Date: 10.03.2008	SO (M) TK (M) NO (M) MD (M) HD (M) ED (M)	NO (F)	SO–NOL married TK–NO: distanced relative NO–NO: brother-in-law–sister-in-law MD, HD, ED–NO: distanced relative	Premeditated murder (s.82)	Eloping with NO's brother-in-law	2004	SO: aggravated life imprisonment reduced to 15 years with application of s.29 and s.62 TK, NO, MD, ED, HD: aggravated life imprisonment reduced to 12 years 6 months imprisonment with application of s.39/1, s.62
70	Kastamonu High Criminal Court 2009/28E, 2009/167 K, Date: 30.07.2009	MK (M)	MG (M) HG (M)	Acquaintance	Murder (s.81)	Spreading rumours about HG's daughter	2008	Life imprisonment reduced to 2 years 8 months 15 days imprisonment with application of s.35, s.29, s.62

71	Kayseri 1st High Criminal Court 2007/146 E, 2007/328 K, Date: 23.11.2007 2009/233 E, 2009/287 K, Date: 02.09.2009	NP (M) EP (M)	MTE (M)	Non-acquaintance	Murder (s.81)	Being in a relationship with NP and EP's mother	2007	EP: life imprisonment reduced to 6 years 8 months imprisonment with application of s.29, s.31, s.62 NP: life imprisonment reduced to 10 years imprisonment with application of. s.29, s.62
72	Kayseri 2nd High Criminal Court 2001/154 E, 2001/227 K, Date: 13.09.2001	EM (M)	BM (F)	Sister-in-law	Murder (abolished Penal Code s.449)	Infidelity	2001	Life imprisonment
73	Kayseri 2. High Criminal Court 2005/76 E, 2010/276 K, Date: 01.10.2010 2011/177 E, 2011/212 K, Date: 30.06.2011	SK (M)	DK (F)	Father–daughter	Murder (s.82)	Eloping	2005	Aggravated life imprisonment reduced to life imprisonment with application of s.62

(*Continued*)

(Continued)

	Court	Defendant (male/female)	Victim (male/female)	Defendant–victim relationship	Offence	Motive	Year of offence	Sentence
74	Kayseri 2nd High Criminal Court 2007/32 E, 2007/181 K, Date: 29.05.2007	BK (M) HK (M) EK (M)	MK (M)	Non-acquaintance	Premeditated Murder (s.81)	Being in a relationship with BK, HK, EK's relative's wife	2006	HK: acquitted EK: life imprisonment reduced to 15 years imprisonment with application of s.29, s.62 BK: life imprisonment reduced to 6 years 3 months imprisonment with application of s.39/1, s.29, s.62
75	Kirsehir High Criminal Court 2007/54 E, 2007/68 K, Date: 17.05.2007	KD (M)	IK (M)	Non-acquaintance	Premeditated murder (s.82)	Eloping with KD's sister	2007	Aggravated life imprisonment reduced to 16 years 8 months imprisonment with application of s.29, s.62
76	Kocaeli 1st High Criminal Court 2007/195 E, 2007/341 K, Date: 18.10.2007	ES (M) YS (M) HS (M)	RS (F) OS (M)	HS–OS: brothers ES, YS–OS: distanced relative HS–RS: married ES–RS: distanced relative YS–RS: brothers–sisters	Attempt to murder (s.81, s.82)	Assumed relationship with HS's wife (RS)	2007	HS: aggravated life imprisonment reduced to 4 years 2 months imprisonment with application of s.35, s.29, s.62 ES: life imprisonment reduced to 3 years 4 months imprisonment with application of s.35, s.29, s.62 YS: aggravated life imprisonment reduced to 2 years 1 month imprisonment with application of s.35, 39, 29, 62

77	Kozan High Criminal Court 2007/282 E, 2008/30 K, Date: 24.01.2008	OA (M)	TC (F)	Brother–sister	Murder (s.82)	Rumours about infidelity	2007	Aggravated life imprisonment reduced to 21 years imprisonment with application of s.29, s.62
78	Manisa 2nd High Criminal Court 2011/246 E, 2012/153 K, Date: 14.05.2012	IE (M)	SE (F)	Married	Murder, customary killing (s.82)	Infidelity	2011	Aggravated life imprisonment
79	Mardin 2nd High Criminal Court 2006/80 E, 2006/350 K, Date: 20.06.2006	MY (M)	FY (F)	Brother–sister	Customary killing (s.82)	Rumours about infidelity	2006	Aggravated life imprisonment
80	Mersin High Criminal Court 2008/267 E, 2008/468 K, Date: 04.12.2008	OP (M)	ZG (F) ZG (M)	OP–ZG (F): divorced couple OP–ZG (M): non-acquaintance	Premeditated murder (s.82)	Rumours about infidelity during the marriage	2004	Aggravated life imprisonment reduced to 20 years imprisonment with application of s.29, s.62
81	Odemis High Criminal Court 2010/172 E, 2011/78 K, Date: 15.03.2011	SE (F) HT (M) HT2 (M) ZE (M)	DE (F)	ZE–DE: father–daughter HT, HT2–DE: uncle–niece SE–DE: mother–daughter	Customary killing (s.82)	Eloping, being in a relationship with several men, rumours about DE's chastity	2010	SE: acquitted ZE, HT, HT2: aggravated life imprisonment reduced to life imprisonment with application of s.62

(*Continued*)

(Continued)

	Court	*Defendant (male/female)*	*Victim (male/female)*	*Defendant–victim relationship*	*Offence*	*Motive*	*Year of offence*	*Sentence*
82	Osmaniye 1st High Criminal Court 2007/153 E, 2009/228 K, Date: 03.12.2009	HD (M) RA (M)	MA (M)	RA–MA: brothers HD–MA: non-acquaintance	Premeditated murder (s.82)	MA's relationship with HD's brother's wife	2007	HD: aggravated life imprisonment reduced to 20 years imprisonment with application of s.29, s.62 RA: aggravated life imprisonment reduced to life imprisonment with application of s.62
83	Sanliurfa 1st High Criminal Court 2005/27 E, 2005/248 E, Date: 31.03.2005	MA (M) BA (M) AA (M) HA (M)	GA (F)	AA, HA, MA–GA: brother–sister BA–GA: nephew–aunt	Murder (s.82)	Eloping, being pregnant out of wedlock	2004	AA, HA: acquitted BA: aggravated life imprisonment reduced to 18 years imprisonment with application of s.31, s.62 MA: 24 years imprisonment reduced to 10 years imprisonment with application of s.62, s.65
84	Sanliurfa 1st High Criminal Court 2005/178 E, 2005/200 K, Date: 04.10.2005	MSD (M)	HD (F)	Husband–wife	Premeditated murder (s.82)	Infidelity	2005	Aggravated life imprisonment reduced to 15 years imprisonment with application of s.29, s.62

85	Sanliurfa 1st High Criminal Court 2005/276 E, 2006/250 K, Date: 06.06.2006	MT (M) MO(M) MO(M) BO(M)	AA (M)	Acquaintance	Premeditated murder (s.81)	Bride exchange conflict	2005	MO, BO: acquitted MT, MO: life imprisonment reduced to 15 years imprisonment with application of s.29, s.62
86	Sanliurfa 1. High Criminal Court 2007/2 E, 2007/95 K, Date: 05.04.2007	MK (M) IK (M) MK (M) IK (M) IK (M) HK (M) AK (M) IK (M) HK (M) HK (M)	EK (F)	Father–daughter Uncle–niece Cousins Brother–sister	Premeditated murder (s.82)	Rumours for having sexual relationship without marriage	12.06.2012	MK: aggravated life imprisonment reduced to life imprisonment with application of s.62 MK, IK, IK, HK, AK, HK: aggravated life imprisonment reduced to 12 years 6 months imprisonment with application of s.62, s.39/1, IK, HK: acquitted IK, MK: non-suit
87	Sanliurfa 1st High Criminal Court 2008/115 E, 2008/246 K, Date: 30.10.2008	SC (M)	IS (M)	Non acquaintance	Attempt to murder (s.81)	Bride exchange conflict	2008	Life imprisonment reduced to 12 years imprisonment with application of s.35/2 and s.62

(*Continued*)

(Continued)

	Court	*Defendant (male/female)*	*Victim (male/female)*	*Defendant–victim relationship*	*Offence*	*Motive*	*Year of offence*	*Sentence*
88	Sanliurfa 1st High Criminal Court 2008/235 E, 2008/310 K, Date: 04.12.2008	IK (M) MK (M) MK(M) IK (M) HK (M) AK (M) HK (M)	EK (F)	IK–EK: father-daughter MK–EK: distance relative MK–EK: uncle–niece IK–EK: cousins HK–EK: cousins AK–EK: cousins HK–EK: brother–sister	Customary killing (s.82)	Loss of virginity before marriage	2008	IK, MK: case closed (death) MK: aggravated life imprisonment reduced to life imprisonment with application of s.62 MK, IK, IK, HK, AK, HK: aggravated life imprisonment reduced to 12 years 6 months imprisonment with application of s.39/1, s.62
89	Sanliurfa 1st High Criminal Court 2009/147 E, 2009/172 K, Date: 13.10.2009	MA (M)	GA (F)	MA–GA (brother–sister)	Customary killing (s. 82/1-a-k-f)	Pregnancy out of wedlock	2009	MA: aggravated life imprisonment reduced to life imprisonment with application of s.62
90	Sanliurfa 2nd High Criminal Court 2008/108 E, 2010/37 K, Date: 03.02.2010	HS (M) MHC (M) YD (M) AC (M) SC (M) HC (M)	SC (M)	Uncle–nephew relationship	Murder (s. 82)	Rumours about infidelity	2008	HS, MHC, AC: aggravated life imprisonment reduced to life imprisonment with application of s.62 SC, HC: acquitted YD: aggravated life imprisonment reduced to 12 years and 6 months with application of s.62, s.39

91	Sanliurfa 2nd High Criminal Court 2008/147 E, 2010/396 K, Date: 28.12.2010	HC (M) VB (M) IB (M) EB (F)	YK (F)	HC–YK: father–daughter VB–YK: uncle–niece IB–YK: uncle–niece EB–YK: grandmother–granddaughter	Customary killing (s.82/1-a-k)	Eloping and getting married without the family's approval	2007	HC: aggravated life imprisonment reduced to life imprisonment with application of s.62 VB: acquitted IB: separated from the case EB: acquitted
92	Sanliurfa 2nd High Criminal Court 2011/224 E, 2011/215 K, Date: 23.09.2011	YD (M)	SC (M)	Distanced relative	Customary killing (s.82)	Rumours about infidelity	2008	Aggravated life imprisonment reduced to life imprisonment with application of s.62
93	Sanliurfa 3rd High Criminal Court 2011/133 E, 2011/144 K, Date: 30.06.2011	DA (F) FA (M) HA (M) AC (M)	NY (F)	Non-related (NY's boyfriend's family)	Customary killing	NY's relationship with the defendant's husband/fathers	2008	Aggravated life imprisonment reduced to life imprisonment with application of s. 62; further reduction to 25 years imprisonment with application of CMUK s.326
94	Seydisehir High Criminal Court 2008/461 E, 2008/485 K, Date: 25.04.2008	ZY (F)	AY (M)	Boyfriend–girlfriend	Murder (s.81)	Denying the fatherhood of ZY's baby and spreading rumours about ZY's chastity	2007	Life imprisonment reduced to 10 years 10 months imprisonment with application of s.29, s.62

(*Continued*)

(Continued)

	Court	Defendant (male/ female)	Victim (male/ female)	Defendant–victim relationship	Offence	Motive	Year of offence	Sentence
95	Siirt High Criminal Court 2010/228 E, 2011/31 K, Date: 27.01.2011	HN (M) TN (M) SN (M) AN (M) AN (M) KN (M) ON (M)	NP (F)	HN, TN, SN, AN, AN, KN: non-related ON–NP: boyfriend–girlfriend	Murder (s.82)	Discovering the victim's premarital sexual relationship before marriage	2007	HN, TN, SN, AN, AN, KN acquitted. ON: aggravated life imprisonment with application of s.82/1-a, reduced to 22 years imprisonment with application of s.31/3 and s.62/1
96	Tarsus High Criminal Court 2010/117 E, 2010/245 K, Date: 03.08.2010	MC (M)	MC (F)	Brother–sister	Murder (s.82)	Eloping, having sexual relationship with several men, rumours about MC (F)'s chastity	2010	Aggravated life imprisonment reduced to life imprisonment with application of s.62
97	Trabzon High Criminal Court 2005/431 E, 2007/93 K, Date: 08.03.2007	MD (F)	New-born baby	Mother–son	Murder against a new born baby (s.82)	Delivering a baby out of wedlock	2005	Aggravated life imprisonment reduced to 25 years imprisonment with application of s.21/2, s.62
98	Trabzon 1st High Criminal Court 2006/291 E, 2007/250 K, Date: 25.09.2007	SB1 (F) SB2 (F)	New-born baby	SB1: mother–daughter SB2: granddaughter–grandmother	Murder against a new-born baby (s.82)	Delivering a baby out of wedlock	2006	SB1: aggravated life imprisonment reduced to 25 years imprisonment with application of s.21, s.62 SB2: aggravated life imprisonment reduced to 8 years 4 months imprisonment with application of s.21, s.39, s.62

99	Trabzon 2nd High Criminal Court 2007/41 E, 2007/27 K, Date: 26.12.2007	RK (M)	DK (F)	Father–daughter	Murder (s.82)	Rumours about DK's sexual relationship with several men	2007	Aggravated life imprisonment reduced to 17 years 6 months imprisonment with application of s.29, s.62
100	Van 1st High Criminal Court 2008/314 E, 2009/475 K, Date: 13.11.2009	KI (F) NI (F)	New-born baby	KI (mother)–baby NI (Aunt)–baby	Murder (s.82)	Delivering a baby out of wedlock	2007	KI: aggravated life imprisonment reduced to life imprisonment with application of s. 62 NI: acquitted
101	Van 1st High Criminal Court 2010/291 E, 2011/267 K, Date: 27.04.2011	SE (M) EE (M) ME (M) ZE (M) SE (F) KE (M)	NE (F)	SE–NE: uncle–niece EE–NE: uncle–niece ME–NE: father–daughter ZE–NE: uncle–niece SE–NE: mother–daughter KE–NE: brother–sister	Customary killing (s. 82/1-d-e-k)	Pregnancy out of wedlock	2006	SE, EE, ME, KE, ZE, SE: aggravated life imprisonment reduced to life imprisonment with application of s.62
102	Van 2nd High Criminal Court 2009/361E, 2013/108 K, Date: 19.03.2013	KC (M)	EP (F)	Spouse	Premeditated murder against a pregnant woman (s.82/1-a-e-f)	Suspected infidelity	2009	Aggravated life imprisonment reduced to life imprisonment with application of s.62

2.2 Motives for honour killings

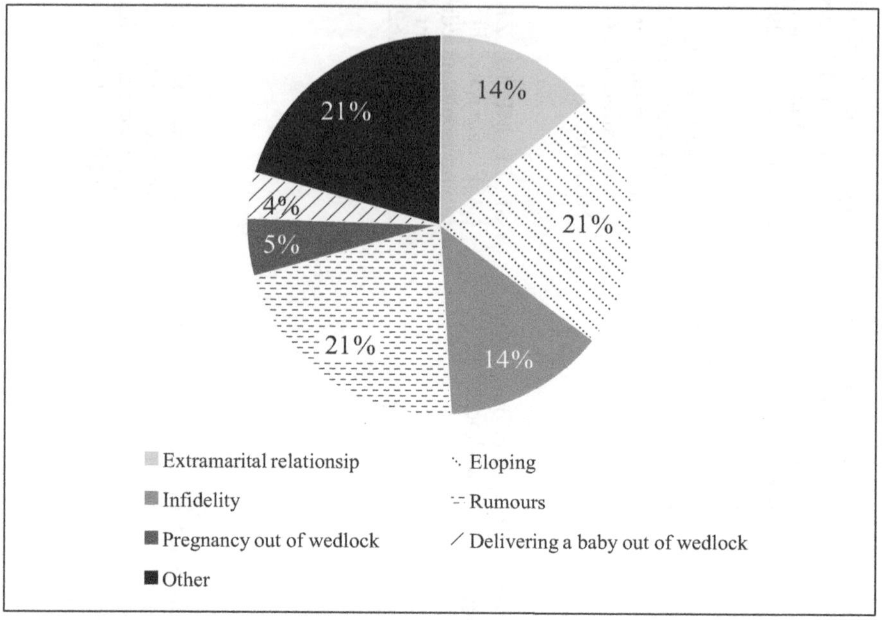

Other: behaving against patriarchal norms, prostitution, homosexuality, getting married without families' approval, being in a relationship after divorce, breach of engagement, abducting, bride exchange conflict.

2.3 Gender of perpetrators convicted of honour killings

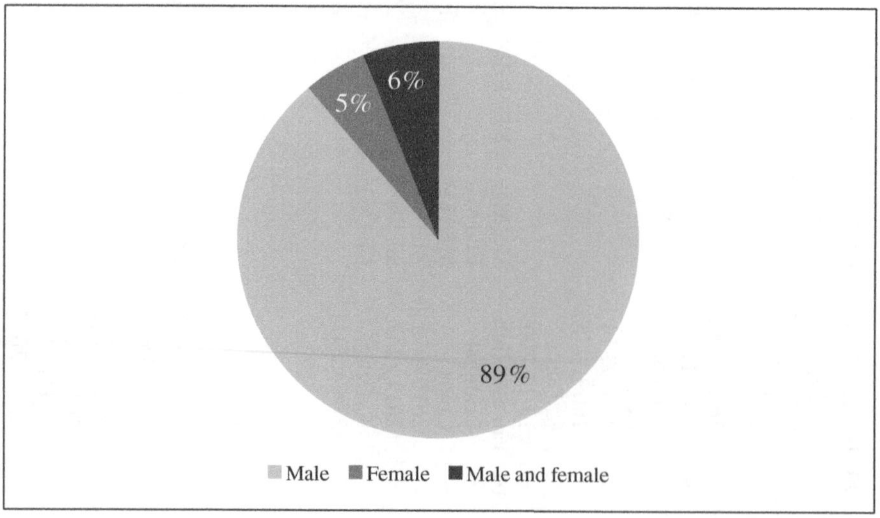

2.4 Gender of victims of honour killings

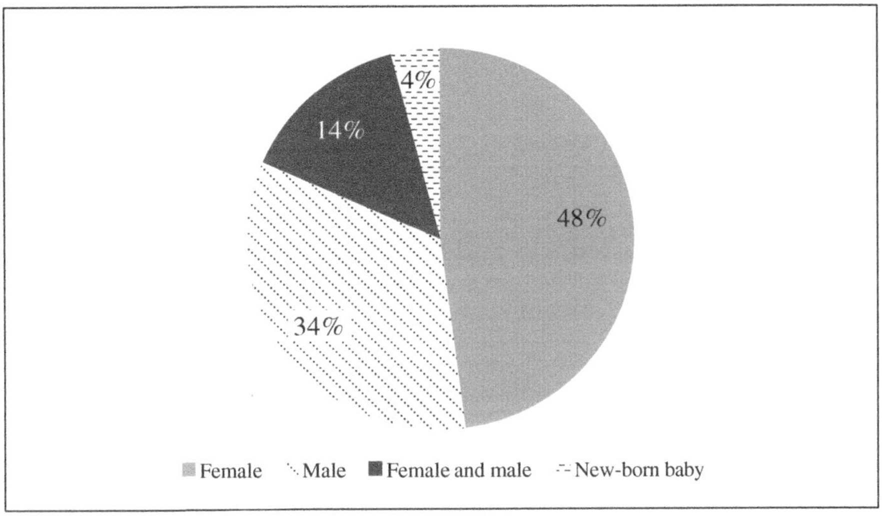

2.5 Courts' legal definitions of honour killings

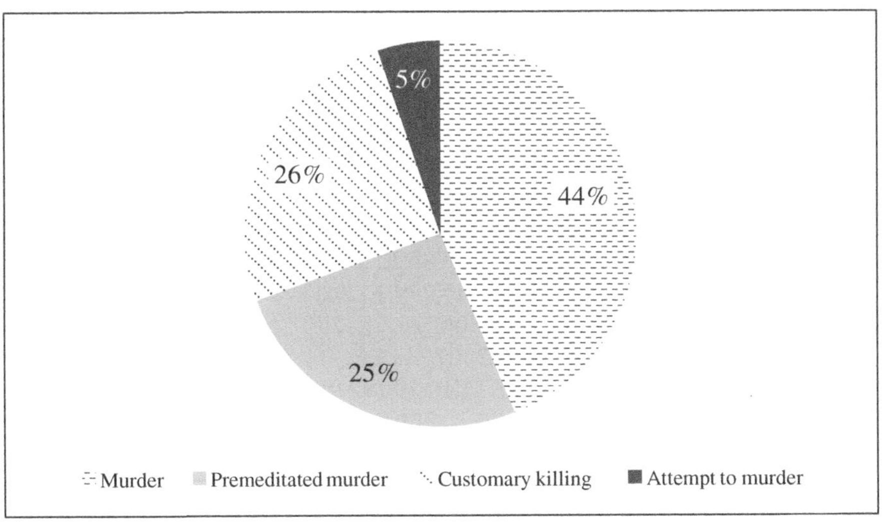

2.6 Defences and other mitigations

Matters of discretionary mitigation (s.62)	89
Unjust provocation (s.29)	42
Attempt (s.35)	9
Minority (s.31)	9
No defence or reduction applied	6

2.7 Numbers of offenders and sentences imposed

Sentence	*Number of offenders in 98 court cases*
Acquitted	60
Less than 10 years	26
10–20 years	55
20 years-life imprisonment	78
Case closed; no sentence decided[1]	8
Total	227

1 Cases were closed either due to the death of the defendants during the trials.

2.8 Turkish case law

The First Degree Court Cases (Alphabetical)

Adana 1st High Criminal Court 2005/144 E, 2008/82 K, Date: 10.03.2008
Adana 1st High Criminal Court 2009/131 E, 2009/600 K, Date: 28.12.2009
Adana 1st High Criminal Court 2011/182 E, 2012/91 K, Date: 02.03.2012
Adana 2nd High Criminal Code 2007/36 E, 2008/167 K, Date: 29.05.2008
Adana 2nd High Criminal Court 2008/432 E, 2009/162 K, Date: 30.04.2009
Adana 3rd High Criminal Court 2011/391 E, 2012/243 K, Date: 11.06.2012
Adana 4th High Criminal Court 2007/85 E, 2008/241 K, Date: 08.07.2008
Adana 4th High Criminal Court 2011/259 E, 2011/256 K, Date: 07.07.2011
Adiyaman 1st High Criminal Court 2007/17 E, 2007/177 K, Date: 13.11.2008
Adiyaman 1st High Criminal Court 2007/114 E, 2007/242 K, Date: 24.07.2007
Agri High Criminal Court 2007/215 E, 2008/191 K, Date: 24.06.2008
Akhisar High Penal Court 2001/80 E, 2001/192 K, Date: 18.10.2001
Aksaray High Criminal Court 2006/367 E, 2008/14 K, Date: 05.02.2008
Ankara 3rd High Criminal Court 2004/545 E, 2005/235 K, Date: 11.11.2005
Ankara 9th High Criminal Court 2009/88 E, 2009/186 K, Date: 23.06.2009
Bafra High Criminal Court 2009/132 E, 2010/43 K, Date: 12.02.2010
Bakırköy 3rd High Criminal Court 2011/310 E, 2012/137 K, Date: 25.04.2012
Bakırköy 5th High Criminal Court 2006/303 E, 2007/458 K, Date: 12.11.2007
Bakırköy 5th High Criminal Court 2007/269 E, 2008/27 K, Date: 04.02.2008
Bakırköy 5th High Criminal Court 2009/260 E, 2009/317 K, Date: 16.10.2009
Bakırköy 5th High Criminal Court 2010/435 E, 2011/64 K, Date: 14.03.2011

Bakırköy 6th High Criminal Court 2006/170 E, 2009/221 K, Date: 16.07.2009
Bakırköy 6th High Criminal Court 2008/76 E, 2009/207 K, Date: 06.07.2009
Bakırköy 7th High Criminal Court 2006/246 E, 2008/170 K, Date: 11.04.2008
Bakırköy 8th High Criminal Court 2009/229 E, 2012/329 K, Date: 05.07.2012
Bakırköy 13th High Criminal Court 2007/526 E, 2007/17 K, Date: 20.11.2007
Bakırköy 13th High Criminal Court 2009/183 E, 2010/96 K, Date: 04.05.2010
Bakırköy 14th High Criminal Court 2007/219 E, 2009/132 K, Date: 14.05.2009
Bakırköy 14 High Criminal Court 2010/179 E, 2012/462 K, Date: 20.12.2012
Bakırköy 15th High Criminal Court 2009/116 E, 2009/217 K, Date: 13.05.2011
Badırma High Criminal Court 2009/181 E, 2010/141 K, Date: 29.09.2010
Batman High Criminal Court 2011/222 E, 2011/236 K, Date: 23.06.2011
Batman 2nd High Criminal Court 2015/343 E, 2017/171 K, Date: 21.06.2017
Bursa 4th High Criminal Court 2008/184 E, 2008/289 K, Date: 17.10.2008
Bursa 4th High Criminal Court 2009/333 E, 2009/350 K, Date: 20.11.2009
Denizli 1st High Criminal Court 2006/289 E, 2007/74 K, Date: 20.02.2007
Diyarbakir Juvenile Court 2006/29 E, 206/333 K, Date: 20.10.2006
Diyarbakir 1st High Criminal Court 2004/6 E, 2006/376 K, Date: 21.12.2006
Diyarbakir 1st High Criminal Court 2006/228 E, 2007/174 K, Date: 20.03.2007
Diyarbakir 1st High Criminal Court 2006/437 E, 2009/115 K, Date: 26.03.2009
Diyarbakir 1st High Criminal Court 2010/247 E, 2010/397 K, Date: 23.09.2010
Diyarbakir 1st High Criminal Court 2010/279 E, 2010/522 K, Date: 28.12.2010
Diyarbakir 1st High Criminal Court 2010/350 E, 2012/66 K, Date: 07.02.2012
Diyarbakir 1st High Criminal Court 2011/140 E, 2011/192 K, Date: 10.05.2011
Diyarbakir 1st High Criminal Court 2011/147 E, 2012/259 K, Date: 08.05.2012
Diyarbakir 1st High Criminal Court 2011/207 E, 2012/280 K, Date: 17.05.2012
Diyarbakir 2nd High Criminal Court 2005/255 E, 2005/308 K, Date: 16.12.2005
Diyarbakir 2nd High Criminal Court 2009/379 E, 2010/617 K, Date: 01.12.2010
Diyarbakir 3rd High Criminal Court 2009/520 E, 2009/531 K, Date: 31.12.2009
Duzce High Criminal Court 2008/29 E, 2009/208 K, Date: 27.08.2009
Elazig 1st High Criminal Court 2006/184 E, 2007/470 K, Date: 13.12.2007
Elbistan High Criminal Court 2006/201 E, 2006/322 K, Date: 19.12.2006
Elbistan High Criminal Court 2008/36 E, 2009/138 K, Date: 16.06.2009
Erzurum 3rd High Criminal Court, 2008/157 E, 2011/86 K, Date: 18.05.2011
Gaziantep 1st High Criminal Court 2010/259 E, 2012/214 K, Date: 25.04.2012
Gaziantep 2nd High Criminal Court 1999/287 E, 2002/323 K, Date: 10.10.2002
Gaziantep 2nd High Criminal Court 2007/396 E, 2008/177 K, Date: 01.05.2008
Gaziantep 2nd High Criminal Court 2008/275 E, 2008/318 K, Date: 11.11.2008
Gaziantep 2nd High Criminal Court 2010/108 E, 2010/377 K, Date: 29.06.2010
Gaziantep 2nd High Criminal Court 2011/408 E, 2012/30 K, Date: 24.01.2012
Gaziantep 3rd High Criminal Court 2006/130E, 2007/159 K, Date: 12.04.2007
Hatay High Criminal Court 2008/363 E, 2009/27 K, Date: 29.01.2009
Igdir High Criminal Court 2011/34 E, 2011/69 K, Date: 05.05.2011
Istanbul 1st High Criminal Court 2011/70 E, 2012/106 K, Date: 16.04.2012
Istanbul 2nd High Criminal Court 2009/118 E, 2009/213 K, Date: 07.07.2009
Istanbul 3rd High Criminal Court 2000/205 E, 2001/131 K, Date: 10.05.2001

Izmir 6th High Criminal Court 2007/359 E, 2009/52 K, Date: 30.3.2009
Karabuk High Criminal Court 2006/122 E, 2008/13 K, Date: 05.02.2008
Karsiyaka 2nd High Criminal Court 2005/91 E, 2007/406 K, Date: 20.11.2007
Kartal 2nd High Criminal Court 2007/372, 2008/116, Date: 10.03.2008
Kastamonu High Criminal Court 2009/28 E, 2009/167 K, Date: 30.07.2009
Kayseri 1st High Criminal Court 2007/146 E, 2007/328 K, Date: 23.11.2007
Kayseri 1st High Criminal Court 2009/233 E, 2009/287 K, Date: 02.09.2009
Kayseri 2nd First Instance Criminal Court 2001/154 E, 2001/227 K, Date: 13.09.2001
Kayseri 2nd High Criminal Court 2007/32 E, 2007/181 K, Date: 29.05.2007
Kayseri 2nd High Criminal Court 2011/177 E, 2011/212 K, Date: 30.06.2011
Kirsehir High Criminal Court 2007/54 E, 2007/68 K, Date: 17.05.2007
Kocaeli 1st High Criminal Court 2007/195 E, 2007/341 K, Date: 18.10.2007
Kozan High Criminal Court 2007/282 E, 2008/30 K, Date: 24.01.2008
Manisa 2nd High Criminal Court, 2011/246 E, 2012/153, Date: 14.05.2012
Mardin 2nd High Criminal Court 2006/80 E, 2006/350 K, Date: 20.06.2006
Mersin High Criminal Court 2008/267 E, 2008/468 K, Date: 04.12.2008
Odemis High Criminal Court 2010/172 E, 2011/78 K, Date: 15.03.2011
Osmaniye 1st High Criminal Court 2007/153 E, 2009/228 K, Date: 03.12.2009
Sanliurfa 1st High Criminal Court 2005/27 E, 2005/248 E, Date: 31.03.2005
Sanliurfa 1st High Criminal Court 2005/178 E, 2005/200 K, Date: 04.10.2005
Sanliurfa 1st High Criminal Court 2005/276 E, 2006/250 K, Date: 06.06.2006
Sanliurfa 1. High Criminal Court 2007/2 E, 2007/95 K, Date: 05.04.2007
Sanliurfa 1st High Criminal Court 2008/235 E, 2008/310 K, Date: 13.10.2009
Sanliurfa 1st High Criminal Court 2009/147 E, 2009/172 K, Date: 13.10.2009
Sanliurfa 2nd High Criminal Court 2008/108 E, 2010/37 K, Date: 03.02.2010
Sanliurfa 2nd High Criminal Court 2008/147 E, 2010/396 K, Date: 28.12.2010
Sanliurfa 2nd High Criminal Court 2011/224 E, 2011/215 K, Date: 23.09.2011
Sanliurfa 3rd High Criminal Court 2011/133 E, 2011/144 K, Date: 30.06.2011
Seydisehir High Criminal Court 2008/461 E, 2008/485 K, Date: 25.04.2008
Siirt High Criminal Court 2010/228 E, 2011/31 K, Date: 27.01.2011
Tarsus High Criminal Court 2010/117 E, 2010/245 K, Date: 03.08.2010
Trabzon High Criminal Court 2005/431 E, 2007/93 K, Date: 08.03.2007
Trabzon 1st High Criminal Court 2006/291 E, 2006/906 K, Date: 25/09/2007
Trabzon 2nd High Criminal Court 2007/41 E, 2007/27 K, Date: 26.12.2007
Van 1st High Criminal Court 2007/139 E, 2009/3 K, Date: 09.01.2009
Van 1st High Criminal Court 2008/314 E, 2009/475 K, Date: 13.11.2009
Van 1st High Criminal Court 2010/291 E, 2011/267 K, Date: 27.04.2011
Van 2nd High Criminal Court 2009/361 E, 2013/108 K, Date: 19.03.2013

The Appeal Court Cases (Chronological)

Department No:1 of the Criminal Appeal Court 1967/1955 E, 1967/2367 K, Date: 13.10.1967

Department No:1 of the Criminal Appeal Court 1980/3237 E, 1980/3424 K, Date: 10.07.1980

Department No:1 of the Criminal Appeal Court 1991/1125 E, 1991/1497 K, Date: 29.05.1991

Department No:1 of the Criminal Appeal Court 1993/1258 E, 1993/1790 K, Date: 29.09.1993

Department No:1 of the Criminal Appeal Court 1993/1716 E, 1993/1812 K, Date: 30.09.1993

Department No:1 of the Criminal Appeal Court 1993/1949 E, 1993/2360 K, Date: 16.11.1993

Department No:1 of the Criminal Appeal Court 1994/216 E, 1994/305 K, Date: 15.02.1994

Department No:1 of the Criminal Appeal Court 1994/1570 E, 1994/1607 K, Date: 17.05.1994

Department No:1 of the Criminal Appeal Court 1994/2021 E, 1994/2441 K, Date: 08.07.1994

Department No:1 of the Criminal Appeal Court 1996/2829 E, 1996/3407 K, Date: 27.10.1996

Department No:1 of the Criminal Appeal Court 1997/2687 E, 1997/3486 K, Date: 04.11.1997.

Department No:1 of the Criminal Appeal Court 1998/422 E, 1998/1809 K, Date: 28.05.1998,

Department No:1 of the Criminal Appeal Court 1998/686 E, 1998/3132 K, Date: 16.06.1998

Department No:1 of the Criminal Appeal Court 1998/3126 E, 1998/3379 K, Date: 09.11.1998

Department No:1 of the Criminal Appeal Court 1998/3774 E, 1999/1328 K, Date: 20.04.1999

Department No:1 of the Criminal Appeal Court 2001/644 E, 2001/1884 K, Date: 03.05.2001

Department No:1 of the Criminal Appeal Court 2001/1529 E, 2001/3150 K, Date: 06.07.2001

Department No:1 of the Criminal Appeal Court 2002/1450 E, 2002/2504 K, Date: 12.06.2002

Department No:1 of the Criminal Appeal Court 2002/936 E, 2002/2584 K, Date: 17.06.2002

Department No:1 of the Criminal Appeal Court 2003/968 E, 2003/1333 K, Date: 10.06.2003

Department No:1 of the Criminal Appeal Court 2003/1097 E, 2003/286 K, Date: 19.11.2003

Department No:1 of the Criminal Appeal Court 2003/2581 E, 2003/1790 K, Date: 11.07.2003

Department No:1 of the Criminal Appeal Court 2004/1751 E, 2004/2314 K, Date: 14.06.2004

Department No:1 of the Criminal Appeal Court 2005/1329 E, 2006/587 K, Date: 10.03.2006

Department No:1 of the Criminal Appeal Court 2007/2927 E, 2007/8501 K, Date: 19.11.2007

Department No:1 of the Criminal Appeal Court 2007/6700 E, 2008/1986 K, Date: 14.03.2008

Department No:1 of the Criminal Appeal Court 2008/1345 E, 2008/3877 K, Date: 17.04.2008

Department No:1 of the Criminal Appeal Court 2009/6048 E, 2009/1039 K, Date: 03.03.2009

Department No:1 of the Criminal Appeal Court 2008/5953 E, 2009/1075 K, Date: 04.03.2009

Department No:1 of the Criminal Appeal Court 2009/2965 E, 2009/1533 K, Date: 24.03.2009

Department No:1 of the Criminal Appeal Court 2008/6646 E, 2009/1558 K, Date: 25.03.2009

Department No:1 of the Criminal Appeal Court 2009/6048 E, 2009/1937 K, Date: 08.04.2009

Department No:1 of the Criminal Appeal Court 2008/7373 E, 2009/2154 K, Date: 15.04.2009

Department No:1 of the Criminal Appeal Court 2008/8227 E, 2009/3039 K, Date: 27.05.2009

Department No:1 of the Criminal Appeal Court 2009/248 E, 2009/3297 K, Date: 08.06.2009

Department No:1 of the Criminal Appeal Court 2008/8385 E, 2009/3412 K, Date: 11.06.2009

Department No:1 of the Criminal Appeal Court 2008/8055 E, 2009/3527 K, Date: 16.06.2009

Department No:1 of the Criminal Appeal Court 2008/359 E, 2009/3640 K, Date: 17.06.2009

Department No:1 of the Criminal Appeal Court 2008/6528 E, 2009/3761 K, Date: 23.06.2009

Department No:1 of the Criminal Appeal Court 2008/9038 E, 2009/3764 K, Date: 23.06.2009

Department No:1 of the Criminal Appeal Court 2008/9234 E, 2009/4140 K, Date: 01.07.2009

Department No:1 of the Criminal Appeal Court 2008/9234 E, 2009/4140 K, Date: 02.07.2009

Department No:1 of the Criminal Appeal Court 2008/9435 E, 2009/4468 K, Date: 09.07.2009,

Department No:1 of the Criminal Appeal Court 2008/9651 E, 2009/4794 K, Date: 15.07.2009,

Department No:1 of the Criminal Appeal Court 2008/5009 E, 2009/5002 K, Date: 22.07.2009

Department No:1 of the Criminal Appeal Court 2008/9934 E, 2009/4994 K, Date: 23.07.2009,
Department No:1 of the Criminal Appeal Court 2009/4558 E, 2009/6033 K, Date: 19.10.2009,
Department No:1 of the Criminal Appeal Court 2008/10847 E, 2009/6194 K, Date: 21.10.2009
Department No:1 of the Criminal Appeal Court 2009/6163 E, 2009/6188 K, Date: 21.10.2009,
Department No:1 of the Criminal Appeal Court 2008/8615 E, 2009/6878 K, Date: 11.11.2009
Department No:1 of the Criminal Appeal Court 2009/190 E, 2009/6887 K, Date: 11.11.2009,
Department No:1 of the Criminal Appeal Court 2009/270 E, 2009/6891 K, Date: 11.11.2009,
Department No:1 of the Criminal Appeal Court 2009/2357 E, 2010/414 K, Date: 27.01.2010
Department No:1 of the Criminal Appeal Court 2009/2357 E, 2010/414 K, Date: 28.01.2010
Department No:1 of the Criminal Appeal Court 2009/5798 E, 2010/1986 K, Date: 31.03.2010
Department No:1 of the Criminal Appeal Court 2009/6525 E, 2010/3023 K, Date: 22.04.2010
Department No:1 of the Criminal Appeal Court 2009/6772 E, 2010/3058 K, Date: 29.04.2010
Department No:1 of the Criminal Appeal Court 2009/840 E, 2010/3970 K, Date: 03.06.2010
Department No:1 of the Criminal Appeal Court 2009/8804 E, 2010/4214 K, Date: 07.06.2010
Department No:1 of the Criminal Appeal Court 2008/6782 E, 2010/4691 K, Date: 22.06.2010
Department No:1 of the Criminal Appeal Court 2009/9808 E, 2010/4917 K, Date: 01.07.2010
Department No:1 of the Criminal Appeal Court 2009/7465 E, 2010/5325 K, Date: 07.07.2010,
Department No:1 of the Criminal Appeal Court 2009/5798 E, 2010/1986 K, Date: 31.03.2010
Department No:1 of the Criminal Appeal Court 2010/4303 E, 2010/6578 K, Date: 12.10.2010
Department No:1 of the Criminal Appeal Court 2009/10191 E, 2010/6617 K, Date: 13.10.2010,
Department No:1 of the Criminal Appeal Court 2008/8285 E, 2010/7220 K, Date: 04.11.2010,
Department No:1 of the Criminal Appeal Court 2010/2637 E, 2010/7269 K, Date: 08.11.2010

Department No:1 of the Criminal Appeal Court 2009/8192 E, 2010/7538 K, Date: 24.11.2010,
Department No:1 of the Criminal Appeal Court 2010/1509 E, 2010/7851 K, Date: 08.12.2010,
Department No:1 of the Criminal Appeal Court 2010/3190 E, 2010/8043 K, Date: 14.12.2010,
Department No:1 of the Criminal Appeal Court 2010/4407 E, 2011/695 K, Date: 15.02.2011,
Department No:1 of the Criminal Appeal Court 2010/4522 E, 2011/1511 K, Date: 15.03.2011
Department No:1 of the Criminal Appeal Court 2010/5426 E, 2011/1760 K, Date: 23.03.2011,
Department No:1 of the Criminal Appeal Court 2009/2858 E, 2011/1787 K, Date: 23.03.2011,
Department No:1 of the Criminal Appeal Court 2010/5786 E, 2011/1972 K, Date: 01.04.2011,
Department No:1 of the Criminal Appeal Court 2011/1811 E, 2011/2444 K, Date: 20.04.2011,
Department No:1 of the Criminal Appeal Court 2011/2688 E, 2011/2667 K, Date: 27.04.2011,
Department No:1 of the Criminal Appeal Court 2010/6241 E, 2011/3025 K, Date: 11.05.2011,
Department No:1 of the Criminal Appeal Court 2010/7469 E, 2011/3272 K, Date: 23.05.2011
Department No:1 of the Criminal Appeal Court 2010/7496 E, 2011/3277 K, Date: 23.05.2011,
Department No:1 of the Criminal Appeal Court 2009/2674 E, 2011/4286 K, Date: 05.07.2011
Department No:1 of the Criminal Appeal Court 2011/5149 E, 2011/6551 K, Date: 02.11.2011,
Department No:1 of the Criminal Appeal Court 2011/2467 E, 2011/6863 K, Date: 17.11.2011,
Department No:1 of the Criminal Appeal Court 2010/3722 E, 2012/2270 K, Date: 28.03.2012,
Department No:1 of the Criminal Appeal Court 2011/5057 E, 2012/3350 K, Date: 30.04.2012
Department No:1 of the Criminal Appeal Court 2011/4322 E, 2012/3639 K, Date: 07.05.2012,
Department No:1 of the Criminal Appeal Court 2012/838 E, 2012/3806 K, Date: 10.05.2012
Department No:1 of the Criminal Appeal Court 2012/1116 E, 2012/4037 K, Date: 21.05.2012
Department No:1 of the Criminal Appeal Court 2012/1475 E, 2012/4900 K, Date: 13.06.2012

Department No:1 of the Criminal Appeal Court 2012/3769 E, 2012/8528 K, Date: 21.11.2012
Department No:1 of the Criminal Appeal Court 2012/3659 E, 2012/9331 K, Date: 12.12.2012
Department No:1 of the Criminal Appeal Court 2012/3490 E, 2013/665 K, Date: 31.01.2013
Department No:1 of the Criminal Appeal Court 2012/4767 E, 2013/1774 K, Date: 06.03.2013
Department No:1 of the Criminal Appeal Court 2012/5546 E, 2013/2471 K, Date: 26.03.2013
Department No:1 of the Criminal Appeal Court 2012/5466 E, 2013/2563 K, Date: 27.03.2013
Department No:1 of the Criminal Appeal Court 2011/716 E, 2013/3268 K, Date: 18.04.2013
Department No:1 of the Criminal Appeal Court 2013/372 E, 2013/3427 K, Date: 30.04.2013
Department No:1 of the Criminal Appeal Court 2013/2120 E, 2013/5542 K, Date: 07.10.2013
Department No:1 of the Criminal Appeal Court 2013/2789 E, 2014/184 K, Date: 22.01.2014
Department No:1 of the Criminal Appeal Court 2013/4853 E, 2014/218 K, Date: 23.01.2014
Department No:1 of the Criminal Appeal Court 2013/5931 E, 2014/184 K, Date: 05.03.2014
Department No:1 of the Criminal Appeal Court 2014/1719 E, 2014/2733 K, Date: 29.04.2014
Department No:1 of the Criminal Appeal Court 2014/923 E, 2014/3551 K, Date: 17/06/2014
Department No:1 of the Criminal Appeal Court 2014/2440 E, 2014/3752 K, Date: 07.07.2014
Department No:1 of the Criminal Appeal Court 2014/1502 E, 2014/3859 K, Date: 15.09.2014
Department No:1 of the Criminal Appeal Court 2014/2480 E, 2014/3931 K, Date: 17.09.2014
Department No:1 of the Criminal Appeal Court 2014/2849 E, 2014/4347 K, Date: 01.10.2014
Department No:1 of the Criminal Appeal Court 2014/4124 E, 2014/4693 K, Date: 22.10.2014
Department No:1 of the Criminal Appeal Court 2014/3932 E, 2014/6444 K, Date: 22/12/2014
Department No:1 of the Criminal Appeal Court 2013/3398 E, 2015/144 K, Date: 21.01.2015
Department No:1 of the Criminal Appeal Court 2014/4735 E, 2015/790 K, Date: 18.02.2015

Department No:1 of the Criminal Appeal Court 2014/5304 E, 2015/3088 K, Date: 12/05/2015
Department No:1 of the Criminal Appeal Court 2015/2328 E, 2015/4272 K, Date: 02.07.2015
Department No:1 of the Criminal Appeal Court 2015/1374 E, 2015/5380 K, Date: 10.11.2015
Department No:1 of the Criminal Appeal Court 2016/3998 E, 2017/3540 K, Date: 25.10.2017
Department No:1 of the Criminal Appeal Court 2016/249 E, 2017/514 K, Date: 21.02.2017
Department No:1 of the Criminal Appeal Court 2017/1971 E, 2018/954 K, Date: 05.03.2018
Department No:1 of the Criminal Appeal Court 2017/3239 E, 2018/4215 K, Date: 17.10.2018
Department No:1 of the Criminal Appeal Court 2018/3283 E, 2018/4629 K, Date: 13.11.2018
Department No:1 of the Criminal Appeal Court 2018/3008 E, 2018/5370 K, Date: 12.12.2018
Department No:4 of the Criminal Appeal Court 1992/1663 E, 1992/2343 K, Date: 31.03.1992
Department No:4 of the Criminal Appeal Court 1994/1307 E, 1994/4739 K, Date: 31.05.1994
Department No:4 of the Criminal Appeal Court 1998/6759 E, 1998/8272 K, Date: 09.11.1998
Department No:5 of the Criminal Appeal Court 1985/2804 E, 1985/3741 K, Date: 09.10.1985
Department No:5 of the Criminal Appeal Court 1990/3391 E, 1999/4351 K, Date: 11.10.1990
Turkish Court of Appeal for the 2nd Circuit 2006/14694 E, 2007/2504 K, Date: 22.02.2007

Assembly of the Criminal Chambers Cases (Chronological)

Assembly of the Criminal Chambers 1973/404 E, 1973/459 K, Date: 04.06.1973
Assembly of the Criminal Chambers 1973/324 E, 1973/537 K, Date: 09.07.1973
Assembly of the Criminal Chambers 1974/16231 E, 1974/415 K, Date: 23.09.1974
Assembly of the Criminal Chambers 1977/1–380 E, 1978/14 K, Date: 23.01.1978
Assembly of the Criminal Chambers 1978/484 E, 1979/58 K, Date: 12.02.1979
Assembly of the Criminal Chambers 1989/1–55 E, 1989/113 K, Date: 20.03.1989
Assembly of the Criminal Chambers 1990/1–176 E, 1990/194 K, Date: 25.06.1990
Assembly of the Criminal Chambers 1993/4–154 E, 1993/183 K, Date: 21.06.1993
Assembly of the Criminal Chambers 1994/1–225 E, 1994/250 K, Date: 31.10.1994
Assembly of the Criminal Chambers 1997/1–8 E, 1997/26 K, Date: 25.02.1997
Assembly of the Criminal Chambers 2001/1–51 E, 2011/42 K, Date: 12.04.2011
Assembly of the Criminal Chambers 2002/1–247 E, 2002/414 K, Date: 3.12.2002

Assembly of the Criminal Chambers 2003/1–173 E, 2003/198 K, Date: 24.06.2003
Assembly of the Criminal Chambers 2009/1–221 E, 2010/61 K, Date: 23.03.2010
Assembly of the Criminal Chambers 2010/111 E, 2010/32606 K, Date: 11.05.2010
Assembly of the Criminal Chambers 2010/3–23 E, 2010/142 K, Date: 08.06.2010
Assembly of the Criminal Chambers 2010/1–150 E, 2010/192 K, Date: 12.10.2010
Assembly of the Criminal Chambers 2010/111 E, 2010/32606 K, Date: 15.10.2010
Assembly of the Criminal Chambers 2011/18 E, 2011/1–10 K, Date: 01.02.2011
Assembly of the Criminal Chambers 2011/1–138 E, 2011/130 K, Date: 14.06.2011
Assembly of the Criminal Chambers 2011/1–52 E, 2011/180 K, Date: 12.07.2011
Assembly of the Criminal Chambers 2011/1–52 E, 2011/180 K, Date: 20.09.2011
Assembly of the Criminal Chambers 2012/1–76 E, 2012/258 K, Date: 26.06.2012
Assembly of the Criminal Chambers 2012/1–76 E, 2012/258 K, Date: 03.07.2012
Assembly of the Criminal Chambers 2013/1–355 E, 2013/456 K, Date: 19.11.2013
Assembly of the Criminal Chambers 2013–1/665 E, 2014/66 K, Date: 11.02.2014
Assembly of the Criminal Chambers 2015/830 E, 2016/630 K, Date: 11.10.2016
Assembly of the Criminal Chambers 2014/357 E, 2017/310 K, Date: 06.06.2017

Other Cases

Opuz v Turkey [2010] 50 EHRR 28
R v Goren (Mehmet) [2001] EWCA Crim 307

Appendix 3
Legislation translations

3.1 Abolished Turkish Penal Code law no: 765 passed on: 01.03.1926 (Official Gazette no. 320 dated 13.03.1926)[1]

S.51: "If a person commits a crime in the heat of anger or under influence of strong grief caused by an unjust provocation, he shall be punished in case the punishment of death is prescribed for the offence, by aggravated life imprisonment; and if aggravated life imprisonment is prescribed for the offence, by aggravated imprisonment for twenty-four years. In other cases the punishment prescribed for the offence shall be reduced by one-fourth. Where provocation is grievous and severe, aggravated imprisonment for twenty-four years shall be given instead of punishment by death, and aggravated imprisonment for not less than fifteen years shall be given instead of aggravated imprisonment. Other punishments shall be reduced by one-half to two-thirds."

S.55: Anybody above the age of fifteen but below the age of eighteen years at the time of commission of an act, shall be punished as follows:

1 Aggravated imprisonment for not less than twenty years shall be imposed instead of punishment of death
2 Aggravated imprisonment for fifteen to twenty years shall be imposed instead of aggravated imprisonment for life
3 Other punishments shall be reduced by not more than one third
4 Punishments of disqualification to hold public office and to be placed under police supervision shall not be applied

Punishments restricting personal liberty, even if the offender serving out a fine, shall be served in reformatories or in a special section of the penitentiaries for adults, if the offender had not completed the age of eighteen years at the time he began serving his sentence. Such a person, upon attaining the age of eighteen years, if the period of the punishment he was originally sentenced to is more than three years, or if a period exceeding two years remains unserved, shall be transferred to a penitentiary for adults. However, persons having shown good

1 This section is quoted from Nevzat Gurelli, *The Turkish Criminal Code* (London, Fred B Rothman & Co 1965).

conduct during the period served, if deemed appropriate, may be kept in special penitentiaries, or in a special section of penitentiaries for adults.

Anybody attaining the age of eighteen by the time the execution of the sentence is to be commenced, if the duration of the punishment is less than three years, and if, considering their past conduct, it is deemed appropriate, shall serve this punishment in special penitentiaries or in a special section of penitentiaries for adults.

S.59: Apart from statutory matters of mitigation, wherever discretionary matters of extenuation in favour of the offender are accepted by the court, aggravated imprisonment for life, instead of death, and aggravated imprisonment for thirty years instead of aggravated imprisonment for life, shall be imposed. Other punishments shall be reduced by not more than one sixth.

S.423: Whoever removes the virginity of a girl who has completed fifteen years of age with a promise of marriage, shall be imprisoned for six months to two years.

In case of marriage, the prosecution and the punishment shall be suspended. However, if a decree of divorce is rendered against the husband within five years after the marriage, the public prosecution shall be restored or the punishment previously adjudged shall be executed.

S.449: If homicide is committed:

1 Against an ascendant or descendant
2 Against the member of the Grand National Assembly
3 Under a brutal feeling or with torture
4 With premeditation
5 Against more than one person
6 Through the means prescribed in Chapter I of Part 7, such as fire, flood, and shipwreck
7 In order to prepare, facilitate, or commit a separate crime even if it cannot be consummated
8 In order to get the fruits of a crime or to conceal the preparation made or that purpose or in the heat of anger resulting from failure to achieve the goal of a crime
9 In order to conceal a crime or to destroy the evidence and traces thereof, or to enable himself or someone to run away from punishment
10 With the motive of blood feud; the offender shall suffer death

S.450: Whoever torments another person physically or damages his or her welfare or causes cerebral damage, without intending murder, will be sentenced to between six months' and one year's imprisonment.

Where the act constitutes a danger to the victim's life or causes constant weakness in one of the organs or senses, or permanent difficulty in speech or permanent injuries to the face, or physical or mental illness for twenty or more days, or prevents [the victim] from continuing his regular work for the same number of days, the offender will be sentenced to between two and five years' imprisonment.

Where the battery causes the victim to suffer a mental bodily sickness which is definitely or probably incurable, or the loss of a hand or foot or of the ability to talk, or sterility, or incapacity of a limb, or permanent alteration of the face, or miscarriage of child, the offender shall be punished by aggravated imprisonment for five to ten years.

If the act did not cause any illness or did not prevent [the victim] from continuing his regular work or these situations did not last for more than ten days, the offender will be sentenced to between two and six months' imprisonment or to an aggravated fine of 12,000 to 150,000 liras, provided that the injured person complains.

If the offence is committed by use of the means specified in Article 457, commencement of legal proceedings is not contingent upon the filing of a complaint.

S.457: If the acts mentioned in Article 456 are committed against the persons cited in Article 449 or if the act is committed by a hidden or visible weapon or harmful chemical, the punishment shall be increased by one-third to a half of the main sentence.

S.462: As regards perpetrators who commit the offences specified in the two foregoing chapters, against the wife, husband, sister, or offspring, at the time the victim is caught while in the act of adultery or illegal sexual intercourse, or while the victim was about to commit adultery or about to engage in illegal sexual intercourse, or while the victim was in a situation showing free from any doubt, that he or she has just completed the act of adultery or illegal sexual intercourse; or against another person caught participating in such acts with one of the aforesaid relatives, or against both, the punishment prescribed for the offence shall be reduced to one-eighth and aggravated life imprisonment shall be commuted to imprisonment. In lieu of aggravated life imprisonment, imprisonment for four to eight years, and in lieu of death, imprisonment for five to ten years shall be imposed.

S.463: If the offences specified in Articles 448, 449, 450, 456, and 457 have been committed by more than one person each of whom acted individually and if the doer of the act cannot be identified, each one of these persons shall be punished by one-third to one-half of the punishment prescribed for the offence they have committed. Offences for which death or aggravated life imprisonment is prescribed shall be punished by aggravated imprisonment for not less than ten years. However, this provision is not applicable to persons who are known to have committed the act jointly.

3.2 Turkish Penal Code law no. 5237, passed on 26.09.2004 (Official Gazette no. 25611 dated 12.10.2004)[2]

S.29 (1) A person committing an offense with affect of anger or asperity caused by the unjust act is sentenced to imprisonment from eighteen years to twenty-four years instead of aggravated life imprisonment, and to imprisonment from

2 This section is quoted from Legislation Online available at https://www.legislationline.org/download/id/6453/file/Turkey_CC_2004_am2016_en.pdf (Accessed 25 October 2019)

twelve years to eighteen years instead of life imprisonment. In other cases, the punishment is abated from one-fourth up to three-thirds.

S.31: (1) The children having not attained the full age of twelve on the commission date of the offense, may not have criminal responsibility. Besides, no criminal prosecution may be commenced against such persons; but, it may be deemed necessary to take certain security precautions specific to children.

(2) In case a person who attained the age of twelve but not yet completed the age of fifteen on the commission date of the offense does not have the ability to perceive the legal meaning and consequences of the offense, or to control his actions, he may not have criminal responsibility for such behaviour. However, security precautions specific to children may be adopted for such individuals. If a person has the ability to apprehend the offense he has committed or to control his actions relating to this offense, then such person may be sentenced to imprisonment from nine years to twelve years if the offense requires aggravated life imprisonment; from seven years to nine years if the offense requires life imprisonment. Two-thirds of other punishments is abated and in this case, the imprisonment to be imposed for each offense may not be more than six years.

(3) A person who attained the full age of fifteen but not yet completed the age of eighteen on the commission date of the offense is sentenced to imprisonment from fourteen years to twenty years if the offense requires aggravated life imprisonment; and from nine years to twelve years if the offense requires life imprisonment. One-half of the other punishments is abated and in this case, the imprisonment to be imposed for each offense may not be more than eight years.

S.35: (1) A person who acts with the intention of committing crime but fails to perform the acts necessary to commit the crime due to a cause beyond his control, is considered to have attempted to commit crime.

(2) In case of attempt to commit crime, the offender is sentenced to imprisonment from thirteen years to twenty years instead of aggravated life imprisonment according to the seriousness of the damage or danger; and imprisonment from nine years to fifteen years instead of life imprisonment. In other cases, the punishment is abated from one-fourth up to three-fourths.

S.39: (1) A person encouraging another person to commit offense is sentenced to life imprisonment from fifteen years to twenty years if subject to aggravated life imprisonment; and from ten years to fifteen years imprisonment if the offense requires life imprisonment.

(2) A person is kept responsible under the following conditions from commission of offense as the party encouraging the offender;

a) To solicit a person for commission of an offense or to support his decision to commit offense or to guarantee help after commission of offense
b) To give idea about how the offense shall be committed or to supply the necessary tools to be used during commission of offense
c) To render support before and during the commission of offense in order to simplify the intended act

S.62: (1) In case of existence of the discretionary matters of mitigation extenuating the punishment in favour of the offender, the offender is sentenced to life imprisonment instead of aggravated life imprisonment; or twenty-five years' imprisonment instead of life imprisonment. The matters of discretionary mitigation are indicated in the court's decision.

(2) While evaluating the matters of mitigation, background, social relations, and behaviour of the offender after the commission of offense and during the trial period, and potential affects of the punishment on the future of the offender is considered.

S.65: (1) Public action is dismissed in case of amnesty. The imposed punishments are abated together with all consequences.

(2) In case of pardon, the convict may be released from penitentiary where he is sentenced to imprisonment or the period of imprisonment is shortened or the imprisonment can be transformed to punitive fine.

(3) The punishment of disqualification from certain rights under judgment is executed despite of pardon.

S.81: (1) Any person who unlawfully kills a person is sentenced to life imprisonment.

S.82 (1) In case of commission of this offense;

a Wilfully
b Ferociously or brutally
c By use of nuclear, biological, or chemical weapons which cause explosion or result with fire, flood, destruction, sinking etc.
d Against any one of the antecedents or descendants, or spouse or brother/sister, or
e Against a child or a person who cannot protect himself due to corporal or spiritual disability, or
f Against a pregnant woman, or
g By virtue of public office, or
h With the intention of concealing or facilitating commission of an offense, or destroying the evidences, or
i Blood feud
j Ethical reasons

the offender is sentenced to aggravated life imprisonment.

S.83 (1) In order to keep a person responsible from a death due to failure to perform an obligation, the failure or negligence creating such consequence should be equal to commissive act in degree.

(2) In order to accept negligence and commissive act as equal elements, a person;

a Should have undertaken liabilities arising out of a legal adaptations or contract to execute a commissive act, and
b His previous performance should constitute a risk against the other's life.

(3) Any person causing death of a person due to failure in performing of a legal obligation or requirement, as a basic punishment, is sentenced to imprisonment

from twenty years to twenty-five years instead of aggravated life imprisonment and from fifteen years to twenty years imprisonment instead of life imprisonment. As for the other cases, the court may decide for imprisonment from ten years to fifteen years, or reduction of punishment.

3.3 Turkish Criminal Procedure Code law no: 5271 passed on 4.12.2004 (Official Gazette no. 25673 dated 17.12.2004)[3]

S.192 (1) Presiding judge or trial judge shall conduct the main hearing, interrogate the accused, and provide for the presentation of evidence.

(2) If one of the related parties objects on the grounds that the presiding judge's order related to a measure concerning the administration of the main hearing is legally inadmissible, the court issues a ruling upon this point.

S.237 The victim, real persons, and legal entities, who have been damaged by the crime, as well as the individuals liable for pecuniary compensation, are entitled to intervene in the public prosecution during the prosecution phase at the court of the first instance at any stage, until the judgment has been rendered, announcing that they are putting forward their claim.

S.307/4 If the motion of appeal on law was filed only by the accused, or by the Office of Public Prosecution on his favour, or by individuals mentioned in Article 262, then the punishment included in the new judgment cannot be more severe than the previous judgment.

3.4 Turkish Civil Code law no: 4721, passed on 22.11.2001 (Official Gazette no. 24607, dated 08.12.2001)[4]

S.1 The law must be applied in all cases, which come within the letter or the spirit of any of its provisions.

Where no written provision is applicable, the judge shall decide according to customary law and, in default thereof, according to the rules, which he/she would lay down if he/she, himself/herself had to act as legislator.

3 This section is quoted from Feridun Yenisey, *Turkish Criminal Procedure Code* (Istanbul, Beta 2009).

4 This section is quoted from Turk Hukuk Sitesi Available at https://www.turkhukuksitesi.com/serh.php?did=11284 (Accessed 25 October 2019)

Index

Note: Page numbers in italics indicate figures; page numbers in bold indicate tables.

For Product Safety Concerns and Information please contact our
EU representative GPSR@taylorandfrancis.com Taylor & Francis
Verlag GmbH, Kaufingerstraße 24, 80331 München, Germany